BIG IDEA SERMONS

PASTOR PAUL CANNINGS, PhD

BIG IDEA SERMONS

52 SERMON GUIDES

FOR BUSY PASTORS AND BIBLE TEACHERS

NASHVILLE, TENNESSEE

Printed in the United States of America

978-1-4627-7462-3

Published by B&H Publishing Group
Nashville, Tennessee

Dewey Decimal Classification: 251
Subject Heading: PREACHING \ PASTORAL THEOLOGY \ SERMONS

Please send your comments and requests for information to the address below: Power Walk Ministries 7350 West T.C. Jester Blvd. Houston, TX 77088 Telephone (281) 260-7402. www.powerwalkministries.org

For more information about speaking engagements please contact us by telephone at (281) 260-7402.

1 2 3 4 5 6 7 • 22 21 20 19 18

DEDICATION

As a boy growing up, I cannot remember a day that my mother did not seek to lovingly influence me to love the Lord. Never once did I feel pounced on with the Bible, yet her life and testimony made me feel that Christ was the best person to fall in love with. At age twelve, I remember surrendering my life to Christ one Sunday evening, to the amazement of my friends in the back bench of the church. That night I went to church to hang out with my friends and found a better friend, Christ.

When I came home I told my mother and she immediately put me in her lap and gave me one of her amazing hugs. She told me how excited she was and immediately began making preparations for me to attend discipleship classes. I must admit that I did not know that I was going to be put to "work" for believing Christ but it was not a matter of discussion. Mother's word was final.

I knew that very Sunday who would be my discipleship leader because my mom was having a long discussion with "Sister Clark," a senior lady at church. Sometimes the conversation became heated, and every now and then I would hear my name whispered. But I knew Sister Clark wanted the best for me. I fell in love with God from watching my mother and the dedication of Sister Clark. She would come to the class, no matter rain or shine, walking or riding her bike.

Even if it was just me in class, my mother made sure I went each Sunday afternoon. Sister Clark was just as devoted. She was always patient teaching me the scriptures. I kept thinking, maybe hoping, that she would cancel class because, at times, I was the only student present. But oh no, she patiently kept explaining the Bible to me. I became a disciple of Christ at this young age directly because of Sister Clark's love and dedication and my mother's early morning devotions. I was so excited to share the gospel that eventually I lead the small group evangelizing each Saturday.

My mother's impact continues because she did a lot to get her family to America so that we could be educated in the States. She sacrificed much for me to finish college, constantly telling me to continue until I received a doctorate degree. It is this guiding influence for spiritual growth and her commitment to family and academics that has served as my foundation. I truly believe she blessed me to serve the Lord.

I dedicate this book to Annie Eleen Cannings, whom we are blessed to call "mom," "momze," and "grandma" for all she has done and meant to me and my family. Love you Mom!

ACKNOWLEDGMENTS

In 1969, as a result of the influence of my parents and my mother's daily morning devotions, I accepted Christ into my life during a church service in Guyana, South America. This moment was and is the greatest event in my life. I would like to thank the Lord God, who sought me and drew me in. He has loved me so much that He has allowed me to be a part of His eternal family.

My wife, Everette, has been an avid supporter in all aspects of my life since our friendship began in 1979 and extending into our marriage on September 6, 1980. I give her my deep gratitude for all her years of sacrifice and encouragement, which has allowed me to remain focused. She has blessed my life in too many ways to list.

Our sons, Paul Jr. and Pierre, and their wives, Tanisha and Monica, respectively. I am blessed to witness their love for the Lord and each other. When I see their families, my heart is strengthened and renewed. I thought that this would always be the delight of my life until we were granted seven grandchildren; Paul III, Natalia, Tylia, Everson, Cholie, Carter, and Kyla. Our grandchildren have become the greatest joys of our lives. I praise the Lord for allowing us to experience such joy.

I also thank my administrative assistant, Gail O'Neal for the hard work she does in order to make so many things possible. Her tireless commitment and service continually makes a difference in peoples' lives. It is because of the staff at Living Word Fellowship Church, serving the Lord faithfully, that I was able to find the time to work on this material.

Special thanks to Miriam Glover for her insight, hard work, and commitment to see this book through to the end. She has edited this work, proofread through much material, and has helped the vision become a reality, as the Lord has ordained.

Special thanks also to Pastor Earl Lewis, and Pastor Lee Skinner for their commitment to Power Walk Ministries. They have been faithful board members and are committed servants of God. It is because they have made many sacrifices for this ministry that we have been able to progress this far. Their labor has not gone unnoticed.

I cannot help but thank God for calling me to serve Him. There have been many difficult days, but each experience has taught me more, has strengthened my resolve, and has caused me to fall more deeply in love with Him. Growing in my relationship with the Lord has been one of the most challenging life experiences I have had, but it has been the single greatest empowering journey of my life.

I thank God for calling me to pastor Living Word Fellowship Church. I thank Him because it has driven me to desire to learn more about the Lord, to draw closer and closer to Him so that I can be what He wants me to be for His people. I love the people the Lord has called for me to serve. We have shared a lot together as a church family and it has blessed each of us to experience God even more deeply.

CONTENTS

Sermon Series 1

Rethink Church

Safeguard the Church

Matthew 16:13–19

General Overview of the Passage

Along His travels, Jesus decided to stop in the middle of Caesarea Philippi, a fully functioning pagan society. The city had Greek mythological influence, pagan worship, and even a place for people to worship Caesar. It was here that Jesus asked a question to His disciples—His most devoted followers and the men He poured His life into for almost three years. The question that He asked is an action that has no completion and whatever people are going to say will continually be said. When disciples provide Christ the answer, what they say will be a repeated action that is continuous with no end in sight. So the wrong answer to the question will continue to be the wrong answer. The right answer will continue to be the right answer.

Peter answers that Christ is the Son of the living God, meaning Christ is deity, the promised Messiah. He is independent of everything yet begotten by the Father. Christ blessed Peter because the revelation of who Christ is in the midst of a pagan, godless world was a supernatural revelation. God revealed to Peter the true nature of Christ.

Christ again uses a mood in this verse that says what He is saying is continuously going to be said. Christ tells Peter that this confession of faith, which was influenced by God, is a revelation from God that demonstrates that Peter is to become a "mass of a rock." This means that the influence of the Holy Spirit upon Peter's life is the same experience that the church is going to be built upon (John 14:16–17; Acts 2:1–13; Rom. 8:1–25). It also means that Peter is going to be the primary leader of the disciples (Acts 10:23–48; 15). Christ, however, is still the person who builds the church (Eph. 1:22–23; 4:11–13). It is Christ who provides salvation. He is the Word and the church is His body; He is the one who calls pastors, and as a result of His death and resurrection the Holy Spirit will come as our Helper and Advocate, our peace and Comforter. So even though this revelation establishes Peter, Christ is the true Rock (1 Cor. 10:4).

The gates of Hades will try to pollute God's Word. Satan sends wolves, false teachers in the church who have selfish ambitions (Acts 20:28–30; 2 Tim. 3:1–9; 1 John 2:18–24). Satan even seeks to imitate Christ (2 Cor. 11:12–15). Christ protects the church that is truly committed to Him because Christ's power is greater than anything Satan can do (Eph. 3:10). Christ supplies the keys to the gate (2 Tim. 3:17; 2 Pet. 1:3–4), but the authority to open and close the gate is in the hands of the disciples.

Historical Background

Establishing Context

Jesus stopped in the most unusual place to ask this question. Caesarea Philippi was a place devoted to the worship of a pagan god called Pan. Herod had a temple set up for the worship of Caesar. "The city was some twenty-five miles from the Lake of Galilee and about seventeen hundred feet higher, hence the need to stop along the way (Matt. 15:21); it lay near the source of the Jordan, at the Old Testament Dan, the northern boundary of ancient Israel."[1]

Christ has always been associated with being the Rock. "He is the Rock, His work is perfect" (Deut. 32:4). "The LORD is my rock and my fortress" (Ps. 18:2). "For who is God, except the LORD? Or who is a rock, except our God?" (Ps. 18:31). "A *living stone* (1 Pet. 2:5)."[2] There are several times He is mentioned as the Rock (Ps. 118:22; Isa. 28:16; Acts 4:10–12; 1 Cor. 2:1–2; 3:11; Eph. 2:20). "The word refers neither to *Christ* as a *rock*, distinguished from *Simon*, a *stone*, nor to *Peter's confession*, but to *Peter himself*, in a sense defined by his previous confession, and as enlightened by the 'Father in Heaven.'"[3]

Jesus talks about Hades and mentions that to get to Hades you have to go down. So it seems like Hades is down in the earth. "According to Jesus, Hades is down (Matt. 11:23), and it is a prison to which He holds the keys (Rev. 1:18)."[4]

Gates are very important to the Jews. They serve as a kind of City Hall for a major city. The elders sit at the gates, as we can see in the case of Boaz and Ruth.

---

[1] C. S. Keener, *The IVP Bible Background Commentary: New Testament* (Downers Grove, IL: InterVarsity Press, 1993), Matt. 16:13.

[2] Vincent Marvin Richardson, *Word Studies in the New Testament* (Bellingham, WA: Logos Research Systems, Inc., 2002), 1:91–92.

[3] Ibid., 91.

[4] Ibid., 1:93–96.

The gates can also be a place of commerce (Deut. 16:18; 17:8; Ruth 4:11). Christ talks about the gates as a place of authority. The same idea is attached to keys. "Keys here refer to the authority to admit into the kingdom[5] (Matt. 23:13), based on the knowledge of the truth about Jesus (16:16)."[6]

What Does the Context Mean?

Even though the disciples walked with Christ and saw all the miracles and heard Him teach, they could not identify Him as the Christ without God's revelation. If the Spirit of God does not illuminate the Word of God, we would not be able to know Christ or be the church (1 Cor. 2:10–15). Bible knowledge alone only puffs up (1 Cor. 8:1). The Word of God needs to be brought to light as we walk in the light. Once the church has experienced Christ it then holds the keys to keeping Satan out of its doors. When Christ is placed first, a church truly becomes "the church of the living God."

It is the church that serves as a covering, protecting the believer from Satan (Eph. 3:10), equipping them with the armor of God (Eph. 6:11–17) and strengthening each believer through spiritual gifts. The church is the only organism that Christ is attached to and will redeem.

Sermon Subject and Title

Sermon Title: Safeguard the Church
Big Idea: The church is an organism that is shaped, empowered, and finds its authority from the lordship of Christ exercised through the ministry of the Holy Spirit.

---

[5] **Kingdom:** This term means "rule," "reign" or "authority" (not a king's people or land, as connotations of the English term could imply). Jewish people recognized that God rules the universe now, but they prayed for the day when He would rule the world unchallenged by idolatry and disobedience. The coming of this future aspect of God's reign was generally associated with the Messiah and the resurrection of the dead. Because Jesus came and will come again, Christians believe that the kingdom has been inaugurated but awaits consummation or completion. "Kingdom of heaven" is another way (Matthew's usual way) of saying "kingdom of God." "Heaven" was a standard Jewish way of saying "God" (as in Luke 15:21). (Glossary terms are from C. S. Keener's *IVP Bible Background Commentary: New Testament.*)

[6] Robert B. Hughes and J. Carl Laney, *Tyndale Concise Bible Commentary,* The Tyndale Reference Library (Wheaton, IL: Tyndale House Publishers, 2001), 411.

SERMON OUTLINE (MATT. 16:13–16)

A. Keep Christ First (vv. 13–16)

1. The church must be made up of people who are saved.
2. Knowledge alone does not put Christ first (John 6:41–43; 1 Cor. 8:1). Pharisees, Scribes rejected Him (John 5:39–40).
3. Christ is first when believers commit to be His disciples. Christ must move from Savior to Lord.
4. Sincere believers of Christ truly come to know Him (2 Cor. 4:4; Anna, Luke 2:36–38; Simeon, Luke 2:25–32; 1 John 2:3–6).

B. Allow the Holy Spirit to Illumine the Word (v. 17; 1 Cor. 2:10–15)

1. Christ told Peter that flesh and blood did not reveal Christ to him, but His Father.
2. The Spirit comes into those who accept Jesus as the Christ (John 10:9; 1 John 4:2; Eph. 1:13–14).
3. The Holy Spirit illuminates our lives to have a true experience of Christ (Rom. 8:9–16).
4. The Holy Spirit helps us to understand the deep things of God (John 14:26; 1 Cor. 2:10–15).
5. Spiritual blindness remains if we do not practice the things we know (Eph. 4:17–23; 2 Pet. 1:3–11).

C. Christ Must Shape and Establish the Church (v. 18a; 1 Cor. 3:10–11)

1. Christ is the Rock, the foundation, the cornerstone and the head of the church (1 Cor. 3:10–15; 10:4; Eph. 2:20–22).
2. Christ builds the church and it belongs to Him.
   a) He is our salvation.
   b) He is the Word.
   c) Spiritual gifts shape the church to be His body (Rom. 12:3–8; 1 Cor. 12).
   d) He calls pastors (Eph. 4:11).
   e) The Holy Spirit guides us into truth (John 14:16–17; 16:13). Jesus is the truth (John 14:6).
3. Satan and his forces use many gates:
   a) Pollute the Word (1 Tim. 4:1–4).
   b) Send wolves into the church (Acts 20:29).
   c) False apostles and workers (2 Cor. 11:13–16).
   d) Selfish ambition (James 3:13–15).
   e) Anger (Eph. 4:26–27).

4. Christ protects the church that is truly committed to Him because Christ's power is greater than anything Satan can do (Eph. 3:10).

D. We Must Use the Keys, His Word (v. 19)

1. The keys (the Word of God) are supplied by Christ (John 17:20–21).
2. The keys open the truths of God for believers. Truth sets us free (John 8:31–32).
3. The keys provide access to the kingdom of heaven (God's rule) within the hearts of believers on earth (Luke 17:21).
4. The keys provide authority to handle church discipline issues (Matt. 18:17; 1 Cor. 5:1–5; 2 Cor. 2:8; Titus 3:10).
5. The keys make sure that whatever is being bound or loosed has been approved in heaven (Matt. 16:19; 18:15–18).

Author's Comments

Comments

What about our church looks like Christ? I cannot recall a time when Christ said to sing songs everyone likes, to make sure worship does not require too much time, to make sure the preacher never talks about money, and that he does not say things that offend those who attend. So why is it that these and other issues are struggles that dominate what many believers seek to receive from church?

In this passage, Christ focuses on the essentials. The essentials to all that a car has are the engine, transmission, brakes, and electrical system. Without these essentials, having a battery and gas becomes useless. Christ does not ask the question before many of the crowds He spoke to, but only to the men He took time to disciple. This is definitely an essential because one of the first things He told His disciples is to go make disciples (Matt. 28:18–20). Christ told Peter that the only reason he recognized Christ is because of the Father illuminating his mind. Christ must always be the head of the church (Eph. 1:22–23). It does not matter who has been in the church the longest, who gives the most, or who speaks the loudest; what matters is that the instructions of Christ, through His Word, are implemented accordingly (John 15:1–111). Another essential is that the Holy Spirit, the Helper of Christ (John 14:16–17), must be in a person's life (they must be saved; Rom. 8:9–11) so that the Word of God can be illuminated (1 Cor. 2:10–15) and the believer can experience the influence and power of God.

Another essential is the Word of God, often called "the keys." Since the believer is committed to be a disciple, they have a heart for the Word like the Bereans (Acts 17:11–12; 1 Pet. 2:1–2). There must be a serious commitment to preach in season and out of season (1 Tim. 3:15; 2 Tim. 4:1–4). The New Testament church structured itself accordingly. "And they continued steadfastly in the apostles' doctrine and fellowship, in the breaking of bread, and in prayers" (Acts 2:42). When these elements are totally functional in the church, Satan is resisted and the believers experience God's powerful protection. When we have the essentials in the church, the music and décor can then lead to celebratory worship.

> Therefore do not be unwise, but understand what the will of the Lord is. And do not be drunk with wine, in which is dissipation; but be filled with the Spirit, speaking to one another in psalms and hymns and spiritual songs, singing and making melody in your heart to the Lord, giving thanks always for all things to God the Father in the name of our Lord Jesus Christ, submitting to one another in the fear of God. (Eph. 5:17–21)

The church must secure the essentials because if it does not, the lampstand is removed (Rev. 2–3). If the Word becomes corrupted, Satan takes over (2 Cor. 11:14–15; 1 Tim. 4:1–4), leaders become wolves (Acts 20:29–30), believers' lives become darkened (Eph. 4:17–21), believers are not healed from struggles or sicknesses (James 5:13–18), believers are misled by those who have only a form of godliness (2 Tim. 3), and the church can become divisive, destroying the lives of those who attend (Rom. 16:17–18; 2 Thess. 3:14–15; Titus 3:9–11). The essentials hold the church together because, as Paul says:

> According to the grace of God which was given to me, as a wise master builder I have laid the foundation, and another builds on it. But let each one take heed how he builds on it. For no other foundation can anyone lay than that which is laid, which is Jesus Christ. Now if anyone builds on this foundation with gold, silver, precious stones, wood, hay, straw, each one's work will become clear; for the Day will declare it, because it will be revealed by fire; and the fire will test each one's work, of what sort it is. If anyone's work which he has built on it endures, he will receive a reward. If anyone's work is burned, he will suffer loss; but he himself will be saved, yet so as through fire. (1 Cor. 3:10–15)

The church may be vibrant, based on our evaluation, but there is no Christ if He chooses to vacate the building:

> And to the angel of the church in Sardis write, "These things says He who has the seven Spirits of God and the seven stars: 'I know your works, that you have a name that you are alive, but you are dead. Be watchful, and strengthen the things which remain, that are ready to die, for I have not found your works perfect before God.'" (Rev. 3:1–2)

This does not mean that the church needs to be boring and the pastor does not seek to keep the message interesting and the service lasts three hours. God does not like a dull church (Deut. 28:47–48). When Christ spoke to the Samaritan woman, He told her to worship Him in spirit (small *s*) and truth (John 4:24). He loved how vibrant the Samaritans were on Jacob's mountain, but they did not use the historical books in the Bible, so they lacked truth. The Jews used all the books but lacked spirit. Christ wanted both.

We must function with a deep commitment to let the church be the church. When Christ's headship is essential and there is one Christ, when the Holy Spirit is not quenched (1 Thess. 5:12–22), when there is one Spirit, and when the Word of God is applied truthfully, all believers grow into the nature of Christ and there is unity (Eph. 4:12–13; 2 Pet. 1:3–4). "There is one body and one Spirit, just as you were called in one hope of your calling; one Lord, one faith, one baptism; one God and Father of all, who is above all, and through all, and in you all" (Eph. 4:4–6). The powerful influence of the Holy Spirit that binds the body together blesses God (Ps. 133).

Application

Unless Christ is the center of everything that is done in the church, there is no point to doing anything. It is like believing a person has experienced salvation but doesn't believe in the resurrection. It is like wanting to live but preferring not to have a heart, lungs, or brain. Is that even living?

Christ must be purely who He is (1 John 4:4), or He is not Christ at all. So when we worship Him, we need to come to know Him and experience Him. Reading the Bible while practicing it is essential; loving others while serving them is essential (John 13:35), so that we become more like Christ and, therefore, become His church functionally.

Illustrate It

It was said that more and more people have less time for church. It's almost as if there are too many alternatives on Sunday. And as people are working harder and longer during the week, Sunday is their only day off. With the world becoming more impersonal, people would rather stay home and watch television.

The church is the only place that Christ is the head of and the place He is directly attached to (Eph. 1:22–23). It is the place to call the elders to pray to be healed; it is the place where you find all the spiritual gifts that serve to strengthen a person in a broken world; it is the place where a pastor/teacher resides to mend broken lives; it is the place where Christ wants His death remembered; it is the pillar and foundation of truth; it is where the nation of God gathers each week; and it is where love matters most.

Why do believers come to it with a watch, a complaint, no time to serve, and with a critique? It is because they have become so influenced by the world that church has lost its taste. It is like a young man in college who drank beer so much that the taste of water became bitter.

> H. W. Beecher says that "some churches are like lighthouses, built of stone, so strong that the thunder of the sea cannot move them . . ." The light that shines from these churches is the light of Christ shining through his believers. Sinners are not reached solely through the church's ceremony, pomp, beautiful music or largeness—they are reached through the Christ-likeness of its individual members.[7]

---

[7] Richard A. Steele, ed., *Practical Bible Illustrations from Yesterday and Today* (Chattanooga, TN: AMG International, Inc., 1995).

Return to Your First Love

Revelation 2:1–7

General Overview of the Passage

Christ speaks to the seven churches through an angel. The identity of the angel is not completely clear. Jesus' message shows Jesus as holding, with a determined grip, seven stars, which represents the seven pastors in these churches (1:20). These pastors serve as lights to the world. They can also be presented as a single cluster of stars that shine as one with one unified message. He holds these stars in His right hand demonstrating a position of honor and equality (the church represents His headship and body). Christ walks among the churches. His walking demonstrates that the Lord continually patrols the churches and is always on the spot when He is needed; His presence is not localized but coextensive with the church. His walking also implies that He provides constant and vigilant supervision. His holding of the stars and His continual walking among the churches also demonstrates His power and authority. We see that He walks with this kind of authority among the seven churches. "As for the mystery of the seven stars which you saw in My right hand, and the seven golden lampstands: the seven stars are the angels of the seven churches, and the seven lamp-stands are the seven churches" (Rev. 1:20 NASB).

Christ, after affirming that He lives among the churches, lets them know about their accomplishments. He compliments them for their hard work that is filled with sweat and fatigue, their endurance, steadfast behavior that is consistent due to their hope in God. He commended them because they did not tolerate evil men, but tested their hearts to see if this was good or evil. Many were proven false, and their longsuffering was not just because of life issues. It was based on their commitment to live for Christ's sake. They did this consistently without tiring of being faithful or giving up because these various tasks were strenuous and exhausting.

Christ knows the details of this church because He said that He was walking among them. He found them lacking a very important element (Rev. 2:4):

"Thou hast 'remitted' or let down thy early love; that is, it is less glowing and ardent than it was at first. The love here referred to is evidently love to the Saviour and the idea is that, as a church, they had less of this than formerly characterized them. In this respect they were in a state of declension."[8]

Christ challenges the church to return to their first love and partake of the "tree of life" so that He does not take away their lampstand.

Historical Background

Establishing Context

"These seven churches (Rev. 1:4, 11) are themselves lampstands (Rev. 1:12) reflecting the light of Christ to the world (Matt. 5:14–16; John 8:12) in the midst of which Christ walks (Rev. 1:13)."[9]

The interpretation for the angel (or messenger) of the church has had challenges. Some people believe it is a reference to the writer of the book as the apostle John. Others believe that John is speaking to the pastors of the church. Some have taken it to be a reference to the bishop over the elders, but the fact that *angelos* is in each church indicates that interpretation would not work. The interpretation that has the least difficulties is that the angel or messenger is the pastor of the church (Gal. 1:8; 4:14; 1 Tim. 5:21).

The church of Ephesus had a very sound reputation for confronting sin, false apostles, and evil men, and were known for their "perseverance" and endurance in the name of the Lord. But, "sound doctrine and perseverance are inadequate without love. Whether love for other Christians (as in 1 John; cf. "works"—Rev. 2:5, 19; "hate"—2:6) or for God (Jer. 2:2) is in view is not clear."[10]

"The 'tree of life' which was first mentioned as being in the garden of Eden is now in the Paradise of God. Although the 'tree of life' was used to symbolize

---

[8] *Albert Barnes' Notes on the Whole Bible,* Electronic Database Copyright © 1997, 2003 by Biblesoft, Inc.; https://www.studylight.org/commentaries/bnb/revelation-2.html.

[9] *Robertson's Word Pictures in the New Testament* (Nashville, TN: Broadman Press, 1985).

[10] C. S. Keener, *The IVP Bible Background Commentary: New Testament* (Downers Grove, IL: InterVarsity Press, 1993).

the law[11] in later Jewish teaching, this vision alludes to Genesis 2:9 and a restoration of paradise (on which cf. 2 Corinthians 12:2–4). Each of the promises in these oracles to the churches is fulfilled in Revelation 21–22."[12]

What Does the Context Mean?

We must preserve the church God built so that we bless Him and are continually blessed. Christ, who continually walks among the seven churches, says that they must totally turn from their ways and eat from the tree of life. If they have a change of heart and go back to the things they first did He will not remove His presence from among them.

Sermon Subject and Title

Sermon Title: Return to Your First Love
Big Idea: God's very nature is love, so being busy doing many great things in ministry without the manifestation of love means nothing.

Sermon Outline (Rev. 2:1–7 nasb)

A. The Way It Was (v. 1)

1. *Holds*—The churches are in Christ's grasp and they will remain there continuously. This is a present active participle.
2. *Right hand*—This is a place of honor and equal dignity.
3. *Walks*—Christ is persistently, vigilantly, and continuously walking among the seven churches. The churches are continuously monitored by Christ.
4. *Says*—This is a message they must pay attention to always. Said in the present tense indicative, meaning what is being said is a continuous act that is habitual.

---

[11] **Law:** "Torah" (the Hebrew word behind the Greek word translated "law") means literally "instruction" and "teaching," not just regulations. It was also used as a title for the first five books of the Old Testament (the Pentateuch, the books of Moses) and sometimes for the whole Old Testament. This commentary uses the translation "law" because it is familiar to readers of most translations, even though the English term's semantic range is much narrower than the Jewish concept. (Glossary terms are from C. S. Keener's *IVP Bible Background Commentary: New Testament.*)

[12] Ibid.

B. The Issues to Resolve (vv. 2–3)

1. *I know*—Christ has a full divine knowledge and experience that provides Him a comprehensive understanding of what is taking place in the church. This is a perfect active, which means that Christ's knowledge is complete and is a set condition.
2. *Labored/perseverance*—The members of the church were diligent in service to the point of fatigue, straining with all their might and never fainting. This is an accusative, which means that Christ's knowledge directly relates to recognizing the service in the church.
3. *Did not tolerate evil men*—They stood up against false apostles who did not demonstrate a godly character. These men continuously and habitually called themselves apostles (present active indicative).
4. They desired a pure and sound church and were faithful to it.
5. *Hated the Nicolaitans*—They did not support those who preached spiritual liberty, ate foods sacrificed to idols, practiced idolatry and immorality.
6. *Perseverance/endured*—It did not matter what trials or tribulation they experienced; they remained steady in their godly character. "Have" is in the present active indicative, meaning they continuously and habitually endured all that was against them.
7. *Did not grow weary*—They were in a set condition of not becoming so weak that they faint (perfect active indicative).
8. *Christ loved them*—He was among them, but He would not lower His standard.

C. We Must Refresh Our Ways (vv. 4–5)

1. *Left*—There is a movement which was continuously away from truly loving Christ.
2. *Their first love*—Compared to Acts 20 and Ephesians—even though they were trying to do the right things to keep the church sound—they had lost their love for Christ and their unselfish desire to do His complete will (Matt. 22:36–40; John 14:15).
3. *Left their first love*—The Jews were committed to laws of Moses and all that Judaism became, but they still crucified Christ. A person can become deeply committed to all the traditions they believe should be a part of the church and neglect the Word of God working in and through their lives.

4. *Remember*—(present active indicative)—This is a continuous act of making sure they do not forget.
5. *Fallen*—They were in a state of decline even though it was a theologically sound church. The perfect active means that their state of decline remains this way.
6. *Repent*—This is a one-time decision to change, to go in a completely different direction, to make a decisive break from present actions.
7. *Consequence*—The taking of the lampstand. Unless they repent, Christ will remove His presence from the church.

D. Live as Overcomers (vv. 6–7)

1. *Who has ears*—This is a believer who continuously wants to hear what Christ has to say.
2. *Let him*—Christ commands them to allow each person the opportunity to make a one-time decision to repent.
3. *Hear*—Must have a mind willing to change.
4. *Tree of life*—The person who repents to Christ experiences all that eternal life provides.
5. *Paradise*—This person experiences rest and eternal bliss, a life of peace.

Author's Comments

Comments

The church of Ephesus was the most important church in Rome. It was a church that experienced a great founder, the apostle Paul (Acts 20:27–31) and great preachers and teachers in Timothy, the apostle John, Apollos, and Priscilla and Aquilla. The church was known for sound doctrine and functioned as a great example to other churches. Their commitment to the Word became more Pharisaic in the sense that they made sure the Word was not polluted, but failed to love Christ and one another. It is like some marriages where the couple becomes committed to their marriage but does not have the same warm love they had for each other when they first met. Even though they are married, are they in love?

Application

We must preserve the church God built so that we bless Him and are continually blessed. Christ, who continually walks among the seven churches, says that they must totally turn from their ways in order to eat from the tree of life.

If they have a change of heart and go back to the things they first did, He would not remove His presence from among them. One of the first things they did was to love God, by obeying His Word, and to love one another.

Illustrate It

At the peak of his career, Michael Jordan's father died. Shortly after this, Michael decided to accomplish his childhood dream—he wanted to play baseball. He played for one season, and even though he was excited to live his dream, he decided to go back to his first love, basketball.

We may love our church, but we are not the head of it. We are the body; Christ is the head. We need to focus on growing up in His nature, through the ministry of the Holy Spirit, because if we abide in Him, His love will abide in us, and as the Father loved Him we will be loved by God as well (John 15:8–10). "Teacher, which is the great commandment in the law?" Jesus said to him, "'You shall love the Lord your God with all your heart, with all your soul, and with all your mind.' This is the first and great commandment. And the second is like it: 'You shall love your neighbor as yourself.' On these two commandments hang all the Law and the Prophets" (Matt. 22:36–40).

Stand for Truth while Disarming the Enemy

Revelation 2:12–17

General Overview of the Passage

Christ says to the pastor that He knows—meaning He has a full knowledge and experience—that Satan remains in this city and has a lot of influence. Christ comes to His church with a sword purposely constructed to cut with both edges (Heb. 4:12). This sword can cut into a person's soul to examine thoughts and motives. It can cut into a person creating so much damage that it creates judgment upon them for all the evil they have done. The impact is complete and can determine their eternal destiny. In the midst of a city where Satan dwells, God speaks to His believers to hear a message from Him. This is a place that He dwells (Rev. 1:20; 2:1), but He is threatening to leave it.

The believers remained focused with clear intent and a strong grip on following God's purposes, His character, and the authority of the name of Jesus Christ. They did not reject or turn against their knowledge and conviction concerning the gospel. They sustained their commitment to Christ even though people who lived in the city were expected to worship the god of Pergumum. This led to Antipas, a member of the church, being murdered. The mob probably did this to honor the god Aesculapius. Antipas, possibly an officer in the church, was praised for being a true, trustworthy, and steadfast servant of God.

Christ, however, said He had a few things against them. The church had become caught up in the teachings of Balaam, who advised the Midianite women how to lead the Israelites astray (Num. 25:1–2; 31:16; Jude 11) when God did not allow him to curse the Israelites. He found a way to get the men of Israel to break two of God's laws, thus causing a just God to respond. Balak, the king, instructed Balaam to curse the Israelites in fear that they might defeat him, whereas the Nicolaitans taught about liberality, which led to believers participating in idol worship, eating food given to idols, and practicing immorality.

They were people in the church who persisted in continually teaching these doctrines with a strong conviction. They persisted in seeking to persuade the believers of the church to believe in these doctrines. This, like in the case of Balaam, had become a trap leading believers into ruin. Apparently, the leadership of the church did little or nothing to stop it. These leaders (Antipas being an example) seem to have been committed to the Lord, but they did not prevent false doctrine from persisting in the church.

Christ instructs them to reject these acts and turn back to a committed walk with Christ. He says that if they did not, He would come quickly. Christ would command a war or fight against these false teachers with the sword of His mouth. Christ seems to indicate that He, personally, is going to bring upon them His judgment.

These believers, who experienced the difficulties of life in Pergamum, were provided by Christ a white stone with a new name inscribed upon it. This means that His judgment of them found them righteous and He would allow them in His presence.

Historical Background

Establishing Context

The church of Pergamum was in a city that was really pagan. It was a place where the god of Zeus was worshipped. It was a rich city but immoral. It was known for its two-hundred-thousand-volume library. It manufactured parchments that became known as *pergamena.* This is where we get the name parchment.

Because of the widespread idol worship they were against Christians. This is why Antipas was brutally murdered. "This adversity led to the slaying of Antipas. Antipas was said to have died either as result of being put in bronze kettle and burnt to death or was attacked by a mob and murdered to honor their god."[13]

False teaching slipped into the church. This was the teaching of Balaam—the same teaching that was experienced in the wilderness. "Balaam could not curse Israel so he got the Moabite women to be with Israelite men. This immorality led to God going against Israel rather than Balaam cursing them."[14] There

---

[13] Keener, *The IVP Bible Background Commentary*, s.v. Rev. 2:12–17.

[14] Ibid.

was also false teaching by the Nicolaitans who wanted the believers to walk contrary to the Word of God by eating food offered to idols. "The Nicolaitans sought to encourage believers to live liberated from the law. This includes eating idol food, practice idolatry and immorality. This N.T. church allowed this kind of teaching."[15] Because the church was tolerating these teachings, Christ warned them that He has "the sharp two-edged sword" (Rev. 4:12b).

"A new name written on the stone . . ." (Rev. 2:17 NASB). There was special significance about these stones. "White stones used for medical purposes were associated with Judea; and perhaps most significant, jurors used black stones to vote for a person's guilt but white ones to vote for innocence. The Old Testament associated change of name with a promise (e.g., Gen. 17:5, 15)."[16]

What Does the Context Mean?

We must be conscious of and must never tolerate false doctrine (1 Tim. 4:1–5). We should never, because of the pressures of new and popular religious movements, compromise the truths of God's Word. It does not matter if this leads to persecution and isolation from the rest of society. As sanctified believers being separated unto God, we should never let feeling so different cause us to give up trusting and believing the truth God's Word provides. Christ will judge those who teach false doctrine and will reward those, who despite the pressures and popularity of false doctrine, live in the truth of His Word as overcomers.

Sermon Subject and Title

Sermon Title: Stand for Truth while Disarming the Enemy
Big Idea: Our commitment to live for Christ does not remove our responsibility for being our brother's keeper by holding members accountable when they teach false doctrine. When we seek to keep the church's doctrine pure, Christ blesses us not just here on earth but also eternally.

Sermon Outline (Rev. 2:12–17 NASB)

A. In Truth, They Stood under Pressure (vv. 12–13)

1. *Church*—God's called-out people separated unto Him (Phil. 2:14–16).

---

[15] Ibid.

[16] Ibid.

2. *Cults*—Stronghold for Satan; like Daniel, commanded to worship false gods; Satan creates confusion while God is peace.
3. *Has the sharp sword*—"Has" here is a present active verb meaning that Christ continuously has this sword.
4. *Sharp sword*—Serves to separate believers from the world, critically examine thoughts and motives, and judge those believing false doctrine.
5. *I know*—Christ has a completed state of knowing and complete understanding of all that is taking place here (perfect active indicative).
6. *Keep the faith*—They persisted in living out the character and nature of Christ; Antipas—trustworthy, reliable, steadfast servant who may have been be a leader in the church.

B. The Truth Challenged under Pressure (vv. 14–15)

1. *Unlike Ephesus*—God had a few things, not one thing (Rev. 2:4), He held as concerns for the church at Pergamum.
2. *Against*—God set Himself to oppose the church.
3. *Hold*—False teachers persisted in their teaching (demonic influence; 1 Tim. 4:1–5), and the church did nothing about it. This is something they are doing continuously to the point it has become a habit (present active accusative). The accusative means that this is the direct reason Christ will set Himself against the church.
4. *False Doctrine*
   a) *Balaam*—Got the men of Israel to be with Moabite women; turned God against a nation.
   b) *Balak*—A king afraid of God's powerful nation sought out a prophet to curse God's people.
   c) *Nicolaitans*—Liberality, idol worship; did not like conservative Christians. They were pressuring them to change by practicing idolatry and living an immoral lifestyle.

C. Overcomers, Blessed by the Truth (vv. 16–17)

1. *Repent*—Regret what was done, turn with determination—once-and-for-all decision (aorist) to do the will of God. This is a command (aorist imperative).
2. *Christ comes quickly*—Christ not threatening to take His lampstand. He will war against the church. Christ's coming is continuous and it needs to be received by these believers (present passive verb).
3. *War against with sword*—Double edge (v. 12); long sword—very destructive.
4. *Overcomers*—Repented, stayed focused like Antipas.

5. *Hidden*—Secure, protected by Christ.
6. *Written*—It is inscribed on the stone and it is permanent and they must receive it once provided (perfect active passive).
7. *White stone*—Spared God's judgment; banquet admission—Messianic feast, not outer darkness.
8. *New nature*—Mature in faith; transformed because they remained faithful.
9. *No one knows*—Only the person who receives this reward has a complete knowledge of what was provided (perfect active indicative).

Author's Comments

Comments

You know people ask, "Is the pastor preaching this Sunday?" or "Which praise group is singing on Sunday?" or "What series is the pastor on?" but I am not sure if they ever ask whether or not Jesus is still in the church. After all, if He cuts Himself off from those who don't abide in Him, how could He be in a church when the people who are the church are not abiding in Him? The believers of Pergamum were once committed to the point of death, but then they began to drift (similar to the Hebrew brethren; Heb. 2:1–4). To drift away from Christ is to eventually be cut off.

It seems like Christ is more aggressive than with any other church mentioned in Revelation in punishing disobedience. He talks about using a double-edged sword (2:12), He is coming quickly (2:16), and He will make war with the double-edged sword that comes from His mouth. It is as if the presence of false doctrine was so strong in the church that Satan got a foothold and established a throne (2:13). It seems like this is the reason why Christ comes with such force. When it has to do with false doctrine, Christ aggressively wants to cut it out (1 Tim. 4:1–5).

Abiding in Christ is directly correlated with abiding in His Word (John 15:8–10). This was Christ's challenge to His disciples before He died. When they did not abide in His Word, they ended up deserting Him. But when they abided in His Word, they fulfilled John 12:23–26:

> But Jesus answered them, saying, "The hour has come that the Son of Man should be glorified. Most assuredly, I say to you, unless a grain of wheat falls into the ground and dies, it remains alone; but if it dies,

> it produces much grain. He who loves his life will lose it, and he who hates his life in this world will keep it for eternal life. If anyone serves Me, let him follow Me; and where I am, there My servant will be also. If anyone serves Me, him My Father will honor."

When a person arrives at this commitment to Christ, true discipleship is born (Luke 14:26–27). Therefore, the heartbeat of a church is their commitment to keep the Word pure. Whether it is what the choir is singing, what the Sunday school teacher is teaching, or whatever the small group ministry is studying, maintaining the purity of the Word of God and living with a loving heart one to another are the crux of all we do.

Application

To tolerate false doctrine is to invite Satan into the church (1 Tim. 4:1–4). He is a savage wolf (Acts 20:29–30) and seeks believers (1 Pet. 5:7–9; Rev. 12:10) to destroy them. Teachers who teach in violation of the church's doctrine must be held accountable in an effort to protect the body from the destructive efforts of Satan and justice executed by Christ (2 Pet. 1–3).

Illustrate It

When President Obama first became president, he went to France to meet the president of France. During his visit, there was a lot being said about the lifestyle of France's president. During one of the times, photographs were being taken making President Obama seem like he was looking at the behind of a woman who was near him. That picture started circling around as if President Obama, in the presence of the president of France, was beginning to behave like that president. When the news outlets eventually saw the real picture, President Obama was looking down because he was trying to help a woman in high-heeled shoes come down the stairs! The angle of the first picture didn't tell the whole story; it made President Obama look like his eyes got the best of him.

I wondered what the discussion was like at the house with his wife while the first picture circulated.

False information can create lots of damage and leave people bitter. The false teaching in the church of Pergamum could lead the church to be controlled by Satan. Satan made this city a place where he felt comfortable establishing his throne. Satan is a slanderer, a liar, and a deceitful worker.

Make Your Amen Count

Revelation 3:1–6

General Overview of the Passage

How Christ addresses the church of Sardis is different from how He begins His address to the church in Smyrna, Pergamum, or Thyatira. The Lord states to the church of Sardis that He holds the seven spirits and the seven stars. "On the 'spirits' and 'stars' (cf. 1:4, 16, 20), the "alive . . . dead" here reverses the imagery of 1:18 and 2:8."[17] Because of what is transpiring in the church, He is addressing only His called-out believers including the "angel of the church." This is because there are only a few people in Sardis who remain committed to the Lord (v. 4). As a result, what He writes to them is engraved with precision and it is legislated by God.

There were a few people in Sardis who did not defile themselves. They chose to live holy, not sinful lives. But only a few. These believers lived by faith, which was demonstrated by the way they conducted their lives. Their reward causes them to wear clothes that do not show defilement. It does not show corruption. The inner commitment of Christ toward them is exposed when they wear white. He who prevails, conquers, proves to be victorious against the odds will not have his name completely washed away from the Book of Life. This Book is God's list of all those who are destined for eternal life (Phil. 4:3; Rev. 3:5; 13:8; 17:8; 20:12, 15; 21:27). The believers, who are few, are the ones who are actually alive. They are alive in the midst of those who seem alive but are dead. These believers remain in the Book of Life that is held in Christ's care, and He agrees with what is written before the Father and His angels. Those who are worthy are those who demonstrate consistently that their spiritual transformation has the same value on the outside as on the inside of their lives.

This church has a good reputation for being a church that is alive and displays evidence of God's presence. But in actuality it is dead. As a result,

[17] Keener, *The IVP Bible Background Commentary*, s.v. Rev. 3:1–2.

Christ commands them to a task they must fulfill. He told them to keep their eyes wide open and remain awake because they need to establish the things that remain. They need to make sure that these things become a strong fixture within the church.

Historical Background

Establishing Context

The people of Sardis believed that it was impossible for anyone to capture the city because of how the land was situated. The only problem was it was captured twice. It had a large Jewish population, many of whom were popular and wealthy. Of all the churches that were addressed, Sardis and Laodicea are the only cities that are now not inhabited. "This verse refers to Jesus' saying preserved in Matthew 24:43 (as do 1 Thess. 5:2; 2 Pet. 3:10). Sardis's acropolis had never been taken by battle, but twice in its history invaders had captured it by stealth unexpectedly in the night."[18]

The church of Sardis was famous among the churches. It was known to be "alive." It is apparent that the people who lived in Sardis believed that the church had spiritual vitality, so it was the place to be. There was indeed a godly remnant in Sardis, and Christ challenges them not to soil their clothes. "He promised that true believers will be dressed in white (cf.[19] v. 18), symbolic of the righteousness of God, that their names will remain in the book of life, and that He will acknowledge them as His own before His Father and His angels."[20]

The Book of Life, generally speaking, was a part of many countries or cities. It was the book that registered the residents as citizens and was used as a part of Jewish life in the Old Testament. It most likely had to do with the registration of people's genealogy. Being erased from the Book of Life may be a threat to the loss of salvation, or it could be (not enough information given to clearly distinguish this) that some may miss the rapture. "In the Old Testament, the book of life represents a register of God's covenant people (Exod. 32:32–33; Isa. 4:3; Dan. 12:1). To be blotted out of His book meant to forfeit the privileges

[18] Ibid., s.v. Rev. 3:3.

[19] **cf. *confer*:** compare (C. S. Keener, *IVP Bible Background Commentary*).

[20] C. E. Arnold, *Zondervan Illustrated Bible Backgrounds Commentary, Volume 4: Hebrews to Revelation* (Grand Rapids, MI: Zondervan, 2002), 272.

of covenant status."[21] "When someone committed a criminal action and was condemned, he lost his citizenship and his name was then erased from the register. This action, using the same Greek verb *exaleiphō*, is attested by several ancient authors and inscriptions. Those who overcome are promised that they will never lose their citizenship in the heavenly city."[22]

What Does the Context Mean?

You have heard these sayings a thousand time, but they are nonetheless true: "Things are not always what they seem to be" and "Not everything that glitters is gold." We cannot get so caught up in what people may say about a particular church. This can cause a person to slowly lose touch with the true interpretation and application of Scripture. We must remain focused on developing the ministries that God has placed in our care. In the midst of all the bad theology that exists, we must remain focused. We must maintain a consciousness of God's continual presence in order to be a blessed assembly of believers.

> According to the grace of God which was given to me, as a wise master builder I have laid the foundation, and another builds on it. But let each one take heed how he builds on it. For no other foundation can anyone lay than that which is laid, which is Jesus Christ. (1 Cor. 3:10–11)

Sermon Subject and Title

Sermon Title: Make Your Amen Count
Big Idea: Christ provides credit where it is due but demands excellence because the church represents His nature and His glory, so those who are faithful must seek to make a difference.

Sermon Outline (Rev. 3:1–6 NASB)

A. Remain Alert (vv. 1–3)

1. *Angel*—The pastor is held accountable for the church being Christ's church (Eph. 4:11–16).

---

[21] Ibid., 273.
[22] Ibid., 272–73.

2. *Says*—What Christ says in this passage is continuously the same and it is definitely true (present active indicative).
3. *Christ* is directly engaged in His church (1 Cor. 12; Eph. 1:22–23):
    a) *Know*—Know is in the perfect active indicative, which means that Christ is completely set in what He knows and what He is going to do. Nothing could change His mind.
    b) *Know*—Christ is constantly among us.
    c) *Know*—He has a full divine understanding of everything.
    d) *Name*—The reputation of this church is that it is physically exciting, but for Christ it is spiritually dead.
    e) *Found*—Christ is constantly examining this church.
    f) *I have not . . . in the sight of God*—Christ knows what God the Father is thinking.
    g) *Deeds not complete*—All the work that is being done is in a state of being incomplete (perfect passive participle). The passive means that they have accepted the condition the church is in.
4. The attitude of an alert believer:
    a) *Wake up*—Christ's command is to make themselves continuously vigilant (Rom. 12:10–12), and watchful (1 Pet. 1:13–15; 5:8)—(present active imperative middle).
    b) *Strengthen*—Christ commands them to be steadfast in purpose and disposition once and for all (Gal. 6:9–10) (aorist active imperative). It is a nominative—this is what they must become.
    c) *Remember*—We must remain constantly focused on what we have learned.
    d) *Receive*—We must remain steadfast, walking by faith (perfect active indicative); the state of remaining steadfast is a set, complete condition.
    e) *Heard*—Be always committed to obey God. What they heard was a one-time decision (aorist) to do (active) what was presented to them.
    f) *Keep*—Christ commands them to continuously and habitually preserve (Ps. 119:11) what they have heard (present active imperative).
    g) *Repent*—Be willing to change whenever God challenges us to change. This is an act of turning around that they are commanded to do once and for all (aorist active imperative).

h) *Come like a thief*—Never forget that God is not afraid to judge us and He comes unannounced.

B. Remain Obedient No Matter Life's Difficulties (vv. 4–6)

1. *You have a few people*—These people are continuously among them and this is the direct reason for His comments in this verse (present imperative, an accusative).
2. *Remain faithful*—Even though it is a challenge; it is not easy to remain faithful in a wicked world and in an unfaithful church.
   a) *Not soiled*—They were willing to deal with sin (1 John 1:8–9; Jude 23).
   b) *Walk*—Be committed to demonstrate a life of faith.
   c) *Walk*—They kept their relationship with Christ fresh.
   d) *Worthy*—Tested and proven deserving of their reward (Col. 1:9–12).
   e) *Overcomers*—Consistently gaining victory over obstacles.
   f) *White*—Remain faithful until we meet our Savior (Rev. 3:18). This is in the dative, meaning this is a robe that was given to them by Christ.
3. Our reward is sure; this is special because they are experiencing many challenges:
   a) *Not erase*—God will not eliminate these individuals' names from the Book of Life.
   b) *Not erase*—The individuals who listen prove to be worthy (20:12, 15; 21:27).
   c) *Not erase*—Those who listen and strengthen the things that remain prove to be genuine.
   d) *Confess*—Christ will present these believers before God as true believers.
4. *An ear let him hear*—Those who truly have a heart for God are commanded to make a one-time decision to remain committed to obey (aorist imperative active).

Author's Comments

Comments

Is it what people say about the church we go to that makes the church qualified to keep Christ in its doors? It does not matter what people believe the church should be or what they describe it to be. The real issue is what the Bridegroom thinks about the bride. Because this Bridegroom threatens to leave does not mean He is planning to divorce His church. We need to be quick to listen to Him as He explains, in this passage, what keeps Him from walking out the door.

Church attendees want to dictate what takes place in their church. They believe they should be heard especially when they believe they donate a lot of money. It does not matter what the Scriptures say—it matters most what they like. In Sardis, many of the people were wealthy and attended church mostly because of the reputation the church had in the city. They did not seem to do an evaluation of how the church fits a biblical description (2 Tim. 3:17). It was how the church satisfied their needs. This is what led to the church's demise. Neither the church nor the city exists today.

I know as a pastor how much pressure people can apply. It is not always for negative purposes. Some people want to see their church grow, and meet its financial needs. Their training is from liberal arts instructions. This training, in some cases, has led them to experience much success in their lives. Renewing the mind can be a challenge because in their view there is no need to change their way of thinking because of their accomplishments. The issue is that Scripture instructs us not to lean to our own understanding (Prov. 3:5–6) because in the New Testament Paul teaches us that this is very dangerous.

> This I say, therefore, and testify in the Lord, that you should no longer walk as the rest of the Gentiles walk, in the futility of their mind, having their understanding darkened, being alienated from the life of God, because of the ignorance that is in them, because of the blindness of their heart; who, being past feeling, have given themselves over to lewdness, to work all uncleanness with greediness. But you have not so learned Christ, if indeed you have heard Him and have been taught by Him, as the truth is in Jesus. (Eph. 4:17–21)

Then Paul tells us to "put off, concerning your former conduct, the old man which grows corrupt according to the deceitful lusts, and be renewed in the spirit of your mind, and that you put on the new man which was created according to God, in true righteousness and holiness" (Eph. 4:22–24).

To some people this makes church boring and irrelevant, to which I say God provides the concepts and He allows us a lot of freedom (John 8:31–32) in the application (Eph. 1:9–11). When the application does not violate the Word of God, the Lord sustains His lampstand.

> For though I am free from all men, I have made myself a servant to all, that I might win the more; and to the Jews I became as a Jew, that I might win Jews; to those who are under the law, as under the law, that I might win those who are under the law; to those who are without law, as without law (not being without law toward God, but under law toward Christ), that I might win those who are without law; to the weak I became as weak, that I might win the weak. I have become all things to all men, that I might by all means save some. Now this I do for the gospel's sake, that I may be partaker of it with you. (1 Cor. 9:19–23)

It is important to read the last part of this passage: "Now this I do for the gospel's sake . . ." All of this is done for the purposes of Christ because it is the same person that wrote: "All Scripture is given by inspiration of God, and is profitable for doctrine, for reproof, for correction, for instruction in righteousness, that the man of God may be complete, thoroughly equipped for every good work" (2 Tim. 3:16–17). Keeping the church Bible-centered does not make it boring; it makes it a dynamic experience of the powerful development of the Holy Spirit in a believer's life. The application of biblical concepts provides a lot of freedom (John 8:31–32) that can bless the variety of needs that may exist in the church.

When the church empties itself of the Word of God, Christ is no longer the head of it (the lampstand is removed) and Satan reigns (Acts 20:27–32; 2 Cor. 11:1–15; 1 Tim. 4:1–5).

Application

Most people join a church they believe meets their needs. That is like finding a hospital that an individual believes fits their self-diagnosis. In the Scriptures, the church needs to be led by Christ, who is the head, and it needs to be shaped in the manner in which the body of Christ works, with Christ as the foundation and the chief cornerstone. When a person finds such a church, then the body of Christ builds them up into the fullness of God. That is the primary need. Once that is accomplished, the Bible states that we will be able to "comprehend with all the saints what is the breadth and length and height and depth, and to know the love of Christ which surpasses knowledge, that you may be filled up to all the fullness of God" (Eph. 3:18–19 NASB). Once this takes place, a person can walk in the light as Christ is in the light (1 John 1:5–7). Once this is accomplished, the fruit of the Spirit flows out of a person's life. These attributes, once established, take care of whatever else a person needs. A believer's need is to find a church that can shape believers to be like Christ. When this takes place, 2 Peter 1:3–11 says this believer does not stumble through life.

Illustrate It

"The *Wall Street Journal* of June 21, 1983, carried a disturbing article on vacant church buildings in Britain. The delicate debate as to what should be done with idle structures intensified when the rector of a parish down the road from All Saints Church 'took the bells down from the tower.' He proposed to melt them. Many citizens from Saltfleetby, England, were incensed, especially Mrs. Aegerter, who lives next door to All Saints and who sweeps and cleans the church regularly.

"This thirteenth-century stone structure is said to be one of 186 old buildings the Church of England has 'mothballed.' They have created a 'Redundant Church Fund,' apparently waiting for a revival, a miracle, or a demographic shift in population.

"Their contemporary poet, Philip Larkin, asked, 'When churches fall completely out of use, what shall we turn them into?' He continues. 'Shall we keep a few chronically on show . . . and let the rest rent-free to rain and sheep?'

"Since 1969, church authorities have indicated that 908 churches are no longer needed; 247 of them have already been demolished, and another 475 buildings have been 'converted' to other purposes. When is a church redundant? Is it not possible for a so-called active congregation to be spiritually empty?"[23]

[23] G. C. Jones, *1000 Illustrations for Preaching and Teaching* (Nashville, TN: Broadman & Holman Publishers, 19867), 123.

Let His Amen Be Our Amen

Revelation 3:14–22

General Overview of the Passage

John is instructed to write to the pastor of the Laodicean church. The trustworthy and steadfast Christ, who is the God of truth, can be contrasted to the untrustworthy, faithless Laodiceans. Christ established all things as the Creator from the beginning (Rev. 1:5, 8). He calls out to believers and challenges them, with complete authority, to change their behavior. "Three things are necessary for this: (1) to have seen with His own eyes what He attests; (2) to be competent to relate it for others; (3) to be willing truthfully to do so."[24]

Christ says He has full knowledge of all of the works of the church of Laodicea, a church the apostle John says is supposed to be energized by their faith. Using the analogy of hot or lukewarm water, which is a major irritant in the city, Christ says like lukewarm water, He wants to spit them out. Just like doctors who used lukewarm water to cause people to vomit, they too cause Christ to want to vomit. The church should understand since the whole city struggled with the lukewarm water. It was a constant irritant for the people. Just like they rejected the water and wanted it either to be hot or cold, He rejects them.

The church says, in an affirming manner, that they are in a state of being very wealthy and believed they were doing very well (after an earthquake thirty-five years before this letter was written, they did not need Rome's assistance). They were very wealthy because they had a medical center, rich wool business (textile industry), and eye salve businesses. This wealth caused them to not fully recognize the spiritual poverty they were in. They felt spiritually proud and self-sufficient, but in God's eyes they were so poor they needed extreme pity.

---

[24] R. Jamieson, A. R. Fausset, and D. Brown, *A Commentary, Critical and Explanatory, on the Old and New Testaments* (Oak Harbor, WA: Logos Research Systems, Inc., 1997).

Even if they applied "Phrygian powder" mixed with oil (eye salve) to heal their eyes, they were still blind and destitute of spiritual clothing (because they were naked, signifying judgment and humiliation) (Rev. 3:18).

Because of their condition, Christ gives them advice to buy gold from Him, which is in a pure state, because then they would be truly rich. This would cause their inner purity to radiate in a white garment. This radiance would be proof that, while they lived in a city that did not know God, they were not polluted by it. This would cover the humiliation that spiritual nakedness could bring upon them. This gold would also allow them to have eye salve that would permit them to perceive the things of God: "*Christ's righteousness* imputed to the believer in justification and imparted in sanctification."[25]

Christ explains to them that, despite their spiritual depravity, He has a continual tender affection for them that causes Him to be concerned for them. He desired them to leave their present state and grow them to spiritual maturity. In order to do this, He must educate them through correction. They needed to become eager to develop their Christian character by turning from their present ways because of a change in heart.

Christ is the one who is knocking. He is the one persistently standing and knocking at their heart's door. This means that He is no longer inside the door and He is doing His best to get the attention of those who are inside the door. If anyone has a heart to obey His voice without question, Christ will go in the door immediately. He does not just come in; He comes to fellowship in the manner of communion (Rev. 3:20–22).

Any church member who shows genuine superiority and overwhelming success to prevail under these circumstances is an overcomer. The person who prevails or conquers the pressure of this environment, Christ will render the privilege of sitting on His throne.

Historical Background

Establishing Context

> Laodicea became important only in Roman times. It was capital of the Cibryatic convention, which included at least twenty-five towns. It was also the wealthiest Phrygian city, and especially prosperous

[25] Ibid., 198.

in this period. It was ten miles west of Colossae and six miles south of Hierapolis. Zeus was the city's patron deity, but Laodiceans also had temples for Apollo, Asclepius (the healing deity), Hades, Hera, Athena, Serapis, Dionysus and other deities. Many Jewish people lived in Phrygia.[26]

Laodicea was a city of economic prosperity and social prominence during the wealthy days of Rome. "It was also known for its textiles (especially wool) and for its medical school and production of ear medicine and undoubtedly the highly reputed Phrygian eye salve. Everything in which Laodicea could have confidence outwardly, its church, which reflected its culture, lacked spiritually."[27]

There were hot springs outside the city. They had a pipe that channeled water from the hot springs to people's homes. The problem was that by the time it got to the house, it often cooled to lukewarm. This became the complaint of many residents in the city who lived comfortably.

There was a medical school in the city that was famous for making "eye salve." It was a medicine that used to help heal people's eye ailments. This is why John said, "The Laodiceans were spiritually blind, John told them that the Lord would have to anoint their eyes with salve that they might see, or know the truth."[28]

What Does the Context Mean?

The church[29] must make the decision to be hot or cold, because to be lukewarm is to become vomit-inducing in the presence of God. It must remove its nakedness by buying pure gold from Christ (Rev. 3:15–18). This would bring

---

[26] Keener, *The IVP Bible Background Commentary*, s.v. Rev. 3:14–22.

[27] Ibid., s.v. Rev. 3:15–16.

[28] Ronald F. Youngblood, ed., *Nelson's Illustrated Bible Dictionary* (Nashville, TN: Thomas Nelson, 1986), 383.

[29] **Church:** The Greek term used in the New Testament reflects the terms often used in the Septuagint to translate the Hebrew word for the "congregation" *(qahal)* of Israel: "church" (assembly) and "synagogue" (gathering). Although some scholars have suggested that Jesus could not have spoken about the church during his earthly ministry, the Dead Sea Scrolls used the Hebrew term for God's community; hence Jesus could use this word in talking about His future community (Matt. 16:18; 18:17). The term was in common use in Greek culture for "assemblies," especially citizen assemblies in cities. (The popular modern surmise that the Greek word for *church, ekklēsia,* means "called-out ones" is thus mistaken; that sense is actually more appropriate for

them back to the Word and cause them to open their eyes to the things of God. They must invite Christ back in. It is not that He had gone far away. He is close by standing, knocking at their door. If anyone invites Him in, He will prepare a meal, develop a genuine fellowship with them, and provide to them what God provided to Him: a throne. If they are sincere about hearing and obeying by following His direction, they will sit on the throne with Him.

Sermon Subject and Title

Sermon Title: Let His Amen Be Our Amen
Big Idea: Everything that glitters is not gold, because it is Christ who determines the true nature of the church. Anyone who responds to His persistent call upon their hearts experiences the great blessing of sitting on His throne with Him.

SERMON OUTLINE (REV. 3:14–22)

A. **Accept His Ways (vv. 14–16)**
   1. *Christ says*—What Christ is saying in this passage is continuously being communicated.
   2. *Christ is faithful*—He has walked among the church—held seven stars. He presents the church as radiant:
      a) They must return to their first love.
      b) Christ blesses Smyrna for trusting Him in persecution.
      c) He judges Pergamum and Sardis.
      d) He protects Thyatira and blesses Philadelphia.
   3. *I know*—Christ has a full knowledge of everything the church is doing. His knowledge is complete and is actively in a set condition.
   4. Make a decision or Christ makes one for us (v. 16).

B. **Amen versus His Amen (v. 17)**
   1. We must limit ourselves to the security the world provides us versus the security He provides. It is His description of us that counts.
   2. Christ views them in a lot of toils and trouble, inner pain, one step from poverty, cannot see the next second (blind even though you have the eye salve; 2 Pet. 1:3–11).

"saints," i.e., "those separated [for God]." Glossary terms are from C. S. Keener's *IVP Bible Background Commentary*.)

3. They have no spirituality—They are without faith; this is why you want to feel materially rich.

C. Accept His Advice (vv. 18–19)

1. *Advice*—Make it a point to constantly respond to His instructions (present active indicative).
2. *Refined*—Get into a fixed mind-set of receiving refined (pure) gold (Matt. 13:44) (perfect passive participle). This is advice they need to receive from Christ.
3. *White garments*—Remain unpolluted in a polluted world (Phil. 2:13–18; Rev. 3:4).
4. *Eye salve*—They need to remove their spiritual blindness by submitting to His Word.
5. *I love*—Christ continuously has a tender affection for these believers (present active).
6. *Approve*—Christ sought to continuously bring their actions under His conviction (present active indicative).
7. *Discipline*—Accept His advice or accept His correction and sometimes scourging. They must make it a habit to do so (present active indicative).
8. *Zealous*—They needed to become very eager to develop Christian character (Phil. 3:12–21).
9. *Repent*—Our change needs to be purposeful from the heart and mind.

D. An Invitation that Is Everything (vv. 20–22)

1. *Stand*—He has set His mind to constantly stand (perfect active indicative).
2. *Knock*—He is constantly knocking. Christ is persistently seeking to guide us in the right direction (perfect active indicative). This is a determined action.
3. *Anyone*—It does not take the whole church; Thyatira is an example.
4. *Dine*—He will make the principal meal. He is excited and ready to be in fellowship with us.
5. *Overcomers*—Prevails, show a genuine desire to supersede what the church is doing.
6. *Hear*—Christ commands those who are willing to repent, because they are ready to change, to become diligent in applying His Word. This is a one-time action that demonstrates a serious commitment to obedience (aorist active imperative).

Author's Comments

Comments

Have you ever been in a relationship where you were excited about a person but the person was not? Your friend or spouse is "just there" and doesn't show the excitement or passion you have? You cannot wait to be with them but their career and other things cause them to come to you only when time allows. This is how Laodicea was.

Christ died for their sins and they accepted Him. In His love and passion for them, He remained at the right hand of the Father so that He can be their lawyer when Satan comes with his list of accusations (Rev. 12:10). They were too caught up in their culture that viewed success through the lens of wealth.

The people of Laodicea were caught up in their riches and successes and were no longer concerned with Jesus' amen. His "amen" was not their "amen" because they saw themselves as self-sufficient. Christ's view of them was completely different. A cup of coffee or tea is better hot than lukewarm. We immediately try to get it warmed up. Lukewarm water was normally spit out and was often used by doctors to cause people to vomit. Christ viewed them as spiritually poor and, therefore, vulnerable to the attacks of Satan and of no value before God. They are "wretched, miserable, poor, blind, and naked" (Rev. 3:17). Their culture was more influential in their lives than Christ.

> Do not love the world or the things in the world. If anyone loves the world, the love of the Father is not in him. For all that is in the world—the lust of the flesh, the lust of the eyes, and the pride of life—is not of the Father but is of the world. And the world is passing away, and the lust of it; but he who does the will of God abides forever. (1 John 2:15–17)

Many people flock to churches that promise that they will be blessed. We chase God so that He can provide us wealth. It is our love for wealth that often drives us to God rather than love for God driving us to serve Him, to grow in Him so that we grow in holiness.

> Therefore we make it our aim, whether present or absent, to be well pleasing to Him. For we must all appear before the judgment seat of Christ, that each one may receive the things done in the body, according to what he has done, whether good or bad. Knowing, therefore, the

terror of the Lord, we persuade men; but we are well known to God, and I also trust are well known in your consciences. (2 Cor. 5:9–11)

This is the heartbeat that pleases God: service. Notice that as soon as the nation of Israel came out of Egypt, we have the book of Leviticus.

Application

If the world shapes our value, it is not different than if a person who is not a jeweler determines the value of a diamond. The value may sound great and we may get excited, but our excitement means nothing. When a true jeweler evaluates the value of the diamond, that is the assessment that really counts. Likewise, God determines the value of churches. His Word defines who we are, which determines how we function in heaven eternally. We need to commit to live for Christ so, like Paul, we no longer live because Christ lives in us (Gal. 2:20).

Illustrate It

During the Iraq War, the Iraqi Special Forces were proclaimed to be strong fighters. In the news, it was clear that American forces were not sure of the outcome. As the war progressed, American forces encountered these soldiers only to find them shell-shocked from all the bombs that were landing around their bunkers. Others had not eaten for days. Even though there were a few holdouts still fighting, it was not as strong a resistance as expected. The American forces were well armed, well trained, and their support systems were functioning well, at least from what we were told here in the States. When the Iraqi soldiers started out, they felt they had everything, but during the battle it exposed how much they lacked. The resources of America kept them overwhelmed.

We may think we are resourceful, but when Satan gets the best of us, we learn how much we lack. When Satan finishes beating on us, he can leave us shell-shocked like the Iraqi soldiers. When our resources come from God, we are ready for anything, as Paul told us when he said, "I can do all things through Christ who strengthens me" (Phil. 4:13). This is why Christ told the folks in Laodicea to buy gold from Him.

Blueprint for Designing the Church

Ephesians 4:11–13

General Overview of the Passage

Christ made a sovereign decision to put men in place who would execute His agenda and establish the New Testament church. Christ uniquely commissioned messengers who were His ambassadors, qualified to serve because they were eyewitnesses. They were dispatched with Christ's authority so that they would accurately obey their commission.

He also gave those who spoke openly the divine message that came directly from God as divine revelation (prophets). This message proclaimed how what was being said relates to future events. Christ also gave those messengers who went from place to place preaching the gospel, proclaiming glad tidings (evangelists). And lastly, He gave those who would tend to His sheep, guiding them in the truth, tenderly caring for them by watching out for them so that they are safe from the enemy (pastors and teachers; Eph. 3:10; 6:11–18). "The gifts in fact are gifted persons: apostles, prophets, evangelists, pastors, and teachers (or pastor-teachers). Apostles and prophets were already mentioned in 2:20 and 3:5 as the foundational gifts to the church. In a strict sense apostles were witnesses of Christ's resurrection and were commissioned by Him to preach."[30]

The pastor and teacher are in place to prepare and train believers so that they are fully furnished and completed as Paul states in Colossians 1:28. This preparation can only take place with those who have consecrated themselves by abstaining from earth's defilement (saints). The equipping process should energize these believers' faith, so that out of their total surrender they serve the

[30] David S. Dockery, *Holman Concise Bible Commentary: The Pauline Letters* (Nashville, TN: Broadman & Holman Publishers, 1998), 579.

Lord faithfully. This includes compassionate love toward those in need in the Christian community.

All of this is done with a focus that each believer lives in the power of Christ's resurrection. This leads to oneness of each believer's faith so that everyone functions with one mind. This unity is in each believer putting their full trust in the knowledge of God with a commitment to do what their convictions have taught them. This faith controls and guides the believer each day and allows the believer to come to a full knowledge of God (Eph. 3:18–19; Col. 1:9–10). These believers arrive at being complete, which is the goal God has set—every believer becoming a completely blameless, adult Christian. This creates a measurement for people to comprehend the big picture of a believer who, at this period in their life, demonstrates a maturity level that looks like Christ (stature; 2 Pet. 1:3–11). This statue is God filling the believer so that they are the sum total of all that God desires for them to be (Gal. 2:20; Eph. 3:14–19; Phil. 3:12; Col. 3:1–4). This believer is one who is totally influenced and controlled by Christ.

> In 1:23 he was seen as filled by God and as filling the church; since here we have no suggestion of what might fill him the phrase is better taken as denoting what he fills, and, as in 1:23, what he fills will be the church, and not "all things" as in 4:10. 3:19 also spoke of believers being filled. There is tension between 1:23 and our verse (and 3:19) in that in the former the filling is already a fact whereas here it is still future.[31]

Historical Background

Establishing Context

The book of Ephesians was written to believers to understand those things that were a mystery (Eph. 1:9) to everyone living during the Old Testament times. The New Testament is clear. The mystery is "the manifold wisdom of God might be made known by the church to the principalities and powers in the heavenly places" (Eph. 3:10). So believers need to expand their knowledge (1:8, 18) and "walk worthy of the calling with which you were called" (Eph. 4:1). We

[31] Ernest Best, *A Critical and Exegetical Commentary on Ephesians* (Edinburgh, Scotland: T&T Clark International, 1998), 399.

are to work it out in the church, through a process, where believers can grow up into the fullness of God.

God establishes offices in order to build up His church in this process. These includes apostles: "the term applies to commissioned agents of Christ authorized in a special way (more authoritatively than others) to declare and propagate His will."[32] "'Prophets' were spokespersons for God, whose role was known from the Old Testament and continued in the church; apostles were to prophets perhaps as prophetic judges (e.g., Samuel and Deborah) or leaders (e.g., Elijah and Elisha) were to other Old Testament prophets—with special rank and authority."[33] There were evangelists, as well as pastors and teachers, who proclaimed the good news of Christ. Pastors are shepherds and overseers of the assembled, whereas teachers "offered biblical instruction to the congregation and trained others to expound the Scriptures as well."[34] Even though this may sound like two offices in the Greek construction, it is one office.

Equipping believers to be able to "walk worthy" originates from people getting their bones set, restoring their life to normality. This causes their bones to be repaired or reconciled to their original position. All of these offices were gifts given by God to help the churches walk in this way.

What Does the Context Mean?

God put together a structure and a foundation for the development of His people. He gave gifted men, beginning with apostles and ending with pastors and teachers. These pastors/teachers must focus on mending broken spiritual bones. Once the equipping of the saints is taking place, they must focus on challenging God's people to work according to their faith for the service of the needs of others so that the church is established for Christ. When He is lifted up, He draws people unto Himself (John 12:32). This was the focus of Christ's prayer (John 17:20–23), which is to establish oneness of the faith—a faith that is steeped in a conviction of the knowledge of God which, in turn, leads a person to experience full maturity in Christ (Col. 1:9–12).

---

[32] Keener, *The IVP Bible Background Commentary*, s.v. Eph. 4:11.

[33] Ibid.

[34] Ibid.

Sermon Subject and Title

Sermon Title: Blueprint for Designing the Church
Big Idea: God's blueprint for the church establishes believers, whom God uses to build His church to impact others.

Sermon Outline (Eph. 4:11–13 NASB)

A. The Foundation God Built (v. 11)

1. *He gave*—It is God's sovereign will that established the foundation for the church (Eph. 2:20).
2. *He gave*—This is in the aorist tense, which means this is something that God has done once and for all. This is His sovereign decision and He is not requesting anyone's input (Eph. 1:9–11). Pastors have all been selected when God established the church. Leaders, whether elders or deacons, need the Scripture's guidance and the gift of discernment to recognize who they are.
3. *He gave*—It is God's sovereign will that established pastors and teachers. The pastor's key role is to:
   a) Feed God's flock (1 Tim. 4:11–16; 2 Tim. 3:16).
   b) Preach the Word, which is critical to the strength of a believer's life (Deut. 8:3; 2 Pet. 1:3–11).
   c) Challenge God's flock to grow (Col. 1:28–29; 1 Tim. 4:11–16; Titus 3:4–8).
   d) Cause them to fall in love with God (Eph. 4:16).
   e) Guide them through the discipline and development the Holy Spirit provides.

B. God-Given Leadership Establishes the Church (v. 12a)

1. The pastor must provide leadership (in the accusative, meaning that is the direct focus for God's gift to the church):
   a) *Equip*—An accusative; this is the direct reason for which pastor/teachers much function. Like a house fully furnished or a boat fully equipped for a journey, the pastor/teacher needs to fully equip the saints to do good (Eph. 2:10; Phil. 2:12–13; 2 Pet. 1:3).
      - Ability to manage day-to-day problems they face.
      - Ability to manage marital issues.
      - Ability to deal with singleness issues.
      - Ability to find strength in critical times.

b) *The Saints*—This is a genitive, so it qualifies the noun. The pastor's work of equipping members of the church is most effective with those who are set aside to Christ (1 Tim. 4:12 NASB—in this verse Timothy is told that what he does is for those "who believe"). The pastor's leadership is more focused on these individuals (Eph. 5–6) because:
   - They are truly consecrated to God (Rom. 8:4–17).
   - They are committed to not conform to the world (Rom. 12:2).
   - They are committed to experiencing the divine nature of God (Gal. 2:20).
   - They can move faster to help others (John 15:1–11).

c) *Work of service*—Challenge believers to commit to ministering to the needs of others (1 Thess. 1:3–5; 5:13–15); use their spiritual gifts (Eph. 4:7).

d) *Build up the body*—Become spiritually profitable for everyone in the church; spiritually strengthening for powerful living.

C. The Church's Mission Is to Establish Committed Believers (vv. 12b–13)

1. *All attain*—Must be focused on God's goal for the church (Col. 1:28–29).
2. *Unity of faith*—Each person has a full trust and deep conviction about Christ so that we function as one person (Eph. 3:16–21; 4:3–6).
3. *Unity of faith*—Each person is committed to apply the convictions taught by the pastor/teacher (James 1:21–25; 2:14–26). Faith is exposed in the application of God's Word (James 2:14–26).
4. *Mature man*—Completely equipped, sold out, fully surrendered to Christ—an adult believer.
5. *Measure and stature*—These believers line up to the divine nature of Christ (Gal. 2:20; Col. 3:1–4).
6. *Fullness of Christ*—Christ has filled the believer with gifts and dwells in them and has full control of their lives (Eph. 3:19; 5:18; Phil. 4:9; Heb. 13:7–8).

Author's Comments

Comments

If you visited the doctor on Friday of last week and he said next Friday is your last day on this earth, how would your schedule this week be affected? How would you relate to your family, friends, and church? The things you value most would take up all your time. The thing Christ values most is His church. He is uniquely the Head of His church, and it is the only people He develops as His own. It is a life-and-death issue for Christ, because we have an enemy who is seeking to kill and destroy us (1 Pet. 5:8; Rev. 12:10). We need to be focused on what is most important to God so that we assist others in our assembly to build the church that Christ builds through us. Paul lays this out for us in the passage, and it needs to become our concentration.

Ephesians 4:11–13 states that Paul is making everything that is positional in a believer functional. In 1:3, Paul states that each believer has "every spiritual blessing in the heavenly places in Christ." In 3:16–19, Paul instructs us that the Holy Spirit is at work in us, Christ is at work in our hearts, and God is breathing the Word into us, so "that you may be filled with all the fullness of God." Then the "pastor and teacher" is charged with providing leadership and teaching to get done what is already in place. It is like going to the gym to build muscles. The gym does not give us muscles; we only exercise what is already there. So it is with the church. The pastor and teacher equip the saints (those already set aside in their hearts for God's purposes, like someone setting aside the time to go to the gym committed to exercising) so that through hard work and commitment to implementing the teaching provided these believers grow up into "the fullness of God."

Many times as pastors, we are focused on numerical growth; I truly understand. Every farmer (Paul says a pastor is like a farmer; 2 Tim. 2:6) when he plants a crop wants to see it grow. However, if this becomes why we do everything, then we are truly off the mark and in sin. The Scriptures teach us that God does not reward us for quantity but for quality (1 Cor. 3:13) and for our faith in Him (Heb. 11:6). As we know "faith comes by hearing, and hearing by the word of God" (Rom. 10:17); thus, how we implement His Word is what makes the difference. Paul was quick to let Timothy know the significance of this when he wrote 2 Timothy 3:17; "that the man of God may be complete, thoroughly equipped for every good work." If it is our heart to live and implement God's Word, then that is what would make the difference (1 Tim. 4:11–16). "Take heed to yourself and to the doctrine. Continue in them, for in doing this you will save both yourself and those who hear you" (1 Tim. 4:16).

The major purpose of the church is to present believers complete in Christ (Col. 1:28–29). This is the main reason the church is structured the way it is, with spiritual gifts being provided by the Holy Spirit (Eph. 4:7; 1 Cor. 12;

1 Pet. 4:7–11). It is for this we must strategically design our mission statements, disciple leaders, hire staff, and structure our messages.

Application

People come from all walks of life with experiences that can be positive and negative. Some people have been abused by relatives, some by husbands or wives, some by churches, and some people have just been through much in their lives. God created the church to be a spiritual hospital to develop believers to grow up into the fullness of God through Christ. We need to go to church with purpose (Heb. 10:23–26) and not just for selfish means. If we go with the purpose of Christ on our hearts, all of our needs will be met (John 12:23–26; Heb. 10:25). When we go for selfish means, we will always have a perceived need that will not be met. Go to church with God's purposes in mind. Because this is His body, when it is healthy, all we can do is be healed.

Illustrate It

My younger brother and I grew up very close. I went to college and he went off to the army. He was very dedicated to what he was doing. One day while playing he said to me, "I can't rump with you anymore." Obviously, I asked why. He said, "I am no longer your little brother, I am a true soldier. There are things I have been taught to do that may just happen naturally at this point and I would hate to know it happened with my brother." That statement startled me.

Over the years when God called me to be a pastor, I wondered, *Can our involvement in the church cause us to be transformed into the fullness of Christ?* It did this for Paul. Paul told us that he had "been crucified with Christ; it is no longer I who live, but Christ lives in me; and the life which I now live in the flesh I live by faith in the Son of God, who loved me and gave Himself for me" (Gal. 2:20). Is this not the intent for which Christ established the church? If someone can be a disciple for military purposes, then why not for Christ? The purpose of being in Christ's body is to grow up into the fullness of God (Eph. 4:13). After all, we have the DNA to make this work (Eph. 3:16–19).

The Pillars of the Model Church

1 Thessalonians 1:1–5

General Overview of the Passage

Paul begins by saying he made it a habit to continuously praise and thank God for all the productive things that were taking place with the Thessalonians. This indicates that since Paul, Silvanus, and Timothy met together they must have been so impressed with the faithfulness of the brethren in Thessalonica, that they constantly brought it up before God.

Paul with firm assurance continuously called to mind the active work that was done with the Thessalonians' whole strength and their unselfish commitment to help believers in need. This work was based on their complete trust in God and with "patience of hope" (1 Thess. 1:3). "The return of Jesus Christ is the dominant theme of both of these Thessalonian letters. Unsaved people are not eagerly awaiting the Lord's return. In fact, when our Lord catches His church up into the air, unsaved people will be totally surprised (1 Thess. 5:1–11)."[35]

These believers demonstrated a faithful persistence to not surrender to the difficulties they experienced. They were steadfast in their faith. This is because they had a desire to do good based on their confident trust in the power and authority of Jesus Christ. "Therefore, from Paul's perspective it was their firmly fixed hope in Jesus Christ that gave them the strength to persevere in their new Christian beliefs and behavior in spite of considerable adversity from their non-Christian fellow citizens."[36]

---

[35] W. W. Wiersbe, *The Bible Exposition Commentary* (Wheaton, IL: Victor Books, 1996), 2:160–61.

[36] Charles A. Wanamaker, *The Epistles to the Thessalonians: A Commentary on the Greek Text* (Grand Rapids, MI: W. B. Eerdmans, 1990), 76.

This Christian community of loving believers had a full knowledge of divine truths. It was based in a complete understanding of what they were taught. These believers, because of their faith and love for each other, experienced a sincere compassion and love from God. They were selected by God with a clear purpose.

Historical Background

Establishing Context

What is taking place here in 1 Thessalonians is recorded in Acts 17. The Jews, upon hearing Paul speak in the synagogue, decided to follow Paul's teaching and accept Christ. A few leading women in the city also became a part of the church. This church became a vibrant church "so that you became examples to all in Macedonia and Achaia who believe. For from you the word of the Lord has sounded forth, not only in Macedonia and Achaia, but also in every place. Your faith toward God has gone out, so that we do not need to say anything" (1 Thess. 1:7–8).

It is amazing that the Thessalonians responded this way. Imagine this city as a major port with many people coming and going. It was filled with immorality, Greek mythology, and idol worshipers. Most of the population was Greeks and some Romans, but the Jewish synagogue was influential and attracted many citizens of Thessalonica who became proselytes. So when Paul came to the city, it was best to go to the synagogue and preach the gospel. The response was great.

What Does the Context Mean?

When Paul, Silvanus, and Timothy prayed for the Thessalonians, they could not help remembering how these believers displayed their faith with such energy. They exerted a lot of energy to the point of weariness. No matter the trouble they experienced, their steady character in Christ caused them to face their difficulties with the expectancy that the Lord Jesus Christ is able to carry them through. God directed His will toward them by choosing to bring them into the family of God. This took place because Paul, Silvanus, and Timothy shared the gospel, with deep conviction, in the power of the Holy Spirit. The people saw the dedication and truthfulness of the gospel lived out by the kind of men Paul, Silvanus, and Timothy proved to be. "Many traveling preachers and philosophers in that day were only interested in making money from ignorant people. But the Holy Spirit used the Word in great power, and the Thessalonians responded by receiving both the message and the messengers."[37]

Sermon Subject and Title

Sermon Title: The Pillars of the Model Church
Big Idea: Thanksgiving is continuous when a church demonstrates a "work of faith, a labor of love, and steadfastness of hope" (1 Thess. 1:3 NASB) in the Lord in response to the gospel.

Sermon Outline (1 Thess. 1:1–5 NASB)

A. Pillar 1: Concerned Leaders (vv. 2–3a)

1. *We give thanks*—This is a present tense, active, indicative in the first person. This means that Paul was so excited about the heart these believers demonstrated, after hearing the gospel, that when he personally prayed he actively and continuously expressed gratitude to God for all the productive things that were taking place in Thessalonica.
2. *We give thanks*—Paul's leadership in reaching these believers stirred a work that became an example to many other churches (1 Thess. 1:7).
3. *Thanks to God*—This is a dative, meaning that Paul viewed this as a work that God had done in them (Matt. 7:15–23).
4. *Making mention of you*—Paul himself could not help, while praying, to continuously remember these believers before God. It became a habitual process when he went before God to pray (present middle, participle).
5. *Prayer*—They continually kept this church's concerns before God because He is the superior power that is authorizing everything beginning with their salvation (1 Thess. 1:5).
6. *Remembering without ceasing*—Paul, Silvanus, and Timothy got together regularly, and when they did they habitually and actively had the Thessalonians on their minds. They made it a habit to focus their prayers on giving God gratitude for the unshakable faith and complete assurance these believers revealed.

---

[37] Wiersbe, *The Bible Exposition Commentary*, 2:161.

B. **Pillar 2: Passionate Believers (v. 3b NASB)**
   1. *Work of faith*—They worked diligently because of their deep conviction in God's Word.
   2. *Work of faith*—Their commitment to God drove them to serve to the point of weariness.
   3. *Work of faith*—This was productive work because of the level of energy and passion that they gave (James 2:15–17).
   4. *Labor of love*—They were weary but still showed unselfish commitment to help those in need.
   5. *Steadfastness of hope*—They fixed their expectation on Christ's return and pressed forward in service despite the adversity.
   6. *Steadfastness of hope*—These believers persistently demonstrated steadiness toward pleasing God because of their faith, love, and hope in Christ.
   7. *Hope in our Lord*—Despite their difficult trials, they still trusted in the power and authority of Christ.
   8. *Presence of our God*—The lived their lives conscious of God's presence.
   9. *Work of faith, labor of love, steadfastness of hope*—Genitive, meaning that these activities are the main characteristics of these believers' faith, which impressed Paul so much that it led him to constantly pray for them.

C. **Pillar 3: The Gospel, the Message that Builds the Church (vv. 4–5 NASB)**
   1. *Knowing*—The "state of affairs" that they are in is that they have a full knowledge and complete understanding that God purposefully selected them. This is a past action that is now complete (perfect active nominative). They have no doubt or question about their relationship with God.
   2. *Beloved*—God directed His selfless and compassionate love toward them. This is a set condition and a completed act by God.
   3. *Choice*—Like the Jews, they are a chosen people of God (1 Pet. 2:9–10).
   4. *Choice*—They were always a part of God's plan for man (Gen. 12:1–3).
   5. *Power*—The power of God that Paul is speaking of is God's ability to overcome all obstacles in the face of danger to make sure these believers hear the gospel. God so wanted these believers He selected to experience His love that He blessed Paul, Silvanus, and Timothy to overcome all obstacles to reach them.

6. *Conviction*—Paul had full confidence and certainty about the message preached. It is because of this that Paul spoke with boldness.
7. *Conviction*—The message was delivered in the power of the Holy Spirit.
8. *Knowing*—The Thessalonians became a great church and a great example to others because God directed Paul, Silvanus, and Timothy to deliver this message despite all the obstacles they encountered.
9. *Knowing*—Their acceptance of this message allowed them to experience God's compassionate love, which in turn empowered them to a "work of faith, a labor of love, and steadfastness of hope" (1 Thess. 1:3 NASB).

Author's Comments

Comments

A man once told his friend that he wanted to save an old house he bought. The friend who is a builder said that he would need to check it out. The builder went to the house and found that behind the walls the wood was rotten and that it might not be safe to save the house. Upon tearing the old house down, the builder hit one of the pillars of the house thinking there were several main beams, only to find out there was only one pillar that kept the whole house standing.

A house should have many pillars that keep it together. You tear down the main pillars, and all the parts become nothing. We may like the songs, the choir robes, suits the pastor wears, or how the building looks, but these are not the main pillars. In this text Paul, the church planter, explains to us what the main pillars are that make a church a true example for all churches.

These believers genuinely accepted Christ. We know this by the fruit that comes out of them:

> "Not everyone who says to Me, 'Lord, Lord,' shall enter the kingdom of heaven, but he who does the will of My Father in heaven. Many will say to Me in that day, 'Lord, Lord, have we not prophesied in Your name, cast out demons in Your name, and done many wonders in Your name?' And then I will declare to them, 'I never knew you; depart from Me, you who practice lawlessness!'" (Matt. 7:21–23).

The fruit that came out of them is an active obedience to God. They did not make excuses about the great tribulation they were experiencing (1 Thess. 3:5; Rev. 3:14–22). When they served, in much tribulation, they did so knowing that Christ will come again and redeem them unto Himself. This steadfast hope that was based on their deep conviction in Christ shaped their character so that even though they were weary they still were persistent in their service and commitment to God. "Beloved, now we are children of God; and it has not yet been revealed what we shall be, but we know that when He is revealed, we shall be like Him, for we shall see Him as He is. And everyone who has this hope in Him purifies himself, just as He is pure" (1 John 3:2–3).

The amazing thing about this church is that Paul, Silvanus, and Timothy did not get to stay too long at this church (Paul was in Ephesus for three years; Acts 20:31). They were not even able to establish leaders (1 Thess. 5:12–13). Members just rose up to help to keep things going. The church of Ephesus was an exemplary church, but with less time for discipleship these believers grew to be "examples to all in Macedonia and Achaia who believe" (1 Thess. 1:7–8). This church, because of the heart of the people upon hearing the gospel, became a model church.

Application

Every building has main pillars that support it. Without these pillars, the building, no matter how beautiful it may be, will fall. This young church heard the message of God and "hit the ground running." We tend to become excited about praise and worship and being at a church where people know each other and get along well. This is great but it is not the mission of the church. If we are going to be the church God called us to be, we need to demonstrate a sincere, energetic work of faith and be willing to serve God to the point of weariness. If the church does not have these key elements, we need to be a catalyst of change. The difference your church can make begins with you.

Illustrate It

The people that we thank God for in the Scriptures and seek to use as models for our walk before God are people who experienced tremendous challenges to their convictions. Let us reflect on just two of these individuals. Daniel made up in his mind that he was not going to disobey God. His commitment to do so only led to a lot of persecution and harassment. I am sure from a human standpoint that this was difficult for Daniel, but he did not move from his convictions, and that led him to experience the power of God in a mighty way. This faith in God was his victory that causes him to be an example today.

The same took place with the apostle Paul. It did not matter that Paul knew that suffering awaited him in Jerusalem. It mattered most that God was sending him there. In each test, throughout the years, Paul was moved around, but he kept trusting God at His Word. Paul's faith took him to places he may not have wanted to go, but it gave him experiences of God he would never have had.

The church will be great, not simply when the music is good or the sermon is wonderful, but when, like the Thessalonians, we remain steadfast in our hope and fervent in our faith. This is what we need most because this is how God's agenda greatly makes a difference in this world.

Don't Drift from the Anchor

Hebrews 2:1–4

General Overview of the Passage

The writer of Hebrews was seeking to point out to these believers that they must give extreme care to understanding the words of Christ "in these last days" (Heb. 1:2). They must give their full attention so that they understand with a heart to obey because these are of the utmost significance.

The Jews, who mostly made up this church, held in high regard God's Word in the Old Testament. It proved to be reliable and immovable, as it was revealed through angels. It is obvious that anyone who disobeyed these words received just penalties, which served to prove even further that these words were authoritative. The author is saying that if rejecting the Word of God that came through angels received "a just reward," then the words that came directly from Christ should be held with even higher regard since Christ is greater than angels!

To make sure they understood that these words were authoritative, the writer reminded them that those who wrote these words had amazing demonstrations of God's power being evident in them. These miraculous events that took place, in and through their lives, were supernatural acts that could have only come from God. As a result, they should not neglect God's delivering power when there was a need for spiritual growth and strength to deal with the many trials they were experiencing. "More spiritual problems are caused by neglect than perhaps by any other failure on our part. We neglect God's Word, prayer, worship with God's people (see Heb. 10:25), and other opportunities for spiritual growth, and as a result, we start to drift. The anchor does not move; we do."[38]

---

[38] Wiersbe, *The Bible Exposition Commentary*, S. Heb. 2:1.

Historical Background

Establishing Context

These believers were going through a lot of abuse (10:32–39; 12:4), and they wanted to turn back to Judaism. The writer tries to encourage them to persevere in the faith because turning back only leads to destruction (10:39). He challenged them to take their spiritual maturity seriously (5:11–14) and take the assembling of themselves together as the responsibility of all believers (10:23–26) with due respect being given to the leaders of the church (13:7, 17). Since they knew the writer well (5:11; 6:9; 13:18–19, 23), he wanted to personally challenge them not to drift from the faith.

> The words "if we neglect" have their primary reference to the Jews of the period in which the writer lived, who had outwardly left the temple sacrifices, had made a profession of Jesus as High Priest, and who under stress of persecution from apostate Judaism, were neglecting attendance upon the means of grace (10:25), allowing themselves to drift by New Testament truth, leaning back towards the first testament, and were in danger of returning to the temple sacrifices, an act that would constitute the sin known as apostasy, from which there would be no recovery.[39]

It seems that the writer of Hebrews is making a reference to the Jewish law (most of the members of this church were Jews) and how neglect of it led to punishment and a lack of rewards from God. "Disobedience or obedience to the law was punished or rewarded. This discipline is discussed at length in Hebrews 12:5–11 (Deut. 28—30)."[40] The laws recorded in the Old Testament were provided to Moses by angels (Deut. 33:2; Acts 7:38, 53; Gal. 3:19). The writer seems to be using this to encourage the members of the church to not drift away from the Words of Christ because the results are basically the same as it was for the Old Testament saints.

> In speaking like this, the writer of Hebrews regarded these miracles as the powers of the coming age (Heb. 6:5) and, in harmony with the

---

[39] Earl D. Radmacher, Ronald Barclay Allen, and H. Wayne House, *Nelson's New Illustrated Bible Commentary* (Nashville, TN: Nelson Publishers, 1999), Heb. 2:4.

[40] Ibid.

early Christians in the Book of Acts, saw them as expressions of the sovereignty of the One who had gone to sit at God's right ("signs," "wonders," and/or "miracles" in Acts 2:43; 4:30; 5:12; 6:8; 8:6,13; 14:3; 15:12; 2 Cor. 12:12).[41]

What Does the Context Mean?

The believers in Hebrews were experiencing tremendous trials and tribulation (10:32–39). Accepting Christ and seeking to live for Him in a mostly Jewish context led to them losing much and having a hard time taking care of their families. This constant pressure made them want to go back to Judaism and turn away from Christ. The writer is seeking to encourage them to continue to run the race that is set before them because many who committed to walk with God suffered in the same way, but over time God provided them tremendous victories. Therefore, the Word that is a true Word must not be neglected. When it is neglected, it leads to us drifting from sincerely walking with God. To drift is to shrink back, which leads to destruction (Heb. 6:4–8; 10:39).

Sermon Subject and Title

Sermon Title: Don't Drift from the Anchor
Big Idea: The Word of God is an authentic Word that must be respected, or we will stray from God and neglect the sanctifying process His Word provides.

Sermon Outline (Heb. 2:1–4 nasb)

A. Remain Alert (v. 1)

1. God's love and care is continuous (Ps. 34:7; Heb. 1:14; 1 Pet. 5:7). He never stops watching over us.
2. *For this reason we must*—This is a continuous, habitual action that is urgently needed and compulsory for each believer, no matter the internal or external pressures.
3. *Pay much closer attention*—There is sense of urgency that just cannot be missed in this passage. It is as if the sky is falling and to escape these actions is required.

---

[41] Ibid.

4. *Pay much closer attention*—This means to continuously and habitually exercise extreme care about the message they have heard.
5. *Do not drift away*—Everything before this verb is continuous to the point of being a habit, but not drifting is a one-time decision and determination (aorist tense).

B. The Anchor—God's Authentic Word Is Unchangeable (vv. 2, 3b, 4a; 6:17–18)

1. *A proven, unalterable Word*—It is a legally binding document; it is reliable, trustworthy, and immovable.
    a) The Word needs to be viewed with urgency.
    b) The Word must be carefully examined before it is applied regularly (Acts 17:11–12).
2. *A proven, unalterable Word*—It is in the nominative, meaning that the direct purpose for which angels were used to deliver the Word was to prove it was authentic. It is the Word coming directly from God (Heb. 1:1–3).
    a) The Word of God was established by Christ (Heb. 1:3; 1 John 1:1–4).
    b) God powerfully identified with the apostles who wrote the Scriptures (Acts 2:22, 43; 4:30; 5:12; 6:8).
    c) God confirmed His word with the apostles (Matt. 11:2–5; John 3:2; 17:20–23; Heb. 6:5) through:
        - *Signs*—Divine power and authority to perform supernatural acts.
        - *Wonders*—Startling and amazing manifestations of God's power.
        - *Miracles*—Power to overcome all obstacles.

C. No Drifting Allowed (v. 3a)

1. *Neglect so great a salvation*—To flee or to become careless about applying God's Word is to decide not to experience the sanctifying process that our salvation provides. These believers knew that God's salvation requires discipline—Old Testament (Deut. 28).
    a) *It was spoken through the Lord*—The message being heard directly from Christ should inspire confidence because of its authenticity (Heb. 1:2–3). It was confirmed by those who were with Him. It is reliable.
        - There is no place to flee from God's discipline (Heb. 10:35–39; 12:4–11).

- The Word needs to be viewed as unavoidable for living (2 Pet. 1:3–4).
- Listening is not enough; practicing is required (Heb. 5:14).
- The Word must be an integral part of our daily lives (Ps. 119:11, 105).

4. *Salvation*—God desires for us deliverance from the power of sin (Rom. 6:12–19) and the lasting effects of sin (Rom. 8:14–25). This is the true deliverance we desire for daily living.
5. *Salvation*—God wants for us to experience the sanctifying power of our salvation (Titus 3:4–8). This is in the nominative because it is the direct reason we must make the one-time decision not to neglect (aorist active) sanctification.
   a) His desire is to provide us abundant life (John 10:10).
   b) The sanctifying process creates a friendship with Christ (John 15:13–14).
   c) Our salvation is an exceedingly bigger deal than ever before.

D. Rely on the Holy Spirit, Who Keeps Us from Drifting (v. 4c)

1. *The Holy Spirit*—The Holy Spirit's express purpose for being in our lives is to guide us to the truth (John 14:16–17), because knowing and living the truth is the expressway to life (John 14:6).
2. *The Spirit's own will*—It is purely the will of God (1 John 1:1–4; 2 Pet. 1:19–21).
   a) The Word of God is an anchor for life (Heb. 4:12; 7:28).
   b) The Word providing the knowledge necessary for salvation (Heb. 4:12).
   c) God's will stimulates faith that rewards us (Heb. 11:3, 6).
   d) Commitment to the will of God prevents us from drifting (Heb. 6:5).

Author's Comments

Comments

I went into my study and found my son listening to the radio. I asked him why he was listening to music while studying. I told him that there is no way he can study because that was too much noise. There is a lot of noise in our lives that sometimes prevents us from even praying, being able to read the Word, or concentrate and listen to a sermon. Noise from stress, loneliness, bills, work, illnesses, and from managing life as a single parent can drive us to seek survival rather than God. Sometimes there is so much noise that praying becomes difficult because we can't concentrate on what to say or even stay awake. Because there is so much noise, we can easily drift away from God by simply not reading His Word, not praying with others, not going to church, and even avoiding family and friends.

This is the issue that is the challenge for the believers in the book of Hebrews (Heb. 10:32–39). They were drifting from their convictions about Christ back to the old covenant system. They were failing to appropriate the blessings of their salvation (Heb. 2:3). Central to those blessings is the authentic Word of God. The authenticity of the New Testament writings was a challenge because, being Jews, they knew of the many confirmations of the Old Testament that continuously proved God wrote it. If they were going to experience the transformational power of their salvation, they needed to hold to the power of all the Scriptures. "The message of salvation was confirmed to the Hebrew readers by the apostles who heard firsthand; their message was certified to the Jewish hearers by apostolic miracles (2:4)."[42] He wanted them to not drift back to what they used to do; as Paul would say, they needed to "press toward the goal" (Phil. 3:12–16).

The process of not drifting may seem easy to talk about, but in real life it can be hard. The reason is that God does not move on our timing. Some trials may continue for years, while evil people seem to be having a great time and living long (Ps. 37:7–40). This is why the writer challenged them to remember who is writing the Scriptures, and who is writing their story. It was not just what they said, it was how they lived (Heb. 13:7) and how God, through supernatural events, manifested His presence with them. It was examining what they were saying against what Christ said as reported through the apostles. Once the Word proves to be true, then the working out of their salvation has found its source.

Salvation is everything when seeking to overcome trials. Being saved initially, by believing in the heart (having a willingness to submit to God's Word; Rom. 10:9) that Jesus died and rose from the dead is just the beginning. There is a sanctifying process (Phil. 2:12–13), and its core is the Word of God (Rom. 8:5–9; 12:1–2). This sanctifying process is where a believer experiences the power within them, which is the ministry of the Holy Spirit (1 John 4:4). It

---

[42] Hughes and Laney, *Tyndale Concise Bible Commentary*, 664.

is the Spirit that came to guide us into truth (John 16:13). It is the Spirit that came to illuminate the Word of God (1 Cor. 2:10–15). So the more we hold to the authentic Word of God, the more the work of the Holy Spirit is triggered in us, empowering us to eventually live more under the influence of the Spirit than under the flesh (1 Pet. 1:3–9). According to James, it is when a believer trusts God through this process that they win the "crown of life" (James 1:12).

The Word of God is central to experiencing the power we need. This is why having a deep conviction in the Word of God leading to a surrendered life is critical to a believer experiencing victory. Because God's timing is beyond our ability, we must trust His Word to avoid drifting. We must have an anchor when there is so much noise.

Application

We may not be able to reduce the noise that comes upon us. We have to work, take care of sick kids and sometimes older parents, pay the bills; we can't just turn everything off. However, when we view the Word of God as providing us direction for everything we need to address in our lives, it becomes more than a good Word to read; it becomes a lifeline for what we face every second of the day. When it is the air we breathe, the issues we experience do not control us because the Word of God is directing us each day (2 Pet. 1:3). Instead of sinking into depression, our walk with God produces the fruit of the Spirit, which despite everything else, leads to joy and peace. Don't drift; remain anchored. This is the lifeline for daily living and the power that strengthens, the wisdom that enlightens, and the transformation that keeps hope alive.

Illustrate It

Prior to the hundred-year storm coming inland in Galveston and Houston, Texas, the newscast was providing many updates. Many communities sent out information especially to those who were right on the coast. They provided them information on shelters and ways to get out of town. As the storm grew closer, police officers went knocking on doors of homes where they knew older residents lived, as well on those on the water. As the winds picked up, the police would go by with loud speakers, driving the streets, telling people they must evacuate. Despite all these attempts being made, it was on the news that there were a few residents who decided to stay. There were even discussions as to whether or not they should be arrested and placed in a shelter for their safety and the safety of others, but nothing was done.

To help people understand the seriousness of the storm, the news showed relentlessly what took place in New Orleans. They also showed comparative storms and the kind of damage those did in Galveston and Houston. No matter what they said and how vivid the pictures, these residents remained in their homes because they were afraid of looters.

The storm came, and when the police went to check on the residents, one home was nowhere to be found and the other was partially destroyed, with the resident nowhere to be found. They had no idea where to even start looking.

God's Word has provided us vivid pictures of how it works in the Old Testament and for the saints in the New Testament. We must pay attention. We have an enemy, Satan who came to "steal, and to kill, and to destroy." We must listen to the voice of our Good Shepherd who came to give us life and life "abundantly" (John 10:10). We may not like what He says, and the contemplation of obeying Him may create fear, but we must still trust His Word and not lean to our own understanding (Prov. 3:5–6).

Paul's Mission . . . Our Commission

Acts 26:12–18

General Overview of the Passage

We find Paul in this passage standing before Agrippa because the Jews persecuted him for bringing a Gentile, Timothy, into the temple. They also persecuted him for going to the Gentiles because some of the Jews believed that he was not supportive of the Mosaic law. Paul explains his call and his salvation experience on the road to Damascus. While Paul was traveling (four to six days' journey) to Damascus under the authority of the chief priest, he saw a bright light from heaven and heard a voice saying to him, "Saul, Saul, why are you persecuting Me?" meaning, "Why do you purpose to be hostile toward me?"

The one who has all authority and power said that He is absolutely and will always be Jesus. This Jesus commanded Paul to get up on his feet and told him to go primarily to the Gentiles and preach the gospel. It is this call that is burning within him and he is seeking to diligently fulfill. Christ takes Paul and places him under His authority to serve Him. Paul is to be a minister who brings light to darkness and announces the facts of the gospel and tells its good tidings.

Christ promises to deliver Paul out of the evil acts of the Jews and from the Gentiles because he is being sent forth on a particular mission with the Lord's authority. The acceptance of this message provided Paul's audience the ability to see the knowledge of Christ, which will open their hearts to a single-minded purpose. Their ability to come to the knowledge of Christ took place because God empowered the Gentiles to make a decisive change of attitude in a positive and acceptable direction for Christ. Their deliberate choice caused a transformation from ignorance, sin, and misery to being able to see and develop an understanding that is never quenched. They will always be in a state of growing and learning. This is because they were delivered from the authority, power, and strength of the prince of the devils who is the adversary to all Christians.

When this was accomplished, they obtained a release from the punishment they deserved for their previous willful and intentional actions against the will of God. This led them to share in the inheritance God had put in place for them. "Spiritually Paul had led many from the darkness of sin (John 3:19; 2 Cor. 4:4; Eph. 4:18; 5:8; Col. 1:13) to light in Christ (John 12:36; 2 Cor. 4:6; Eph. 5:8; Col. 1:12; 1 Thess. 5:5). This salvation releases from Satan's power (John 8:44; Heb. 2:14) and gives forgiveness of sins (Acts 2:38; 5:31; 10:43; 13:38; Eph. 1:7; Col. 1:14) and a spiritual inheritance (Rom. 8:17; Col. 1:12) with those who are sanctified, that is, those who are positionally set apart to God by His redeeming work (cf. 1 Cor. 1:30; Heb. 10:10; 13:12)."[43]

The transformation and deliverance that took place occurred among those who are set apart, and consecrated to God. These believers withdraw from fellowship with the world because they have accepted and trusted, with conviction, the divine truths of God that eventually produces in them good works.

Historical Background

Establishing Context

This is about Paul's conversion on the road to Damascus, but where it takes place is very important. Damascus is a hundred and fifty miles from Palestine and had a large Jewish population. When Paul saw the bright light, it was amazing because it was in the middle of the day!

Christ said that Paul was "kicking against the goads," an expression that comes from a Greek proverb in reference to fighting a god. It also related to when a young ox is first yoked and it would buck trying to get the yoke off of its neck. If the ox was yoked to a wagon, "a studded bar with wooden spikes served the same purpose. The point was that the ox had to learn submission to the yoke the hard way. Before his encounter with Jesus on the Damascus road, Paul was resisting God in a similar manner (1 Tim. 1:13)."[44]

"For two years Paul was being tried by Jewish leaders. Many Roman leaders had heard Paul's case over that two-year period. Paul speaks his case in this passage in the presence of military personnel and King Agrippa. Paul believed

---

[43] John F. Walvoord, and Roy B. Zuck, *The Bible Knowledge Commentary: An Exposition of the Scriptures* (Wheaton, IL: Victor Books, 1983–c1985), 2:424.

[44] Radmacher, Allen, and House, *Nelson's New Illustrated Bible Commentary,* Acts 26:14.

that King Agrippa had some knowledge of the Old Testament and believed it. He was taken to King Agrippa because Festus wanted his advice on Paul's case. The length of the address was implied in Paul's opening statements (26:3). The address was delivered to one who knew a great deal about the Jewish religion."[45]

What Does the Context Mean?

Christ met Paul in the midst of his passion to keep people from turning from the God of the Jews to Christ. Christ turned this passion into a mission that reached the Gentiles with the gospel. He wanted them to understand the gospel, to stop being controlled by Satan, to experience the inheritance of Christ (Holy Spirit—Eph. 1:13–14), and to live under the complete power of the Holy Spirit, separated from the world because of a lifestyle commitment to faith.

It is for this reason that Paul was being tried by the Jews who continually pursued him. Paul is not going to turn away from his God-ordained call because of the powerful spiritual experience he encountered on the road to Damascus.

Paul's mission was clear, his message was sure, and his passion to fulfill what Christ put on his heart was not going to change. The only thing Paul had left to do was to defend his case.

Sermon Subject and Title

Sermon Title: Paul's Mission . . . Our Commission
Big Idea: Paul's mission, when confronted by Christ, became our commission for Christ.

Sermon Outline (Acts 26:12–18 NASB)

A. Saul's Encounter with Christ (vv. 12–15)

1. *Journey*—Saul was on a six-day mission to destroy Christians and the church. This is in the present tense, nominative, passive; meaning this was always going to be Paul's intent and it is the direct purpose for this trip. He believed this was God's desire for him.

---

[45] William Barclay, *The Acts of the Apostles* in The Daily Bible series, rev. ed. (1976; repr; Philadelphia, PA: The Westminster Press, 2000), 178.

2. *Brighter than the sun*—Paul did not run from the meeting. He faced the meeting with questions. His passion for God kept him focused.
3. *Brighter than the sun*—Christ had an appointed time when He would meet Paul. The church had now scattered (God used Paul as the catalyst). The prediction in Acts 1:8 of going into all the world was now being fulfilled, so it was time for Paul to join the movement. By the time we get to the end of Acts, Paul has reached the uttermost parts of the world (Acts 28:28–31).
4. *A voice saying*—Christ knew everything. He was going to speak until Paul listened. It is the purpose of this meeting (present tense, active, accusative).
5. *Persecuting me*—Christ took what Paul was doing personally (Matt. 25:34–40).
6. *Kick against the goads*—No matter how hard Paul tried to destroy the church, it continued to spread. Present tense here means Paul had no intention of stopping his intense persecution of the church.
7. *Kick against the goads*—No one can stop what God is going to do.
8. *Kick against the goads*—God is patient and will continually work with us.

B. Paul: A Change Agent for Christ . . . Our Commission (vv. 16–18)

1. *I am Jesus*—We must see Jesus as completely sufficient for everything.
2. *I am Jesus*—He must be the recognized authority and power of our lives.
3. *For this purpose*—God has a purpose for our lives; He is persistent (Adam was made with a distinct purpose).
4. *Appoint you*—Christ had determined beforehand to do this in Paul's life.
5. *Minister*—We are slaves for Christ. The needs of others are greater than ours (Phil. 2:1–5). We all have spiritual gifts that God provided at the point of salvation (Eph. 1:3; 4:7) for the purpose of serving others (1 Pet. 4:7–11).
6. *Rescuing you*—God did not guarantee a smooth ride.
7. *I am sending you*—When we decide to be change agents, we function under the authority of God.
8. *I am sending you*—God's direction for our lives is not something that is up for discussion. Once it is decided, the purpose (determined by

our spiritual gift) defines our lives. *Sending* here is in the present tense, active, indicative; it will always be this way for Paul.

9. The awesome blessing of deciding to be a change agent (most of these, not all, are either in the aorist or the accusative—meaning they are one-time actions with a direct purpose):
   a) *Open your eyes*—(open: aorist; eyes: accusative)—Christ first wants us to understand His Word and open our hearts to experience Him (John 6:44; Rom. 10:17; 1 Cor. 2:10–15).
   b) *Turn*—(aorist)—This is a decisive, deliberate, and new direction for all those who accept Christ.
   c) *Darkness*—(genitive—they once possessed darkness; John 3:19–21)—Paul by the power of the Holy Spirit will be empowered to influence unsaved Gentiles to make a decision to turn from sin and ignorance to an understanding that is never quenched.
   d) *Turn to the light*—This is a light that always shines because "Jesus is the light," so it is He who comes into our hearts (John 1:6–13). This is the direct reason for which darkness was removed (an accusative).
   e) *Dominion of Satan*—(genitive—possessed by the influence of Satan; Eph. 2:1–2)—Once they have turned, they are released from the evil power and influence of Satan.
   f) *Receive forgiveness*—(receive: aorist—Salvation is a one-time act of God, John 3:16; forgiveness: an accusative)—The decision to come to Christ releases them from the punishment of sin (1 John 1:9).
   g) *Inheritance*—(an accusative)—Each person is then blessed with the gift of the Holy Spirit (Eph. 1:13–14).
   h) *Sanctified*—They lose a taste for the world. They are now separated unto Christ. They are constantly experiencing the set focus of the work of the Holy Spirit (2 Cor. 3:18;Phil. 1:6—perfect passive).
   i) *Faith*—(dative—faith was provided to us, Rom. 10:17, and it is faith that God uses to transform us)—They will gain the power to live a blessed life of obedience before God (Heb. 11:6).

Author's Comments

Comments

My son took me a long time ago to see *The Matrix*. He believed that the executive producer of this movie had to be a Christian. The movie reminded me how life can control us each day. We get so caught up in the day-to-day issues that we become like a hamster in a wheel, running the rat race, over and over. In the midst of all this, there is a war going on (Eph. 6:10–17).

Morpheus, the leader of the rebels who fought against the power of evil, believed there was a person who would come and provide a powerful deliverance from their enemy. There is a war going on daily between good and evil, and Morpheus believed this deliverer would be their savior. After this young man went through his transformation, he started finding out all about himself and was soon able to defeat the enemy. As a result of this, he now establishes himself replacing Morpheus and is leading the fight against the enemy at a higher level than ever before.

There is a war going on! A Morpheus—John the Baptist—looked for the Messiah who came as a man doing awesome miracles and causing people to follow him. He was transformed—dying on the cross, rising from the dead, and sitting at the right hand of the Father in a gloried body. He is at war for us, fighting off the attacks of Satan every day (Rev. 12:10). He wants to make a difference so people who decide to live in darkness will see the light. He uses His army—saved people who have been transformed from the darkness to light—so that by His power they can fight off the attacks of the enemy. These people, like Paul, are commissioned to save those who remain in darkness.

We have become so caught up in the world that Christ has become more of a means to experience all the material goods the world has to offer. His transformation for us should be so profound that we become passionate to see it take place for others. I love how the Macedonians responded after they experienced Christ:

> Moreover, brethren, we make known to you the grace of God bestowed on the churches of Macedonia: that in a great trial of affliction the abundance of their joy and their deep poverty abounded in the riches of their liberality. For I bear witness that according to their ability, yes, and beyond their ability, they were freely willing, imploring us with much urgency that we would receive the gift and the fellowship of the ministering to the saints. And not only as we had hoped, but they first gave themselves to the Lord, and then to us by the will of God. (2 Cor. 8:1–5)

Think of how transformed the world would be if we, the living "salt and light," had the same passion as Paul did (Matt. 5:13–16; 24:14).

Application

Like Paul, we must be committed to share the gospel. When an individual is saved, he is delivered and given the potential to live powerfully in a dying world. Our passion for Christ should create such excitement that we want to share it with others. It should not matter what challenges we experience, especially in these last days. This must be a serious commitment because in these last days what took place for Paul could become what many believers experience as we are already seeing in some parts of the world.

> "You will be brought before governors and kings for My sake, as a testimony to them and to the Gentiles. But when they deliver you up, do not worry about how or what you should speak. For it will be given to you in that hour what you should speak; for it is not you who speak, but the Spirit of your Father who speaks in you." (Matt. 10:18–20)

Unless we are determined like Paul to serve God, these struggles could cause our love for God to grow cold (Matt. 24:9–14).

Illustrate It

What truly fascinates me about war stories are heroes. It is fascinating because of what they put on the line for the love of their country.

In the movie *Saving Private Ryan*, a sergeant puts his life on the line to save one person in the midst of a tremulous war. He and his men encounter one battle after another and lose good men along the way. The sergeant would not turn back because he had orders he must fulfill. They finally found Private Ryan and saved his life only for the sergeant to lose his.

Paul met Christ on the road to Damascus and was given orders. He was told how hard the journey would be to take the gospel to the Gentiles, but Paul did not flinch (Acts 9:15; 2 Cor. 6:3–10). Paul's determined persistence and deep commitment to the faith keeps saving Gentiles each day.

We sing the song that we are soldiers in the Lord's army, but do we really mean it?

Sermon Series 2

Giving that Blesses

Remember God!

Deuteronomy 8:11–18

General Overview of the Passage

The nation of Israel has seen many people die in the wilderness over the past forty years because of their obedience to God. Entering the Promised Land is not something they have earned. The Promised Land is provided because of God's unconditional covenant with Abraham.

As the Israelites got ready to enter the Promise Land, God provided them this challenge. They are charged to not forget to give careful attention to the laws of God. This includes putting a hedge around the terms of their contract with God's law. If they do not submit to God's will, they will soon forget the One who made a covenant with them and is always near them. Thus, Moses' major point is that they must do everything to not forget what God taught them in the wilderness. This is important because if they fail to trust God completely and to not trust God for His word or to not worship Him as the only one and true God, then what God has provided to them, in fulfillment to what He said to Abraham, would be taken from them.

> God led them through an emotionally terrifying wilderness experience. It was terrifying because there were fiery serpents and scorpions and there was no water. He did care for them, however, by providing water, protection, and food. He put them in an environment they had never experienced. He did this to bring them into submission (humble,; apostle Paul, 2 Cor. 12:7–10). By applying much pressure through the many trials, God tested the quality of their character. God did this because He was planning to bring them many great benefits in the end and He did not want their hearts to become entangled with riches and forget Him (Matt. 6:24). The essence of forgetting God is the failure to keep his commands (8:11). Pride is the danger of success (8:14), for there is always the temptation to think that what has been achieved

> is the result of human effort rather than the gift of God. Proud self-sufficiency would be the Israelites' undoing (8:17–19), causing them to become like the nations that were destroyed before them (8:20).[1]

If God does not respond to them in this manner, then once they are in the land they would set their minds and their emotions to believe that all this was done based on their ability. They may believe it was their authority, their control of their circumstances, their strength, and their hard labor that brought them prosperity. It was God's faithful work that made all of this possible. This was done because God is true to His covenant and will establish it just because He made a pledge and an oath to do it.

Historical Background

Establishing Context

Moses is now repeating the law before this new congregation of Israelites. He is letting them understand the heart of God so that once they get into the Promised Land and experience all that God has reserved for them, they do not forget who provided it and turn away from Him.

> The provision of manna was a test to see if Israel would depend on the Lord's word (cf. comments on Ex. 16:4). Such dependence is humbling (cf. Deut. 8:3). The people could avoid pride in their wealth and strength if they would constantly remember the LORD and the lesson of the wilderness: all of life is a gift from God and nothing is possible apart from Him (v. 18).[2]

God also warns them not to worship other gods because this will turn their loyalty away from Him. "Israel was to acknowledge that Yahweh—not the fertility gods of Canaan—was the source of all blessings in the land. Israel was also to acknowledge that blessing as a product of God's grace, not their righteousness."[3]

---

[1] R. B. Hughes and J. C. Laney, *Tyndale Concise Bible Commentary* (Wheaton, IL: Tyndale House Publishers, 2001), 73.

[2] J. F. Walvoord and R. B. Zuck, eds., *The Bible Knowledge Commentary: An Exposition of the Scriptures* (Wheaton, IL: Victor Books, 1983–c1985), 1:278.

[3] E. H. Merrill and D. S. Dockery, eds., *Holman Concise Bible Commentary* (Nashville, TN: Broadman & Holman Publishers, 1998), 65.

God spent forty years teaching them what He is saying in this passage while they buried their relatives and friends, who disobeyed Him—an experience God vividly provided so they would never forget God.

What Does the Context Mean?

They are under a conditional covenant. If they do as God instructed, they shall be blessed. If they disobey God, He will not bless them (Deut. 28). Forty years has passed and God has sustained them through all of this. They are going from manna to prosperity in a moment of time once they cross the Jordan. They are going from the same diet to a multitude of food. There will be no need for manna, so they are not visibly dependent on God as before. So it can become easy for them to think they are the ones who are taking care of themselves. Before this takes place, God reminds them that if they do this, He will not bless them. They must worship Him only and surrender to His will.

Sermon Subject and Title

Sermon Title: Remember God!
Big Idea: Remembering God's faithfulness determines the nature of future blessings.

Sermon Outline (Deut. 8:11–18 NASB)

A. Don't Forget His Ways (vv. 11–14)

1. *Beware not to forget*—this is an action that must be executed because it is a command (imperative):
   a) *Forget* is in the imperfect meaning; this is an action that began in the past, continues in the present with no plans to stop it in the future. It is perpetual.
   b) We must do our best to learn from the lessons of the past—God's lesson from David (1 Sam. 17:31–40).
   c) We forget when we fail to guide our present choices by truths we have learned in the past.
   d) Failing to observe His commands, His laws, and His decrees, is a failure to give the lessons of the past a significant place in our present.

2. Lord God—The One who sustains His covenant and is supreme over all gods. It is in Him we must find our being (Acts 17:28).
3. God wants us to always remember that He is our provider.
4. We need to always seek to guard the Word that God provided to us (Ps. 119:11; 1 John 2:3–6).
5. God does not want His people to forget His:
    a) *Commandments*—God's Word dictates how He relates to us.
    b) *Statutes*—His moral and civil laws.
    c) *Ordinances*—In the Old Testament, His religious laws. In the New Testament it is baptism, the Lord's Supper, and guidelines for how the church functions.
6. If we choose to forget what we should remember, the following takes place:
    a) *Hearts*—Our worldly passions outweigh our will to obey God (1 John 2:15–17).
    b) *Proud*—We get high on ourselves as if we accomplished everything. This characteristic becomes who they are and this person no longer remembers anything God has done ("you will forget"—perfect action).

B. Remember His Faithfulness (vv. 15–17)

1. God brought them through a wilderness experience that was frightening. There was no way they could have navigated through the wilderness without Him.
2. Even though He knows these experiences are bad, He is attentive and cares for us through them all.
3. *Fathers did not know*—No one but God knows the "valley and shadow of death." This is a set state of being (perfect action of the verb).
4. *Humble*—He allows us to experience trials so that we live a submissive life before God (Deut. 8:1–6; 2 Cor. 12:7–10). It is a Piel infinitive—this is the end result that God sought.
5. These trials make our dependence on God a vivid experience (Deut. 8:1–6).
6. Trials Confirm:
    a) Our faith (Exod. 20:20).
    b) Our commitment (Deut. 8:2).
7. After God proves our faith and commitment, He does what benefits us (Heb. 11:6).

8. *Say in your hearts*—Use human wisdom and follow what our desires instruct us to do (James 3:13–18).
9. If God blesses us before He tests us and develops godly character:
   a) We would think it is our ability that causes us to accomplish His blessings.
   b) We would think that we controlled our destiny.
   c) We would think that it is our creative ability that achieves our accomplishments.
10. God blesses us because He is true to His Word.

C. Bless God as a Sign of True Remembrance (v. 18)

1. *You shall remember*—Our inner thoughts of recalling all that God has done for us should become (especially after forty years of sustaining them) the only manner in which we think about the goodness and power of God.
2. *Giving us power to make wealth*—It is God's ability and capability that makes all things possible. Everything we have God put it in place (Luke 12:22–34; James 1:17).
3. *Swore*—God will always be true to His Word.
4. Giving helps us not to forget God's goodness, and it's a statement that we remember He is our Blesser. He gave us wealth (Deut. 8:10). It expresses our level of dependence on Him.
5. Giving tells God we know where our blessing came from and it reminds us not to forget.
6. Giving is remembering Him by the way we keep His Word.

Author's Comments

Comments

Giving to God can seem unreasonable with gas prices, food prices, and other costs of living items constantly going up. How can we give when we have the same amount of money, but prices increase? Under these circumstances, it can become even more disconcerting when we read passages of Scripture like Malachi 3:8, "Will a man rob God?" He did not say steal from God, as if it is done in secret for God to find out. No, it is to take from God while He is fully aware of what is going on. We are challenged even more when in books like Haggai, God says He put holes in purses (1:6) and problems in houses because believers refuse to obey Him. Is God taking from us or just requiring us to trust

Him to continue to give to us each day? This conflict exists among many believers and many times God seems like the enemy, when He is actually the only true loving and supportive friend we have (John 15:14).

God went to pains to teach the Hebrew people this lesson of dependence on Him, so it must be of tremendous importance that we learn it. This, I believe, is why this chapter we are studying begins with: "So He humbled you, allowed you to hunger, and fed you with manna which you did not know nor did your fathers know, that He might make you know that man shall not live by bread alone; but man lives by every word that proceeds from the mouth of the LORD" (Deut. 8:3). Jesus would explain to us the same thing in John 6:35: "And Jesus said to them, 'I am the bread of life. He who comes to Me shall never hunger, and he who believes in Me shall never thirst.'" David would say in Psalm 37:25, "I have been young, and now am old; yet I have not seen the righteous forsaken, nor his descendants begging bread." Those who walk conscious of God's Word, who trust Him, and who are surrendered to His will, He blesses (Ps. 112:1–3; Prov. 24:3–5). A person who lives with this mind-set is a true worshipper. A true worshipper has to be restrained (Exod. 36:1–7) when it comes to giving because they know without a doubt: "Every good gift and every perfect gift is from above, and comes down from the Father of lights, with whom there is no variation or shadow of turning" (James 1:17). When Paul matured, his view of God became so great (Phil. 4:13) his perspective about riches changed (Phil. 3:4–9) and his focus became attached to one thing: ". . . that I may know Him and the power of His resurrection, and the fellowship of His sufferings, being conformed to His death, if, by any means, I may attain to the resurrection from the dead" (Phil. 3:10–11). What became of greater importance to the apostle Paul is the very thing God was seeking to teach the Hebrews in this message delivered by Moses: ". . . that He might make you know that man shall not live by bread alone; but man lives by every word that proceeds from the mouth of the LORD" (Deut. 8:3).

Wealth, as we saw with the Hebrews in the Promised Land, can easily remove our dependence on God.

> Do not love the world or the things in the world. If anyone loves the world, the love of the Father is not in him. For all that is in the world—the lust of the flesh, the lust of the eyes, and the pride of life—is not of the Father but is of the world. And the world is passing away, and the lust of it; but he who does the will of God abides forever. (1 John 2:15–17)

Worrying about "making ends meet" can cause us to drift from growing in Christ: "Now the ones that fell among thorns are those who, when they have heard, go out and are choked with cares, riches, and pleasures of life, and bring no fruit to maturity" (Luke 8:14). The entire purpose of His death is lost (John 10:10; 15:14; developing life in us and a true friendship with Christ) just because we became more dependent on human resources than God's provision (Matt. 6:24).

Giving makes a strong statement about our relationship with God. "Now may He who supplies seed to the sower, and bread for food, supply and multiply the seed you have sown and increase the fruits of your righteousness, while you are enriched in everything for all liberality, which causes thanksgiving through us to God" (2 Cor. 9:10–11). Giving is making a strong statement that God is remembered in everything because His kingdom is first and foremost (Matt. 6:9–10; Luke 12:31, 34). He is not taking from us, but blessing us with life and empowering us to experience His provision without worry and stress because we are confident about where our help comes from (Matt. 6:25, 34). Our financial decisions are guided by His Word, as we exercise wisdom, and in difficult times we can trust Him because we know He "is able to do exceedingly abundantly above all that we ask or think, according to the power that works in us" (Eph. 3:20).

Application

God takes giving to Him very seriously. To not give to the one who provides all things is to disrespect Him, and this does not demonstrate true worship. Worship is to highlight God's "worthship." Not showing gratitude for all He has done is no different than asking one of your children for one French fry after you bought it for them and they say no. It is no different if you ask the same child to bring you a glass of water and they say no. The child could not provide for himself and yet he shows no gratitude to the one who cares for him! The same child saying "I love you" somehow no longer seems sincere—"God loves a cheerful" and bountiful giver (2 Cor. 9:6–15) because they are saying thanks.

Illustrate It

The story is told of O. J. Simpson who always wondered how rich people could commit suicide until one day in the midst of his fame and fortune he felt alone and lost, and wondered what had become of his life. He just seemed to be running from one thing to the next. O. J. Simpson had forgotten what he had said about rich people committing suicide until that day when he considered it when he had everything before him.

"For what will it profit a man if he gains the whole world and forfeits his soul? Or what will a man give in exchange for his soul?" (Matt. 16:26 NASB).

It is interesting that the Scriptures teach us that God is willing to bless us if we fear Him and walk in His ways. In passages such as Psalm 112:1–3, Psalm 128, and Proverbs 24:3–5, God promises to take care of those who are wise, walk in His knowledge, and fear Him. Once a person accepts God's promises and becomes a sincere giver, God establishes and sustains them.

Faithfulness Blesses

Luke 16:10–13

General Overview of the Passage

The focus of this passage is not to demonize money or wealth, but to provide a godly perspective of the earthly resources as Christ did in reference to the rich young ruler (Matt. 19:16–26). "Earthly wealth is not only trivial and unreal; it does not belong to us. It is ours only as a loan and a trust, which may be withdrawn at any moment. Heavenly possessions are immense, real, and eternally secure."[4] The person who is steadfast to fulfill what was entrusted to them in a very little thing (Matt. 25:14–31) is also faithful with much. The person who is dishonest and untrustworthy in a very little thing will be dishonest in much.

If a person has not been trustworthy or steadfast in fulfilling the required expectations of a task as it relates to wealth (all kinds of possessions that have material value), especially when it is acquired in a dishonest manner, no one demonstrates confidence in them. "If a believer is not faithful in the small matters pertaining to this world, they cannot expect God to commit the true riches of His grace."[5]

In this passage, Christ explains that no domestic servant who serves in a submissive manner can comply with two masters. This servant who tries to serve two masters will end up committed to one and eventually despise the other. It is impossible to serve two masters, especially when their masters are in vastly different directions. "Once a man chooses to serve God, every moment of

---

[4] A. Plummer, *A Critical and Exegetical Commentary on the Gospel according to S. Luke* (London: T&T Clark International, 1896), 386.

[5] *Barnes' Notes*, Electronic Database (Biblesoft, 1997).

his time and every atom of his energy belongs to God. God is the most exclusive of masters. We either belong to Him totally or not at all."[6]

Historical Background

Establishing Context

Mammon in the Scriptures has a particular meaning. *Mammon* is an Aramaic word for possessions or money."[7]

Jesus lived in a day that is not unlike ours. The Pharisees were very covetous (Matt. 23:14; Titus 1:11). They taught that everyone, if they are walking right with God, would expose God's favor by the wealth they accumulate. While teaching this, they stole money from the people they were supposed to protect, especially the widows. They laughed at the teachings of Christ because He did not teach that God's blessings are displayed in wealth. Jesus did not teach it was a sin to be wealthy but that the "world's attitude toward wealth and failure to use wealth to the glory of God"[8] was a sin. "It is not a sin to be wealthy, for godly men like David and Abraham were wealthy, nor is it a sin to enjoy one's wealth (1 Tim. 6:17); but it is a sin to have the world's attitude toward wealth and fail to use wealth to the glory of God."[9]

During the time of Jesus' ministry, there were slaves and sometimes two masters owned one slave. They would try to share a slave because the two persons could not buy one each. In most if not all cases one master was unsatisfied because it was difficult for the slave to serve them both. This problem is the backdrop to Christ's teaching this principle.

What Does the Context Mean?

The meaning of the whole parable is about faithfulness with whatever is provided to us. If God provides a lot, then we must remain good stewards in submission to His authority. If God blesses us with a little, we must be faithful with the amount provided.

---

[6] W. Barclay, *The Gospel of Luke*, The Daily Study Bible series, rev. ed. (1975; repr., Philadelphia, PA: The Westminster Press, 2000), 209.

[7] C. S. Keener, *The IVP Bible Background Commentary: New Testament* (Downers Grove, IL: InterVarsity Press, 1993), s.v. Luke 16:9–13.

[8] Ibid.

[9] Ibid.

It is even worse if a person cannot be faithful with material resources that were acquired dishonestly. If a person could not faithfully manage resources attained dishonestly, then there is no way anyone would trust them. The same is true of resources someone is managing that belongs to someone else. As a result, it is not how much a person has that leads to greater blessing, but how faithful a person is with what is provided to them.

Being faithful with a small or large amount of resources requires such attention and concentration that it is impossible to execute how the resources are to be managed if the person has two bosses leading them in two different directions.

Sermon Subject and Title

Sermon Title: Faithfulness Blesses

Big Idea: It is not the faithfulness of God that is in question, but our faithfulness to Him. Our faithfulness to God is demonstrated when we respectfully use His resources, whether it is a little or much. God blesses us when He serves as our master and we are faithful with whatever He provides.

Sermon Outline (Luke 16:10–13 NASB)

A. The Rewards of Faithfulness (v. 10)

1. *He who is*—This is a person who has always been faithful with little and is committed to be endlessly faithful.
2. *Faithful*—Even though they have little (2 Cor. 8:1–5) they are dependable, reliable with the little they have (Prov. 10:4; 21:5). This is a nominative, meaning it is the subject of the verb. This is the focus of this passage.
3. *Faithful*—They are committed to consistently and steadfastly fulfill what God wants them to do with the little they have (Matt. 25:14–31). "Faithfulness is not determined by the amount entrusted but by the character of the person who uses it."[10]
4. Because the nature of their character is trustworthiness, they will do a great job with much.

---

[10] Notes from the *NIV Study Bible* (Grand Rapids, MI: Zondervan, 2011), s.v. Luke 16:10.

5. A person who is dishonest and untrustworthy with less does the same with much.

B. God the Financial Planner (vv. 11–12)

1. *Wealth*—All kinds of possessions that have material value (1 John 2:15–17).
2. *Unrighteous wealth*— Proverbs 28:19–20, 22; 1 Timothy 6:6–10; James 5:1–6
3. *True riches*—Exists as a result of the goodness and will of God (James 1:17).
   a) True riches are a blessing from God (Prov. 10:22).
   b) True riches are gained as a result of diligent hands (Prov. 10:4; 13:14; 21:5).
   c) True riches are attained as a result of a righteous life (Ps. 112; Prov. 10:16).
   d) We must use our wealth:
      - To take care of our senior parents (1 Tim. 5:1–5).
      - To be responsible to our families (1 Tim. 5:7–8).
      - To give to the Lord's church (Luke 6:38; 2 Cor. 9:8–10).
      - To help those in need (1 John 3:16–20).
      - For His kingdom purposes (1 Tim. 6:17–18).
      - To bless God's preacher (Gal. 6:6–9; 1 Tim. 3:3—pastors cannot be greedy or lovers of money; Ezekiel 34; 1 Tim. 3:3–4; 2 Pet. 2:2–3).
   e) True riches from God never fail (Matt. 6:19–20).
4. *Another's*—Can mean a lack of faithfulness in managing the wealth at your job.
5. What God has in store for us is in heaven (Luke 6:38).

C. Christ Only Blesses Faithfulness to His Agenda (v. 13)

1. No one can continuously be under two different agendas (James 4:4; 1 John 2:15–17).
2. To remain focused, they have to reject one in order to give their will to another.
3. God is an exclusive master.

Author's Comments

Comments

I don't need to say that we are living in troubled times. It is not trouble only because of wars and rumors of wars, but it can also be difficult times financially. If life is about material things, then Christ misled us when He said that He provided life and life abundantly (John 10:10). This becomes even more difficult to believe, because while Christ was on earth He said He had nothing (Luke 9:58); and when He ascended into heaven (Acts 1:9–11), He left the disciples with nothing (Acts 3:6). Enjoying life or experiencing a productive life on earth cannot be as a result of material resources (Matt. 6:19–20).

To some people, gaining financial freedom is about politics and knowing a lot about money. It does not hurt to know about financial management and portfolios. However, God's structure is different and it simply requires faithfulness.

In God's structure, a person can start with little. In His structure, it matters most who is the master (Matt. 6:24), and second, how faithful we are with the little we have. The love for money can cause us to forsake God (1 Tim. 6:10). "We can't serve God and money simply because we have to choose between the vastly different courses each calls for."[11]

Faithfulness is not just doing something consistently, being on time or being at one's post. It also involves being determined to fulfill what it is expected and to remain steadfast until the task is completed. This is why it is important to have one master and to have a master who does not do things dishonestly. This is not just about money. It concerns everything that God has blessed us to acquire. This is why the passage uses the word "wealth." "Blessed is the man who fears the Lord, who delights greatly in His commandments. His descendants will be mighty on earth; the generation of the upright will be blessed. Wealth and riches will be in his house, and his righteousness endures forever" (Ps. 112:1–3).

Faithfulness to God leads to blessings.

---

[11] L. O. Richards, *The Bible Reader's Companion* (Wheaton, IL: Victor Books Logos Research Systems, 1996), electronic ed., 667.

Application

Our faithfulness determines our blessing. Whatever resources God provides, we must see them as coming from above. As a result, we should manage with the consciousness that Christ expects us to be good stewards.

When my children were small, they would invite friends over and my wife and I would always be very careful to return the children to their parents better or in the same way we received them. It was especially important since these children did not belong to us. Whatever God provides to us, we must be good stewards of it because "Every good gift and every perfect gift is from above, and comes down from the Father of lights" (James 1:17).

We are technically not managing what is ours, but managing what belongs to God. As a result, we must take care of it. Our faithfulness to respect His will, as we manage these resources, blesses us.

Illustrate It

Bernie Madoff, in his desire to get wealthy, lied to his clients and made off with millions of dollars of their wealth. He enjoyed lavish living, owned several planes, homes, cars, and went on exotic vacations. Eventually his Ponzi scheme caught up with him, and he was indicted and placed in jail. His followers wanted to get rich quick. The stock market was not good enough following the standard methods; they wanted more. There seems to have been enough greed to go around, but Mr. Madoff was greediest of them all.

The saddest news in this entire story is that his son killed himself in 2010 because he could not get past what his dad did.[12] "For what will it profit a man if he gains the whole world and forfeits his soul? Or what will a man give in exchange for his soul? For the Son of Man is going to come in the glory of His Father with His angels, and *will then repay every man according to his deeds*" (Matt. 16:26–27 NASB, emphasis mine).

If a person makes God their master, they experience life and life abundantly (John 10:10).

[12] https://nypost.com/2010/12/11/bernie-madoffs-son-mark-commits-suicide/

God's Formula for Successful Living

Psalm 128:1–6

General Overview of the Passage

God prospers those who fear Him, and according to the psalmist, God also makes them happy. This is because they have made it a pattern in their lives to submit to the divine will of God. These "God fearers" reverence God by being committed to His Word for all their decisions. Being a "God fearer" is essential to everything covered in this passage. "The fear of God is an attitude of respect, a response of reverence and wonder. It is the only appropriate response to our Creator and Redeemer."[13]

In verse 2 the psalmist changes from "everyone" to personalize it to the person he is writing to, the individual. When a righteous man eats the fruit of his hands, after putting in long, hard, and exhausting work (Eccles. 10:15), he shall be emotionally satisfied and come to a point of bliss or complete happiness. God's blessings could—but not always—also include economic benefit that practically serves the family so that it is a delight for them. Laboring in independence of God is vain work (Ps. 127:2), but working in reverence to God and in obedience to His ways is fruitful (Ps. 128:3). This attitude also blesses the person's family.

A man's wife becomes fruitful and resourceful in the house (faithful and dedicated to the home, unlike the wayward wife in Prov. 7:11). When the family is around the table, which is blessed by God's faithfulness because of a God-fearing father, it symbolizes not only their love and care, but also great family fellowship. We see each of the children happily communicating at suppertime, as each retells his day's experiences. The happy family is the blessed family, the

---

[13] E. D. Radmacher, R. B. Allen, and H. W. House, *Nelson's New Illustrated Bible Commentary* (Nashville, TN: Nelson Publishers, 1999), 732.

holy family. "It speaks to us of the fact that eating together *around your table* becomes both the sign and the symbol of the perfection of loving and joyous fellowship that is the will of God, and which indeed reflects the family nature of God himself as Holy Trinity."[14]

It is from Zion (God's place of worship) that the Lord provides gifts that lead to prosperity, goodwill, and happiness. The Lord does this from Zion because He desires a relationship with His people and has all authority and power to execute the process. God's blessings establish well-being not just for the God-fearing family, but also for the community. This experience lasts all the days of a sustained, prosperous, and healthy life. The psalmist's desire is that this man experiences his children's children and also a harmonious state that is absent of external or internal strife.

Historical Background

Establishing Context

"The psalm is generally regarded as postexilic. The incorporation of the formula of v. 6b into the poem and probably the mixed form of the psalm support this view. In the collection it is a companion piece to Psalm 127, with its common interest in the family and hard-won harvest."[15]

This psalmist identifies with a family going up to Jerusalem. When they arrive, the father puts his hands on the head of the animal, transferring the sins of the family to the animal. This man hopefully has prepared the sacrifice in proper order (for example, prepare the animal, make sure it is ceremonial in order and has submitted to God's structure) because he fears God.

An olive tree is valuable to the Jewish community because of what it can offer the family and the community. The man who was helped by the Samaritan on the road to Jericho had olive oil poured into his wounds. "An olive tree was versatile, useful for its wood, leaves, and oil; it also symbolized well-being (Gen.

---

[14] George Angus Fulton Knight, *Psalms: Volume 2,* The Daily Study Bible Series (Louisville, KY: Westminster John Knox Press, 2001, c1982), S. 283.

[15] Leslie C. Allen, *Psalms 101–150, Revised,* Word Biblical Commentary, vol. 21 (Dallas, TX: Word, Inc., 2002), 243.

8:11) and splendor (Hosea 14:6). It tenaciously produces new shoots even after being cut down."[16]

For a person to be promised long life is a tremendous blessing because the life expectancy was forty-five and the mortality rate for infant births was fifty percent. So for a person to see their grandchildren was clearly an act of God. What seems to be implied in the passage is that the children are born healthy and in each case safely. This is uncommon in their day, leading to many special family gatherings. "The feasts of ancient Israel were family affairs. As families made their way to the holy city for the annual festivals, they would encounter other families and mutually celebrate the goodness of God in their lives."[17]

What Does the Context Mean?

It is best for a man to fear God and to walk in His ways. This not only provides financial blessing; it also produces a good home, great worship, and a long life. Righteousness is a commitment to the divine will of God. It is not that the person is perfect. A righteous person is someone who when corrected quickly adjusts their will to match the will of God because they have an awesome adoration and trust for Him.

In those days there was no Social Security for senior individuals. It was an agrarian culture, so as a person aged, working the fields and cleaning the house would have been extremely difficult. To have children who were willing to support their parents would have been vital for the survival of senior parents. This is why Naomi, at the death of her husband and sons, went home to die. Most women, during those days, had no technical skill or vocation. It would have just been a matter of time before she dies. In contrast, a righteous man with a fruitful wife would view their children and grandchildren as olive plants and would be embraced as a true blessing.

God is a loving God, willing to provide for His children, but like a Father, God expects us to live in reverence of His holiness, righteousness, authority, and power.

---

[16] J. H. Walton, *Zondervan Illustrated Bible Backgrounds Commentary (Old Testament): The Minor Prophets, Job, Psalms, Proverbs, Ecclesiastes, Song of Songs* (Grand Rapids, MI: Zondervan, 2009), Vol. 5, 426.

[17] Radmacher, Allen, and House, *Nelson's New Illustrated Bible Commentary*, s.v. Ps. 128.

Sermon Subject and Title

Sermon Title: God's Formula for Successful Living
Big Idea: A man who fears God is a man who makes God's Word the source that determines his lifestyle, which in turns blesses him and his family.

SERMON OUTLINE (PS. 128:1–6)

A. **Fear God (v. 1)—Mental**
   1. To be *blessed* means to live in happy bliss—God is in control.
   2. A "God fearer" is someone who understands the power and authority of the Lord.
   3. A "God fearer" is someone who lives with a conscious respect for the Lord each moment of the day.
   4. A "God fearer" is a God worshipper.
   5. *Fearing God* is an essential characteristic in order to receive gifts from the one who has a covenant with us and has power and authority.
   6. *Walk in His ways* means to have our lifestyle (everyday decisions) controlled by God's divine will.
   7. "Say to the righteous that it shall be well with them, for they shall eat the fruit of their doings" (Isa. 3:10).

B. **Work Hard (v. 2)—Emotional**
   1. In verse 2, the psalmist changes from an "everyone" approach to personalize it; he now writes and speaks to one person.
   2. Emotional satisfaction—when a person is willing to work until they are weary, God blesses them to enjoy well-being and contentment (Prov. 10:4; 13:4; 21:5; Eccles. 5:10).
   3. Their hard work also provides them economic benefit that is excellent and is practically beneficial.
   4. Laboring in anxious independence of God is vain (Ps. 127:2).
   5. Working in obedience to God is fruitful (Ps. 128:3).

C. **Take Family Seriously (vv. 3–4)—Social**
   1. The wife will be faithful, productive, and resourceful (Prov. 31).
   2. *Children like olive plants*—will produce fruit, become of financial benefit to their parents, will bless them (anointing oil), and will be there when they are sick (oil for wounds).
   3. *Around your table*—Loving family fellowships.
   4. *Behold*—Pay attention to what a blessed man looks like.

5. A blessed man reverences God's authority and He does not take God's love for granted.

D. Be Committed to Church Life (v. 5)—Spiritual

1. *Blessed* (different Hebrew word)—gifts of goodwill from God; leads to prosperity and happiness; comes from Zion (place of worship; it is where the temple is).
2. *From Zion*—a person experiences all economic benefit; giving to God faithfully (Mal. 3:8–12).
3. Zion is the center from which all blessings flow.
4. It is this economic benefit that impacts the community (Mal. 3:8–12).
5. These blessings never fail; they last all the days of a blessed man's life.

E. Enjoy God's Blessings (v. 6)—Personal

1. This blessed believer experiences long life.
2. *A blessed believer lives in peace*—harmonious living and an absence of strife from the inside and out.
3. A blessed man has well-being and satisfaction.

Author's Comments

Comments

Do you trust God for His promises or do you trust the world for its economic strategies? The world tells you to go to school to gain an education, build a career, find time when you can for your family, and enjoy the fruit of your labor. Go to church when you can and serve God if you have time. The Bible describes this life as vanity. Most people die from stress and related illnesses when God offers peace, joy, love, and strength to endure hard times as a fruit of the Spirit's dwelling in us (Gal. 5:22). From this life, He promises to bless us and our families (Ps. 112; Prov. 24:3–5). There is a lot less stress with God's plan and it produces a more secure level of success that lasts forever. "I know that nothing is better for them than to rejoice, and to do good in their lives, and also that every man should eat and drink and enjoy the good of all his labor—it is the gift of God" (Eccles. 3:12–13).

I know, as a pastor, it is hard to get believers to surrender to these principles. Example: "So He humbled you, allowed you to hunger, and fed you with manna which you did not know nor did your fathers know, that He might make you know that man shall not live by bread alone; but man lives by every word that proceeds from the mouth of the LORD" (Deut. 8:3). Placing God first in everything is what leads to all the earthly blessings believers desire. When this is preached, it so goes against everything the world teaches and raises all kinds of suspicions. Believers cannot find time, or some believe the church is seeking to get more money from them. Others view God's principles as impractical; they think they need to focus on doing all they can to make it because "God helps those who helps themselves." To this the psalmist says they work in vain (Ps. 127:1–2). Solomon, who had just about all the earthly goods anyone can desire, says, "He who loves silver will not be satisfied with silver; Nor he who loves abundance, with increase. This also is vanity" (Eccles. 5:10).

The Scripture repeatedly drives home the point of this passage (Ps. 128) because God is life and is the provider of all of life's blessings. This is still true today; Christ came to give life (John 10:10), and this is why believers seek Him first (Luke 12:31) and abide in Him, because to not abide in Him means life eventually comes to nothing (John 15:5). Conversely, to abide in Him means He grants the desires of a believer's heart (John 15:7).

> Do not love the world or the things in the world. If anyone loves the world, the love of the Father is not in him. For all that is in the world—the lust of the flesh, the lust of the eyes, and the pride of life—is not of the Father but is of the world. And the world is passing away, and the lust of it; but he who does the will of God abides forever. (1 John 2:15–17)

When a person fears God and lives with a heart to honor Him each day, God produces His life in and through their lives (Gal. 2:20), and since His life is everything, God's blessings becomes their gift.

God's formula for success is learning to be a true disciple of God. It is learning to love Him, to trust Him so that we reverence Him each day we live (Luke 12:29–34). We do not do this with a motive to be blessed. We reverence Him because the more we love Him and learn about Him, the more we surrender to Him. Our surrender leads to truly experiencing Him daily, and this becomes the greatest blessing we seek because this is the only one that matters eternally.

> Then Peter answered and said to Him, "See, we have left all and followed You. Therefore what shall we have?" So Jesus said to them, "Assuredly I say to you, that in the regeneration, when the Son of Man sits on the throne of His glory, you who have followed Me will also sit on twelve thrones, judging the twelve tribes of Israel. And everyone

who has left houses or brothers or sisters or father or mother or wife or children or lands, for My name's sake, shall receive a hundredfold, and inherit eternal life." (Matt. 19:27–29)

Application

Walking righteously before God is everything. To live our lives without a reverence of God leads to a life of stress, frustration, and anxiety (Ps. 127:1–2). Does God shape your family structure, your day, the manner in which you work and worship Him? Or is He someone who is important only on Sundays? This attitude determines the quality of our homes and our blessings.

Illustrate It

I was called to the bedside of a very ill woman who was a member of our church. Sandra was a faithful member who sincerely loved her family. By the time I arrived, her son and her daughter and their children were all at her bedside. As she took her last breaths, the family began to kiss her, hug each other, and talk about their mother in such loving terms.

I shared the story of a time when I stayed near the bedside of someone dying and I was the only one there. There was no one in sight to say goodbye. In contrast, to see Sandra's family reminiscing about their mother, telling her to say hello to their dad and how they miss him, confirmed what family should be all about. I encouraged them to be the family they said she taught them to be and remain close, because at the end of your life, you should be able to count on your family. Sandra lived a rich life because she made loving God and loving her family the most important things in her life.

Sermon Series 3

Programmed for Victory

Don't Quit; Victory Ahead

1 Peter 1:6–9

General Overview of the Passage

Despite the pain and difficulties these believers were experiencing, Peter challenged them, just like James did for believers experiencing similar circumstances—to live carefree like a lamb skipping through a field knowing that the shepherd is watching over them. They can maintain this mind-set, because the many trials they are going through are nothing compared to eternity. "The trials may come from God or under His permissive will from Satan, or may be the result of our own wrong doing. The word emphasizes the diversity rather than the number of the trials."[1]

If a believer is able to remain focused in the Lord's discipline, it will continuously provide evidence of the level of a believer's faith. Under the scrutiny of a believer's faith, God determines whether or not the refining process is necessary.

This process, when a believer keeps the faith, in the midst of each testing, exposes the nature of God in and through their lives. The display of the attributes of Christ is a result of the believer's persistent commitment with great confidence to trust God's Word. This leads to an even greater level of joy and a greater display of the maturity of Christ in the believer's life. The purpose of God allowing these trials is so that the person can be totally removed from any inhibitions that may hamper their full surrender to God.

Peter, who once while under great duress walked away from Jesus, now encourages believers who are suffering to remain focused by keeping the faith. This is the same point James made. Trials are seen as occasions for joy (James 1:2). These Scriptures are true, but in reality, when difficulties come, most believers struggle to feel a sense of joy and, like Peter, feel afraid and desire to back away from God. It is because of the lessons Peter learned (not just in the

---

[1] K. S. Wuest, *Wuest's Word Studies from the Greek New Testament: For the English Reader* (Grand Rapids, MI: Eerdmans, 1984, 1997), s.v. 1 Pet. 1:6–7.

time of Christ but also in the beginning stages of the Jerusalem church) that he can now encourage these believers to keep the faith.

Historical Background

Establishing Context

These believers were experiencing much suffering. Some commentators believe that this was during the time of Nero, a Roman emperor. Peter is "exhorting and testifying that this is the true grace of God in which you stand" (1 Pet. 5:12). "Testing could be joyous rather than grievous because these readers knew in advance the goal of the testing: when they had persevered to the end, the final deliverance would come."[2]

Due to the fact that they were in a place where metal was melted in many furnaces around the city to provide military armor for the Roman soldiers and for new buildings, the believers would easily relate to being refined by fire. They would know, because of the jewelry makers in the city, that fire was also used to purify gold.

Setting the focus for their suffering, including the fact that Christ also suffered and is now glorified because He remained focused on the purposes of God, serves to encourage these believers to stay the course and remain focused on Christ.

What Does the Context Mean?

God's permissive will allows Satan to test us. God works this out for our good and His glory. When we continue in His Word despite what we may experience, our faith in Him is tested and that process refines us (James 1:2–4). This is because when we hold fast to God's Word in trials we "work out [our] own salvation" (Phil. 2:12). The Spirit of God transforms us as we renew our minds (Rom. 12:2), and whatever we experience works out for our good (Rom. 8:28). This is why we are more than conquerors through Jesus Christ (Rom. 8:37–39). The writer of Hebrews puts it this way:

> Therefore we also, since we are surrounded by so great a cloud of witnesses, let us lay aside every weight, and the sin which so easily ensnares

---

[2] C. S. Keener, *The IVP Bible Background Commentary: New Testament* (Downers Grove, IL: InterVarsity Press, 1993), 1 Pet. 1:3–8.

us, and let us run with endurance the race that is set before us, looking unto Jesus, the author and finisher of our faith, who for the joy that was set before Him endured the cross, despising the shame, and has sat down at the right hand of the throne of God. For consider Him who endured such hostility from sinners against Himself, lest you become weary and discouraged in your souls. (Heb. 12:1–3)

Sermon Subject and Title

Sermon Title: Don't Quit; Victory Ahead
Big Idea: To demonstrate the proof of our faith when tested produces godly character that glorifies and honors God at Christ's return.

Sermon Outline (1 Pet. 1:6–9 NASB)

A. Faith Is Fail-Proof (vv. 6–7)

1. *In this*—Rejoicing takes place because of total surrender and complete trust in God (1 Pet. 1:5; Phil. 4:4–9).
2. *In this*—Knowing that God has placed a hedge around us (Ps. 34:7; Heb. 1:14)—"who are kept by the power of God through faith" (1 Pet. 1:5).
3. *Now for a little while*—Compared to eternity, trials are for a particular season (Luke 4:13; Gal. 6:9–10).
4. *You can greatly rejoice*—Rejoicing is a habitual attitude (1 Thess. 5:16; Phil. 4:4) of exceeding gladness that serves as an expression of confidence in God.
5. Faith is necessary because trials can bring us to mental anguish (extreme pain and distress of the mind).
6. Faith is necessary because we have no control over:
   a) How many trials (1 Pet. 4:12)
   b) What kind of trials
   c) How long they last
7. Proof of faith:
   a) Christ's examination of our convictions (Deut. 8:1–10; 2 Tim. 3:14–15).
   b) A sustained belief in God's Word (Heb. 11).
   c) Exposes our complete trust in Him (Heb. 11).

d) *Tested by fire*—True faith refines us.
e) *Found*—This is a discovery process that took place after much scrutiny.
f) *Result in praise and glory*—The excellent nature of Christ is developed in us and exposed through us. "I have been crucified with Christ; it is no longer I who live, but Christ lives in me; and the life which I now live in the flesh I live by faith in the Son of God, who loved me and gave Himself for me" (Gal. 2:20–21).
g) It leads to a joyous welcome home in heaven (Rev. 3:21).
h) It provides the crown of life (James 1:12).

B. Keeping the Faith Leads to an Inexpressible Joy (vv. 8–9)

1. *Have not seen Him*—To not see God yet continually obey Him stimulates spiritual maturity (Heb. 11:1–2).
2. To not see God but believe brings blessings (John 20:29).
3. *You love Him*—To continuously and habitually obey God's Word despite the obstacles these believers encountered.
4. *Believe in Him*—To walk in complete confidence and boldness that God is our deliverer.
5. *Believe in Him*—To fully surrender to God through His Word.
6. *You greatly rejoice*—To demonstrate true expressions of gladness.
7. *You greatly rejoice*—An attitude of complete trust leads to worry-free life. An example of joy is a lamb skipping around in a field carefree because the shepherd is present (Ps. 23).
8. *Inexpressible*—Because of the circumstances that many trials provide, words cannot explain why they had joy in their trials.
9. *Full of glory*—We mature to be like Christ (Gal. 2:20). This means we experience the fruit of the Spirit (Gal. 5:23–25).
10. *Outcome of faith*—Faith has a product. It is the working "out your own salvation with fear and trembling" (Phil. 2:12).
11. *Salvation*—Trials that stimulate faith deliver us from fear, worry, and weakness. We find strength as a result of the character of Christ fully developing in us.
12. *Soul*—We are delivered from the deepest troubles in our life.
13. Trials teach us to live triumphant over everything from the inside out (Rom. 8:18, 28, 37–39; Phil. 4:13).

Author's Comments

Comments

Faith is challenging because it is perfected when tested. A believer can know the Word of God, but when trials come they can easily succumb to their feelings of stress, worry, and negative thoughts that may their minds. Especially when trials persist, it is easy for doubt to dispel faith.

These believers have a government that is against them, people that don't like them, wives struggling with unsaved husbands, problems in the church because of the attitude of some, apathy in the use of their spiritual gifts, pride for some, and for others a feeling that Satan had devoured them. Peter had to help them keep from quitting in the midst of their tests by challenging them to remain sober and to live a pure and humble life before God. From Peter's own experience he learned what it took for these believers to gain victory. They must "resist [the devil], steadfast in the faith, knowing that the same sufferings are experienced by your brotherhood in the world. But may the God of all grace, who called us to His eternal glory by Christ Jesus, after you have suffered a while, perfect, establish, strengthen, and settle you" (1 Pet. 5:9–10).

Victory is not experienced in the midst of the race. Victory is at the finish line (Heb. 12:1–3). In the midst of the race we are being refined but at the end of the refining process we will be "anxious for nothing" (Phil. 4:6) and can "rejoice always" (Phil. 4:4), be content in all things (Phil. 4:11–12), can accomplish "all things through Christ" (Phil. 4:13) because we have grown from being conquered to being conquerors (Rom. 8:37). The circumstances may not change on the outside, but everything within us is "love, joy, peace, longsuffering, kindness, goodness, faithfulness, gentleness, self-control" (Gal. 5:22–23). At this point in our spiritual maturity, the other circumstances no longer can cause the flesh to direct our spirit because we now walk in the power of the Holy Spirit (Gal. 5:25; 1 John 4:4).

Application

When a believer is faced with trials, he should not to worry or become anxious, because God's uses trials to grow us to maturity (James 1:2–4). God only disciplines those whom He loves (Heb. 12:6). Believers must remain committed to obeying God's Word because each trial is focused on testing their deep commitment to God—their faith. Trials refine our faith, expose our love for Christ, and work out our salvation (Phil. 2:12). This is why trials can be counted joy (James 1:2), because when a believer keeps the faith, he "no longer lives, but Christ lives in me; and the life which I now live in the flesh I live by faith in the Son of God, who loved me and gave Himself up for me" (Gal. 2:20).

Illustrate It

There were two football players with great dreams to be NFL prayers. Before the spring/summer ended, the coach demanded that the players come to college early so that they can practice three times a day. One of the players, with great dreams, grumbled and said, "Man, I sure am not looking forward to that." The other player kept silent. He thought to himself, *That is not a problem because I am going to work out all summer.* For most of the summer, the first player worked a job and worked out from time to time because he felt that once he gets back, he is going to have to practice three times a day. The other player worked a part-time job so that he would have time to work out and be completely ready for the season because he intended to keep his starting position and continue to improve on the field.

Upon return, both players saw each other and began to talk again about how great it would be to play in the NFL. It was their senior year, so they had to work very hard just to be recognized. The second player who worked really hard during the summer maintained his starting position while the other was struggling to maintain his position. The player who was struggling to keep his position began to complain and sometimes became sick in practice while the other player succeeded in impressing the coaches. The player who impressed the coaches spent time after practice watching film and would sometimes go to the coach's office to learn the playbook better.

God is clear that He made man to give Him glory. For us to expose the very nature of Christ like the apostle Paul did takes the practicing of God's Word. When a believer trusts God throughout this process and surrenders all to God, no matter how difficult it is, they experience God. They see Him working in and through their lives in a powerful manner. Some believers hope for the best without giving God their best. We must be like this hard-working player so we work out our salvation in fear and trembling (Phil. 2:12).

Steps to Surviving Storms

1 Peter 1:13–16

General Overview of the Passage

Peter wanted to instruct believers how to live in difficult times so that they can effectively experience all that God has in store for them in this life and the life to come. They must be sober and alert and prepare their minds for action so that as obedient children they will not be shaped by the world. This is an attitude that leads them to successfully overcome each trial. These trials strengthen their relationship with God because the trials are purifying (1 Pet. 1:3–9). This allows them to achieve God's greatest desire, which is to be holy as He is holy.

Peter did not remain sober. He became more interested in who will sit on the right or the left of Christ's throne (Mark 10:35–40). He did not want to hear that Christ would die, especially after being told by God, in the presence of all the other disciples, that Jesus is the Christ "the Son of the living God" (Matt. 16:13–23). The pressure of watching Christ being taken away led Peter to cut off the ear of one of the soldiers who arrested Jesus. Fear so overwhelmed Peter during Christ's trial that he denied Christ three times, and after Christ's death hid himself in fear of being persecuted by the religious leaders. Peter became drunk with stress, worry, and fear because of the pressure of the crowds and his personal agenda; and instead of following Christ, he conformed to influences of the world. Peter's experience—and what he learned from it after Christ restored him—makes him the best person to guide these believers as they live in the midst of such difficult experiences.

Peter exhorts them to be encouraged in the realization of God's love (cf. Heb. 12:12–13). "Be sober" rather than panic (repeated in 1 Pet. 4:7; 5:8). "Recall Peter's embarrassing realization of his own sinfulness and truancy when suddenly confronted by the risen Christ while fishing on the Sea of Galilee one morning (John 21:7)."[3] When difficulties come and keep coming with more and more intensity, this process preserves the mind and strengthens lives.

Historical Background

Establishing Context

Because of all the suffering these believers were experiencing, Peter uses an analogy the believers can relate to. When they were in a hurry, going on a long journey, or were in the midst of eating the Passover meal, the Jews would gather their long, loose robes and tuck them in their belts. Just as the Jews prepared themselves physically, these believers, because of all the suffering they were experiencing, needed to put all their mental faculties to work and prepare their minds to focus on the expectation of Christ's return

The purification process of these believers should "result in praise and glory and honor at the revelation of Jesus Christ" (1 Pet. 1:7 NASB). The challenge to be sober, fixing their hope on Christ again, is at the revelation of Jesus Christ. Since this is their hope, they, like a lamb being offered to slaughter or a high priest going before the very presence of God, must remain consecrated, undefiled, and set aside for devoted service to God, abstaining from defilement.

> Israel was called to be holy as God is holy and thus to live in a manner distinct from the ways of the nations (Lev. 11:44; 19:2; 20:7, 26). The daily synagogue prayers also stressed holiness to God; hence the idea would have been one of the most familiar to Jewish readers and to Gentiles who had learned Scripture from them.[4]

What Does the Context Mean?

In the midst of persecution that placed much pressure on the lives of believers, Peter exhorts them to remain sober. This is something that Peter did not do when Christ was arrested. Christ told Peter everything that would take place; and Peter, in the midst of duress, did not remain sober. Peter challenges these believers to remain sober and commit to live holy, even though they were suffering for their commitment to Christ. They must not allow the suffering to

---

[3] C. F. Pfeiffer and E. F. Harrison, eds., *The Wycliffe Bible Commentary: New Testament* (Chicago: Moody Press, 1962), s.v. 1 Pet. 1:13–14.

[4] Keener, *The IVP Bible Background Commentary*, s.v. 1 Pet. 1:13.

cause them to return to their former manner of life. They need to be obedient to Christ despite pressure to do otherwise. The believers in the book of Hebrews were given the same challenge:

> But recall the former days in which, after you were illuminated, you endured a great struggle with sufferings: partly while you were made a spectacle both by reproaches and tribulations, and partly while you became companions of those who were so treated; for you had compassion on me in my chains, and joyfully accepted the plundering of your goods, knowing that you have a better and an enduring possession for yourselves in heaven. Therefore do not cast away your confidence, which has great reward. For you have need of endurance, so that after you have done the will of God, you may receive the promise:
>
> "For yet a little while, and He who is coming will come and will not tarry. Now the just shall live by faith; but if anyone draws back, my soul has no pleasure in him."
>
> But we are not of those who draw back to perdition, but of those who believe to the saving of the soul. (Heb. 10:32–39)

Sermon Subject and Title

Sermon Title: Steps to Surviving Storms
Big Idea: A mind fixed on Jesus is a life that is not at risk of being overcome by the world.

Sermon Outline (1 Pet. 1:13–16 NASB)

A. We Must Prepare Our Minds for Action (v. 13)

1. *Therefore*—Because the return of Christ was not known to the prophets of old or angels, these believers must prepare their minds for action.
2. *Therefore*—A heavenly inheritance awaits us (1 Pet. 1:3–4), Christ's return is unknown, and since trials are persistent, believers must set their minds for action.
3. *Gird your minds*—(2 Cor. 10:3–5; Phil. 4:8–9)—This is in the aorist tense, which means it is a past once-for-all-act; we must function in a sober state of mind, once and for all, so that we are not distracted with life's worries or fears.

4. *Sober*—We must make it a habit to make sound judgments with clarity of mind (1 Thess. 5:6, 8; 2 Tim. 4:5). This is a present active participle.
5. *Hope*—It is to be a hope that is complete in its character—an assured expectation.
6. *Hope*—Maintain a consecrated devotion to service with the expectation that Christ will do what He said He would do.
7. *Grace brought to you*—Christ provides generous spontaneous gifts based totally on what He desires to provide, not based on anything we earned.

B. The Attitude that Leads to Success (vv. 14–15)

1. *Obedient*—*Obedience* here means complete surrender to do whatever God instructs us to do.
2. *Children*—God views us as dependent on Him for everything and we must therefore live with the faith of a child (Matt. 18:1–6).
3. *Fashion*—The word *fashion*[5] in the Greek text refers to the act of assuming an outward appearance patterned after worldly passions (Eph. 4:17–24).
4. *Former lusts*—Lust refers to the desire for things that are contrary to the will of God.
5. *Conform to the former lust*—We must no longer present ourselves to the worldly passions that once influenced or controlled us. To counter this, we must submit ourselves with child-like faith to God's instruction (2 Tim. 3:14–15).
6. *Called*—This is to respond to a divine invitation to set oneself apart from the world.
7. *Called*—Each believer is divinely called to salvation (John 6:44; Eph. 1:3–4) with a spiritual gift to serve God (1 Pet. 4:10–11).
8. *Holy*—(1 Thess. 4:7)—This is a believer who is set apart from the worldly passions, consecrated and devoted to God. Peter calls all these believers to display the character of God since they have been born again (1 Pet. 1:3) for this purpose (1 Pet. 1:4–9). This is an aorist tense—this decision is a one-time act because it is purposeful.
9. *All*—It is the totality of everything we do, whether big or small.

C. We Must Fully Trust God's Prescription for Surviving Difficult Times (v. 16)

1. *Written*—Past completed action having presented the results (perfect passive indicative). This is similar to the word for *legislate* or attached

[5] *Nuggets*, 26–28.

to a command that is engraved. Peter is letting them know that what he is saying to them is legislated by God and it is a completed act. No one can change it.

2. *Holy*—We must make our ambition to live separate, consecrated, and devoted to the Lord's will and to the service of our God. To be holy is the victory that survives all storms.

Author's Comments

Comments

It is not easy, especially for people who were addicted to sinful passions, to think of this passage becoming a reality in their lives. Living the Christian life for these individuals is hard enough. Just developing the discipline for Bible study, attending worship regularly, and serving God consistently, living out Christian principles at work, at home, and among their friends is a challenge. What these individuals seem to not account for is that there is a work already established in them that they must exercise (Heb. 5:14). Once they practice God's Word (Peter's call for obedience), the Spirit of God becomes a more intimate experience that then empowers them to stay focused. It is like going to the gym and exercising. I am not creating muscles; I am exercising what is already there. The more I do so, the more I experience the potential that was always there. This is very similar to Paul saying, "Therefore, my beloved, as you have always obeyed, not as in my presence only, but now much more in my absence, work out your own salvation with fear and trembling; for it is God who works in you both to will and to do for His good pleasure" (Phil. 2:12–13).

This is why this process begins with a once-and-for-all decision to be "sober minded" and obey God like a child obeying their parents. It is Paul who said; "For what I am doing, I do not understand. For what I will to do, that I do not practice; but what I hate, that I do" (Rom. 7:15). As a result, Paul states:

> For those who live according to the flesh set their minds on the things of the flesh, but those who live according to the Spirit, the things of the Spirit. For to be carnally minded is death, but to be spiritually minded is life and peace. Because the carnal mind is enmity against God; for it is not subject to the law of God, nor indeed can be. So then, those who are in the flesh cannot please God. But you are not in the flesh but in the Spirit, if indeed the Spirit of God dwells in you.

> Now if anyone does not have the Spirit of Christ, he is not His. And if Christ is in you, the body is dead because of sin, but the Spirit is life because of righteousness. But if the Spirit of Him who raised Jesus from the dead dwells in you, He who raised Christ from the dead will also give life to your mortal bodies through His Spirit who dwells in you. (Rom. 8:5–11)

This is why we cannot go on presenting the members of our body to sin, but must make a decisive decision to present our bodies to righteousness (Rom. 6:12–18). The eyes never got saved (Matt. 6:22–23), the tongue never got saved (James 3:1–12), the mind still has to be renewed (Rom. 12:2), and we must have holy hands to worship God (1 Tim. 2:8). Presenting our members leads to a worshipful lifestyle (Rom. 12:1). It is this lifestyle that stirs the ministry of the Holy Spirit. As we practice the Word (exercising our spiritual muscles), we are led to live in the Spirit and not in the flesh (Gal. 5:16–24).

Peter is moving these individuals in this direction because he is seeking to empower them (1 John 4:4). "What then shall we say to these things? If God is for us, who can be against us?" (Rom. 8:31). "Abide in Me, and I in you. As the branch cannot bear fruit of itself, unless it abides in the vine, neither can you unless you abide in Me" (John 15:4). Driving us to holiness is a survival technique.

Even though it may seem hard to be sober-minded in a very trouble world, and to develop a consistent life of obedience to God's Word, it is not as hard as it may seem. The only thing that may be hard is coming to the realization, with the options we have before us, that living each day is about Christ and Christ alone. It is only through Him we can have life and "life abundantly" (John 10:10).

Application

Trials and difficulties cause our emotions to sometimes explode. When this takes place, we must commit to keep God's Word (1 John 2:3–6) in our hearts so that we do not sin (Ps. 119:11) against God. Sometimes a person can be so disoriented at the loss of a loved one, who is a believer, that they can become despondent and stop going to church, reading their Bible, and praying. Christ promises us that we will see each other again and told us not to mourn as those who have no hope (1 Thess. 4:13). So we weep (Rom. 12:15) and mourn, but we must remain sober, remembering that God cares and has prepared a place for all who die in Christ.

No matter the problems we experience, we must remember that it is not our job to resolve them. It is our job to obey God no matter the issue, and trust God to work things out for our good (Rom. 8:28). This is the example we see with men like Abraham, David, Daniel, and so many others. They trusted God to work it out as they obeyed His Word each and every day.

Illustrate It

I was watching the NBA finals a few years ago when the San Antonio Spurs were playing the Miami Heat. The game seemed to be a sure win for San Antonio with just about two minutes left on the clock. Miami called a time-out and put together a strategy to win the game. When Miami passed the ball back in, it seemed like they were determined and ready to efficiently execute their plays.

Miami, with just seconds left on the clock, managed to execute perfectly on offense and defense, so that when everyone thought the game was over, they came back and won. Miami went on to win the series because they discovered a level of playing ability they did not know was there until the level of adversity moved them to search deeper.

Our struggles should make us better, not bitter. We should become stronger, not weaker. Our faith should grow, our hope should be our present help, and our confidence in Christ should lead to a full surrender.

God's Edition of an Extreme Makeover

1 Peter 2:9–10

General Overview of the Passage

Even though Israel was God's chosen nation in the Old Testament (Gen. 12:1–3), reaching all mankind was always God's plan, as Genesis 3:15 explains; "And I will put enmity between you and the woman, and between your seed and her seed; He shall bruise your head, and you shall bruise His heel." The last part of this verse directs us to the anticipated death of Christ for all mankind (John 3:16). God's purpose is further exposed when God selected Abram in Genesis 12:3: "I will bless those who bless you, and I will curse him who curses you; and in you all the families of the earth shall be blessed." Paul picks up on this thought in Romans 4:16–17 when he says how all the families of the earth will be blessed:

> "Therefore it is of faith that it might be according to grace, so that the promise might be sure to all the seed, not only to those who are of the law, but also to those who are of the faith of Abraham, who is the father of us all (as it is written, 'I have made you a father of many nations') in the presence of Him whom he believed . . ." It is the same writer who calls both Jew and Gentile a family unto God. (Eph. 3:14–15)

The purpose of what took place with the Jews is to help us to understand how God works with us all. "So let no one judge you in food or in drink, or regarding a festival or a new moon or sabbaths, which are a shadow of things to come, but the substance is of Christ" (Col. 2:16–17).

The Old Testament showed how God works with the Jews to lead us to understand how God works with His "holy nation" in the New Testament. The person who ties this all together is Christ (Eph. 2:11–14). The Old Testament is not as clear as the New Testament about the afterlife, but it talks about the dead going into the bosom of Abraham. The New Testament, however, makes it clear that when believers die, they go directly into the presence of God (2 Cor. 5:1–10). The "holy nation" that Peter references is in essence the New Testament church.

It has always been God's plan to make us one (John 10:14–16). The person who pivots it all is Christ:

> Therefore remember that you, once Gentiles in the flesh—who are called Uncircumcision by what is called the Circumcision made in the flesh by hands—that at that time you were without Christ, being aliens from the commonwealth of Israel and strangers from the covenants of promise, having no hope and without God in the world. But now in Christ Jesus you who once were far off have been brought near by the blood of Christ. (Eph. 2:11–13)

It took Peter a while to understand this, so Christ had to give him a vision on the rooftop in Acts 10:9–16 and send him to Cornelius's house so that Peter would grow in his comprehension. "Then Peter opened his mouth and said: 'In truth I perceive that God shows no partiality. But in every nation whoever fears Him and works righteousness is accepted by Him'" (Acts 10:34–35). This revelation resolved the heated dispute we see in Acts 15. This resulted in the gospel being preached to all nations by Paul who finally is formally commissioned to go to the Gentiles with Barnabas (Acts 15:13–35).

Peter's growth process met challenges in Galatians 2:11–14. As Peter grew, he recognized the true meaning of Isaiah 28:16 and 8:14, and Psalm 118:22. As a result, Peter is better able to relate to this church that is a mixture of Jew and Gentile.

Historical Background

Establishing Context

Because the church is made up of Gentiles, and some Jews, Peter quotes Exodus 19:6. This is evidence that Peter's struggle recorded in Galatians 2:11–14 is truly over. This is now God's nation, and since everyone is to be holy because God is holy (1 Cor. 6:19–20; 1 Pet. 1:16), the nation is a holy nation to God. This is the church, which is the body of Christ, created with His death and resurrection (1 Pet. 1:3–5). As a result, the church is now the people that are "God's own possession." This is reassuring to these believers who were suffering and feared God was not defending them, His people, in the midst of tremendous persecution.

These believers were once pagans, enslaved to sin; they were once in darkness, having no knowledge of the salvation provided by God (Col. 1:13). Now—like Israel, who was enslaved in Egypt but delivered by God—these believers had been delivered by God from darkness into His "marvelous light." They can now walk in the light (1 John 1:5–7). This gives them hope when they reflect on how Israel suffered but God never left them nor forsook them. He always had a plan and worked it out for their blessing and His glory. Peter uses Christ as another example of this (1 Pet. 2:21–25).

What Does the Context Mean?

God saved us through Jesus Christ, transformed us into a new creation and positioned us to be "a chosen race, a royal priesthood, a holy nation, a people for God's own possession." One of God's purposes for blessing all believers in this manner is so that we can once again experience what it is like to live in the image of God (2 Cor. 3:18). When this experience becomes a living reality, God's purpose for creating us is once again exposed: "Worthy are You, our Lord and our God, to receive glory and honor and power; for You created all things, and because of Your will they existed, and were created" (Rev. 4:11 NASB). It does not matter what our ethnicity is because once a person is saved they are in the family or God and are part of a "chosen race." "There is one body and one Spirit, just as you were called in one hope of your calling; one Lord, one faith, one baptism; one God and Father of all, who is above all, and through all, and in you all" (Eph. 4:4–6).

> "When the Son of Man comes in His glory, and all the holy angels with Him, then He will sit on the throne of His glory. All the nations will be gathered before Him, and He will separate them one from another, as a shepherd divides his sheep from the goats. And He will set the sheep on His right hand, but the goats on the left. Then the King will say to those on His right hand, 'Come, you who are blessed of My Father, inherit the kingdom prepared for you from the foundation of the world.'" (Matt. 25:31–34)

Just like God fought for the nation of Israel in the Old Testament, He does the same for us in the New Testament. When Israel suffered, it was not because God did not care (Deut. 8:1–7).

Sermon Subject and Title

Sermon Title: God's Edition of an Extreme Makeover
Big Idea: As God's chosen, royal, holy priesthood, we must "walk in the light as He is in the light."

Sermon Outline (1 Pet. 2:9–10 nasb)

A. God's Extreme Makeover: From Darkness to Light (v. 9)

1. *We were called out of darkness*—Living in error and ignorance:
   a) Disobedient and slaves to sin (Eph. 2:1–3).
   b) Controlled by Satan (Eph. 2:1–3).
   c) Following the lust of the flesh and the eyes (Eph. 2:1–3; 1 John 2:15–17).
   d) Called out—a divine specific call with a specific purpose. This is in the aorist tense so it is a once-and-for-all act.
2. *His marvelous light*—(1 John 1:5–7)—Our makeover (2 Cor. 5:17):
   a) He chose us while we ran from Him (1 Pet. 2:9; Rom. 3:11).
   b) We are His possession and He graciously dwells in us (1 Cor. 3:16; 6:20; 7:23–24).
   c) He made us His royalty. We are in Christ who is the King of kings (Eph. 2:6; Col. 3:3–4; Rev. 17:14).
   d) Priesthood—we offer up spiritual sacrifices directly to God (1 Pet. 2:5; Rom. 12:1).
   e) In God's eyes, we are separated from the world (Eph. 1:3, 20; 2:6; 3:10).
   f) In God's eyes, we are to serve Him with devotion (Acts 2:42–44).
   g) In God's eyes, we turn away from things that defile us (Eph. 4:20–24).
3. *Proclaim the excellences of Him*—Our purpose in life has changed:
   a) We must declare things that are unknown to the world (Matt. 28:19–20).

   b) We must be committed to put a lot of energy into living out our God-given character (Eph. 4:20–24).
4. *A chosen race*—Israel was called out from every other race; set aside to God. It is the same with those who have accepted Christ. We are chosen (John 6:44; 10:15–18; Rom. 3:11; Eph. 1:3–4) and are all a part of one family unto God (Eph. 3:14–15).
5. *A chosen race*—Christ's death and resurrection broke the dividing barrier and made us one (Eph. 2:11–22).
6. *Royal priesthood*—We are now king-priests before God because we are now allowed into the Holy of Holies (Heb. 7:5–9; 10:18–22).
7. *Royal priesthood*—We are offering up spiritual sacrifices daily (Rom. 12:1; Heb. 10:18–22).
8. *Holy nation*—We are consecrated through the blood of Jesus and set aside as God's own possession (Eph. 1:14) so that we now live in His presence daily (Eph. 1:20; 2:6; 3:10; 6:12).
9. *Proclaim*—We must declare to some people what is unknown. We must decide once and for all to make Him known to those who do not know Him.
10. *The excellences of Him*—Expose God at His best for us—salvation. We must tell with energy how this God-given power shaped our character to be the light to the world (Matt. 5:13–16; Phil. 2:12–13).

B. God's Extreme Makeover Establishes a Portrait of a Christian (v. 10)

1. *We were once not a people*—We were lost in sin and doomed for hell. Sin put us all in one group—sinners.
2. *He made us the people of God*—We are His valued possession just like Israel was.
3. We have the same significance as Israel did in the Old Testament.
4. *Received His mercy*—God showed sympathy for our doomed state, without hope for eternal life (Eph. 2:13–14); the story of Hosea and Gomer (Hosea 2:23).
   a) We once deserved condemnation because of our unbelief (John 3:18, 36; Eph. 2:1–3). We no longer are under the sentence of judgment (Eph. 2:4–7).[6]
   b) His mercy made us His chosen, a royal priesthood, and holy.

---

[6] Earl D. Radmacher, Ronald Barclay Allen, and H. Wayne House, *Nelson's New Illustrated Bible Commentary* (Nashville, TN: Nelson Publishers, 1999), s.v. 1 Pet. 2:10.

5. We are now privileged to have a direct relationship with God.
6. We now have His seal, the Holy Spirit (Eph. 1:13–14) living in us (Eph. 3:16).

Author's Comments

Comments

How many times have you read in the Scripture that we are holy and, in Christ, we are perfect (His "royal priesthood") before God? But in our hearts we know of the sin that keeps us repenting and the mistakes we make that keep us seeking godly advice.

A child wanted to prove to his mother that he could help her with the chores around the house. So he woke up early and started cleaning his room and went into the kitchen to help fix the Tupperware neatly. He was so excited that he had completed everything before his mother awoke that he could not resist knocking on her door. He told his mother all that he had done for her and she was very thankful. He held her by the hand and took her to his bedroom and the mother did her best to compose herself when she saw the mess he created. When he told her he cleaned the kitchen, she almost went into panic mode. Although his intentions were good and the love of his mother was great, his desire to do his best only exposed his insufficiency. Our desire to please God many times exposes our need for God. We need His "makeover," not ours.

What is so powerful is that God reached us when we were not seeking Him (Rom. 3:11) and drew us to Himself (John 6:44; we received mercy—1 Pet. 2:10). He did not do this just to get us into heaven, but to establish a relationship that was lost when Adam sinned (John 15:13–14; Rom. 5:6–21). The purpose of our salvation is to deliver us from the power and influence of the flesh so that we develop an intimate relationship with God as we walk in the Spirit (Rom. 6; Gal. 5:16–26). The purpose of our transformation is so that the power within us becomes greater than the negative forces around us each day (1 John 4:4). These forces should only serve to expose the weaknesses of the flesh, creating a greater dependence on the work of the Spirit (bring Scripture to our remembrance—John 14:26; conviction—John 16:7–11; illumination—1 Cor. 2:10–15; walk in the truth—John 16:13, etc.). I love the way Paul states it in 2 Corinthians 3:18: "But we all, with unveiled face, beholding as in a mirror the glory of the Lord, are being transformed into the same image from glory to glory, just as by the Spirit of the Lord"—("a chosen race . . . a holy nation . . . a people for God's own possession" 1 Pet. 2:9 NASB). This is why the true evidence of our salvation is the fruit we bear. "You will know them by their fruits. Do men gather grapes from thorn bushes or figs from thistles? Even so, every good tree bears good fruit, but a bad tree bears bad fruit. A good tree cannot bear bad fruit, nor can a bad tree bear good fruit. Every tree that does not bear good fruit is cut down and thrown into the fire. Therefore by their fruits you will know them" (Matt. 7:16–20; please read from verse 15–23). The focus of our salvation is for us to demonstrate the very nature of Christ so that those around us see Christ and no longer ourselves.

Christ is one person with one body. When we walk in the Spirit, we functionally (not just because of our position in Christ) become one church in different locations fighting only one enemy, Satan. As a holy nation, it would be impossible for Satan to pollute the earth because the gospel message would be the light to the world (Matt. 16:13–20; John 17:13–26).

Application

The transformation Christ is performing in us should unify us—"a chosen race . . . a holy nation . . . a people for God's own possession" (1 Pet. 2:9 NASB). We should become better focused so that we define ourselves the way Christ has reshaped our lives rather than what the culture says about us. There should be less racism in the church and more love from the fruit of the Spirit. Homes should be more unified because God's holiness dominates the life of each couple so that they are more Christ and the church than husband and wife. Instruction to children raises them in the Lord rather than damaging them because they are being provoked.

When we pray, the transformation process should cause us to experience great responses since God promises that when we abide in Him, He grants us the desires of our heart (John 15:7). We should experience God mightily because we are in His presence through Christ and are now His children. We are in His throne room in Christ, directly in His presence, so we can live and pray with boldness. Our shortcomings are growing experiences, not reasons to feel defeated.

> "So I say to you, ask, and it will be given to you; seek, and you will find; knock, and it will be opened to you. For everyone who asks receives, and he who seeks finds, and to him who knocks it will be opened. If a son asks for bread from any father among you, will he give him a

> stone? Or if he asks for a fish, will he give him a serpent instead of a fish? Or if he asks for an egg, will he offer him a scorpion? If you then, being evil, know how to give good gifts to your children, how much more will your heavenly Father give the Holy Spirit to those who ask Him!" (Luke 11:9–13)

God's extreme makeover should be a light in a dark world.

Illustrate It

A few years ago, there was a program on television called *Extreme Makeover: Home Edition* that took people's houses and transformed them into beautiful houses that exposed the dreams of parents and their children.

The television program found families who were going through difficult times and were not able to make the necessary adjustments to their houses. There was a family whose father, because of an accident, was confined to a wheelchair. The house was not designed for wheelchair access, so getting around the house was difficult. Many people, builders, electricians, plumbers, landscaping companies, a variety of vendors, and people from various communities would come out and work to rebuild the home within a few weeks. When the family returned from a paid vacation they were amazed at the transformation of their home.

Like this family, as Gentiles, we were unable to transform our sin nature to holiness, but thanks be to God He made us into a new creation. This transformation established a nation of Jews and Gentiles who are now consecrated to God—"a holy nation," all experiencing His mercy for His glory.

Experience God's Favor in Troubled Times

1 Peter 2:18–20

General Overview of the Passage

In this passage, Peter addresses household slaves and servants, some of whom might be well educated and hold responsible positions. Peter challenges them to make themselves continuously subordinate to their masters. This submission does not necessarily involve them agreeing with their masters. Peter wants for them to give complete respect to their masters' authority. They must reverence them and seek to please them by being careful in how they respond. This response is not just for those who are kind to them, but also those who are unscrupulous and dishonest.

This kind of behavior demonstrates a free-hearted generosity to their master while not expecting anything in return. The purpose of this kind of behavior in the midst of continued abuse is so that the servant remains faithful to God. This is an incredible challenge because their abuse could have been physical and mental ("bear up"—a superimposed burden—also means to continuously bear up under something that is evil that stimulates pain in their lives; 1 Pet. 2:19 NASB). Peter could have written this as a reflection of the Lord's teaching in Luke 6:32–34 and is reiterated in 1 Peter 2:21–25:

> Peter is not just describing the beating that the slaves experienced but also the beating he saw Christ experience before His crucifixion. This whole passage, 1 Peter 2:19–24, bears the mark of Peter's memories of the scene of Christ's last sufferings (see Introduction)—the blows of the servants, the scorn of the high priest, the silent submission of Jesus, the cross, the stripes.[7]

[7] Marvin Vincent, *Vincent's Word Studies in the New Testament,* Vol. 2 (Grand Rapids, MI: Wm. B. Eerdmans Publishing Co., 1965), s.v. 1 Pet. 2:20.

A reputation for God is not established if a believer continuously and deliberately acts in ways that violate the principles of God. This does not gain favor from God. If a believer is subordinate to his boss in obedience to God while experiencing evil, God provides for them His bountiful love and protection.

Historical Background

Establishing Context

At the time of the writing of this letter many households had slaves. There were massive estates where there were thousands of field slaves and household slaves. Some of these slaves were abused because there were not laws that controlled how slaves were treated. They were expected, since they were owned, to do whatever their masters told them to do. Almost all owners treated their slaves as socially inferior. Many of these slaves came to a saving knowledge of Jesus Christ, but their masters did not. When some of the masters learned that some of their slaves were saved, they made things worse for these slaves. A large population of the church were slaves, so it was important for Peter to address them so that they, even in the midst of their unjust treatment, would represent Christ as holy nation unto God.

> This passage addresses household slaves, who often had more economic and social mobility than free peasants did, although most of them still did not have much. Field slaves on massive estates were more oppressed; given the regions addressed (1:1) and the nature of household codes they are probably not addressed here and at most are peripherally envisioned.[8]

Peter identifies Christ as one who unjustly suffered. By teaching the slaves how Christ functioned under these circumstances Peter hoped to teach the slaves how to please God despite the difficult circumstances they were experiencing. Peter even seems to sympathize with them in 1 Peter 2:21.

---

[8] V. H. Matthews, M. W. Chavalas, and J. H. Walton, *The IVP Bible Background Commentary: Old Testament* (Downers Grove, IL: InterVarsity Press, 2000), s.v. 2 Kings 23:1.

What Does the Context Mean?

Many of the slaves came to Christ but returned to unjust masters. This struggle seemed to make some of the believing slaves want to rebel. Peter's charge to them was that when a person suffers it is better for them to suffer for doing good than for doing what is wrong. Peter even seems to sympathize with them when he says, "For to this you were called, because Christ also suffered for us, leaving us an example, that you should follow His steps" (1 Pet. 2:21).

God rewards a person for suffering for righteousness. "But even if you should suffer for the sake of righteousness, you are blessed . . ." (1 Pet. 3:14). So these believing slaves must endure their suffering patiently (commit to endure righteously) because this gains favor with God. Christ left them an example by the manner in which He endured His suffering righteously and was blessed by God.

> "You have heard that it was said, 'You shall love your neighbor and hate your enemy.' But I say to you, love your enemies, bless those who curse you, do good to those who hate you, and pray for those who spitefully use you and persecute you, that you may be sons of your Father in heaven; for He makes His sun rise on the evil and on the good, and sends rain on the just and on the unjust. For if you love those who love you, what reward have you? Do not even the tax collectors do the same? And if you greet your brethren only, what do you do more than others? Do not even the tax collectors do so? Therefore you shall be perfect, just as your Father in heaven is perfect.'" (Matt. 5:43–48)

Sermon Subject and Title

Sermon Title: Experience God's Favor in Troubled Times
Big Idea: Experiencing God's favor in troubled times takes place because a servant, in obedience to God, chooses to endure suffering with a clear conscience when their master's treat them unjustly.

SERMON OUTLINE (1 PET. 2:18–20 NASB)

A. The Mind-set that Finds Favor (vv. 18–19)

1. *Servants*—Whether a person is on a job or at the church or serving in their community, this mind-set applies.

a) *Be submissive*—This is a present passive, meaning a person must continuously make it a habit to receive what the position brings their way.
   - You don't have to respect what they do but accept their instructions.

b) *With all respect*—Must commit to bring oneself under the authority of those whom God has allowed to be in positions of authority. The sense here is to exercise reverence for the person's position of authority.

c) *Not only those who are good*—Must not only reverence those from whom a person receives profitable benefits or only those who have a good heart.

d) *And gentle*—Masters who were forbearing or showed self-restraint. Those masters who were not trying to punish them or create strife.

e) *Also those who are unreasonable*—These masters are crooked or perverse.

2. *Favor*—This mind-set ensures generous, free-hearted gifts from God if a believer (Col. 3:22–25):
   a) Maintains a continuous awareness (consciousness) of the righteousness of God (1 Pet. 3:13–14).
   b) Endures the emotional load and mental anguish that persecution brings while trusting God's Word.
3. *Conscience toward God*—Whatever the servant decides to do, it should be done with a conscious awareness of God's divine will (Col. 3:22–23; 1 Pet. 3:13–16) even if they:
   a) *Bear up under sorrows*—Some of their masters could have been physically abusing them creating physical and mental anguish.
   b) *Suffering unjustly*—Their masters cared nothing for God's moral standards.
4. The high priest and Pharisees were corrupt, but Jesus still demonstrated respect for God's structure (1 Pet. 2:21–25).

B. The Benefit of Enduring Troubled Times (v. 20)

1. There is no benefit before God if a believer sins under harsh treatment (1 Pet. 3:17):
   a) *Sin*—Purposefully, willfully habitually violates the standards of God.

2. The attitude that generates spontaneous, free-hearted blessings from God:
   a) *What is right*—Must commit, no matter what, to do what is beneficial to the kingdom of God. Do what brings God glory (Col. 3:17).
   b) *Suffer for it*—Peter could have Christ on his mind when he writes this (1 Pet. 2:21–25). Christ endured suffering continuously because He "must be about [His] Father's business" (Luke 2:49). He must do what is right no matter the physical or mental abuse. He is now at the right hand of God with everything below His feet (Phil. 2:9–11).
   c) *Endure*—This means to bear up under a load for a particular journey to a particular destination. To endure emotional pain and mental anguish for the purposes of God (1 Pet. 3:13–16).
      - *Bearing up* is a present tense active verb; this means this principle is actively being applied.
      - To bear up under punishment while maintaining their Christian character (1 Pet. 3:13–16).
3. *Favor with God*—No one, no matter their position of authority, or power they may possess, can stop God from generously bestowing His gifts upon us.
4. *Favor with God*—The believer did not earn the gift, because it is a free-hearted gift from God. This is provided to the suffering believer when they choose to accept what God allows because He views it as necessary (1 Pet. 1:6) to obtain the outcome of their faith (1 Pet. 1:9; living stones—1 Pet. 2:5). His focus is for them to be holy as He is holy (1 Pet. 1:15–16).

Author's Comments

Comments

I must admit that in reading this, especially being an African-American, I thought it was an incredible request. Even if God chooses to instruct us this way, I would hope He would at least provide a timetable when we will be blessed for this kind of suffering described in this passage! Surprisingly, He does not. What is clear is that God expects us to trust Him because He is faithful, He cannot lie (Heb. 6:18), and is always true to His promises.

This process is truly representative of what Peter stated in 1:6–7: "In this you greatly rejoice, though now for a little while, if need be, you have been grieved by various trials, that the genuineness of your faith, being much more precious than gold that perishes, though it is tested by fire, may be found to praise, honor, and glory at the revelation of Jesus Christ." God uses these circumstances to build character (Rom. 5:1–5; James 1:2–4), and create, as in the case of Daniel, a true representation of His power in an unfair and evil environment.

No one survives this without the support of other believers (1 Pet. 2:9–10; 4:7–11). We must lean on the spiritual gifts of others to strengthen and encourage us. This is why Peter says we must remain sober (1:13–15) and vigilant (5:7–11). If we allow our emotions to get the best of us, we may not remain mentally alert, and Satan can get the best of us.

Remaining focused on God's purposes is everything (1 Pet. 2:21) because it is not all about making money on the job (God will provide for our needs according to His riches; Phil. 4:19 ESV). It is about being a light in a dark world. It is about working out "[our] own salvation with fear and trembling" (Phil. 2:12). It is about growing to spiritual maturity so that we are complete in Christ (Col. 1:28–29; James 1:2–4). Sometimes we are too focused on creating temporal rewards than heavenly rewards (Luke 12:33–34). Remember, only what we do for Christ lasts (1 Cor. 15:58).

Application

The believers were working for unsaved supervisors who were often abusive or unfair. Peter instructs them to be subordinate even when their masters were evil. When believers function in this manner, they experience the favor of God. They must function daily with an awareness of God because this keeps them focused to bear up under injustice. There is no profit for suffering for sinful behavior; it is better to not sin and endure the pain so that God provides the believer with His unmerited favor. Obeying God and trusting God is always its reward (Heb. 11:6).

Paul says we do not work for those in authority, but to bring God glory, and for this He blesses us whether those in authority are good or evil (Col. 3:22–25).

Illustrate It

Pete had become lost in the desert and had been chasing mirages. He thought to himself, *I'll follow this last one.* It was a deserted town with a well in the very center. His mouth parched from the intense heat, he ran to the well with his last ounce of energy. He vigorously pumped the handle only to find that no water came forth. Then, he looked up to a note nailed to the post. It instructed its readers to "look behind the rock where a five-gallon container of water will be found" and warned against drinking or using it for anything besides priming the pump. Every ounce was needed, and not even a drop could be spared, the note emphasized. "After pouring the water down the pump, pump the handle vigorously and all the water you desire will come forth," the note said. One last instruction was to please fill the water can and place it behind the rock for the next weary soul who might happen to come along.

How hard it is for people to give up a "sure thing" for something they cannot see at the time. Pete had a sure thing in the bucket of water and yet was instructed to pour it "all" down the pump.[9]

---

[9] *A Treasury of Bible Illustrations* (Chattanooga, TN: AMG Publishers, 1995), 132.

Surviving Suffering

1 Peter 3:13–17

General Overview of the Passage

After reassuring these believers that God is concerned for them because His eyes, ears, and face are toward them (1 Pet. 3:12), Peter challenges these suffering saints to press forward. Once they remain zealous to do what benefits others, those who treat them badly—possibly creating bodily injury—will be unable to do so because God will continue to protect them from being destroyed (2 Cor. 4:7–12). Even if they should continuously and actively experience something evil causing pain, it must be because they are committed to live in conformity to God's divine will. This demonstrates the power of having the spiritual state of the kingdom of God in their hearts (blessed—happy and successful because of divine favor). Because of the level of their suffering, they must not become timid or shrink back because of the power of their opponents or allow themselves to be distressed. It is not uncommon for Christians to suffer because of their commitment to Christ or their commitment to holiness (2 Tim. 3:12). To be distressed or become intimidated should only be the standard behavior of the unsaved.

They must maintain their commitment to God by consecrating themselves to Christ as true believers are expected to in the midst of a polluted world. They must keep Christ in their hearts as the one with all authority and power who is master of the souls (the Lord should dominate every day of our lives—our possessions, our occupation, our marriage, our spare time—nothing can be excluded). This focus must be maintained in their day-to-day lives. This keeps them sober and alert, allowing them to experience the powerful outcome of their faith (1 Pet. 1:9, 13–15). It is this that brings God praise (1 Pet. 1:7). It also blesses them with protection by the power of God (1 Pet. 1:5).

As a result, they need to be ready to put together information like a person defending themselves in a court of law. This needs to be done for everyone who is seeking answers from them. Their defense must be based on the confident expectation of the anticipated coming of God. This includes the wholesome dread of displeasing God, a fear that causes them to seek Him for wisdom and understanding. This consciousness based on the fact that God is always in control should inspire holy boldness (2 Tim. 1:7). This boldness may intensify their pain as in the case of Christ (1 Pet. 1:21–25). If it is God's will for them to experience these attacks, it will not only bless them, it will work out for what is best: "And we know that all things work together for good to those who love God, to those who are the called according to His purpose" (Rom. 8:28).

Historical Background

Establishing Context

There were many things that plagued these believers. They were being persecuted in their day-to-day life; there were issues in the church challenging them to recognize that they are one holy nation unto God; the need to instruct women how to dress since they lived in the liberal culture of Rome; slaves needed to remain focused on how they served their masters as Christians; wives who got saved needed to know how to respect their husbands who were unsaved; husbands who were saved needed to love their wives as Christ loves the church; the believers needed to live godly lives in a polluted world and faithfully serve in church based on their spiritual gifts. With the persistent pain of these trials, especially the persecution against the church, Peter sought to encourage them because the persecution was very challenging. He sought to keep them focused so that they remained productive no matter what they faced.

> Peter alludes to the language of Isaiah 8:12, where God assures the prophet that he need not fear what the rest of his people feared, but should trust in God alone (Isa. 8:13). The setting of the Isaiah quotation is significant. Ahaz, King of Judah, faced a crisis because of an impending invasion by the Assyrian army. The kings of Israel and Syria wanted Ahaz to join them in an alliance, but Ahaz refused, so Israel and Syria threatened to invade Judah! Behind the scenes, Ahaz confederated himself with Assyria! The Prophet Isaiah warned him against ungodly alliances and urged him to trust God for deliverance.

> "Sanctify the LORD of hosts [armies] himself; and let him be your fear, and let him be your dread" (Isa. 8:13).[10]

It is this attitude that Peter saw demonstrated by Christ when Peter stood quietly by as Christ was brought before the Sanhedrin. He saw Christ suffer because He was committed to His Father's will. Peter writes about this in chapter 2:21–25:

> For to this you were called, because Christ also suffered for us, leaving us an example, that you should follow His steps: "Who committed no sin, Nor was deceit found in His mouth"; who, when He was reviled, did not revile in return; when He suffered, He did not threaten, but committed Himself to Him who judges righteously; who Himself bore our sins in His own body on the tree, that we, having died to sins, might live for righteousness—by whose stripes you were healed. For you were like sheep going astray, but have now returned to the Shepherd and Overseer of your souls.

It is this example that teaches us, while we live out the will of God, how to survive suffering.

What Does the Context Mean?

As Christians, we are faced with crises, and we are tempted to give in to our fears and make the wrong decisions. But if we "sanctify Christ as LORD" in our hearts, we need never fear men or circumstances. Our enemies might *hurt* us, but they cannot *harm* us (meaning they cannot destroy us). Only we can harm ourselves if we fail to trust God. Generally speaking, people do not oppose us if we do good; but even if they do, it is better to suffer for righteousness's sake than to compromise our testimony. Peter discussed this theme in detail in 1 Peter 4:12–19. Instead of experiencing fear as we face the enemy, we can experience blessing if Jesus Christ is Lord in our hearts. "The word 'happy' in 1 Peter 3:14 is the same as 'blessed' in Matthew 5:10ff. This is a part of the 'joy unspeakable and full of glory' (1 Pet. 1:8)."[11]

---

[10] Warren W. Wiersbe, *The Bible Exposition Commentary* (1989; repr., Wheaton, IL: Victor Books, 1996), s.v. 1 Pet. 3:13.

[11] Ibid.

Sermon Subject and Title

Sermon Title: Surviving Suffering
Big Idea: Being zealous for what is good while suffering leads to God's blessings.

SERMON OUTLINE (1 PET. 3:13–17 NASB)

A. Do Not Fear Their Intimidation (vv. 13–14)

1. *Who is there to harm us*—Who is actively in place, in the future, to badly treat, maybe create bodily injury, to the saints who placed their trust in God? This is a rhetorical question, implying that no harm done to their bodies will outweigh God's blessings.
   a) *Zealous*—(nominative)—They must become eager, desiring earnestly, burning with zeal to please God and to do what benefits others. This is because they are blessed for suffering for what is good.
   b) God promises to protect us (1 Pet. 3:8–12; Rom. 8:31, 37–39; 8:28—those who love Him, obey Him).
   c) Our actions can successfully protect us from being injured or thrown down due to evil (Matt. 24:9–11).
   d) *Suffer*—We may continuously experience emotional and mental pain due to evil being done against us. This is a present active indicative verb, meaning they made it a habit to create suffering.
   e) Christians suffered not only because of their confession of Christ, but also because of the purity of their lives. This seems like rebellion to the heathen.
2. A mind-set that protects us:
   a) *Righteousness*—Don't forsake the divine standards of God while enduring painful times. Our behavior needs to be in conformity to what God desires for us to do.
   b) *Intimidation*—We must not fear the power or authority others may seem to have. We must not shrink back from obeying and seek our own means of protection like the brethren did in the book of Hebrews (Heb. 10:32–39). The writer warns them that this could lead to their destruction. There is no armor on the back of a believer (Eph. 6:13–17).
   c) We must not fear man so much that our fear of God loses its influence on our lives (Gal. 1:10).

d) We must not run away.

e) *Trouble*—We must do our best to not allow our minds to become full of anxiety, doubt, or distress (2 Cor. 10:3–5).

3. Actions that preserve us:

   a) An eager spirit to do what benefits others.

   b) *Blessed*—God will provide happiness and prosperity for those who endure (Pss. 112; 128).

B. Be Always Ready to Give a Defense for the Hope within Us (v. 15)

1. *Sanctify*—Do not allow the troubled situations to pollute you.
2. *Hearts*—Allow Christ to have complete authority, even over the hidden parts of our hearts and will.
3. *Make a defense*—Don't have to be timid or quiet—need to prepare themselves as if they were making a defense of their case in a court of law.
4. *Hope*—We must be ready to present with confidence our case when challenged.
5. *Reverence*—We must maintain awe and respect for God while we function in hostile situations. Must maintain respect for the structure we are responding to (1 Pet. 2:13–17).
   a) We fear God so little because we fear man so much (Gal. 1:10). The consciousness of the presence of the Lord Christ should impart a holy boldness (2 Tim. 1:7) and inspire the believer to witness a good confession.

C. Keep a Good Conscience (v. 16)

1. A good conscience maintains peace in our hearts; and this provides confidence to face battles without.
   a) When we have a conscience that is clear, we have a constant awareness of God that in difficult times strengthens us. When our conscience is not clear, our minds are divided and it weakens our resolve.
   b) Maintain a constant awareness of God so that our thoughts distinguish what is good or bad.
2. *Slander*—(present passive indicative)—When people speak thoughtless evil words, it will come to nothing. These individuals slander in a continuous manner with no plans to stop.
   a) Our Christian character and its benefit to other people will put slander to shame.

D. Only Suffer for What Is Good (v. 17)

1. *Better*—(present active participle)—God views this as advantageous and useful to our spiritual development (Heb. 12:4–11). This is always the result when they suffer for doing right.
2. *If God should will it so*—This is something that God has to allow as in the case of Job.
3. *To suffer*—Going through emotional and mental stress may be God's purpose and good pleasure for us to experience (James 1:2–4;1 Pet. 2:21–25).
   a) Those who honor God's will (1 Pet. 2:15) have the comfort to know that suffering is God's appointment (1 Pet. 2:21; 4:19).
4. *For right*—To live by the standards of God no matter what evil people do to us. "The just shall live by his faith" (Hab. 2:4).
5. We have much to gain when we suffer for living out God's character (Joseph, Daniel became great; Paul said it taught him how to live in the power of the resurrection; 2 Cor. 12:7–10; Phil. 3:9–10).

Author's Comments

Comments

One day, while in high school, I was in a chemistry lab when one of the students caused a fire to burn out of control. The student became afraid and ran, and many of the other students turned around and, seeing the fire, began to run too. For whatever reason, I stood there for a minute, and during that time a student jumped over his desk and proceeded to put out the fire. Fear, which caused almost everyone to run, would have allowed the fire to burn down the lab or possibly the school, but the "mind-set of a survivor" keeps the class moving forward. The steps to being a survivor when we are suffering can truly lead us to experience God powerfully.

We must first understand that we live in an evil and polluted world (Phil. 2:14–17) and we will experience suffering. God states that we will have tribulation (John 16:33). So when trials come, we must discipline ourselves not to act as if something strange were taking place (1 Pet. 4:1, 12). We must gird up our minds of action and be alert, always remembering that we are not the only ones suffering (1 Pet. 1:13–15; 5:8–10).

We must remain committed in the midst of trials to live a life that is set aside, committed to the principles of God. The psalmist and Peter assure us that it is the focus which leads to our protection and blessing (Ps. 34:17–19; 1 Pet. 3:14). Paul says it leads to victory: "What then shall we say to these things? If God is for us, who can be against us?" (Rom. 8:31). This is why Peter says, "For it is better, if it is the will of God, to suffer for doing good than for doing evil" (1 Pet. 3:17). There are numerous examples of this in the Scriptures. Just to name a few, look at Joseph, David's interaction with Saul, and Daniel. "Though the adversary, through physical suffering or material hardship, would distress those who were 'eager to do good,' no real harm can come to those who belong to Christ."[12] Christians should overcome fear by sanctifying Christ as their Lord.

We must not be ashamed to speak up. Before Christ's crucifixion He responded to the religious leaders on a number of occasions. In Matthew 23:14–29, what Christ said may seem somewhat offensive; He spoke the truth but He never retaliated physically or exchanged insults for insults (1 Thess. 5:15). God expects us to provide an answer with a clear conscience (1 Pet. 3:15–16).

We can survive the pain that trials may bring, but we must make sure that the trials we are going through are because we choose to obey the will of God.

Application

Sometimes the church can be a difficult place to serve God. Friendliness of a woman to a man can be misinterpreted even though both individuals functioned in a respectful manner, a choir director's choice for a person to sing a song can be misinterpreted, a pastor's sermon can be misinterpreted because someone believes he was targeting them personally, etc. This could lead to believers becoming discouraged or frustrated and may even lead to them being isolated from the church. This is why it is imperative that all believers develop this "survival mind-set." Without serving in the local church a believer cannot grow spiritually (Eph. 4:1–16). The same is true for trials and suffering we may encounter as we live for Christ on our jobs, community activities, or extended family. We must always focus on suffering for what is good.

Illustrate It

A friend of mind was in the midst of the genocide in Rwanda, Africa. He hid under his bed with his wife and four kids for days. Some days, soldiers came

[12] John F. Walvoord and Roy B. Zuck, *The Bible Knowledge Commentary* (Colorado Springs, CO: David C. Cook Publishing, 1983), 850 (s.v. 1 Pet. 13–14).

into his yard looking to kill him and his entire family. They wanted him dead because he was known for starting churches all over Rwanda. He has always had a heart for his people. As the days went by, he realized that eventually these soldiers would break into his house, so he knew he had to run away.

He gathered his family and left in the middle of the night and headed to the Congo in search of a refugee camp. On his way he met a fellow pastor and his wife and family. As they walked along, they ran into a company of soldiers who pulled them to the side. Upon questioning them they took the other pastor to the side and cut his throat. My friend had to help the pastor's wife and children go on from there.

Eventually they came to the refugee camp in the Congo. When he got into the camp someone recognized him and offered him a house for him and his family to stay in. He turned it down and said: "Many of my members and people I know are in the camp. I must stay and minister to them." My friend Dr. Faustin Ntamushora now leads his own ministry called TL Africa, doing what God has always called him to do, and his people respect him highly because he suffered with them and did it with integrity and compassion. God blessed him to earn a doctorate degree from Biola University so that he trains pastors in several countries in the continent of Africa.

The best victories take place for those who keep the faith in the midst of the biggest setbacks they may experience.

Strength for Today

1 Peter 4:7–9

General Overview of the Passage

Peter challenges the believers that "since Christ has suffered in the flesh, arm yourselves also with the same purpose . . ." (4:1 NASB). They must walk in the will of God, because the difficulties attached to the end times are near. The nearness of the end times must never leave the mind of the believer as they function from day to day. As a result, he commands them to be coolheaded and remain balanced in their thinking. They must remain alert for all the negative influences that can consume them—even their own passions or rash decisions. This is so they can maintain a clear mind for prayer.

They must also make a willful decision that, despite all the distractions they may have, they will eagerly seek to serve each other's needs. They must actively strain or stretch themselves to sacrificially serve the actual needs of all the saints. This is essential because it continuously covers individual actions of violating the principles of God. This kind of love does not stir up sins; it covers them.

They must welcome strangers, since it is difficult for these strangers to afford lodging expenses or they could not find lodging. The people Peter is writing to don't have hotels and rest houses easily accessible, which is why Peter encourages these suffering Christians to care for each other even if the person is a stranger. These are times of persecution and suffering. These strangers should find, in Christians, loving people who do not speak harshly or complain because they may be demanding or overstay their welcome. The times are evil and it would get worse as Christ nears return, so extended kindness is necessary.

The dominant factor is love. God's love must make everyone stretch and strain themselves as they seek to obey Him. Love is not touchy-feely; it is obedience to God's Word as it relates to other people, even enemies! "Beloved, let us love one another, for love is of God; and everyone who loves is born of God and knows God. He who does not love does not know God, for God is love" (Matt. 22:36–40; 1 John 4:7–8).

Historical Background

Establishing Context

Jesus brought in a whole new era that He consummates with His return: "The end of all things is near" (1 Pet. 4:7 NASB). There are no more covenants to establish, no more major exiles, and what Christ needed to do, He stated on the cross, was finished.

"In many Jewish traditions (including Dan. 12:1–2), the end of the age would be preceded by a period of great suffering; the impending end, therefore, calls for exhortations to perseverance in seriousness and prayer."[13] This is why the need for a supportive church is critical. What these believers were experiencing was a sign of the end of the times. So they need to remain fervent in prayer and employ the spiritual gifts that God provided at the point of salvation. This is not a time for complaining against each other. This was a time to be hospitable. "Hospitality was receiving others, especially taking in travelers of the same faith who needed a place to stay. As generally in the ethical ideals of antiquity, lodging and provisions were to be provided generously, not grudgingly."[14]

Because of the level of suffering that these believers may experience, complaining against each other, rather than being hospitable, would compound the vast needs among them. A healthy church body can therefore remain sober, focused on making "sound judgments," praying for each other so that each believer functions in the strength of the Spirit within them.

What Does the Context Mean?

A calm and collected spirit is conducive to the act of praying. It results in effective prayer. The Christian who is always on a tear, whose mind is crowded with fears and worries, who is never at rest in their heart, does not do much praying. This section provides us with a brief, positive indication of the practical demands of Christian discipleship.

1. Watch out for impending consummation.
2. Christians, therefore need to keep their heads and not get carried away by self-indulgence or excitement.

---

[13] Keener, *The IVP Bible Background Commentary: New Testament*, s.v. 1 Pet. 2:12.
[14] Ibid.

3. Christians ought to preserve the mental alertness necessary to sustain effective prayer.
4. Give priority to an active expression of love.
5. Faithfulness in stewardships of gifts.
6. Seek to glorify God through Jesus Christ.

The awareness of the impending judgment and that there is life after death should disturb their complacency, and make them face daily living in a new sense of eternal values.

Sermon Subject and Title

Sermon Title: Strength for Today
Big Idea: Believers find strength for today when, in the midst of increased suffering, each person remains sober minded for the purpose of prayer, committed to loving and serving each other without complaint. This is also strengthening because these praying, loving believers are committed to make sound judgments while being hospitable to one another. This is the church that strengthens believers and glorifies God.

Sermon Outline (1 Pet. 4:7–9 NASB)

A. Preserve the Mind for Prayer (vv. 7; 5:7–8)

1. *End of all things*—Trials and difficulties will increase (Matt. 24:4–14).
2. *End of all things is near*—The end is a past action that is complete. It is now the "state of affairs." This means that when Christ said, "It is finished," what will take place from that time forward is the "state of affairs."
3. *Sound judgment*—Evaluate what is going on against Scripture (Phil. 1:9–11; 2 Pet. 1:3–4). Peter is commanding them to do this (imperative mood).
4. *Sober spirit*—We must not allow the troubles of this life to stop us from thinking wisely (Eph. 5:15–17).
5. *Sober spirit*—We must not allow ourselves to wonder or speculate (2 Cor. 10:3–6).
6. *Sober spirit*—Must always remain alert so we can view things through God's eyes (1 Pet. 5:8).

7. *Purpose of prayer*—A clear mind allows us to pray effectively. This is an accusative, meaning it is the direct purpose for being sober.
8. *Purpose of prayer*—A mind not filled with worries or anxiety prays more effectively (Phil. 4:4–6).

B. Be Fervent to Love One Another (vv. 8–9)

1. *Above all*—The most important thing a believer can do (John 13:34–35; 1 Cor. 13:1–3). This is a genitive, and thus is the primary purpose.
2. *Fervent*—We must persistently stretch and sometimes strain ourselves to care for each other (Matt. 24:9–13).
3. *Love*—There is no greater attitude to put on but the attitude of love (1 Cor. 13:3; John 13:34–35).
4. *Love*—We must commit to obeying God when responding to each other (1 John 4:11–12).
5. *Love*—His attitude empowers us to forgive and establishes less need for complaining.
6. *Covers*—This attitude empowers us to not be overwhelmed with each person's weaknesses. This is a present tense, active indicative, which means that this must be continuous and habitual.
7. *Love covers*—Working together in difficult times keeps everyone strong (Ps. 133; Matt. 12:25).
8. *Hospitality*—This attitude must extend to strangers (Matt. 10:40–41; Heb. 13:1–2).
9. *Complaining*—To complain is to misuse the tongue. It is sinful (Col. 3:13).

Author's Comments

Comments

Peter's audience was going through a lot. Peter several times had to remind them to remain sober (1 Pet. 1:13; 4:7; 5:8). They had an issue with an abusive government (2:13–17), their jobs (2:18–20), their families (3:1–7), and people slandering them (3:8–17). Peter challenges each believer to remain clear minded for prayer, and to be committed to continuously love others through the ministry of hospitality. Hospitality must abound without complaint because this would allow each believer to forgive one another. This attitude then extends to faithful service that is based on spiritual gifts provided by the Holy Spirit.

All of this is easier said than done. However, all of this is necessary for each believer to survive. A difficult world along with an unhealthy church is certainly not a good combination. As believers, we must meet the challenges God places upon us to establish a healthy spiritual hospital for the wounded and broken. After Peter explains how this church deals with their individual issues, he instructs the church "to live above 'see' level" so that believers grow in Christ's body for His glory.

Can this kind of love and hospitality be seen as a weakness by others and be exploited? Of course. The Bible is clear to say that wolves will come in among us (Acts 20:29), so it can even get worse. It is John who said, "If anyone comes to you and does not bring this doctrine, do not receive him into your house nor greet him; for he who greets him shares in his evil deeds" (2 John 10–11). So wisdom is always required. This is probably why Peter commands them to "be of sound judgment" (1 Pet. 4:7 NASB). Each issue has to be evaluated against the will of God and focused on God's purposes, not influenced merely by a desire to be nice.

This passage of Scripture is the structure that must mold our hearts so that the love God requires strengthens everyone involved. "A new commandment I give to you, that you love one another; as I have loved you, that you also love one another. By this all will know that you are My disciples, if you have love for one another" (John 13:34–35). A commitment to discipleship, which is directly related to loving God and keeping His commands (John 14:15). The Word of God shapes how we love, and wisdom guides and protects.

Application

When a person is going through a lot of struggles, what kind of member do they become? Do they isolate themselves from everyone? Do they stop serving? Do they begin complaining against everyone? Or do they demonstrate trust and obedience to the will of God and continue to use their spiritual gifts for service and despite their pain love and pray for others? The litmus test to a sincere faith is in the answer to these questions.

Illustrate It

I was talking to my brother, who is an Iraq veteran, and I asked him if he was ever concerned being out in the desert in "no-man's land" in a tank that only got about five miles to the gallon. He laughed and reminded me that I did not know what I was saying. I said to him that I just wanted to know because, if he was under attack, how could he make the proper adjustments when he could not even move. He laughed again and said he was there to fight and he trusted that the tankers would bring gas. That was their job. The planes would drop ammunition, and that was their job. Proper planning may lead to no need for ammunition, and that was his job. He was there to fight the enemy, and he was bent on getting that done effectively—not losing any of his men, and returning to base knowing that he accomplished his mission. I went on to ask why he would stick his head out of the tank in a war. He laughed again, tapped me on the back, and said, "Paul, you got a mission to do, and taking care of snipers is the job of another sniper." My brother trusted the system so well that he remained focused on what he was there to accomplish.

We are in a war and we need the system God put in place in the church to work. We need to not complain against one another but find ways to work together. This empowers each believer, especially those Peter is writing to.

Spiritual Protection for Satanic Attacks

1 Peter 5:6–11

General Overview of the Passage

A person in need of physical treatment and relief chooses a particular surgeon, and therefore submits himself or herself under his "operating hand," in hopes of enjoying the promised benefit in due time. Believers must make the single decisive act of humbling themselves under God and throwing their troubles to the loving, caring hands of God. This decisive act demonstrates their trust in God to exalt and deliver them in due season. They function in this manner because God continuously has them as the object of His concern.

Because these individuals need to be decisive, they cannot allow themselves to become drunk with worry. They must remain calm and collected in spirit so that their state of mind is clear to make good decisions (1 Pet. 1:13; 4:7). Peter commands believers to remain watchful and alert because Satan functions with hostility, constantly striving with great desire to falsely accuse and slander them. He is like a lion constantly roaring, like a hungry beast whose lifestyle is committed to darkness. He desires to completely destroy those he attacks.

Peter now commands us to oppose the devil, holding to our orders from God like a body of heavily armed infantry formed in ranks and files close and deep. His audience must remain steadfast with complete confidence in the divine truth of God, fully trusting God for His Word. This is why they must remain sober. They must do this with the full knowledge of understanding that many other Christians are experiencing the same kind of pain from persecutions. These persecutions are occurring continuously.

After believers have experienced this same kind of pain from persecutions, the God who provides bountiful, freehearted, unearned, and unmerited favor gives a divine invitation to experience all the attributes His eternal divine nature provides. God will set, figuratively speaking, broken bones and readjust dislocated lives, causing believers to become well-grounded in their faith and love for God. This process allows believers to become more capable to deal with difficult experiences, so they can better endure trials. This affords for the fullest grounds for confidence and courage.

The way God powerfully cares and fights for each person in the midst of awful persecutions causes Peter to end this passage on a great note of praise: "To Him be . . . dominion forever and ever. Amen." The "amen" adds the emphatic endorsement that God is the only who that is due praise and glory.

Historical Background

Establishing Context

The suffering that the believers were experiencing was humiliating. A woman had to respect her husband who was not saved and possibly not a spiritual leader in the home. A slave had to respect a master who was abusing him or her. Believers were being slandered and were instructed to only function in such a manner that is pleasing to God. All of this and more could lead believers to find it difficult not to fight for themselves just so they survive emotionally. Peter told the people that this leads God to fight for them as they demonstrate their surrender to Him.

> Here the sense includes embracing and accepting the suffering until God provides the way out (cf. Jer. 27:11). On present humbling and future exalting, see comment on Luke 1:52–53 and 14:11; the cries of God's people during unjust sufferings had always moved him to act on their behalf (Exod. 2:23–25; 3:7–9; Judg. 2:18; 10:16).[15]

Lions in these times were viewed as vicious beasts. Nero used lions to attack Christians in public arenas. Many Christians died from being eaten by lions. The picture Peter paints of not allowing Satan to devour them is very vivid to these believers.

The "devil" is literally the "slanderer," carrying the same connotation as the adversarial accuser. Jewish teachers saw this in the book of Job (where he was going to and fro on the earth"—1:7). Satan sought in this present age to turn

---

[15] Keener, *The IVP Bible Background Commentary: New Testament*, s.v. 1 Pet. 5:6.

people to apostasy from the truth, although his power was limited because he ultimately had to answer to God.

What Does the Context Mean?

When faced with difficulties, a believer must fight against any desire to function independently from God. Difficulties should draw us closer to God. When we make the choice to surrender to God, we must make a decisive decision to put all our cares upon Him—meaning not just troubled situations, but our anxieties as well. These difficulties and worries can provide Satan an opportunity to influence and impact our lives (Luke 8:14), limiting our spiritual growth. Christ loves us and is always in control. He promises never to leave us nor forsake us, and when we trust Him, the trial leads to spiritual transformation that causes the believer to become "perfect" (1 Pet. 5:10). This allows the believer to have a powerful relationship with God, that matures them and gives God glory.

Sermon Subject and Title

Sermon Title: Spiritual Protection for Satanic Attacks
Big Idea: The persistent attacks of Satan lead to spiritual growth when believers humble themselves and cast all their anxieties to God remaining firm in their faith.

Sermon Outline (1 Pet. 5:6–11 NASB)

A. Trust God's Mighty Hand (v. 6)

1. *Humble ourselves*—This is a one-time decision (aorist) to bring ourselves under the authority of God. Peter commands (imperative) us to do so. We must remember our limitations as human beings.
2. *Mighty hand of God*—This is in direct relation (an accusative) to us humbling ourselves. God is powerful and has all authority, and as our warrior He can deliver us from our troubles or discipline us. We must remember that He is in control (Rom. 8:28). Nothing will stop God from accomplishing His purposes.
3. *Exalt*—In due season, when we humble ourselves, God reestablishes us to a position of privilege and honor (Gal. 6:9–10).

B. Trust that He Truly Cares (v. 7)

1. *Casting*—A believer must make a single decisive act (aorist tense) of throwing or hurling their troubles to God.
2. *Casting*—Because we know that God is in control, we can once and for all give our troubles to Him.
3. *Anxiety*—Anxiety is distress in view of possible danger or misfortune, and has a direct correlation to casting (an accusative).
4. *Cares*—We can cast because God continuously and actively (present active indicative) has us as the object of His concern (1 Pet. 3:12).
5. *Cares*—We must trust that He heard us and will work things out for our good (Rom. 8:28).
6. We must learn to wait on God (Isa. 40:27–31).
7. God becomes the person we focus on because He carries all our worries (1 Pet. 3:12).

C. Remain Firm in the Faith (vv. 8–9)

1. *Be sober*—We are again (1 Pet. 1:13–15) commanded by Peter to not allow ourselves to become drunk with worry, especially since God is in control.
2. *Alert*—He commands us to once and for all (aorist active imperative) be actively vigilant and watchful. (Peter fell asleep no matter how many times Christ requested him to stay awake.)
3. *Alert*—We must maintain a clear mind for good decision making because Satan is constantly at work.
    a) We need to remember how powerful Satan is because this can cause us to lean to God's power.
    b) *Devil*—All of Satan's actions in this verse are in the present active indicative. He is constantly active, habitually focused on destroying us.
    c) *Devil prowls about*—Satan is our enemy and he slanders us before God daily (Rev. 12:10).
    d) *Like a roaring lion*—Satan is constantly seeking to do evil, and is fiercely hungry, aggressively seeking to destroy us (present active indicative). He is never satisfied.
    e) *Seeking*—Satan is constantly striving (present active indicative) with a great desire to destroy us with the worries and cares of this life (Luke 8:14).

4. In order to resist the devil, we must remain firm in the faith (faith is in the dative, so it is directly correlated to resisting Satan):
   a) *Firm*—We must arm ourselves with a deep conviction about the true Word of God (2 Pet. 1:3–4). This is a nominative, meaning this is what we must become.
   b) *Firm in the faith*—Live with complete confidence that God's Word will come to pass (2 Tim. 3:14).
5. *Knowing*—Our faith should take us to a state of full knowledge and understanding that we are not the only ones suffering (perfect active nominative).
6. *Knowing*—Unlike Elijah (1 Kings 19:9–10, 18), our faith should remind us that there are others who are suffering just like us (1 Pet. 4:12–16). This is because we did not run away thinking that we are alone in our pain.
7. *Accomplished*—We must accept that this is constantly repeating itself (present passive) all around the world. Satan has no new tricks.

D. Remember God Is Only Refining Us (vv. 10–11; 1 Pet. 1:7)

1. *After suffering for a little while*—Our pain from persecution is necessary (1 Pet. 1:6), but it is only for a little while compared to eternity.
2. *The God of all grace*—This is a genitive which means God is the one who shapes how all grace abounds—grace being a generous, free-hearted, unearned, and unmerited gift of kindness.
3. *Called us to His eternal glory*—God once and for all provided to us a specific divine invitation to experience His divine nature. This is a transformation process that is refined, through trials, so that we become just like Him (Col. 3:1–4; James 1:2–4). God through Christ does this (all future tense) by:
   a) *Perfecting us*—This means to take broken bones, realign them and restore them to their perfect place. God takes us broken (humbled) from trials and tribulation to become just like Him (2 Cor. 3:18). This is why James says to count it joy (James 1:2).
   b) *Confirm*—Approaching trials "firm in the faith" leads us to become well-grounded in the Word.
   c) *Strengthened*—With broken lives mended and convictions strong, we become more capable of being able to endure trials while dealing with difficult experiences.

d) *Established*—Means to have a solid immovable position. Believers become immovable in their faith and trust in God.

4. *Amen*—This is an emphatic endorsement to all the above.

"For His anger is but for a moment, His favor is for life; Weeping may endure for a night, But joy comes in the morning" (Ps. 30:5).

Author's Comments

Comments

God never exalts anyone until that person is ready for it—first the cross, then the crown; the suffering, and then the glory. Like a trained athlete winning gold at the Olympics, Moses was shaped by God for forty years before God sent him to deliver the Israelites from Egypt. David ran from Saul for twelve years before becoming king. Joseph was under God's hand for at least thirteen years before God lifted him to the throne. Paul served without full acceptance by the apostles for fourteen years (Gal. 2:1). One of the evidences of our pride is our impatience with God (Peter, Matt. 16:21–23), and one reason for suffering is that we might learn patience (James 1:1–6). Here, Peter was referring to words he heard the Master say: "For whosoever exalts himself shall be humbled; and he that humbles himself shall be exalted" (Luke 14:11). "Therefore let him who thinks he stands take heed lest he fall" (1 Cor. 10:12).

Even though all the above is true, no one desires this process, because we are all expecting Christ to provide us a life of joy and peace. We may not say this, but our disappointment when we are going through trials implies it. One of the benefits of the kind of relationship with God, described in this passage, is knowing that God desires to take care of our burdens (Ps. 34:17–19). The hope is that God would so strengthen us that our maturity develops so much strength that no matter the pressure we may experience on the outside, it does not disturb the spiritual transformation we experience on the inside. For me, the apostle Paul, outside of Christ, is the best model. His maturity was so powerful (Gal. 2:20; Col. 3:1–4) that even if he was threatened with death he would view it as gain (Phil. 1:21), and was anxious for nothing. If he was suffering, the pain did not deter him from the hope of experiencing the promised crown (Rom. 8:18; 2 Tim. 4:6–8). Being penniless was met with contentment, and no matter what he experienced he genuinely gave thanks (1 Thess. 5:18). No matter the pain

Paul experienced, the transformation process produced strength. This is the victory that overcomes everything.

Application

Satan is busy. We can either become obsessed with all that he does or take refuge in God. Taking refuge in God means we must remain humble before Him, willing to accept discipline from Him. We must cast our worries and cares on Him, trusting Him to care for us.

Satan is always busy seeking whom he can destroy. Faith is the best resistance to his attacks because "faith comes by hearing, and hearing by the word of God" (Rom. 10:17). It is the word that does not return void (Isa. 55:11). The best example is Christ being attacked by Satan (Luke 4:1–8). All Christ did was quote Scriptures. Satan cannot overcome the powerful nature of "the word" (Heb. 4:12). It is the very nature of Christ.

So when trials come, we can be distracted by the pain or become absorbed in the transformation process that spiritual growth brings (1 Pet. 1:3–9). This leads to "You are of God, little children, and have overcome them, because He who is in you is greater than he who is in the world" (1 John 4:4). This is why no matter what we experience we must keep our eyes fixed on Christ (Heb. 12:1–3; 1 Pet. 2:21–25), who is "the author and finisher of our faith."

Illustrate It

Years ago as our mission group was in a Jeep in the safari, they saw three lions attack a pack of zebras. As the lions came near the pack, one of the zebras ran away from the rest of the zebras, for what reason no one knows. The lions immediately took off after him and eventually caught up with him and took him down.

It was sad to see, especially since the other zebras stopped running and turned and looked back as one of their own was killed. It seemed to everyone that the lions expected one of the zebras to stray from the pack.

It is interesting in this letter that Peter is emphasizing the need for the brethren to trust God's love, goodness, and power. They must remain in His Word, and they must remain together as a church supporting one another. It is after emphasizing the importance of this that Peter discusses how to combat Satan, who is like a lion. Our culture teaches us to deal with our issues on our own. Gossip in the church restricts us from wanting to share our struggles. As believers, we must trust God's structure and believe God to rescue us from a very evil adversary.

Sermon Series 4

God and Me

Live Blessed Rather than Stressed

Numbers 13:25—14:10

General Overview of the Passage

After forty days, the spies returned to provide Moses a comprehensive review of the land God had ordained for them. They spent forty days carefully examining all that was taking place in the Promised Land. The spies reported much the same—God did not lie. They also brought back physical evidence of the fruitfulness of the land (Num. 13:27). "This confirmed the exact wording of God's promise about the land (Exod. 3:8, 17). It is a tragic irony that the spies were speaking of the very nations already named in God's promise to Abraham (Gen. 15:18). God had already indicated that the Amorites were 'filling up' their iniquity and were being reserved for his judgment, which Israel would execute (Gen. 15:16)."[1]

Despite the fact that God confirmed everything the spies said, they deemed the invasion impossible and threw in the towel. They spent all their time thinking about why going into the Promised Land was impossible, rather than focusing on what the Lord required them to do. They had already defeated Egypt, a country greater and stronger. In fact, they won without ever lifting a sword. They saw the glory of the Lord on Moses, the glory of the Lord of the "Tent of Meeting," and they saw water come from a dry rock, yet they still didn't believe.

Fear entered into the picture, and the report changed from a statement of God's faithfulness to the obstacles they saw against man's ability. This report exposes that the land is fully populated on every side, not by nomads but by people who have lived there for centuries and have firmly established themselves. God allows these people to be giants, knowing that the Israelites just left a land

[1] D. A. Carson, *New Bible Commentary: 21st Century Edition,* 4th ed. (Leicester, England: Downers Grove, IL: InterVarsity Press, 1994), s.v. Num. 13:26.

of people who, for the most part, were short. He allowed the land to be fortified, knowing the Israelites were not seasoned warriors. God tested their hearts (Deut. 8). This land is before them after they spent 400 years in Egypt—some of it as slaves—and two years in the wilderness eating "corn flakes" and drinking water. God wanted the people to walk by faith and become exposed to who He really is. The greater the obstacles, the more they learned about His power and His might. Caleb and Joshua remained resolved, while the people grumbled and rebelled against God.

Historical Background

Establishing Context

The forty-day journey demonstrates how thorough the spies search was and possibly created anxiety among the people as they had to wait so long to see them. "The scouts' forty-day exploration of the land accords with the approximate time such a journey would have taken on foot. The number forty is often used in the Bible for an indefinite period in excess of a month. Having trekked from the Desert of Zin all the way to Lebo Hamath and back again means they would have covered from 350 to 500 miles while reconnoitering the hill country and valleys."[2]

The walls of Jericho were tall, about fifty feet high. So were the people! "There we saw the giants (the descendants of Anak came from the giants); and we were like grasshoppers in our own sight, and so we were in their sight" (Num. 13:33).

The land flowing with milk and honey is a way of describing how rich the land is for the people. "The phrase *flows with milk and honey* is a slogan of redemption, a slogan expressing God's goodness in His promise of the land of Canaan (Num. 14:8; 16:13, 14; Exod. 3:8, 17; 13:5; 33:3; Lev. 20:24; Deut. 6:3; 11:9; 26:9, 15; 27:3; 31:20). *Milk* probably refers to goats' milk; *honey* refers to bees, which were especially associated with the propagation of fruitful pastures and fields in Canaan. The phrase evoked visions of pleasure and plenty for the Israelites. Canaan was a good land, and enjoyment of the land would follow faithfulness to God."[3]

---

[2] J. H. Walton, *Genesis, Exodus, Leviticus, Numbers, Deuteronomy*, vol. 1 of the Zondervan Bible Background Commentary series (Grand Rapids, MI: Zondervan 2009), 359.

[3] V. H. Matthews, and M. W. Chavalas, and J. H. Walton, *The IVP Bible Background Commentary: Old Testament* (Downers Grove, IL: InterVarsity Press. 2000), electronic ed., s.v. Num. 13:26.

Everything God said hundreds of years before it took place were true. They had a God they could trust.

What Does the Context Mean?

The spies came back with a report that supported all that God said about the land, but ten of the spies saw the obstacles rather than the opportunity to finally settle their families. The people believed the spies and decided that they were not going into the land and needed someone else to lead them back to Egypt. Moses, Aaron, Caleb, and Joshua prayed before God and addressed the people, letting them know that the land belonged to God, and the protection of the people in the land had been removed. The people must not rebel against God, but rather trust in Him and go in and possess the land. The congregation, controlled by fear, decided to stone them. Whenever people allow fear to reign in their lives, they cancel faith and live stressed.

Sermon Subject and Title

Sermon Title: Live Blessed Rather than Stressed
Big Idea: God's power has no obstacles, so any time we experience difficulties, the only thing required is faith.

Sermon Outline (Num. 13:25–14:10 nasb)

A. **God Is True to His Word (vv. 25–27; 1 Pet. 1:23–25; Heb. 4:12)**
   1. Everything the Lord said the land would be it was (Num. 13:27; Gen. 15:16–21; Exod. 3:8, 17).
      a) He said it hundreds of years earlier and it is exactly as God said it would be (Gen. 15:12–21).
   2. Do not rely on man's philosophy or human ability but on God's Word (Prov. 3:5; 16:9; Col. 2:6–9).

B. **God Empowers Us to Overcome Obstacles (vv. 28–33)**
   1. Eight spies focused on the problems they saw in the land rather than the possibilities (Num. 13:28–29).
   2. God did not reduce the obstacles when this group arrived or when they came back forty years later.
      a) It is interesting that Rahab said the people were more afraid of them than they ever could have been of the people (Josh. 2:8–11).

3. The glass is half empty (Num. 13:28–29, 31–33; 14:1–4):
   a) They said that "we" (their own ability) cannot do it (v. 31). Moses said the Lord will give the land to Israel (Num. 10:29).
   b) The report was bad because they added to what they saw in order to control the people and influence them so that they no longer desired to enter the land (Num. 13:32–33).
   c) Fear entered the hearts of the people, and all of a sudden Egypt looked better (Num. 14:1–4).
   d) How can they turn the hearts of the people so quickly?
      - Eyewitness account from ten spies.
      - Fear of the unknown.
      - Strength and size of the people
   e) It is easy to forget what God has done.
3. The glass is half full (Num. 13:30; 14:5–7):
   a) *Then Caleb*—in the midst of the uproar Caleb speaks.
   b) *By all means let us go up*—no matter the obstacles we must come together and go up; *We shall overcome it.*
   c) They prayed for the people rather than fight for their positions (14:5). Compare with 14:4.

C. The Lord Is Faithful Never to Leave Us or Forsake Us (vv. 8–9)

1. *If the Lord is pleased with us*—If we find favor in His sight, He will bless us (Num. 14:8; Rom. 8:31; James 5:16).
2. *He gives it*—He puts it in place—His action, His initiative, He provides the results to us.
3. Do not prevent His goodness. Do not flagrantly disobey God and disrespect His authority (Heb. 6:4–8; 10:32–39).
4. *They shall be our prey*—God has long promised to give them over to us.
5. *Their protection has been removed*—God's shadow no longer covers them. *The Lord is with us*—Their cup of iniquity was now full (Gen. 15:16).

Author's Comments

Comments

Here is a nation who saw God's powerful movement at the Red Sea each day as He fed them, rested over the Holies of Holies, and met Moses at the Tent of Meeting, but when it came time to deal with giants, they resisted God's commands. They were provided every reason to trust God. They had His Word, His powerful, magnificent miracles, but they did not choose faith. This led to more stress than rest.

From a human standpoint, I understand! The giants were not just tall; they were war-tested and enjoyed war. Jews, generally speaking, are not naturally mostly tall. So to go from slavery to warriors before men who are tall and seasoned warriors is intimidating. God, however, never places us in intimidating situations without history and His Word.

The reason this is extremely important is because often the issues we experience are really between God and Satan. Satan is a huge force because he is not trying to defeat us more than He is seeking to stop God's purposes. Since he knows God's purposes and magnificent power, his obstacles are going beyond our ability (Satan is a powerful angel; Ezekiel 28; Isaiah 14—look at what he did to Job in a short space of time). They can only be resolved by God. Satan knows that God seeks to work through us to teach us to live by faith and not by sight (2 Cor. 5:6–7; Eph. 6:11–12), so he does everything possible to discourage us. If we do not exercise faith, Satan knows we have no ability to defeat him; doubt does not provide us any results (James 1:6–8—he created doubt with Eve). When we view what we face through our ability, it creates doubt and drives fear, leading us to resist to God. Maybe this is why John writes, "The whole world lies under the sway of the wicked one," (1 John 5:19). John also says, "You are of God, little children, and have overcome them, because He who is in you is greater than he who is in the world" (1 John 4:4).

Any giants we encounter must automatically lead us to spontaneously reflect on what God is saying. This is the difference between the spies and Joshua and Caleb. Joshua and Caleb believed God, so the problem was never theirs to resolve; they just saw themselves as participants in God's resolution of the issue. Their convictions concerning God's promises were greater than their fears. What they saw did not change their convictions; it only directed them to trust God more.

What is God seeking to get you to do that your level of faith prevents you from doing? Who or what is your giant?

Application

The biggest fight any believer may face in this life is the fight of faith (1 Tim. 6:12). We are living in a world that is in the power of the evil one, so obstacles are normal (1 Pet. 4:12; 1 John 5:19). We must put our energy to learning God's instructions, since God promises to not give us more than we can bear. Then we can allow Him to achieve His purpose as James outlines in James 1:2–4. When a trial comes, a believer needs to run to faith. God says that He "has given to us all things that pertain to life and godliness" (2 Pet. 1:3), so when issues arise we must remember we have everything we need to exercise faith. John adds: "greater is He who is in you than he who is in the world" (1 John 4:4 NASB). The believer must remember that the Word is a Word of life, not just knowledge. The result is that we grow spiritually and make room for the fruit of the Spirit as a result of the trials God blesses us to endure (James 1:12). This produces joy, rather than stress, and blesses us to live as overcomers, rather than underachievers (Rom. 8:31, 37).

Illustrate It

Several years ago, the New Orleans Saints made it to the Super Bowl. No one thought that they had a chance to win the game. They were fighting their way through the game and were close at the half. When the team came out for the second half of the game, the coach called an on-side kick, which they recovered. From that point on, New Orleans was on their way to winning the game. All of this took place after a storm that just about destroyed New Orleans.

The Detroit Pistons were in the NBA championship game. No one thought that they had the caliber of players to compete at this level. The players did not listen to anyone. They just went out on the court and implemented their playbook and followed the leadership of their coach.

Too many times, we let intimidation control our faith, rather than the other way around. The only fight we have is the fight of faith (1 Tim. 6:11–12). Is God's Word true? Can He do the impossible? We must put our faith to work. This is when we learn who God really is and live more in the fruit of the Spirit than the weakness of the flesh.

For Thine Is the Glory

1 Peter 4:10–11

General Overview of the Passage

Each believer has obtained from God an undeserved gift. Each believer is required by the Lord to serve based on this spiritual gift for the glory of God with no expectation of any thanks. It is the needs of the other believer that come first (Phil. 2:1–5) which when executed leads to a powerful experience of the strength and spiritual development of all believers.

Each believer must continuously manage these gifts so that they use them faithfully without expecting thanks (it is a free generous gift with no expectations). Each believer is not just a slave in use of the gift; they are also managers. They must find ways to serve God and to manage their time to use it (1 Cor. 4:1–2). Each believer's use of their gift is for the well-being of other believers. This is possible because this gift is a free-hearted gift that is unearned and unmerited based on the spontaneous generosity of God for us (Eph. 4:7). No one earned their gift or deserved to receive it. It is provided by Christ through the Holy Spirit (Titus 3:4–8). Believers must be good managers of their gifts so that the church does not reduce the effectiveness of the execution of God's agenda for helping those in need, bringing glory to God. Whatever gift a believer has and therefore puts to work, they must do so in order that God's nature is fully exposed. The purpose of this is that in all things God's innate light would continuously shine forth through the person of Jesus Christ. This reflects Christ in all His excellence, His divine nature, and power and authority, which, in turn, establishes a strong and productive church.

Historical Background

Establishing Context

"To the people in the early church community believed that the coming of the age where Gentiles and Jews worship together as one another is marked by the Holy Spirit entering into the lives of believers as was experienced by the disciples. The manifestation of the Holy Spirit is evidence when believers experienced their spiritual gift."[4]

> Peter viewed these gifts as essential for the strength of the church especially since believers were experiencing a number of issues that create difficult struggles and for some even death. Peter never tells us in this letter which gifts he might stress, for he gives only two categories, the one who "speaks" and the one who "serves." In this he divides gifts as Luke says that Peter did in Acts 6:2, where "word of God" is contrasted with "wait[ing] on tables.[5]

What Does the Context Mean?

We are stewards of God's grace. Everything God has provided to us, we must be good stewards of, focused on glorifying God (1 Cor. 4:1–2; Rev. 4:11).

Each believer must remain clear-minded for prayer and be committed to continuously love other believers through the ministry of hospitality. Hospitality must abound without complaint because this would allow each believer to forgive one another. This attitude then extends to faithful service that is based on spiritual gifts provided by God's free gift of the Holy Spirit for each believer. As each believer speaks or serves, they must do so as a result of the power of God, so that everyone's service magnifies and demonstrates the true nature of Jesus Christ.

Sermon Subject and Title

Sermon Title: For Thine Is the Glory

---

[4] C. E. Arnold, *Zondervan Illustrated Bible Backgrounds Commentary, Volume 4: Hebrews to Revelation* (Grand Rapids, MI: Zondervan, 2002), 142.

[5] Ibid.

Big Idea: God is glorified when spiritual gifts are employed under the direction and empowerment of the Holy Spirit.

Sermon Outline (1 Pet. 4:10–11 nasb)

A. His Gift (v. 10)

1. *Each one*—Every believer has a spiritual gift.
2. *Receive a special gift*—Meaning they have already obtained it.
3. *Gift*—Given by God based on His manifold grace (Eph. 4:7). A gift that we should not compare with others. It is the Lord's decision for His purposes (2 Cor. 10:12–13). His spiritual enablement for His special duties.
4. *Employ it*—Put it to work; work while it is day; night will come (John 9:4).
    a) The stronger Christ's body—the church—the better off everyone is (Eph. 4:12–13).
5. *Service*—Work as a slave serving tables.

B. His Stewards (v. 10)

1. *Good*—Work empowered by the Holy Spirit benefits everyone in the church.
2. *Steward*—We have to manage ourselves in time so that we make time to employ our gift (1 Cor. 7:32–35).
3. *Grace*—Unmerited gift freely, spontaneously, and generously bestowed without any need to return it:
    a) God's grace is best displayed in service.

C. His Strength (v. 11a; Col. 1:28–29)

1. *Speaks*—Whoever dare break the silence; Mosaic laws (Acts 7:38), writers of OT (Rom. 3:2), Christian doctrine (Heb. 5:12), teachings of Christian teachers (1 Pet. 4:11).
2. *Utterances*—Christian teachers; we must manage this gift clearly because teachers will be judged more strictly (James 3:1).
3. *Strength*–When we are serving using our gift, we are empowered by God to bring Him glory. This is the mighty power of God, the Holy Spirit, working in us (Col. 1:28–29).
4. *Supplies*—His provision.

D. His Glory (v. 11b)

1. *Glorified*—The character of Christ is brought to light.

2. *Glory*—Excellence in His divine nature, coinciding with His self-revelation.
3. *Dominion*—God in His power and might, strength, and His authority.
4. The church becomes a living organism empowered by the Holy Spirit, magnifying the nature and purposes of Christ through the church.

Author's Comments

Comments

We live in a society that is addicted to people and obsessed with self. Being a community of believers becomes extremely difficult when trying to establish fellowship in a church. Preachers have not set a good example in this area; we compare and compete just like many parishioners. The lasting question is: "Has what we achieved in this life made a lasting difference in the lives of other believers because we have faithfully served the Lord's church?" It is only what we do for Christ that will last (1 Cor. 15:58).

Just like these believers in this passage, many people come to church hurting, broken from sexual abuse, divorce, spousal abuse, suffering from depression or low self-esteem. When they attend church, God has joined and held together His body (Eph. 4:16) with the gift of encouragement, knowledge, wisdom, service, giving, etc. When the gifts are brought to light and each church attendee is focused "to stimulate one another to love and good deeds" (Heb. 10:24 NASB), parishioners can be built up so that "we all attain to the unity of the faith, and of the knowledge of the Son of God, to a mature man, to the measure of the stature which belongs to the fullness of Christ" (Eph. 4:13 NASB). Without spiritual gifts being activated, the church is not built up spiritually, unity is not achieved (Eph. 4:4–6, 13), and the love that Peter is seeking to achieve does not become an integrated part of the church (Eph. 4:16). As a result, "in all things God may be glorified' (1 Pet. 4:11) is not manifested.

Spiritual gifts, along with establishing a loving community of believers, are essential for a healthy church that magnifies and glorifies God.

Application

Everyone wants to go to a church that serves them effectively. The question is, *How many people want to serve so that by their service each member is blessed?* Every day God is at work protecting us, providing for us, and sustaining this massive ball called Earth. We should be so thankful that serving Him and giving to Him should never be a sermon we need hear. How much time has our Lord found in our calendars this week? Are we just consumers or are we investors? How many of us correct our children when they find it hard to bring us a glass of water because of all we do for them? As stated, God does so much that it should be viewed as an exciting opportunity to serve Him.

Illustrate It

My mother attended a small church in Dallas. Each Sunday she noticed the church was not as clean as it should be. My mother took it upon herself to start cleaning the church, so every Saturday she would go to the church to clean, including the restrooms, and make sure everything was ready for Sunday. My mother did this on her own initiative, never expecting anyone to thank her, and was happy to do so. She did this for years with no encouragement or support because her heart was to please God. This gift of service saved this small church money and removed any distractions that may have been there in the midst of worship.

High Yield Returns

Matthew 25:14–30

General Overview of the Passage

In the above passage, the master represents Christ and the servants represent believers who are entrusted with the responsibility of serving Christ. Each believer will have to give an account for their stewardship of what God entrusted to them (1 Cor. 4:1–2). They will be blessed based on their faithfulness to Christ. The parable of the talents illustrates the faithfulness required of God's servants. "The fact that the master traveled to a far country indicates that there would be ample time to test the faithfulness of the servants."[6]

As we review the parable, we find the land owner is going on a journey where he will stay a while. He summons his subordinates to come before he leaves. These subordinates are owned by him (this is the lowest term in the scale of servitude—one who gives himself to the will of another), and he knows them very well. He gave a sizable amount of his money to them and left. The amount of the money is based on their capability. Their capability is the strength to overcome any form of resistance, dangers, or obstacles they may face as they seek to accomplish this task.

The slave who received the five talents and the one with two talents both went out and, by hard labor, earned a profit on the talents provided. The slaves, while doing this, were still able to live in the master's home. One of the slaves did not do anything. He wrapped the talent in a napkin and dug a hole and put it in the ground. The unprepared slave misjudged the character of the owner and did not take advantage of his investment opportunities.

Christ's "servants" here mean all who, by their Christian profession, stand in relation to Him with entire subjection. His "goods" mean all their gifts and

[6] Earl D. Radmacher, Ronald Barclay Allen, Wayne H. House, *Nelson's New Illustrated Bible Commentary* (Nashville, TN: Thomas Nelson Publishers, 1999), s.v. Matt. 25:14.

endowments, whether original or acquired, natural or spiritual. All that slaves have belongs to their master, so Christ has a claim to everything and demands its appropriation to His service, especially since we are "bought at a price" (1 Cor. 6:20).

The master returned after being gone for a long time. When he returned, his focus was to settle accounts. The slaves who had obtained five and two talents came bubbling over with enthusiasm, sparkling with excitement and reported that they had profited five more talents and two more talents, respectively. The master responded to these slaves that they did excellent and they proved to be useful and of benefit to others. They proved to be steadfast, dependable, and reliable. As a result, he will appoint these two slaves to a position of authority that will cause them to manage more responsibilities in his kingdom. They must, therefore, enter into the gladness and excitement the master has. "A number of scholars believe that the noun *joy* here is used with the meaning 'feast' or 'banquet.' The footnote in NJB ('The happiness of the heavenly banquet') goes beyond the context of the parable itself. In this case, *enter* seems to indicate physically coming in (to the house where the banquet was)."[7]

The third slave came to the master with the same talent he gave to him and accused his master of being rough, harsh, stringent, and even violent. He claims that because of the master's attitude, he was terrified and went outside to bury the talent. The master responded by saying that the man is wicked (malicious, and purposefully desired to cause injury and distress) because he falsely accused his master and did not do what was expected. Instead of admitting that he was wrong, he acts as if the master should have given him credit. He also contradicted himself because if he knew the master was harsh he would have done something. This man was not only wicked, but lazy! The master took away the talent because the slave was not useful (Luke 19:23–25; 1 Cor. 3:10–15) and gave it to the most productive of the slaves.

Historical Background

Establishing Context

The context for the story is found in Matthew 21:33–22:14 and chapters 24–25.

---

[7] UBS Handbook series (United Bible Societies, copyright © 1961–1997).

In Jerusalem there were wealthy landowners. They placed their wealth in the hands of free men who served as their accountants. Because of the mode of transportation in the days of Christ, some of these landowners went on trips that took a long time as they sought to expand their businesses and develop trade. Because most people were familiar with these landowners, Jesus explains this story using them as His reference because it would be easy for people to relate.

In those days there were also bankers who sat at money exchange tables. They were called moneychangers. They lent money at great interest rates. So when the person returns to get their money, they would get it back at a profit and the moneychanger would make a profit as well on money that was technically not his. This is why "Jewish teachers used to say that anyone who immediately buries money entrusted to him is no longer liable, because he has taken the safest course possible in protecting the money."[8]

A talent is "a monetary term as that unit of weight used of the metals that served as money—gold, silver, or copper. A talent of silver represented some 20 years' wages for a day laborer and thus was worth far more than the $1,000 suggested in the NIV notes."[9] This immediately reveals the wealth of the landowner. It explains why he would be comfortable leaving this large sum of money, why he could afford going on a long trip, and how well he knew his servants by the amount he entrusted to each one.

What Does the Context Mean?

The master entrusted his slaves with his resources based on their ability, and two of them faithfully served his interest. One of the slaves was wicked and lazy and did not want to see his master prosper, so he hid the talent and accused his master of being a shrewd businessman profiting from other people's work. The master responded by taking away his talent and giving it to the one with the greatest ability. Christ blesses us for being faithful to advance His kingdom work. He blesses us to serve Him faithfully so that as a result of our service He can multiply His church and our fruit.

---

[8] Ibid.

[9] Lawrence O. Richards, *The Bible Readers Companion* (Wheaton, IL: Victor Books, 1991), electronic form by Logos Research Systems, 1996, 627 electronic ed.

Sermon Subject and Title

Sermon Title: High Yield Returns
Big Idea: Serving God is a divine call. He blesses us with spiritual gifts, which is His investment in our lives and for His kingdom. Our use of His investment is connected to our earthly and eternal blessings.

Sermon Outline (Matt. 25:14–30 nasb)

A. Recognize We Are on His Timetable (vv. 14, 19)

1. *Go on a journey*—The Master provides ample time for each believer. He did not announce when he would come back (Matt. 25:13). This is a present active; this is an ongoing journey.
2. *He called*—This is a specific request and it is only done one time (aorist active).

B. Remember We Own Nothing (v. 14)

1. *His own possessions*—As Master, He has power and authority to demand what we have done with His resources. We are stewards, so nothing really belongs to us (James 1:17; this is in the accusative; His own—this is the direct purpose of the master calling them—the same for us, we are called and given a spiritual gift).
   a) Christ owns everything; this means He has a claim on everything. Our spiritual gifts are sustained by the Holy Spirit.
   b) They lived in their master's house while using his money.
   c) We are His workmanship (Eph. 2:10).
   d) We are bought with a price (1 Cor. 6:20).
   e) Naked we came . . . naked we return (Job 1:21).
2. *His own slaves*—His slaves belong to him. The talents belong to him.

C. Realize He Is a Wise Investor (vv. 15–18)

1. He gave to each person based on their ability. He only gave one talent to the man who buried it. The master did not intend to waste any of his resources.
2. *Based on their ability*—Their capability is the strength to overcome any form of resistance, dangers, or obstacles they may face.

D. Sustain an Attitude that Produces Great Yields (vv. 19–23)

1. *Slave*—He accepted his role and viewed his master as his master (Matt. 25:19–21; called him master).

2. *Entrusted*—The master took the entrusted resources seriously. Notice the slaves did not compare among themselves (2 Cor. 10:12–13).
3. *Traded*—The two faithful servants immediately sought to be profitable.
4. *See*—Upon the master's return, there was no hesitation from the faithful servants in calling attention to what they had done.
5. *Gained*—The servant worked hard until he became profitable. Aorist because this was a one-time gain. They could not get anymore.
6. Excited to be profitable. They came to their master bubbling over with enthusiasm, sparkling with excitement.
7. *You were*—(active)—means they were constantly living a faithful life.
8. *Faithful slave*—This is a slave that was steadfast to the master's trust, dependable and reliable.
9. His master never took the money back to give it back to him (Matt. 25:28; Eccles. 5:18–19). The master did not need it. He simply chose to bless the slaves while he was gone.

E. Be Aware of the Attitude that Is Self-Destructive (vv. 24–28, 30)

1. *Could have put it in the bank*—Could have gone and traded with the moneychangers. The lazy slave just went away (Matt. 25:18).
2. *Wicked and lazy*—Showed no enthusiasm for serving his master. Just focused on doing whatever he normally did.
3. He did what was safe; he put the talent in a napkin (Luke 19:20) and buried it.
4. *Said to the master*—(present active)—What he is saying he is always going to say. This describes his nature. It is what it is.
5. He was evil because he blamed his master for his attitude (Matt. 25:24).
6. *Afraid*—Fear removes faith (2 Tim. 1:7). Instead of doing what the master wanted (faith), he did what was safe (wicked). He knew what he was doing was wrong, but he still did it. He accused his master of being rough, harsh, stringent and violent.

F. Remember Faithful Service Produces Great Rewards (v. 29)

1. *Well done*—They measured up to the master's intended purpose.
2. The man with one talent lost everything and it was given to the man with ten.
3. *Enter into his joy*—(Matt. 25:20–21); gladness and excitement; heavenly banquet; feast (joy).
4. They would be in charge of many things in glory—position of authority and greater responsibility.

Author's Comments

Comments

If Christ were to come today, what would be your report? Don't forget: He comes in a split second when we gather to meet Him in the air. We don't know the day or the time when Christ will return nor when He will call us home (Eccles. 3:2; Matt. 25:13). What will be our report for the life, resources, protection, and faithfulness He has entrusted to us? Does God's investment in us provide great yield for His kingdom?

One of the things that fascinates me in this passage is the amount the landowner gave to the lazy servant. He could have given him whatever he chose and he only gave him one. It speaks volumes about the level of stewardship also exercised by the landowner. He was not going to waste his money on someone who would not even take it to the moneychanger's table.

It seems like Christ did the same thing when He told the disciples to distribute the five loaves and two fishes. "Then He commanded them to make them all sit down in groups on the green grass. So they sat down in ranks, in hundreds and in fifties" (Mark 6:39–40). The same thing took place after Moses selected his leaders (Exod. 18:21). Christ may not require us to serve the same amount of people, but He does require faithfulness and for us to be good stewards (1 Cor. 4:1–2).

We are not just provided financial resources; He gave us spiritual gifts. First Peter 4:10 teaches that we must employ them in serving one another. We must put our gifts to work and serve energetically. The pastor must provide this work for church members to do so that the church grows up spiritually and the members love each other (Eph. 4:12–13, 16). When the church is spiritually productive, it impacts the world for God's glory and protects believers from Satan (Eph. 1:22–23; 3:10; 6:11–17). Just as in the case of the landowner, we must give an account for what was deposited in our care. "Each one's work will become clear; for the Day will declare it, because it will be revealed by fire; and the fire will test each one's work, of what sort it is. If anyone's work which he has built on it endures, he will receive a reward. If anyone's work is burned, he will suffer loss; but he himself will be saved, yet so as through fire" (1 Cor. 3:13–15). "For we must all appear before the judgment seat of Christ, that each one may receive the things done in the body, according to what he has done, whether good or bad. Knowing, therefore, the terror of the Lord, we persuade men; but we are well known to God, and I also trust are well known in your consciences" (2 Cor. 5:10–11).

We will give an account for the work we have done, whether good or worthless. So, it is imperative that we have "high yield returns."

Application

Whatever Christ has entrusted to us we must be diligent in using to serve Him. If it is five loaves and two fish, we must put it in His hands (follow His Word in the way we use His gift), and when we are faithful with a few things, He will bless us with more. We don't need to compare ourselves (2 Cor. 10:12–13); we need to remain focused on running the race He set before us. We must be faithful with what we have.

We need to stop making excuses. We talk about our limited time when we are on God's clock, the kind of people at the church when there is no one that is perfect, the length of service, or the pastor's sermon when we shop forever and watch long movies. It is time to work for God, especially since the days are evil and we are the salt and light of the earth (Matt. 5:13–16).

Illustrate It

NFL football player Dexter Manley faced the end of his career completely broke. He only survived because his girlfriend was kind enough to take care of him. He made millions, and completed high school and college, but could not read. It was not that he did not have everything available to him; he just chose not to invest it.

Magic Johnson played for years in the NBA and did very well for the Lakers. Even though his career was cut short, Magic is doing exceptionally well as an entrepreneur.

The difference between these two men is that one squandered his money and did not apply himself at school, so there was no career after football. The other (Magic Johnson) worked to make his money work for him.

God has blessed us with free public education and an ability to apply ourselves. He has given us spiritual gifts at the point of salvation. The question is, *What are we doing with His gifts?*

All-Sufficient Grace

Romans 6:14–19

General Overview of the Passage

We should know from experience and by divine knowledge that we cannot continuously and habitually hand over our bodies (in which the Holy Spirit lives, 1 Cor. 6:19; 1 John 3:5–8) to sin without some penalty. The price we pay is that we become controlled by sin and enslaved to it. This enslavement leads to death (Rom. 6:23, 1 Cor. 11:30; Heb. 6:1–8; 1 John 5:16). However, the opposite takes place if a person subjects himself to God's will by conforming to His righteous standards. A believer's conformity to God's righteous standards allows them to experience the imputed righteousness of God. This is imputed in the life of the believer as a result of justification.

The believer was a slave of Satan before salvation, but since being saved, is a slave of the Lord Jesus. Christ's righteousness imputed to believers justifies them before God and provides them strength to live by the standards of God (Rom. 8:9–11). This transformation changes who they serve because they are now living in a new nature. The evil nature which compelled them to serve the devil has its power over them broken. Although the believer still sins at times, it is not the normal pattern (Rom. 7:14–25; 1 John 3:4–10). The believer eventually hates sin and endeavors to keep it completely out of their life (Rom. 8:5–8, 12–16). In the event the believer commits an act of sin, they confess it to the Lord Jesus, who removes the sin out of their life as a result of His cleansing blood (1 John 1:8–9).

Paul praises the believers because they have freely and generously subjected themselves to the divine will of God and have done so with an entire mental and emotional commitment to God. This is great because they were once mastered or owned by sin (1 Cor. 3:23; 7:22). Now, they have given themselves over to the instruction and doctrine of God. As a result of their liberation, they are slaves to righteousness.

Paul says that he only instructs them in this manner because the flesh—the domain of the fallen nature—is weak and is open to all kinds of wickedness. So, just as they once put themselves in servitude to sin, they must now place themselves in servitude to righteousness. This leads a believer to be set apart for a life of holiness consecrated to God.

Historical Background

Establishing Context

Many Romans had slaves. This was a standard practice, so it would be easy for those in Rome to relate to what Paul is saying in this passage. If they were slaves to one master, they could not be a slave to another at the same time.

> Slavery was one of the best-known institutions in the ancient world. Almost 35–40 percent of the inhabitants of Rome and the peninsula of Italy in the first century were slaves; and the situation in the provinces may have been comparable. So Paul's analogy would have been one that all his readers could immediately have identified with. Making the analogy even more exact is the fact that people in the ancient world could sell themselves into slavery (e.g., to avoid a ruinous debt).[10]

The Jews believed that because they had the law, and the Gentiles did not, there was no way they could sin like the Gentiles. Since they could not sin like the Gentiles, sin could not have mastery over them. But Paul brought a new argument to the table: no one is under the law anymore. We are all under grace. It is not the law that saves us—it is the grace of God that saves us.

Therefore, when our time arrives to stand before God, full of the dirt and blemishes of our sin, it is faith that blesses the process, not the law. Whether Jew or Gentile, we are all living by grace.

> Not under law means not under the Law of Moses. Yet the believer with God's help, the believer under grace, fulfills the law (3:31; 13:8–10). The Mosaic system consisted of external laws that revealed the sin prevalent in human hearts. In contrast, God's grace places the believer in Christ, and the Holy Spirit in the believer. Therefore, a Christian

[10] Arnold, *Zondervan Illustrated Bible Backgrounds Commentary*, 3:38.

does not have to sin; he or she can resist temptation and do what is right (2 Cor. 3:15–18).[11]

What Does the Context Mean?

Sin was not the master over the believers in Rome because they were not under the law that kept them in bondage to sin (Rom. 3:20). They were now covered by grace. Under grace, they now have the freedom to not function as slaves to sin. When they present their bodies to live, based on the standards of God, and still sin, they can confess their sin and experience the all-sufficient grace of God. But, grace does not abound so that they sin more (Rom. 6:1–2). Grace abounds so that a believer can commit to a life of obedience and righteousness without feeling controlled by sin. Sin under the law did not just separate them from God, it made them spend a lot of time going to the temple to experience God's forgiveness. But under grace a believer is free to experience the love of God provided as a result of Christ's death and resurrection (Eph. 2:8–10).

Paul is glad they have committed to the instruction they have received so that they, being freed from sin, can become slaves to righteousness. The presentation of themselves to be slaves to righteousness will lead them to holiness, setting them apart for God (Rom. 12:1–2).

Sermon Subject and Title

Sermon Title: All-Sufficient Grace
Big Idea: God provides grace so that the sanctifying process leads to a greater ability to live righteously. This is something living under the law could not produce.

Sermon Outline (Rom. 6:14–19 NASB)

A. Grace Liberates Us from the Power of Sin (vv. 14–15)

1. *Sin*—An organized power that influences the members of our body to act in willful disobedience to God (Eph. 2:1–3).

[11] Radmacher, Allen, and House, *Nelson's New Illustrated Bible Commentary*, s.v. Rom. 6:14–15.

a) *You are not*—The inward desire to sin; this desire is continuous to the point of becoming a habit (present active indicative). It should not dominate us (Rom. 3:20) because we are not under the law.
b) During the time of the law, nothing inside a person changed, so all the law did was make them more aware of the sin that was in them. Every time they sought to obey the law, sin made it difficult, so the law became a burden.
c) After being transformed (Rom. 6:12), a believer should not make a decision to sin (aorist active subjunctive).

2. *Master*—The law must not have dominion over or exercise lordship over.
3. *Grace*—A free spontaneous, generous gift that totally depends on the giver's heart and does not require the receiver to repay. This grace frees us from the bondage of sin, because we can freely confess sin without paying its penalty.

B. Grace Frees Us to Be Obedient from the Heart (vv. 16–17; John 14:15)

1. *Know*—They should have a complete knowledge from experience because they live in a city that has a lot of slaves. They should be in a completed state of knowing (perfect active indicative).
2. *Present*—Continuously hand themselves over to sin to the point that it becomes a habit (present active indicative).
3. *Sin*—Willful acts of committing intentional sin in rebellion against the principles of God.
4. *Slaves*—To give themselves to the will of their desires so that they are swallowed up by sin. This is the direct object (nominative) of presenting oneself to sin.
5. *Obedience*—Willing submission to the service of a master. To willingly yield ourselves over to Christ.
6. *Righteousness*—Obedience to God's divine standard leads to a righteous life.
7. *From the heart*—To commit to obey God leads to a sincere wholehearted desire to do the will of God.
8. *Teaching to which you are committed*—Instruction or tutoring that delivers a person into the control of someone else, the Holy Spirit (Rom. 8:9–16).

C. Grace Delivers Us to Holiness (vv. 18–19)

1. *Free from sin*—Because of the process described in Romans 6:17, a believer is liberated from willfully and intentionally sinning against God. They are liberated from being controlled by the sin nature. This is a one-time act that a believer experiences (aorist passive participle).
2. *Slave or servant*—Being liberated from being under bondage of sin allows a believer to live in continuous obedience to God.
3. *Righteousness*—The desire to live in obedience to God leads to righteousness. Righteousness is living up to the divine standards of God because of the imputed righteousness that is now in us. This imputed righteousness allows our spirit to connect with the work of the Holy Spirit. Because of grace, they are no longer living under condemnation, so they are free to continually apply themselves to the transforming work of God (Rom. 8:1–17).
4. *Weakness*—Paul is speaking to this process knowing that the flesh has no strength to ward off sinful desires that can haunt a believer. The believer has to totally rely on the work of the Holy Spirit in their lives (Rom. 8:9–17).
5. *Flesh*—Covers the entire domain of our fallen nature; consistently in opposition to the Spirit of God. This is why someone in the flesh produces sin. The flesh highlights man's weakness (Rom. 7:14–25; Gal. 5:16–24).
6. *Members*—Agents of the body (there is a connection to the old nature); the eye (Matt. 6:22–23), the tongue (James 3:4–9), the mind (Eph. 4:17; James 3:13–17).
7. *Impurity*—The same focus and energy that was given to sin—especially in relationship to sexual sin—believers must become just as focused to present their bodies to righteousness.
8. *Sanctification*—The commitment to present members of one's body to righteousness establishes a life of holiness and consecration to God.

Author's Comments

Comments

A young boy frustrated his mother because he kept hanging around other boys she knew would influence him to do wrong. This mother loved her son and spent time teaching the Scriptures and taking him to church, but the boy, when given the opportunity, went looking for his friends. They had grown up together, from elementary to high school, and had played on the same sports teams. The more time he spent around them, the more he began doing what they did. He enjoyed these activities until he was deeply convicted by a sermon he heard. The boy went to his mother, confessed, and asked forgiveness, which he quickly received. He began becoming more involved in the things of God and grew stronger. God's grace is truly sufficient.

Presenting ourselves to God (Rom. 12:1) is a decision we must make until the desire to do the will of God becomes greater than the desire to sin. This war exists in all Christians (Gal. 5:16–19). It is the same war that Paul mentions he experienced in Romans 7:14–25. As a result, the desire to experience the inner power of the Holy Spirit must be the focus. This transformation to holiness is certain because of the all-sufficient grace of God.

This process is not achieved when a believer just goes to church for the sake of going to church. This transformation takes place when a believer commits to living a "spiritually minded" life (Rom. 8:5–8). This begins with a commitment to renew the mind (Rom. 12:2), meaning the believer always adjusts their minds to whatever God says about a particular issue (2 Pet. 1:3–4). With much prayer and submitting to the Spirit, they turn away from using common sense (Eph. 4:17–22). They learn what spiritual gift God provided, as they do the work of service (Eph. 4:12) in the church (1 Pet. 4:9–11). This process stimulates spiritual maturity (Eph. 4:13) leading to greater experiences of conviction as the Spirit establishes greater influence on their lives. This discipleship process and service is the sanctifying process that leads to righteousness and holiness. This is why the grace of God is empowering.

Application

The grace of God is a powerful process to righteousness. For example, because there is an out of bounds on most sports fields, athletes are forced to make decisions, while remaining in bounds, to win the game. They may make mistakes and get penalized, but they are allowed to stay in the game (for the most part). The more athletes apply themselves to the game and mature as players, the better they become. Christ leads us to maturity and blesses us to finish the course even though we sin along the way. He blesses us to confess our sin, with a true repentant heart, to experience His grace. Using this analogy, because of grace we are allowed to focus more on the perfecting of our faith than going to hell because of our sin. The process of perfecting our faith sanctifies us for righteous living.

> Therefore we also, since we are surrounded by so great a cloud of witnesses, let us lay aside every weight, and the sin which so easily ensnares us, and let us run with endurance the race that is set before us, looking unto Jesus, the author and finisher of our faith, who for the joy that was set before Him endured the cross, despising the shame, and has sat down at the right hand of the throne of God. (Heb. 12:1–2)

Illustrate It

Within the last fifty years, many more laws have been passed in every state across the union. Despite of all these laws, the numbers of brutal crimes have increased drastically. Most cities are in the process of hiring more police officers and have added cameras on many street corners. In some cities, police officers are now carrying machine guns, not pistols. This is because police officers are attacked more than at any time in American history. Neighbors are putting up more and more cameras. It seems like if we have more laws, more officers, and cameras, we should have less crimes.

There are not less crimes because the law does not change a person's heart. Laws expose people's hearts (Rom. 3:20). When Christ came into our lives, He made us into a new creation because righteousness was imputed through the Holy Spirit's presence. We are now empowered and can grow to walk under the guidance of the Spirit (Gal. 5:25). When this takes place, we need grace, not the law.

Paul wanted Jews to understand that the law only exposed a person's heart; it did not fix it. Christ's death allows us to work out our salvation in fear and trembling as we walk by faith, not by the law (Phil. 2:12).

The Proof of Discipleship

Matthew 28:19–20; John 8:31-32; 15:8–10

General Overview of the Passage

"Therefore go," because our Lord has so ordered; because He has promised to impart all the needed strength; because He is worthy of homage, faith, the obedience of all men; because all things are now under Christ's feet (Eph. 1:22–23), and He has all authority which was rendered to Him for heaven and earth. This is an order that must be obeyed. He ordered His leaders (the original disciples) to make disciples. People do not naturally desire discipleship. It is a desire God must create. This lifestyle is something that is modeled in one's day-to-day lifestyles. This process must be for all nations. Each disciple must make a public declaration that they now identify with Christ in baptism.

The disciples must continually and habitually seek to influence the understanding and shape the will of the hearer with their communication of biblical knowledge. The commandments must be taught in a way that would persuade them to continually keep, guard, and preserve all the disciples had taught them. Christ then promises to be with these disciples at all times.

Jesus spoke to those He knew would keep the faith and function with confidence based on His Word. If those who believe stood steadfast and persevered in His word, then their "followship"—learning and application of God's Word—will be revealed. "Whether John speaks of the word remaining in the believer or the believer remaining in the word, the meaning is essentially the same."[12]

Believers need to come to a full understanding and conform to the revealed will of God. It is this reality clearly before their eyes that will liberate them from the law, sin, and death. This freedom is only established by Christ (John 8:36) as we are sanctified by the truth (John 17:19).

---

[12] UBS Handbook series (United Bible Societies, copyright © 1961–1997).

Historical Background

Establishing Context

In Jesus' day, when disciples had completed their studies and training with their rabbi, they left and met up with their own group to repeat and discuss what they had just learned. The difference with Jesus' disciples is that the people they discipled were challenged to live like Christ.

> Many Jews outside Palestine sought converts among the "nations" (which can also be translated as "Gentiles" or "pagans"). But only a few converts ever studied under rabbis, so the idea of making Gentiles full disciples—followers of Jesus who would learn from and serve him—goes beyond this Jewish tradition. Isaiah predicted that Israel would be a witness to (or against) the nations in the end time (e.g., 42:6; 43:10; 44:8).[13]

Disciples of Jesus are those who demonstrate a serious commitment to learn from Christ, to keep His Word, and to walk in His ways. Jesus modeled this for His disciples. He now challenges them to do this throughout the world.

To be baptized publicly is to make a strong statement about an inner commitment to Christ. It is serious—spiritually and physically—because the Pharisees who crucified Jesus are still around working hard for Jesus to not even be a memory. It is a spiritual sign identifying that the Holy Spirit now lives in the life of the believer. From the time of baptism forward, whatever characteristics come out of the believer that reflect Christ is created by Christ and the believer is blessed. "Jewish literature only called God omnipresent; Jesus' claim that he would always be with them, coupled with his being named alongside the Father in baptism (Jewish people did not baptize in the names of people), constitutes a proclamation of his deity."[14]

What Does the Context Mean?

People need to be challenged to put aside their unbelief, trust Christ's power, and make discipleship a way of life. All that we are trying to achieve in our lives is lost when we attach ourselves to the world. We can attain these

---

[13] C. S. Keener, *The IVP Bible Background Commentary: New Testament* (Downers Grove, IL: InterVarsity Press, 1993), s.v. Matt. 28:19–20.

[14] Ibid.

things and more if we abide in Christ. Seeking Christ first brings blessings (Luke 12:31).

Sermon Subject and Title

Sermon Title: The Proof of Discipleship
Big Idea: A disciple is a person who is being liberated from the "old man" to the "new man" so that the "new creation" becomes a living reality each day.

SERMON OUTLINE (MATT. 28:19–20; JOHN 8:31–32; 15:8–10 NASB)

A. Christ's Desire Is for Us to Be His Disciples (Matt. 28:19–20; Acts 10:34–35)

1. *Go make*—The purpose of going is to create a desire within those who accept Christ as their Savior to come to know Him as their friend (nominative—this is the subject of the verb).
2. *Make*—It is to cause people to be disciples. Create an environment that would stimulate people to want to know Christ. Christ commands us to make a one-time decision to focus this way (aorist imperative active).
3. *Disciples*—Develop an environment that stimulates a willingness to be accountable to others (James 5:16) as well as a commitment to learn and apply Christian doctrine so that believers are daily followers of Christ.
4. *Observe*—To continue steadfast in their teachings, dwelling in the Word while building a fortress around it (Josh. 1:5–9; Ps. 119:11). This is a present active indicative, meaning this is a continuous action that becomes a habit.
5. *Teach them*—Must continually seek to influence their understanding and shape their will (present active indicative).

B. Discipleship Is a Life-Changing Experience (John 8:31–32; John 5:39–40)

1. *Jesus was saying*—What Jesus is saying in the passage is forever this way. It is in the imperfect active indicative—a past active that continues in the present and the future and is truly this way.
2. *Believe*—Jesus speaks to people who were committed to keep the faith and function with confidence trusting God for His Word. These believers were committed to Christ's teaching with no desire to change. This

is in the perfect active which is a set condition. This is a conviction that is essential to this process.

3. *Continue*—Despite setups and setbacks, these believers were committed to stand steadfast and persevere in His Word (2 Pet. 1:3–4).
4. *You are*—Anyone who continues in these things, Christ says, will continuously be His disciples (present active indicative).
5. *Truly*—By remaining steadfast in God's Word, these believers expose the true reality of their present profession of faith.
6. *Disciples*—Demonstrate a commitment to learning and applying Christ's doctrine, making them followers for life.
7. *Know the truth:*
   a) To abide in the Word of God is to know the truth (John 8:31; John 15:8–10; 17:17).
   b) A full understanding of the revealed will of God.
   c) The truth frees a believer from the law of sin and death (Rom. 3:20; 1 John 5:16).
8. *The truth makes you free* (it liberates):
   a) It frees us from fear (2 Tim. 1:7).
   b) It increases our faith (Rom. 10:17).
   c) It frees us from self (Luke 14:26).
   d) It frees us from worrying about others' opinions about us (1 Cor. 10:31).
   e) It frees us from sin (Rom. 6:15–19).
   f) It frees us from the power of the law (Rom. 3:20; Gal. 5:26).

C. A True Disciples Glorifies God (John 15:8)

1. *Bear much fruit*—A believer who commits to abide in God's Word continuously allows the inner working of the Holy Spirit. This visibly shapes the character of God into the character of the believer (Gal. 2:20—present active subjunctive).
2. *Prove*—Experience a state of being, demonstrated by conduct. This is when the state of discipleship has come into existence (1 John 3:7; Heb. 13:7).
3. *Disciples*—Committed to learning and applying Christ's doctrine, making them followers for life.
4. Paul, who experienced Christ in this way, says that he no longer lived (Gal. 2:20) and that he "can do all things through Christ who strengthens [him]" (Phil. 4:13). Paul was a high achiever as a result.

Author's Comments

Comments

It is easier to be a member than to be a disciple. It is easy for a person to come to church each Sunday, but at the same time enjoy their comfort zone so that any time anything is done to move them outside that zone they resist it. Could you imagine what it was like for Peter, James, John, or even Paul when Christ met them and their lives were turned upside down? If they were content to attend church with no passion to be disciples, the world would lack models that can be light in the midst of darkness. The purpose of their salvation would be lost because Christ came to provide us abundant life (John 10:10) and to become our friend (John 15:13–14). The purpose of the church is to present everyone complete in Christ (Eph. 4:12–13; Col. 1:28–29). Discipleship is a process that leads to a powerful life that blesses the believer and glorifies God.

If discipleship does not take place, churches will become ineffective social gatherings where everyone settles into "the usual." The New Testament church was being persecuted, scattered, forced to do church discipline, and instructed to go into the world. This led to the spread of the gospel to Judea, Samaria, and the outermost parts of the world. Today, we have thousands more churches but not the same impact. Our families, communities, and world are deteriorating. God wants high achievers for Christ.

How does a believer know when they have settled into a comfort zone? When trials produce bitterness and resentment, not change, a person has settled into a comfort zone. When after months or years of "following" Christ a believer is basically the same husband, wife, father, mother, or single, that person has settled into a comfort zone. When the fruit of the Spirit is more of a Sunday experience than a Monday-through-Friday lifestyle, a person has settled into a comfort zone. This kind of life does not provide them what God has designed them to experience when He made them into a new creation (2 Cor. 3:18).

Discipleship sets us free from the bondage of sin. This is because it stimulates the maturation of the Holy Spirit in the lives of believers. Instead of the believer walking in the flesh, the believer becomes so empowered by the Holy Spirit that they live Spirit led (Eph. 5:15–18). The Holy Spirit overcomes the flesh so that the believer lives free from the effect of sin (Rom. 8:9–17). This is the call of Christ to the church.

Application

The church is commanded to make disciples—it is not an option. To fill the pews is not enough. We must drive believers to become true followers of Christ who are committed to apply His Word to real-life situations every day. This leads to spiritual growth so that a believer no longer lives; it is Christ that lives (Gal. 2:20). This powerful experience of Christ every day (Eph. 3:14–19) empowers a believer to be a high achiever in whatever they seek to do (Josh. 1:5–9).

We can only do all things "through Christ who strengthens" us (Phil. 4:13). We need to abide in Him. It is this that allows us to bear fruit.

Illustrate It

Remember when Michael Jackson put on his sequined glove, red jacket, and white socks and did the slide? People went wild, cheering and imitating his every move. Some folks can sing his songs word for word with a voice and tone that mimics him exactly. These people never dressed, sang, or danced that way before, but upon listening to Michael, their world transformed overnight.

Christ can get us to talk like we have never talked before, to love like we have never loved before, and shape our character into one that reflects Him. When we fully surrender to Him, He will shape us into what He desires us to be.

It Is All in the Family

Romans 8:14–17

General Overview of the Passage

We find in this passage of Scripture Paul continuing the discussion that began in verses 5–11 concerning the flesh (the part of a person that is easily influenced by sin and sets itself in opposition to the Spirit, 7:18; Gal. 5:17). The flesh is like a sponge; it is quick to become absorbed with sin. A believer should not set their minds on the things of the flesh because they are not continually under its obligation to do its will.

The flesh leads to our destruction and it is hostile toward God because it is not willing to submit to the Word of God. Paul says this because he is seeking to convince the Jews and Gentiles that the Spirit of God is already here and they need to live dependent on His work. To stop living under the flesh, a person must die to themselves (Luke 14:26). The focus is not merely to try to kill the flesh; the focus is on what the Spirit is influencing us to do. When we focus on the powerful influence of the Spirit, we put to death the deeds of the body and we live in the newness of the life of God. Paul then says that all who choose to be continually led by the Spirit prove to have the character and likeness of God (sons—John 1:12; 15:13–15; Gal. 3:26; Eph. 3:14–15), and prove not to be slaves in bondage to the flesh, but adopted children (Gentiles saved by grace) who are continually led by a tender, loving Father (the mind is important and that is why it must be renewed). This causes us to constantly, spontaneously desire and cry out for God, "Abba! Father!" as we experience Him each day. God's Spirit continues to control our spirit, which causes us to share everything attached to God and Christ, even Christ's suffering. The person who continually allows the Spirit to influence their spirit will allow God and Christ to be seen in their excellence (exposes the divine excellent nature of God; Titus 3:4–8).

Historical Background

Establishing Context

"Sons of God," relates to people who God called His own. "The plural 'sons of God' is less often used of the people of Israel, but it occurs often enough to justify our thinking that this background has influenced Paul's use of the phrase here (see Deut. 14:1; Isa. 43:6)."[15] The beautiful thing that is very exciting is that God views us as His own children. He works with His children from the inside out using the Helper, who permanently resides in us (John 14:16), leading us to a full experience of Him (Eph. 3:16–19).

"As a legal act, Roman adoption (Rom. 8:15) had to be attested by witnesses; the Spirit is here the attesting witness that God adopts believers in Jesus as his own children."[16] This is similar to Israel leaving Egypt because Israel was and is God's adopted child.

"Abba! Father!" is a very intimate way of referring to God. We hear Christ speak this way on the cross. "On 'Abba' see comment on Mark 14:36; although only a few Roman Jews spoke Aramaic, Jesus' special address for his Father as 'Papa' had become a name for God in early Christian prayers (Gal. 4:6), perhaps by Jesus' design (Matt. 6:9)."[17]

What Does the Context Mean?

This passage teaches what we need to do to allow our lives to be influenced and controlled by the Spirit. We must die to the deeds of the flesh and allow the Spirit to influence our spirit. This is the very thing Christ said in Luke 14:26: "If anyone comes to Me and does not hate his father and mother, wife and children, brothers and sisters, yes, and his own life also, he cannot be My disciple." We are not under any obligation to obey the flesh's impulses, especially since we are not slaves but sons of God as a result of being adopted by Him to do His will. Because we are His adopted children, we do not have to fear. We need to nurture a relationship with Him that would lead us to spontaneously

---

[15] Arnold, *Zondervan Illustrated Bible Backgrounds Commentary, Volume 3: Romans to Philemon*, 47–48.

[16] Keener, *The IVP Bible Background Commentary: New Testament*, s.v. Rom. 8:14–17.

[17] Ibid., s.v. Rom. 8:15.

cry "Abba! Father!" When we are led by the Spirit, we function as sons of God, and therefore, as heirs of God and Christ.

Sermon Subject and Title

Sermon Title: It Is All in the Family
Big Idea: Being led by the Spirit causes our spirit to integrate with the Holy Spirit, transforming us to be like Christ. This moves us from being slaves to being His sons. As His sons, we share His inheritance, and if we endure the process, we also share His glory.

SERMON OUTLINE (ROM. 8:14–17 NASB)

A. Adopted, "Abba! Father!" (vv. 14–15)

1. *Adoption*—New family relation with all rights, privileges, and responsibilities; all the privileges including inheritance rights (Eph. 2:17–19; 3:14–15).
2. *Led by the Spirit*—Means to continuously carry gently.
   a) This is because we are saved Rom. 8:9, 14–17).
   b) As believers, we are putting to death the deeds of the body, the sin nature (Rom. 9–10, 13).
   c) *Spirit minded* (v. 5)—Not led by the flesh with all its desires, but committed to the Word of God (Rom. 6:12–19; Col. 3:1–3).
   d) We humbly submit to God's conviction (John 16:7–10).
   e) Praying in the Spirit (Rom. 8:26).
   f) Obedience to God (Heb. 5:14). Brings our spirit alive to righteousness (Rom. 8:10; 1 John 3:4–8).
   g) The Spirit testifies with our spirit (Rom. 8:16).
   h) It puts to death the misdeeds of the body (Rom. 6:16–18; 8:13).
   i) As a result of all the above, we are no longer afraid of God (Rom. 8:15; 2 Tim. 1:7).
3. *Sons*—Likeness to God's character (8:15; Gal. 3:26).
   a) No longer slaves (6:16–17).
   b) Live in power of the Word so we no longer live in fear of God (2 Tim. 1:7). Perfect love casts out fear (1 John 4:18).
   c) No fear, because we live by grace (Rom. 6:14).

4. *Cry*, to scream—The word *cry* is emphatic—the exuberance of the child's emotions. We continuously and habitually cry out to God emphatically with childlike faith (present active indicative).
5. *Abba* (Daddy or Papa) *Father*—(Gal. 4:6)—In this word, we find a child's tenderness, trust, and love. Expressive of an especially close relationship to God.

B. Children of God (v. 16)

1. *The Spirit and our spirit testify*—When we are being led by the Spirit, He connects with our spirit because we are committed to righteousness (Rom. 8:10). The Holy Spirit's impact on a person's life does not mean they no longer function outside of their personality traits ("testifies with our spirit").
2. *Children of God*—This stresses the dignity and character of the relationship. Our personality remains the same, but our character becomes that of Christ (Gal. 2:20; Col. 3:1–4).

C. Blessed of God (v. 17)

1. *Heirs*—All that God has is in our power; our inheritance divided by lot (John 1:12; Rom. 9:4; Gal. 3:29; 4:4–7).
2. *Fellow heirs*—Personal equality based on an equality of possession—our spirit, His Spirit.
3. *Endure hardship*—This does not eliminate suffering; it sometimes increases it (Ps. 34:19). Our willingness to suffer for His sake draws us closer to the Savior's heart (8:18; James 1:2–4; Rev. 3:21).
4. *Glory*—To receive great honor together with someone else—"to be honored together with, to be exalted together with." To share in the excellent nature of Christ (2 Pet. 1:2–4).

Author's Comments

Comments

There is no greater joy than being born into the family of God. There is hope for deliverance in troubled times; God sustains our strength and resolve; the peace of God protects our minds when we experience overwhelming circumstances; and knowing that God hears our prayers gives us comfort and hope for a better tomorrow. This should keep us seeking God daily.

Being born into a family is to experience everyone in the family and become an active part of all that the family does and is. This moves to us to obey, to serve, to accept discipline, and to be concerned about other family members. This process matures us to become a representative of all the family is. Don't just be born into the family of God; be a part of the family so that the Spirit of God (Eph. 3:14–19) is a daily experience, the love of Christ drives you to obedience, and the power of God shapes you to represent His image before the world (2 Cor. 3:18). Our lives should be all about the family.

Not many believers want to hear about the suffering part of this process. Sanctification can be difficult enough since it is a constant dying to ourselves (John 12:23–26). Most Olympic gold medalists experience some form of pain, no one winning the Super Bowl did not suffer, and most individuals in reaching the height of their career experience some form of suffering. In Philippians 3:7–10, Paul says:

> But what things were gain to me, these I have counted loss for Christ. Yet indeed I also count all things loss for the excellence of the knowledge of Christ Jesus my Lord, for whom I have suffered the loss of all things, and count them as rubbish, that I may gain Christ and be found in Him, not having my own righteousness, which is from the law, but that which is through faith in Christ, the righteousness which is from God by faith; that I may know Him and the power of His resurrection, and the fellowship of His sufferings, being conformed to His death.

It is this process that refines us (1 Pet. 1:3–11), blesses us to become overcomers (Rom. 8:37), and allows us to share Christ's glory: "To him who overcomes I will grant to sit with Me on My throne, as I also overcame and sat down with My Father on His throne" (Rev. 3:21). It is for this purpose we must "press toward the goal" (Phil. 3:12–16).

Application

Many people practice religion, but do we practice Christ? When we are convicted of sin, do we repent, or go through a list of excuses? When Christ illuminates His Word so that we finally understand it and the Spirit of God brings it back to our remembrance, do we allow it to dominate our lives? Are we using our spiritual gifts or talents when serving in church? How we answer these questions determines who leads us—the Spirit of God or our common sense. We must commit to experience God, and not just live for His blessings.

Illustrate It

The Seattle Seahawks were the 2014 defending Super Bowl champions, so everyone wanted to beat them. At the beginning of the season, they did not look good. Their record showed it. Their quarterback remained confident and kept working hard. A lot of commentators said a lot of negative things about the team, but it did not seem to rattle them. His goal is simple; he wants to win at least six Super Bowls, and to that end, he will keep working.

They practiced, practiced, and practiced, and the Seahawks made their run. They made it to the Super Bowl. The commentators' language changed and the team's skeptics came back around. The city became excited once again, because the players did not give up.

Our Super Bowl has already been won, and the Holy Spirit's presence within us is our victory. Practice, practice, practice the Word of God and watch how it works out. We become more used to the Spirit's influence than to the lure of the flesh, so that every day is a Super Bowl experience.

“Would You Be My Friend?”

John 15:12–17

General Overview of the Passage

In this passage of Scripture, Christ makes a rule that must be acted on. He is expecting us to consider the needs of other brethren and seek to help them in their time of need based on the example He has provided. For instance, He explains to us that there is no greater love than the one Christ showed when He demonstrated complete surrender to God’s command to die on the cross. Christ did not forsake what God ordered. It is because of God’s love that Christ sacrificed Himself so that He can call those who believe in His name and abide in His love. They are friends because they are willing to follow His commands in the same way. Read John 15:10: “If you keep My commandments, you will abide in My love, just as I have kept My Father’s commandments and abide in His love.”

When we function as His friends, He no longer refers to us as those who have to fight desires that go against His will (slaves) in order to remain loyal to Him. Rather, we are His friends, and we listen to Him and obey, which exposes us to Christ through the ministry of the Holy Spirit (John 14:16–27) and establish an intimate experience of Him. This intimacy (John 14:17), leads to answered prayer and the development of a character that is representative of a true friendship with God.

Historical Background

Establishing Context

A friend in those times meant loyalty that may have included death. These are people who shared their possessions to help each other survive daily. This is a person who protects the private information of another. “It describes that 'inner circle' around a king or emperor. (In John 3:29, it refers to the 'best man' at a wedding.)"[18]

Love for one another was not signified by mere feelings. The proof of love in John's time was demonstrated by acts of love. It seems like John is influenced by the times he lived in because "supreme duty of friendship may involve self-sacrifice for one's friend even to the point of death."[19]

In John's day, a disciple picked who he wanted to follow. It is portrayed in John's disciples trying to figure out if they should follow John or Christ. Jesus tells them that for Him it was the reverse, because He selected them.

What Does the Context Mean?

Jesus Christ knew He was on His way to Calvary and wanted His disciples to remain focused. He knew the trauma ahead. After His ascension, there would be even more tribulations for them to experience, so He wanted for them to remain "in His love." This means to abide in His Word, which leads to intimacy through the ministry of the Holy Spirit that matures their relationship from slaves to His friends. There is a greater benefit to being Christ's friend than being His slave. Christ will reveal everything to them based on God's instruction. An experience of God is one between a Father and son rather than a slave and his master. This leads to a better positioning for prayer requests to be heard. When Christ is our friend, we can boldly make our requests known to God.

Sermon Subject and Title

Sermon Title: "Would You Be My Friend?"
Big Idea: Christ's sacrificial love should stimulate a willing desire for believers to love Christ and to love one another as they faithfully obey His commands.

Sermon Outline (John 15:12–17)

A. The Love that Defines the Friendship (vv. 12–13)

1. *This is*—This is a present active verb, meaning what Christ is saying here will always be this way. This must become a habit in each believer's life.

---

[18] Keener, *The IVP Bible Background Commentary: New Testament*, s.v. John 15:12–13.
[19] Arnold, *Zondervan Illustrated Bible Backgrounds Commentary*, 2:145–46.

2. *My command*—This command is coming directly from Christ.
3. *Commands*—A specific principle that is a general rule of action. This is how we abide in His love (John 15:10).
4. *Love*—Obeying Christ's commandments leads to love for the brethren (John 15:12, 14, 17; 1 John 3:16–19). Christ obeyed God and died on the cross exposing God's love for us. This love is also in the present active because it is continuous and habitual.
5. *As I have loved you*—Christ's love for us is a decision He made once and for all. How we love is defined by how Christ loves us (Matt. 22:36–40).
6. *Lay down*—Continuously focus our day-to-day living toward doing the will of God, even if it means denying ourselves for our friend (1 John 3:16–18).
7. *Friends*—A display of true loyalty with a commitment to the same purposes.
8. We are Christ's friends because we choose to draw near to Him by listening to His Word. When we obey His commands, we become His disciples. As His disciples, we bear much fruit, which draws us even closer to Him.

B. The Nature of the Relationship (vv. 14–15)

1. *Call*—Expresses the inward thoughts and feelings of the one calling. Christ is calling us from His heart. This is a continuous action that is habitual (present active indicative).
2. *No longer slaves*—Not being driven to give up our will to a master (pruning; John 15:1). No longer a struggle, but a desire (Rom. 6:12, 15–19; 8:12–17). The desire to follow Christ comes from the inside out. This is an accusative, meaning he is discussing what He is no longer doing.
3. *Know*—A slave does not go to a complete settled state (perfect active) of having a full and complete knowledge, a divine understanding of the master's will.
4. *I call you friends*—Christ calling us His friends is the way this will always be. This is a perfect active indicative means it is a completed action or a set state or condition. A friend is someone who knows intimate details of the other person's life. They mutually share possessions and are loyal to each other.

5. *Heard*—To hear with understanding (the Holy Spirit; 1 Cor. 2:10–15), and a commitment to do His will. This is in the aorist tense, meaning what Christ heard from the Father He only needed to hear once.
6. *Father*—Intimate relationship with God; someone who cares and is the vinedresser (John 15:1).
7. *Know*—Christ reveals to His friends a complete knowledge and divine understanding of all that the Father has told Him to teach His disciples. Everything Christ is going to say to His disciples He said once and for all. This action is real because it took place in time and space (it is an indicative).

C. The Benefits of the Relationship (vv. 16–17)

1. *You did not choose Me*—"There is none who understands; there is none who seeks after God" (Rom. 3:11).
2. *Appointed you*—He called us for the purpose of bearing fruit. The character of Christ is the visible expression of the Holy Spirit working inwardly and invisibly in the believer (Phil. 2:12–14). This appointment is a decisive act (aorist).
3. *Remain*—No matter how difficult the obstacles we experience, we must be committed, endure, and remain steadfast. This friendship is not for a day. When we are friends with Christ, the ministry of the Holy Spirit producing fruit is continuous (present active verb).
4. *Ask*—As a friend of Christ, we do not need to beg.
5. *Name*—This means that God's answer would be based on His character, His reputation, and His purposes (John 15:7).
6. *Give*—Because we are His friends, God will put all of this in place for us.
7. *I command*—This is specific directive from God, and what He is saying must become a habit in our lives (present active verb).
8. *Love for one another*—We must direct this will toward how we have love one toward another.

Author's Comments

Comments

Would you prefer to be a slave to Christ or His friend? A friend experiences a closeness that a slave never gets. A slave gets orders; a friend shares with the desire of their friends. A friend always has the back of the other and will support the friend even to the point of death. Would you rather experience Christ as your friend or only as your Savior? This friend "sticks closer than a brother" (Prov. 18:24).

It is this relationship Christ sought when He confronted Peter after the resurrection in John 21:15–17. When Christ asks, "Simon, son of John, do you love Me more than these?" (in verses 16 and 17 "love" is "*philo* and *phileis*" respectively), He is speaking of a friendship love. Christ's greatest desire is to recreate what was lost in the Garden of Eden (Rom. 5:12–21; 2 Cor. 3:18).

Application

Our relationship with Christ should not be religious. God desires for His relationship with us to be a friendship. God's desire moves us from membership to discipleship, from being saved to working out our salvation with fear and trembling (Phil. 2:12).

Our children can be born into our family, but that does not mean they will live by the principles we seek to instill in their lives. This is a process that requires time, unconditional love, an exemplary life before them, and accountability. As the children see this lifestyle and continually try to model it, they become like their parents and mature. When they mature, the parents no longer need to correct them, so they develop a deep friendship.

Christ requires our time in worship, service, and quiet time before Him. He expects leaders in His church to be examples for His people (Heb. 13:7) and willing to humble themselves and submit to the conviction of the Holy Spirit or the accountability of other brothers or sisters in Christ (James 5:16). His focus of being a brand-new creation is for us to become like Christ, having a sincere friendship with God and with other believers (Gal. 2:20).

Illustrate It

During the furious attacks of Hitler on England in World War II, the English did their best to defend themselves. No matter how hard they tried, Hitler did serious damage in the middle of the night on many factories and homes. England's Prime Minister, Sir Winston Churchill, sought help from an ally, their sister country the United States of America. America responded and was able, working with England's Air Force, to protect England from being destroyed.

America proved to be a true friend because her men and women of the military were willing to combat and, if needed, lay down their lives for a friend.

Sheep and Goats

Matthew 25:31–46

General Overview of the Passage

Christ's return will expose His divine nature because He will come in all His glory. He will sit on a throne with external splendor, brilliance, and radiance. He will assemble all nations as one group before Himself. Then Christ will move the sheep (valuable animals) to His right and the goats (rebellious animals of no value) to the left. "Sheep probably symbolize those who trust in—that is, 'follow'—the Savior in obedience (John 10:3–4, 27); goats, those who are belligerent, unruly, and destructive (Ezek. 34:17–19; Dan. 8:5, 7, 21)."[20] Authority was given to Christ to execute judgment because He is the Son of Man who died for our sins (Phil. 2:9–11).

Matthew continues to portray Christ as the king who extends the throne of David. He says that Christ the King, upon His return, brings close to Himself those who are spoken well of by His Father. These blessed sheep will receive a gift from God that has tremendous value. It is all that God has reserved for them that He prepared before earth was ever established. The preparation is set and continues from the past to the present. In Matthew 25:35–36, Christ describes to the sheep on His right that whether He was hungry, thirsty, a stranger, naked, or in prison they responded in love, with the heart of someone nursing the sick.

The sheep on the King's right are now called righteous because they functioned in conformity to the justice of God and lived by His standards. A righteous person is justified by faith, and they show their faith by their works. They faithfully performed the deeds mentioned that were in conformity to the laws of God, which is pleasing to the King. The sheep were surprised to learn whom they served especially since Christ Himself (Matt. 25:37–39) stresses the unselfishness of their motives. The sheep did not know that they were directly serving

---

[20] Marvin Vincent, *Vincent's Word Studies in the New Testament* (Grand Rapids, MI: Wm. B. Eerdmans Publishing Co., 1965; electronic ed. Biblesoft, 1997, 2003).

Christ when they were serving the poor and marginalized, which demonstrates how committed they were to be obedient to His calling on their lives. They were totally focused.

On the other hand, Christ literally told the goats to get away from Him because they were cursed. Christ placed them in eternal judgment, but the righteous receive eternal life.

Historical Background

Establishing Context

The judgment being made in this passage is not the Great White Throne Judgment. These are the nations gathered before Him, meaning Gentiles and Jews where Christ judges each person. It is vividly clear that Jesus has absolute authority. The right side is normally viewed as the good side (Christ at the right hand of God). The left side normally represents the wicked.

> This section explains to us how Jesus Christ will judge the Gentile nations. The word *nations* in Matthew 25:32 means "Gentiles," and it is in the neuter gender in the Greek. This means that the nations will be gathered before Jesus Christ, but He will judge them as *individuals.*[21]

The judgment is characterized with sheep and goats. They have some bodily similarities, but they have two different natures. Sheep are very particular about what they eat; goats eat just about anything. Sheep like being out in the cool of the night; goats like shelter. This is why Palestinian shepherds separated the sheep from the goats at night. Sheep drink from still waters; goats drink any water at all. Jews viewed sheep as good and goats as trouble. "Sheep" is a consistent image of God's people, whether the reference is specifically to Israel or to Jesus' disciples. Goats do not occur often in the New Testament, but in the Old Testament seventy percent of the references concern their use as animals for sacrifice, such as the goat offered for sin sacrifice and the scapegoat, where in a symbolic way sin was removed from the community and sent to the region of desert or death (Lev. 16:8–10, 26).[22]

---

[21] Keener, *The IVP Bible Background Commentary: New Testament*, s.v. Matt. 25:31.

[22] Arnold, *Zondervan Illustrated Bible Backgrounds Commentary: Matthew, Mark, Luke*, 1:157.

Some people believe that the sheep are those believers who have been imprisoned for serving God or have gone through tremendous hardships for serving the Lord, while the goats are those who have been oppressing the Jews. However, "There does not appear to be any significant reason why the goat was selected to contrast with the sheep, except for the symbolism that will be attached to both in a surprising manner."[23]

What Does the Context Mean?

God views all saved believers as His sheep. This passage explains how He would respond to us for faithful service. This passage also portrays Jesus as judge on His glorious throne extending blessings of God and eternal life to His sheep that are righteous. He also provides eternal punishment for the goats on His left because they proved to be worthless.

The heart of those who are righteous is highlighted by the fact that they did not even know when they were serving Christ in this manner. They did not do it for credit; they did so out of their hearts. These righteous people are given eternal life.

Sermon Subject and Title

Sermon Title: Sheep and Goats
Big Idea: Faithfulness or lack of faithfulness is always under God's watchful eyes, and it determines our eternal rewards.

Sermon Outline (Matt. 25:31–46 nasb)

A. From Savior to Judge (vv. 31–33)

1. *Glory; glorious*—Jesus is seen in His divine glorious nature, angels around Him; He is exposed with great light, splendor, and radiance. His glorious return is not continuous; it is in a "blink of an eye" and no more (aorist subjunctive).
2. *Nations*—Every nationality.
3. *Gathering*—This gathering is in the future, but no one gets to choose whether they will be there on not.
4. *He will put*—Christ is in complete control of all that is taking place.

---

[23] Ibid.

5. *Sheep*—Symbolize those who trust in Christ, follow Him, and are obedient (John 10:3–5, 27).
6. *Goats*—Those who are belligerent, unruly, and destructive (Ezek. 34:17–19; Dan. 8:5, 7, 21).
7. *Right*—A place where Christ is seated (Rev. 3:21–22). To be at the King's right means to hear from His lips.

B. Inherit the Blessing (v. 34)

1. *Son of man* (Matt. 25:31), *King* (v. 34)—The throne of David is reestablished (not the Great White Throne Judgment). This is the only time in Matthew when Christ is called King.
2. "Sheep on His right, come." They are welcome because they have a fellowship with Christ even before this meeting. He is their Savior, the Judge and King. Christ commands His sheep, once and for all, to do what He says (aorist imperative active).
3. *Who are blessed*—To be well spoken of; to bring someone to a desired relationship with God. It has tremendous value; it is the kingdom of God (Matt. 13:43). This blessing, once enacted, never changes. It is a completed action that is in a set condition (perfect). It is eternal. It is in the passive voice, meaning it is something we receive.
4. *Father*—The author of everything. A tenderness and care is implied. Shows a special relationship. He is the author of their faith.
5. *Inherit*—To receive a considerably valued gift that has been earned, as one's own, and to possess it.
6. *Inherit*—Christ commands them to take once for all time.
7. *Prepared for you*—This blessing was already set in place (perfect tense) and takes no more actions to experience. The sheep are only there to accept it (passive voice).

C. The Attitude that Leads to Blessings (vv. 35–40)

1. *I was*—Repeats over six times. The pain of those who hurt is always before God and He is excited to see His sheep serve their needs.
2. *You gave*—All these actions are interestingly in the aorist tense. It is not a continuous effort. It is based on the fact that the sheep saw a need and responded.
3. *I was*—When Christ uses the phrase "I was," it is in the imperfect active. The desire to help those in need is endless but the act of service is a one-time act.

4. *Visited*—They examined everything closely and were willing to nurse the sick.
5. Sheep's character shows compassion, service, and unselfishness; they provided physical help (clothing, medicine, food, and drink), social help (shelter and fellowships for strangers), and emotional help.
6. *Righteous*—Notice He did not say the sheep on the right; He said the righteous on the right. This means those who faithfully performed the deeds mentioned. They did so in conformity to the laws of God, which pleased the King. A righteous person is justified by faith and they show their faith by their works (Hab. 2:4; James 2:14–26).
7. Astonishment is expressed by the righteous. Service is spontaneous, grateful, and humbly rendered, completely forgotten.
8. *Hunger, thirst, and sickness*—Even though the service was provided, the righteous knew that these individuals still needed help.
9. *Brothers*—Christ identified with those who are a part of the Christian community because they are in fellowship with Him.
10. *I say to you*—What Christ is verbalizing to them is continuously this way.

D. The Attitude that Leads to Condemnation (vv. 41–45)

1. *Depart from Me* (Matt. 25:41), *Go away* (Matt. 25:46)—Christ commands them to get out of His presence.
2. *You gave me nothing*—The goats' decision not to give was a one-time act demonstrating they have no desire to ever do this.
3. *Accursed*—"You that are under God's curse. Get out of My sight! God will call down evil on you." Once everyone stands before God, their position is permanent. This is a perfect active.
4. *Eternal fire; eternal punishment* (Matt. 25:46)—prepared for the devil and his angels.

E. The Eternal Rewards (v. 46)

1. *Righteous*—These are those who lived by faith (Hab. 2:4).
2. *Eternal life*—The life that is God's and hence not affected by limitations of time.

Author's Comments

Comments

This passage of Scripture highlights how meticulous Christ is about how, whom, and when we serve His purposes. When have we seen someone in need, but busy schedules led us to ignore them? What excuses are we quick to assert when challenged in this manner? Faith does not allow excuses. Faith only requires obedience, which leads to rewards. These believers' love for Christ led them to serve Him. What does our love for Christ move us to do?

We may say we have faith, but James says that faith without works is dead (James 2:14–26). As we know, faith is not a notion, an impulse, or something we feel strong about. Faith is concrete, not subjective, because it is directed by the Word of God (Rom. 10:17). So when someone is in need, faith directs it: "By this we know love, because He laid down His life for us. And we also ought to lay down our lives for the brethren. But whoever has this world's goods, and sees his brother in need, and shuts up his heart from him, how does the love of God abide in him?" (1 John 3:16–17). "Now we exhort you, brethren, warn those who are unruly, comfort the fainthearted, uphold the weak, be patient with all. See that no one renders evil for evil to anyone, but always pursue what is good both for yourselves and for all" (1 Thess. 5:14–15). It is for these and many more reasons these individuals are surprised they are being blessed by Christ. These individuals did as the Old Testament directed them so that they, at the point of their death, can go into Abraham's bosom (Exod. 22:25; Lev. 19:15). They obeyed God to live a righteous life before Him and have their sins forgiven. So now that Christ not only welcomes them into His presence, but blesses them, they are surprised.

These individuals' willingness to serve the Lord and submit to His Word, no matter the sacrifices, demonstrates they are true followers of God. This is why serving God is a choice that comes from a heart that is committed to God. Our commitment to God leads to schedule changes, time management adjustments, and clear focus for life (Eph. 5:15–18).

Application

Serving our Lord is expected of all believers. We are also given spiritual gifts in order to serve in the power of the Holy Spirit. Christ states in James that to neglect those in need is to not have faith (James 2:14–17). When we live and serve, we must remember God is holding us accountable. Only faith is rewarded (Heb. 11:6). The church of Laodicea was criticized for their lack of service (Rev. 3:14–22). Serving God is not an option. Even though being saved gets us into heaven, serving Him allows us to receive the rewards Christ has set aside for us, so that we live in all He has prepared for us.

Illustrate It

ESPN once aired a feature on Jerry Rice, one of the greatest receivers in all of football. His work ethic was virtually unmatched. He worked out before practice, after practice, and just about every day in the off-season. A story circulated for years told of how a teammate of Jerry came to clean out his locker a week after they had won the Super Bowl and saw Jerry Rice on the practice field running wide receiver routes. He was not showboating to get into the Hall of Fame or to keep his position on the team. He simply loved the game.

Now contrast this with Allen Iverson of the NBA team, the Philadelphia 76ers. He missed a lot of practices and was often late to scrimmage games. Although he had great skills on the court, he was routinely criticized for his lack of discipline.

Jerry Rice had a long NFL career and went on to the Hall of Fame. Iverson went to China to play, and it was told on the news that after all the money he made he was now struggling to manage his financial responsibilities.

When, as sheep, we love the Lord, we will serve Him faithfully, consistently giving Him our best. Being a sheep on the right is first a result of knowing the Shepherd's voice and loving who He is. It is being faithful to serve Him and to work for His glory just because we love Him and because He loves us. Solomon said in Ecclesiastes 11:9:

> Rejoice, O young man, in your youth, and let your heart cheer you in the days of your youth; walk in the ways of your heart, and in the sight of your eyes; but know that for all these God will bring you into judgment.

No Substitute for the Shepherd

Psalm 23

General Overview of the Passage

David's master is the Lord because He has full authority over him; He is the one who maintains His covenant over the people of Israel and is David's Shepherd. He is a tender, loving, caring leader who provides nourishment for David. Because God is David's Lord and Shepherd, David never lacks; God's grace sufficiently meets his every need.

> David who sometimes views Christ as His rock and shield now presents Christ as his guide, physician and protector. Jesus identified Himself as that expected "Good Shepherd" (John 10:14). He is also called the "Great Shepherd" (Heb. 13:20) and "the Chief Shepherd" (1 Pet. 5:4). Because the Lord was David's Shepherd, his needs were met.[24]

When David says that God "makes me lie down," what he means is that God makes him rest from exertion, with a sense of security. In His abundant care, God faithfully provides for His people. "'Pastures of tender grass,' are mentioned, not in respect to food, but as places of cool and refreshing rest."[25] Since sheep are afraid of fast-flowing streams, still waters are much more restful. God's provision of still waters has a soothing effect and calms the sheep.

To lead sheep represents a shepherd's loving concern, similar to leading a helpless person by the hand. This represents spiritual refreshment and, therefore, causes David to lack nothing.

---

[24] Robert Jamieson, A. R. Fausset, and David Brown, *A Commentary, Critical and Explanatory, on the Old and New Testaments* (Oak Harbor, WA: Logos Research Systems, Inc., 1997), s.v. Ps. 23:3.

[25] Ibid., s.v. Ps. 23:2.

God revives and refreshes my spirit and tenderly leads me along the right path (attached to God's will; well-worn path), which offers safety and well-being (this causes David to be secure and prosperous). This is a path that is the unswerving adherence to the standards of God. Paths mean a way that are "right with him," making sense to him.

Walking through the "valley of the shadow of death" was intimidating for sheep. David may have, at times, felt like he was going through the "valley of the shadow of death." He may have considered that this is the way sheep feel when they walk through this valley and a shadow comes over them making the sheep think it is night time. Nights are often scary for sheep because they have no defense mechanisms to fight off hungry predators. David explains that a person has to make a choice not to fear. This is where the rod that directs the sheep when and where to go comes in to play, as well as the staff that protects them. The rod and staff reassures the sheep and reinforces confidence within them as they go through the valley.

In the midst of all that can be troubling or intimidating to David, he says that God anoints his head with oil. This is olive oil that was provided to refresh guests who may have come from a long journey.

Because of all the Good Shepherd does, David is convinced that God's kindness, mercy, favor, and God's loving generosity will pursue him all the days of his life. As a result, he will have lengthy stays in the temple of his master and it will last forever. The Lord, being his Shepherd who faithfully cares for David, will lead David so he lacks nothing, especially in the temple of God.

Historical Background

Establishing Context

Sheep depend on their shepherds for everything. They can go without water for long periods of time, but when they find water, they drink a lot of it. They cannot run fast and are defenseless. They depend on the shepherd to protect them. David understands this and says to the reader that there are a lot of things the Shepherd is doing for the sheep. Because God is "the Good Shepherd," David knows that he would not go lacking for anything, especially since the Master knows that the sheep is completely dependent upon Him. "In contrast to goats, which are quite independent, sheep depend on the shepherd to find pasture and water for them. Shepherds also provide shelter, medication and aid in birthing. In summary, they are virtually helpless without the shepherd."[26]

The rod and the staff served different purposes. "The rod was a club worn at the belt, while the staff was a walking implement that doubled as a weapon in time of need (1 Sam. 17:35) and guided and controlled the sheep."[27]

The valley of the shadow of death was a burial site for enemy soldiers that were killed (Ezek. 39:11, 15). It was also a place where they burned trash and disobediently performed child sacrifices to worship Molech. When a shadow came over it, darkness covered the valley, even though it was daytime. Sheep were afraid of the dark because of predators. It was surrounded with dense forest, so the sheep did not know what would come after them.

David seems to indicate that the house of the Lord is saying that this is the temple, but David goes on to say "forever." To dwell in the house of the Lord means that David was talking about the dwelling places for the priest and that he would occupy those places forever.

"'Goodness' throughout one's lifetime (23:6a) means continuous enjoyment of worship in the temple, a longing expressed in Mesopotamian hymns and prayers as well (see comments on 27:4). In ancient Sumer, worshipers dedicated statues to stand in the temple, symbolizing the individual's continuous presence before their god."[28]

What Does the Context Mean?

It is the almighty Lord of Hosts who serves as David's shepherd. As a result, David does not want for anything. David is able to rest in His provision of blessings and quiets his soul in waters that are still. He revives his spirit and focuses David back to things of the Spirit that would guide him into righteousness for the sake of God's character. This spiritual revival keeps David from fear that can overwhelm him because of his surroundings. God's protection and guidance becomes David's comfort in the midst of evil. God also provides for

---

[26] V. H. Matthews, M. W. Chavalas, and J. H. Walton, *The IVP Bible Background Commentary: Old Testament* (Downers Grove, IL: InterVarsity Press. 2000), electronic ed., s.v. Ps. 23:2.

[27] Ibid.

[28] J. H. Walton, *The Minor Prophets, Job, Psalms, Proverbs, Ecclesiastes, Song of Songs*, vol. 5 of the Zondervan Illustrated Bible Backgrounds Commentary series (Grand Rapids, MI: Zondervan. 2009), 5:341.

David even when people are seeking to harm him and treats him as an honored guest, never needing anything, because God keeps pouring into his cup. All of this demonstrates that God's goodness and mercy is pursuing David all the days of his life, and as a result, David worships God forever. Allow God to be your shepherd.

Sermon Subject and Title

Sermon Title: No Substitute for the Shepherd
Big Idea: Allowing the Lord to shepherd us daily leads to a continuous experience of His "goodness and lovingkindness" following us, which results in our lack of want. Our needs are fulfilled. This intimate relationship with God is a continual worship that extends into heaven.

Sermon Outline (Ps. 23 NASB)

A. He Is My Shepherd (vv. 1–2)

1. *Lord and my Shepherd*—His master who has full authority over his life, a tender, loving, caring leader who has been his rock, his shield, anointed him king, protected him against Saul, and established him king.
2. *Want*—David never goes lacking because God's grace is sufficient to meet the needs of His people.
3. *Makes me lie down*—Because He is Lord and Shepherd, He makes him rest from exertion with abundant care.
4. *Lead*—Leading someone by hand who is helpless and needs to be guided in the right direction.
5. *Quiet*—Sheep were afraid of fast-flowing streams. Smooth waters calmed the sheep.
6. Sheep all had a need to feel safe, because in the midst of the pastures were threatening wild beasts making them feel helpless.

B. He Is My Healer (v. 3)

1. *Restores*—Revives and refreshes his spirit. Brings David's spirit back to God's original intent.
2. *Guides*—Tenderly leads him along the right path; attached to God's will (a well-worn path); this offers safety and well-being, causing David to be secure and prosperous.

3. *Path of righteousness*—God leads David to unswervingly adhere to His standards by convicting him when he sins (2 Sam. 12), guiding him into the right path.
4. *Name's sake*—In accordance with God's revealed character.

C. He Is My Protector (v. 4)

1. *Walk through the valley of the shadow of death*—Ravines overhung by high, steep cliffs filled with dense forest; they inspired dread to the timid, and caused someone to be prey to wild beasts.
2. *Not fear*—After he evaluates everything intelligently, he made a choice not to fear, but to trust the good Shepherd.
3. *God is with me*—God remains with David, no matter what trouble he experiences.
4. *Rod*—Authority rules. He protects (used for counting, and protecting sheep—drive away wild animals).
5. *Staff*—Provides support while they walk and steers them when needed. This fills David with confidence despite the danger that surrounds him.
6. *Comfort*—David, because of God's care, can exhale deeply.

D. He Is My Provider (v. 5)

1. *Prepare*—God arranges and sets in order provision.
2. *Before, presence*—In David's face; in front of him God provides David reassurance.
3. *Anointed*—This is to rub a guest's head with olive oil (social custom for welcomed guest) as he welcomed his guests. Despite the position of his enemies, God organized the table and then treated David as a special honored guest.
4. *Cup overflows*—Never-ending flow of drink (this is good for someone being restored). There is more than enough.

E. He Is My Companion (v. 6)

1. *Goodness*—God's kindness, mercy, practical or economic benefits. This includes his favor, loyalty, and benevolence.
2. *Lovingkindness*—This is God's steadfast, loving generosity.
3. *Follow*—Pursues or hunts him down.
4. *Life*—All the days when he has health, prosperity, and vitality because of God's faithfulness as his Shepherd.
5. *Dwell in the house of the LORD forever*—The Lord's faithful care of David (who had a lot of trouble in his life) leads David to lengthy stays in the temple of God.

Notice David starts this psalm with LORD and ends with LORD. Despite God being his shepherd He is always his Lord.

Author's Comments

Comments

I know my country works hard to protect me, and the more I learn all that it takes, the more appreciative I am to be a citizen of America. The Lord is my Shepherd, and the more I learn about Him, the more appreciative I am. He shows me His love with each passing day.

Could you imagine a little shepherd boy out in the field, sometimes for days and full nights, caring for his father's sheep? He loved them so much that he would fight off a lion and a bear. It is his love for his sheep that reminds him of God's powerful love for him.

In the Old Testament God seeks to train the nation of Israel to think this way as He guides them through the wilderness. In Deuteronomy 8:3–4 God says:

> "So He humbled you, allowed you to hunger, and fed you with manna which you did not know nor did your fathers know, that He might make you know that man shall not live by bread alone; but man lives by every word that proceeds from the mouth of the LORD. Your garments did not wear out on you, nor did your foot swell these forty years."

The same idea is in the New Testament. Christ conveys this same concept of God's commitment to faithfully shepherding us. He says in Luke 12:22–30 that we must not worry about what we need to eat or what we need to drink or the clothes we need to wear. Christ teaches that to live this way is to live like a non-saved person (Luke 12:30).

Paul, with similar life experiences to David, no longer viewed his life as lacking anything, although most of us would say he needed everything from a physical standpoint. Similarly, God had to empty Moses of himself for forty years in the wilderness, redesigning him as someone who would so trust God that he would put a stick over the Red Sea believing God to make the difference.

God became so endeared to these men, and many like them in the Scriptures, that their full surrendered lives demonstrate how God shepherds us into a place of no lack at all. This experience always drives sincere worship and devotion to God.

Application

When we go to sleep at night, do we believe that God is our Shepherd? When we lose a job, do we believe that the Lord is our Shepherd? When our children run out the door to catch the school bus, do we believe that the Lord is our Shepherd? When we lay down on the surgeon's table, do we believe that God is our Shepherd? When we mourn the death of our parents, do we believe the Lord is our Shepherd? When we believe in the nature of Christ, it reminds us of who we are to Him and it should lead us to trust Him each and every moment of the day.

Illustrate It

A blind man and his dog developed a powerful relationship. The more the blind man was around the dog, the more he learned to depend on and trust the dog. The dog was trained to be in place for the blind man and do whatever he needed. The dog never turned on the blind man and always protected him. The dog never led the blind man into any kind of danger. When the dog sensed danger and communicated with the blind man, the blind man trusted him and followed him wherever he led. The dog was light to the blind man's darkness.

The Lord is our shepherd and we need to trust Him, because without Him we walk in darkness. Jesus is the light . . . not a light but *the* light.

Sermon Series 5

Back to the Basics: Marriage and Parenting

God's Blueprint for the Family

Genesis 1:26–28

General Overview of the Passage

After making everything, on the sixth day God created man (Col. 1:15–17). Mankind is to be the image of God. Mankind must reflect God's ability for knowledge, righteousness, love, holiness, and dominion over all creatures. This same process is extended into the New Testament where believers are expected by the power of the Holy Spirit to be "conformed to the image" of Christ (Rom. 8:29), and as Paul modeled for us (Gal. 2:20), we must live in His likeness.

Not only is mankind made in God's image; he is also made in God's pattern, matching the specifications of the Creator. "Let us make man *as* Our image" (the Hebrew preposition in this phrase can be translated *as*). "In ancient times an emperor might command statues of himself to be placed in remote parts of his empire. These symbols would declare that these areas were under his power and reign. So God placed humankind as living symbols of Himself on earth to represent His reign."[1] This imagery helps us to understand what God meant when He stated that man would have dominion over the earth.

God brought from nothing the forming and establishing of mankind to be the copy of His essential nature. It is in this image God set mankind in place. God created man with the capacities that image those God has. For example, God can multiply anything, and He gave man the opportunity to multiply and enjoy intimacy.

For man to be made in God's image means that he has a free will, mirrors God's characteristics, and has the capacity to love like God. Likeness means that man's substance has a representation of the characteristics of God. Man has eyes, God sees; man has a heart, God loves; man has a mind, God thinks; man

[1] Earl D. Radmacher, Ronald Barclay Allen, and H. Wayne House, *Nelson's New Illustrated Bible Commentary* (Nashville, TN: Thomas Nelson Publishers, 1999), s.v. Gen. 1:26.

has hands, God holds all things together. "The two words used in the text differ in nuance, with 'image' referring to the something that contains the 'essence' of something else, while 'likeness' is more connected to 'substance,' expressing a resemblance at some level."[2] The making of mankind is God's decision. He structured mankind with a purpose in mind and designed mankind with the ability and the capacity to fulfill His purposes.

Historical Background

Establishing Context

"This is the high point of the text, that toward which the passage drives from the beginning. In the viewpoint of Scripture, there is nothing grander in all of God's creation than mankind, whom He has made in His image to reflect His glory."[3]

"The Hebrew name for God in Genesis 1 is *Elohim*—the name of God that links Him with creation. The basic root of the name is *El* which means 'mighty, strong, prominent.'"[4] Colossians 1:15 states that, "all things were created through Him and for Him." Man, then, being the image of God, is given the capacity, with God's help, to accomplish the task God places before him and to be like Christ (Gal. 2:20). "It is clear that man, as God made him, was distinctly different from the animals already created. He stood on a much higher plateau, for God created him to be immortal, and made him a special image of His own eternity."[5]

What Does the Context Mean?

Marriage is God's idea. Man and woman are designed for God's purposes (Acts 17:28; Rev. 4:11). The nature of God was placed in mankind and is necessary for marriage to be at its best. In the New Testament, the image and likeness is attained through Christ (2 Cor. 3:18), and the marriage is stated

---

[2] J. H. Walton, *Genesis, Exodus, Leviticus, Numbers, Deuteronomy,* vol. 1 of the Zondervan Illustrated Bible Backgrounds Commentary series (Grand Rapids, MI: Zondervan, 2009), 21.

[3] Radmacher, Allen, and House, *Nelson's New Illustrated Bible Commentary*, 6.

[4] Walton, *Genesis, Exodus, Leviticus, Numbers, Deuteronomy,* 20.

[5] Charles Pfeiffer, *The Wycliffe Bible Commentary: Old Testament* (Chicago, IL: Moody Press, 1962, 2009), s.v. Gen. 1:26.

by the apostle Paul to represent Christ and the church (Eph. 5:32). It is this process that channels God's blessings as mankind follows God's instructions (Mal. 2:13–16). The original design of man to experience God's eternal nature is essential for a productive and successful marriage.

Sermon Subject and Title

Sermon Title: God's Blueprint for the Family
Big Idea: The spiritual nature of a married couple determines the strength and the effectiveness of the family.

Sermon Outline (Gen. 1:26–28 nasb)

A. **God's Blueprint (vv. 26–27)**
  1. *God said*—This is God's idea; God spoke specifically to provide direction. What God said in the passage is true.
  2. The making of marriage is "God's thing."
  3. *Make man*—Man is formed based on God's structure for mankind. This structure is designed to remain the same until eternity.
  4. *Image:*
     a) Man is designed to share in the nature of God (2 Cor. 3:18; Gal. 2:20). "For whom He foreknew, He also predestined to be conformed to the image of His Son, that He might be the firstborn among many brethren" (Rom. 8:29).
     b) Man is given the ability or capacity for knowledge, righteousness, and love, and will live forever, whether in heaven or hell.
     c) The spiritual development of couples is essential to the sustained growth of a good marriage.
        - The fruit of the Spirit is everything you want in a marriage (Gal. 5:22).
        - Man represents Christ's headship (1 Cor. 11:3) and love in a marriage (Eph. 5:25).
        - Marriage represents the relationship of Christ to the church (Eph. 5:32).
        - Any husband who has the Spirit of God will not mistreat his wife (Mal. 2:15).

- If a man mistreats his wife, his prayers will not be answered (1 Pet. 3:7).
- A wife is told to model spirituality rather than just other adornments (1 Pet. 3:1–6).
- A woman is preserved in the bearing of children (1 Tim. 2:15).

5. *Likeness*—Synonymous to "image." Mankind represents the exact specifications outlined by God.
6. *Created*—Mankind must be sustained by God in order to maintain his existence (John 15:5; Heb. 1:3).
   a) A man who builds his house independent of God builds it in vain (Ps. 127).
   b) A man who fears God is blessed; his marriage and children are blessed, and he is given long life (Ps. 128).
7. *Created*—God's creative work is set and can never be changed.
8. *Male and female:*
   a) The closeness of the Trinity is duplicated.
   b) The ability to multiply is representative of the Trinity's creation of all things.
   c) Intimacy highlights a covenant relationship between husband and wife (1 Cor. 6:16; Heb. 13:4). Anything different is dealt with severely by God (1 Cor. 6:18).

B. The Family God Blesses (v. 28)

1. *Blessed*—When man commits to God's plan, God provides man goodwill leading to prosperity and happiness. God's blessing upon this home is perpetual (imperfect active).
   a) A person's family is blessed because they commit to God's purposes (Ps. 128; Prov. 24:3–5).
   b) God blesses his house and his descendants (Gen. 17:16; Ps. 112:1–3).
   c) *Subdue*—Man will be provided the ability to rule with authority everything God planned. God gave men the ability to be a manager, and challenges men to provide for their homes (1 Tim. 3:4), as the wife preserves what they have put together as his helper (1 Tim. 5:14).
2. God blesses this kind of family because they are executing His plans, modeling His structure, revealing His image and likeness while building His church.

Author's Comments

Comments

Any individual can purchase a new car that has no defects and still cannot drive it without keys. They can get the keys, but if they disconnect the battery cables, the car still would not work. They can connect the cables and put the keys in the ignition of this new car, but without gas it still does not work. After picking up a new car from the dealership, the person must have the keys, a good battery, and gas. No matter how wonderful a driver they may be, how beautiful a home they own, how intelligent they feel, the design of the car determines whether it works or not. And that, fundamentally, requires keys, a battery, and gas.

Likewise, it does not matter the number of credentials that each person may bring to a marriage; the question remains: "Is God's fingerprint on their lives?" Before Paul can state that marriage is about Christ and the church (Eph. 5:32), he reestablishes the blueprint. The church, he says, is fitted into, "one body and one Spirit, just as you were called in one hope of your calling; one Lord, one faith, one baptism; one God and Father of all, who is above all, and through all, and in you all" (Eph. 4:4–6). But because we must walk in a worthy manner (Eph. 4:1), all that God has done in us must become a functional reality. As a result, God put together the church. He is the head of it, and it has dominion over all the earth (Eph. 1:22–23; it can keep Satan out of the home, Matt. 16:18–19; Eph. 3:10). This church, being the body of Christ, led by the pastor-teacher, causes a believer to functionally develop into the fullness of God (Eph. 4:12–13). So when the believer functions in spiritual wisdom and knowledge (Eph. 1:17–20) rather than their own understanding (Eph. 4:17–19), they walk in the Spirit as they get rid of the old man (Eph. 4:20–24). This development leads them to become drunk with the Spirit (Eph. 5:15–18). To be drunk in the Spirit means a marriage that is at its best and can even ward off the attacks of the enemy (Eph. 6:12–18). Remember, he is the one who led Adam and Eve to sin, separating them from God (Gen. 3:1–7). "But we all, with unveiled face, beholding as in a mirror the glory of the Lord, are being transformed into the same image from glory to glory, just as by the Spirit of the Lord" (2 Cor. 3:18). It is not so much what we bring to the marriage that makes it a powerful experience; it is what we work out (as of result of wisdom, knowledge, and discernment) from the inside out. We do this in fear and trembling (Phil. 2:12–13) as a result of our commitment to be faithful to the local church.

The blueprint for marriage is designed by how the Trinity works within us (Eph. 3:14–21).

Application

Too many couples are more focused on each other than growing in Christ. It is no different than trying to play basketball without a ball. It does not matter the ability or capabilities of everyone on the basketball court; if there is no ball, there's no game. If couples are not focused on where this all starts—the "image and likeness of God"—it does not matter what they bring to the table; marriage does not work. Marriage must have God's fingerprint at its core.

Illustrate It

When an architect agrees to design a building, he will first meet with the owner or key leader to seek to understand the concept of the owner. This stage is called the "envisioning stage of architectural design." Sometimes this can take all day, filled with lots of questions and interviews with key people in the company, family, or church. Once this stage is complete, lots of sketches go back and forth between the architect and the owner.

Once the design of the building meets the leader's expectations, the concept becomes a drawing. The architect employs a pool of many people who have to function like a family to get the project approved. The project may go through many redesigns to get it within a particular budget. Once that is done, the company, with guidance from the architect, hires a contractor. The contractor then bids the project to numerous subcontractors who come and erect the building.

God is the owner of marriage because He initiated its formation. God the Father, God the Son, and God the Holy Spirit came together as the architects. Once the design was complete, the Bible says that all things were brought into being by Christ (Col. 1:15–18). Christ functioned as the contractor who is responsible for erecting the institution of marriage. This is why Paul said that marriage refers to Christ and the church (Eph. 5:32). The Holy Spirit empowers marriages because He is the one who blesses a believer to work out their salvation (Phil. 2:13). He functions like a subcontractor erecting the design of the marriage from the inside out as the Helper of Christ.

The source that shapes and empowers all marriages finds its core in the work of the Godhead.

One Purpose and Design

Genesis 2:15–18

General Overview of the Passage

After God had set up everything in the garden the way He wanted, He placed Adam in its midst. Adam was to have a relationship with Him, meaning Adam was made to live forever and with the capacity to love, to live a holy and righteous life. God had equipped him to manage the garden. Adam was given purpose and direction; he was to carefully guard God's garden as a service to God. The garden was a place where Adam and Eve fellowshipped with God in the "cool of the day."

The Lord commanded Adam, as Adam's superior, and Adam obeyed because of his inner commitment. God communicated this spoken word assigning or appointing Adam to this task. God told Adam that he may consume from any tree, as God directed, but he must not eat from the "tree of the knowledge of good and evil." "The Hebrew word here, *yada*ʿ, suggests a wide range of ideas, but basic to them is both the capacity to make distinctions and to experience all the garden had to offer. As long as Adam and Eve "knew" only good, they remained innocent, choosing and experiencing only what was right in God's sight. They did not even see opportunities to do wrong! "'The Fall' introduced the capacity to see evil choices as well as good ones and with it the desire to try both!"[6] Adam's responsibilities are clearly defined, giving him his spiritual (Gen. 2:9) and physical (Gen. 2:15) purpose before Eve was created.

The Lord, who has all authority, appointed Adam to a new structure. God said that it is not pleasant or beneficial for man to continuously and endlessly be alone. Man being alone would not accomplish the purposes of God. For example, a man cannot have children without a wife. God decided, without any input from man, that He would create the woman to be a designated helper, providing divine aid both physically and spiritually. A wife being designated as man's helper does

---

[6] L. O. Richards, *The Bible Reader's Companion* (Wheaton, IL: Victor Books, 1991; electronic ed. by Logos Research Systems, 1996), 27.

not imply subordination, for the same word is used to describe Christ as God's helper. The concept strongly supports equality of women (same in 1 Pet. 3:7; "a fellow heir"). This is important if God's plans will be accomplished. It is for the purpose of executing God's purposes that man is given headship.

It is important to note in the text the word *suitable*. This is first attached to the function that Adam and Eve are provided by God, which is to be "fruitful and multiply" (Gen. 1:22). They must rule over the earth that begins with filling the earth with the image and likeness of God (children) and then by learning how to cultivate the garden (Gen. 2:15). Managing the earth begins with learning to manage their home base. In order for all of this to work, Eve must be made "bone of my bones and flesh of my flesh" (Gen. 2:23). Eve must be constituted to Adam. She is God's design suited for God's purposes. So God's design is for God's purposes, not Adam's and Eve's. Man not being alone is not just about companionship; it is to execute God's plan effectively. "Literally, *a help answering to him, or one who answers*. She was to be one who could share man's responsibilities, respond to his nature with understanding and love, and wholeheartedly co-operate with him in working out the plan of God (ref. Gen. 2:21)."[7]

Historical Background

Establishing Context

After God made man He gave him purpose. "The garden of the Lord (Gen. 13:10; Ezek. 28:13), indicates, it was in fact a temple in which he worshipped God, and was daily employed in offering the sacrifices of thanksgiving and praise."[8] Adam was not provided instruction on headship because Adam was living without a sin nature. His purpose was more focused on the implementation of God's agenda outlined in Genesis 1:26–31. For this purpose, He needs a helper. "The description of her as 'corresponding to him' means basically that what was said about him in Genesis 2:7 was also true of her. They both had the

---

[7] C. F. Pfeiffer, *The Wycliffe Bible Commentary: Old Testament* (Chicago, IL: Moody Press, 1962), s.v. Gen. 2:18.

[8] R. Jamieson, A. R. Fausset, and D. Brown, *A Commentary, Critical and Explanatory, on the Old and New Testaments* (Oak Harbor, WA: Logos Research Systems, Inc., 1997), s.v. Gen. 2:15.

same nature. But what man lacked (his aloneness was not good) she supplied, and what she lacked he supplied."[9]

Before the fall of mankind, man was required to work. This is the nature of God demonstrated every day as He sustains the earth by His word (Heb. 1:3). "It should be noted that even before the fall man was expected to work; paradise was not a life of leisure unemployment. . . . Work is intrinsic to human life."[10]

Adam and Eve were born without sin, so committing evil was not a concept within them. They didn't even see opportunities to do wrong. All the Fall did was provide them the opportunity to make choices between good and evil. There was nothing evil or magical about the tree. There was nothing about the tree that would stir up evil in them. It was simply a choice—and they made the wrong one.

What Does the Context Mean?

The Lord directs, structures, and determines the outcome of marriage. We must learn His intent and submit to it in order to have His results. The woman is an equal companion to carry out God's purposes. Adam and Eve coming together is the working out of God's plan and purposes and how that affects the family structure so that each individual is blessed and God is glorified.

God defines what our expectations are in marriage. We are not designed to be exactly alike, but to be opposites, so that the man and woman complete each other and fulfill the purposes of God.

God also provided spiritual direction by telling them what not do and what to do in reference to the "tree of life" and the "tree of the knowledge of good and evil." The spiritual direction would determine his relationship with God. This ultimate need is highlighted by Paul in Ephesians 5:32 where marriage is represented as Christ and the church. As you can see, marriage is first for God's design and purposes.

Sermon Subject and Title

Sermon Title: One Purpose and Design

---

[9] John F. Walvoord and Roy B. Zuck, *The Bible Knowledge Commentary: An Exposition of the Scriptures* (Wheaton, IL: Victor Books, 1983-c1985), 1:31.

[10] G. J. Wenham, *Genesis 1–15,* vol. 1 of Word Biblical Commentary series (Dallas, TX: Word, Inc., 2002), 67.

Big Idea: Obeying God's direction by submitting to God's design for marriage establishes a partnership that glorifies God and blesses those who love Him.

SERMON OUTLINE (GEN. 2:15–18 NASB)

A. God's Purpose for Marriage (vv. 15–17)

1. Christ centered.
   a) *The LORD God*—The Lord, the one who seeks a covenant relationship with man; God, the Supreme Being. Christ, who is God's Helper (John 14:16), executes and sustains this plan (Col. 1:15–18).
   b) *The LORD God*—It is God's decisions and plans (Eph. 1:9–11).
   c) *The LORD God*—Christ organizes the structure of the home based on this plan and then names it after Himself (Eph. 5:32).
      - The home is centered on Christ (1 Cor. 11:3; Eph. 5:32).
      - Without Christ being the center of the home, the home loses its purpose (man: Christ; woman: church)
      - When husbands and wives keep the way of the Lord, God blesses their home (Pss. 112; 128; Prov. 24:2–5). The opposite is also true (Mal. 2:13–14).
      - Parents are directed to lead their children to God (Deut. 6:4–9; Eph. 6:3–4). The purpose is for these children to "be fruitful and multiply; fill the earth and subdue it; have dominion over the fish of the sea, over the birds of the air, and over every living thing that moves on the earth" (Gen. 1:28). God blesses this process (Pss. 112:1–3; 128).
2. His purpose is seen in the ability He provides for us to work (Eccles. 3:14, 22; 7:17).
   a) *He took*—God did not ask Adam's permission; He shaped Adam's focus for life (Gal. 2:20). What God said to Adam is always going to be the same (imperfect active).
   b) *He took*—God made Adam outside the garden (Gen. 2:7–8) so taking him into the Garden of Eden had purpose.
   c) *He took*—The garden was made after man, demonstrating it was designed for man to take care of.
   d) When He took Adam, he was single and without a companion (1 Cor. 7:32–35).

e) *Cultivate*—Work the garden; labor like a slave in service to God. Paradise was not a life of leisure and unemployment. One of the primary characteristics about a man is that he is not afraid of hard work.
   - He expects us to be good stewards of His blessings.
   - We must work to be productive (Prov. 10:4; 13:4; 21:5; Col. 3:22–25).

f) *Keep*—Adam's instructions were to preserve with careful attention what God had put in place (Gen. 2:8–9).
   - When God has full control of our lives (Josh. 1:5–9), He blesses us and expects us to manage it well (Luke 12:48—"to him who much is given much is required").

3. We can freely desire a relationship to God. The tree of the knowledge of good and evil; man's decision—free will:
   a) As long as Adam and Eve "knew" only good, they remained innocent—a life pleasing to God.
   b) *God commanded the man*—Shows Adam's need to be a leader and prevent this choice from taking place. Adam chose not to lead when mankind failed (notice Adam was with Eve the entire time Satan was talking).
      - Adam listened to his wife in breaking God's commands. Job did not listen to his wife who told him to curse God and die. So Job experienced the blessings of God (Job 2:9–10). This leadership is for the purposes of God (1 Cor. 11:3), so that the man of God leads his wife away from sin to righteousness (Eph. 5:26). When both of them walk in the Spirit, they would experience the fruit of the Spirit that includes patience, love, joy, and kindness (Gal. 5:22–24).
      - Free will gave them a choice and Satan tempted them. Even though they were born good, a delayed decision gave Satan room to manipulate them.
      - The Fall introduces the capacity to choose evil.
      - Walking with God is a decision we must make (John 14:15; 15:1–10; James 1:22–25).
   c) God places churches in the midst of our lives to guide us back to the fullness of God (Eph. 4:12–13).

B. God's Design for Marriage (v. 18)

1. *The* Lord *God*—The Lord God spoke in reference to the man (Gen. 2:15–17) and now does the same in reference to the woman. All of this is stimulated and directed by Him.
2. The Lord God arranged for the family to be successful.
3. When a single woman is going to seek a man, she must first be focused on God's purposes.
4. *Make*—God fashioned woman without consulting with Adam. She is God's design for man.
   a) This is in the imperfect, which means that until a man knows his God-directed purpose it is difficult for the woman to become suitable in the relationship.
   b) When many women try to lead their man, they become exhausted and frustrated in the relationship the older it gets. This is because they are outside of their design. Some women like this because they feel safer when they are in control.
5. *Not good for man to be alone*—it is not pleasant or beneficial.
   a) "Let us make man"—Starting out the eternal plan God is speaking of creating both man and woman. The structure of the Trinity leads to man having a wife and then children. This can only be fulfilled when the woman is a suitable helper (Gen. 1:26–31).
   b) "Be fruitful and multiply"—Man cannot be alone, because it takes male and female to fill the earth.
   c) "In our image and likeness"
   d) Man cannot cultivate and keep the garden or multiply and represent God's likeness without the woman, so it is not beneficial or productive for him to be alone.
6. *A helper suitable:*
   a) Means "corresponding to him"—same nature—what man lacked, the woman supplied; what she lacks, man supplies ("bone of my bone, flesh of my flesh").
   b) The woman completes man and man completes the woman (1 Cor. 11:7–12).
   c) They are opposite to each other but complement each other. Whatever the man manages (1 Tim. 3:4–5), it is done in an understanding way (1 Pet. 3:7) and the woman preserves it (1 Tim. 5:14).

If this is not maintained the garden does not get cultivated to where it benefits the home (Ps. 127:1–2).

d) Opposites attract and form good partnerships.

e) Marriage is a union of equals, each respecting as well as caring for the other, and each committed to be the other's helper.

7. This leads to one identity because they cannot find identity without the other (Eccles. 4:9–10; Prov. 31:10–31).

Author's Comments

Comments

Marriage was not designed first and foremost for us; it was first designed by God to highlight His nature and His glory. If anyone gets married to get all their needs supplied, they will be miserably disappointed (1 Cor. 7:28). Marriage was not designed by God for selfish desires to be satisfied or for a couple to worship each other because they feel in love. A car cannot function like a boat. That is not its design. A man cannot stay under water for long periods of time like a fish without any oxygen tanks. That is not his design. Marriage will not be a blessing to both people if God's design does not dominate their lives and their plans. In this passage, God continues to teach what His sovereign design is for marriage.

Many people take the statement "it is not good for the man to be alone" straight to the book of Song of Solomon. We need to complete the verse: "I will make a helper suitable for him." The last part of the verse states that God will make (create out of nothing something). So after the man is put in the garden and given specific instructions about spiritual matters (tree of life and good and evil), and physical matters in terms of how to cultivate the garden, then the man is made a "helper suitable." It is for this reason that it is not "good for the man to be alone." Notice the operative phrase is "it is not good"—meaning it produces no pleasant or economical benefit to the plan of God or to the plans of man. Lovemaking (Song of Solomon) automatically, in most cases, produces the design: "Be fruitful and multiply, and fill the earth." You cannot redesign God's design. He is too superior and powerful. This puts people in the flesh trying to accomplish something that God did not design. This is impossible!

Notice that after God made everything, He immediately said it was good, but when it came to man, He only made reference to good when Adam's suitable helpmate was made (Gen. 2:18). God's plan outlined in Genesis 1:26–31 was designed for a husband and wife working together for His glory and purposes.

This is what makes marriage good, blessed, and enjoyable (the fruit of the Spirit; Gal. 5:22–24). This is why Solomon, who wrote the Song of Solomon, says in Proverbs 18:22: "He who finds a wife finds a good thing, and obtains favor from the LORD." Usually, when a man actively seeks after God's purposes, he seeks a wife, because it is only a wife (this term is defined by God—check the sermon outline) that can be a suitable helper in accomplishing God's purposes.

There is a progression that takes place for a man to become a husband and a woman to become a wife. Marriage includes sexual attraction (Gen. 1:27–28); they are first male and female (the marriage bed is honorable before God; Heb. 13:4). Here is the crux that establishes their covenant (Gen. 2:24; Matt. 19:4–6) and when broken, destroys it (Matt. 19:9; 1 Cor. 6:16–19).

However, before we can get to marriage in Genesis 2:23–25, the male must become a man (Gen. 2:15). God takes the man into the garden—not just a male—before He can make this man a "suitable helper." He has purpose before he is given a woman. When God brings her to him, she is a woman—not just a female—before she can be considered to be his wife. Marriage requires maturity and spiritual growth both on the part of the man and the woman.

Application

Marriage is not first for man's pleasure but for God's divine purposes. When couples come together in marriage, they need to focus first on God's purposes, rather than their own. Their plans that define the vision for their home, how many children, will the wife work or not once children come, how will they discipline their children, serve in the local church, etc.—these issues must be addressed. All of these should be defined by their commitment to live for God's glory as they submit to His divine will (Rev. 4:11). Wealth and riches are produced from this commitment (Pss. 127:1–2; 128; 112:1–3). God must always be first (Luke 12:31–32).

Illustrate It

Larry Bird was once asked how he was able to make as many shots as consistently as he did. He responded by saying that each day, except his day off, he took one thousand basketball shots in practice, especially in the off-season. He ran regularly and trained consistently. He understood that his role was to be a shooter. What made Larry a great asset to his team was that he understood his role and worked hard to do a great job.

Adam and Eve never complained about the role God gave them. They accepted it and executed it daily. Until sin came, everything was perfect.

The True Meaning of "I Do"

Genesis 2:21–25

General Overview of the Passage

God put Adam to sleep, and in a powerful movement, God selected out of Adam a rib. The man's life is now being shared by Eve. God did not start with dust for Eve; He started with a rib. This means she is now dependent upon him as he is dependent upon her. This is why it was not good for him to be alone because he needed help. Neither one is fully complete without the other (1 Cor. 11:7–16).

God, who has all authority over his servant, continues by constructing and establishing all that was necessary for the design of the woman. Her design directly corresponded to man's life because she is for him and he is for her. God is putting into place what He had purposed and it shall come to pass.

After spending all day naming animals, Adam immediately recognized that Eve corresponded to him. "As the Creator instituted marriage, it was a sacred relationship of man and woman, with deep mystery at its center proclaiming its divine origin. The loving heart of God doubtless rejoiced in the institution of a relationship that was to be high, clean, holy, and pleasant for mankind."[11]

Adam now says words as an act of communicating a command that he is assigning to marriage. Adam said that Eve had the body frame and substance that corresponded to his own. Adam then goes about loudly getting her attention and after personal evaluation provides a name that is specific to her. He called her this name because there was a powerful movement of God when He selected a rib out of Adam. "He makes a play on the Hebrew words *ishshah* ('woman') and *ish* ('man') as another way of acknowledging the intimacy of their relationship. This is the first time these standard words for man and

[11] Pfeiffer, *The Wycliffe Bible Commentary: Old Testament*, s.v. Gen. 2:22.

woman have been used in the story."[12] The name defines how perfectly matched they are.

When the relationship between a man and a woman becomes husband and wife, because of their sexual union, the man must provide leadership in putting aside his father and his mother to formulate a very close relationship with his wife. The verb "be" is a timeless motion. So the man being with his wife is endless. Once the man and woman are separated unto themselves, they are totally exposed with no barriers between each other.

Historical Background

Establishing Context

There are five things that tie the woman to the man and define their relationship. She is his helper. The history of the word is that it was used to define a designated divine aid that provides support both physically and spiritually.

The second word is the rib. It is a Sumerian word that means life. The rib is protection for the lungs, and the lungs manage a man's breath, which is considered his soul. The ribs protect a man's life.

The third thing that took place is that Adam named the woman Eve. "Here the first man names the first woman in a similar fashion. Though they are equal in nature, that man names woman (cf. 3:20) indicates that she is expected to be subordinate to him, an important presupposition of the ensuing narrative (3:17)."[13]

The fourth aspect of this relationship is that the man and woman are to cleave together. In Matthew 19:4–6, Jesus explains this as sexual union. This also means, "And sticks to his wife. This phrase suggests both passion and permanence should characterize marriage."[14]

The fifth aspect is "were both naked . . . and were not ashamed" (Gen. 2:25). The man and woman are to remain open and vulnerable to each other. "Perhaps then it might be better to translate here, 'they were unabashed' or 'they were not disconcerted.' They were like young children unashamed at their nakedness."[15]

---

[12] Donald E. Gowan, *From Eden to Babel: A Commentary on the Book of Genesis 1–11* (Grand Rapids, MI: W. B. Eerdmans Pub. Co., 1988), 48.

[13] G. J. Wenham, *Genesis 1–15,* Vol. 1 (Dallas, TX: Word, Inc., 1998), 70.

[14] Ibid., 71.

[15] Ibid.

All of this, unlike the making of the man (Gen. 2:7), was done in the garden.

What Does the Context Mean?

Adam was not allowed to take Eve as his partner until he was placed in the garden with clearly defined responsibilities, which he soon learned were impossible to do without a helper. God completed man by putting Adam to sleep and took a rib from his side to make Eve. Adam accepted God's gift without question and highlighted how they perfectly corresponded to each other for God's purposes. He then became prophetic and said that the man shall lead the movement from the parents to create intimacy in the marriage so that they can be open and engaged in each other's lives. Marriage, as a result, is a God-made institution with permanence and a design that is focused on establishing a tribe, a nation, a people unto God.

Adam now knows that God has completed him and his purpose, based on God's design. This purpose is permanent. As with the garden, which God created and commanded Adam to cultivate, God creates Eve, and Adam must now make the marriage achieve God's purposes. Adam takes leadership by first naming her and then became intimate with her. She now belongs to him and he to her.

Sermon Subject and Title

Sermon Title: The True Meaning of "I Do"
Big Idea: God's design for marriage is for it to function in unity leading to an intimacy that binds a couple together forever.

Sermon Outline (Gen. 2:21–25)

A. God's Design for Marriage (vv. 21–22)

1. The man before marriage:
   a) Outside the garden, even though man is saved he is purposeless. He is simply a living being.
   b) Inside the garden, God is in control of man's life—"God took the man . . ."
   c) Man finds purpose (Matt. 25:14–30; 1 Pet. 4:10), and this created the need for God to provide a "helper suitable."

2. Adam on his own could not find a helper; God did it for him.
3. *Deep sleep to fall upon the man*—God did not need his input.
4. God supplies His plans and purposes. Man participates in God's plans and serves God.
5. Without God's intervention, man could not do anything about his need for a suitable helper.
6. The "helper suitable for" the man (Gen. 2:20)—"He took one of his ribs" (Gen. 2:21).
7. *Fashioned:*
   a) Notice that this has a different development than was done for the man (Gen. 2:7). In order words, man starts out as nothing but dust.
   b) *Rib* means "life" or "clay"; it protects the lungs. God breathed life into man and Eve keeps it (1 Tim. 5:14).
      - "God breathed" into man (Gen. 2:7). The life of the marriage begins with the man—"wash his wife with the word" (Eph. 5:26–27; notice God did not say "teach." This is an intimate process that prepares her to be presented before God without blemish). It is a "Word of life" (1 John 1:1; Phil. 2:15).
   c) "Helper suitable" completes God's purposes for man:
      - He manages his house; it does not say his wife. The woman is told to preserve what has been set up with her help (1 Tim. 5:14). This does not mean she cleans the house and the man does not. Since the man was expected to work, he would be the one mostly out of the house, so the woman's responsibility was to make sure their plans continue while he is gone.
      - Keeping his children under control. He preserves them from evil (Eph. 6:2–4; Heb. 12:7–8); the wife complements this by sharing in having them (1 Tim. 5:14) and bringing them up (1 Tim. 5:10). They are not going to act right all the time, but they must not be out of control.

B. God's Purpose for Marriage (vv. 23–24)

1. "This is now bone of my bone . . ." (Eph. 5:28–30):
   a) For the first time, Adam speaks.
   b) From the womb of a woman comes flesh, and from Adam's rib comes the woman's flesh (1 Cor. 11:11–12). Adam and Eve being one flesh is in the perfect active, meaning this is the way it will always be.

- Love wives as their own bodies (Eph. 5:28–30). The husband must do things for their wife as they do for themselves.
- Loving a wife means to love oneself.
    - Must nourish and cherish.
    - Members of one body.

2. God wanted for the man and the woman to function in unity—spiritually, physically, and in purpose.
3. *For this reason:*
    a) For the first time, Adam leads.
    b) This is the only reason a man must put his parents second, not forget them (1 Tim. 5:8).
    c) *Be*—timelessly with and ever-present existence.
    d) *Joined* ("Cleave")—The words *be joined* is like paper that is glued together. They are one but yet two individual personalities (Eph. 5:31).
    e) She is now Adam's wife.

C. God's Design and Purposes Fulfilled (v. 25)

1. Naked and Not Ashamed:
    a) An inner attitude of trust and openness.
    b) No fear of being manipulated or abused.
    c) No barriers, no self-consciousness.
    d) Sexual intimacy.

Author's Comments

Comments

The world will define the Lord's message as backwards, old-fashioned, and out of step with the times. Some people may say we need to find new ministers that are more in step with the times (2 Tim. 4:3–4). But the Scriptures state who all of God's structure is an administration suitable for the fullness of times (Eph. 1:11), and it also instructs the preacher to follow the rules (2 Tim. 2:5).

God's plans are not backwards; they are perfect. From God's perspective, what does "I do" mean? It means that Adam was not asked how to form Eve. He was put to sleep and God did what He knew was best. Eve was designed for God's purposes just like Adam. She can bear children, she is physically weaker and naturally more tender than man because man was designed to work and teach and correct the children (Eph. 6:4) while she nurtures them (she can also breastfeed). God made them a complement so He made them different. "I do" means I am committed to implement God's plan for God's glory and our blessing (Pss. 127; 128; Prov. 24:3–5).

This is not old-fashioned, because when people submit to God's order there is less divorce, less angry children who grow up fighting, and society is more productive. If the other way of doing things is so much better, why aren't our homes, our government, and our country better?

Truth is not just "conservative." Truth is simply the truth. It is not concepts; it is a person, Christ (John 14:6). It does not inhibit anyone because it is empowered by God, and since it does not return void it, it blesses those who trust it (John 8:31–32).

Application

The man's role and the woman's role are not old-fashioned because they are attached to God's divine plan. God's plans never get old because God has no beginning or end. The world should not define how we view God as conservative, moderate, or liberal. God's Word is the truth, it is the pillar of the church, and it is liberating, not confining (John 8:31–32). The church must maintain a deep commitment to preserve and protect the greatest of human relationships, marriage, which serves as an illustration of Christ and the church.

Illustrate It

In order for a man to carry out the purposes God has created him to achieve, a woman is someone he cannot live without. She drives him to be more like Christ because her role is to image the church (Eph. 5:32). As a result, there is a need for him to lead the marriage and the home because he is responsible for presenting the wife as a radiant bride (Eph. 5:27). This is critical, especially when it is established as he washes her with the Word. This brings into reality, even after sin came into the world, humanity being in the image and likeness of God. The birth of children expands that role because he must now instruct and discipline them (Eph. 6:4). So the person he must live with now allows him to multiply what they are doing for the next generation.

Virus Protection Needed

Genesis 3:1–7

General Overview of the Passage

Now that God has put everything in place, Satan approaches Eve with Adam present (Gen. 3:6). The serpent by its very nature was crafty. (Satan had already been removed from God's presence, Ezek. 28:13–19, and is now seeking to destroy God's plans.) He was more skillful than any other beast of the field. Moses states how crafty Satan was and then says "which the LORD God had made" (Gen. 3:1). Moses emphasized that God created Satan His own power. Note that God, knowing that this incident would take place, does not stop it. But because God made everything, it is still under His control and domain.

He allows man, made in His image, with a free will, with clear direction from Him, and with the option of the tree of life (2:9) before him, to make his own decision. God did not try to keep Satan out of His garden and put Satan to the bottom of hell; He allowed all of this to take place. Later, God, through the Holy Spirit, led Christ out to be tempted by Satan (Matt. 4 and Luke 4). Notice, through the power of the Holy Spirit, Christ was also led to this temptation and His lasted forty days—yet He did not sin (Rom. 5:12–21). Mankind has free will so it has to be his decision whether to obey or disobey God.

Satan told Eve a twisted version of a message; he changed God's words to corrupt Eve from the moment he spoke. He was a liar from the beginning (John 8:44; Satan is crafty in making truth seem to be a lie and a lie to seem to be to truth). When Eve repeats what God said, it shows that Adam did tell Eve what God told him, but Eve did not keep what her husband told her. She also left out the word "freely" (they did not have to ask His permission before they ate). Eve added words to what God said and even left out a word: "surely" die. She was not clear about God's commands.

Sin, because of Adam and Eve's state of being created innocent, had to be impressed upon them from an outside temptation. Satan brought forth that temptation. Eve approached this tree as if something was poisonous about the tree. He insinuated a doubt as to her sense of the divine will and appeared as an angel of light (2 Cor. 11:14), offering to lead her to the true interpretation. Instead of being startled by the reptile's speaking, she received him as a heavenly messenger.

Satan inferred that God had kept back some information from her that she ought to know. God is the one, according to Satan, who has unworthy motives. Satan did the same thing when he consulted God in reference to Job (Job 1:9–11; 2:4–5). God has the full knowledge. Satan tempts Eve into believing if she has the same understanding of right and wrong that God has, she would have a better relationship with God.

When Eve carefully examined or inspected the fruit and realized that the fruit seemed as good as everything she has seen thus far, and believing she has an acceptable understanding because she has the full knowledge of what to do, she ate it. "Physical practicality (good for food), aesthetic beauty (pleasing to the eye), and the potential for gaining wisdom—to be "in the know"—these draw a person over the brink once the barrier of punishment is supposedly removed."[16] She then gave Adam the fruit, and he too ate it. Notice, the verse says "he ate it," meaning that both of them did not just take a nibble, but instead they consumed it. Please notice God had built in grace. God did not say they could not touch the fruit or pick the fruit; God said they could not eat.

Their eyes were opened. They discovered that they were naked. All of a sudden with no one around but the two of them, they were ashamed (cf. Gen. 2:25). Their lovely naïveté was now replaced by evil thoughts, and they covered themselves with fig leaves.[17]

Historical Background

Establishing Context

Adam and Eve had obviously delayed picking from the "tree of life," and Satan finds them by the tree of the knowledge of "good and evil." Satan did not draw them to the tree (Christ had to be led out into the wilderness to be tempted). It seems when Eve took and ate the fruit she was already there.

The discussion with Satan shows that Eve was fully informed. She did not lack any information. Adam did his job and taught his wife. However, when the

---

[16] Radmacher, Allen, and House, *Nelson's New Illustrated Bible Commentary*, s.v. Gen. 3:6–7.

[17] Ibid.

serpent is talking to his wife, Adam fails and does not say anything. When they both consumed the fruit, their sin made them conscious of their nakedness. "Fig leaves are the largest found in Canaan and could provide limited covering for the shamed couple."[18]

What Does the Context Mean?

Satan is always seeking to change God's order. Instead of marriage between a man and woman, Satan wants it to be between people of the same gender, or between more than two people, or to allow for divorce under any circumstances. To change God's order is to usurp God's authority and manipulate His Word. The correct interpretation of God's Word is critical to warding off Satan. When doubt is created (James 1:5–8) and common sense is engaged, Satan does not need to do anything (Prov. 3:5–6). Whatever order God has created, we must remain in it for God's glory.

Satan approached Eve rather than Adam. He immediately attacked God's order. Eve shared the fruit with Adam. Instead of Adam trusting in God's word and refusing the fruit, he accepts their conversation and ate the fruit. When this takes place, Satan has accomplished his purpose, which is to get man to sin, thereby corrupting all mankind.

Sermon Subject and Title

Sermon Title: Virus Protection Needed
Big Idea: A lack of a godly leader and commitment to God's Word, in the first family, allowed Satan to lead the world into sin.

Sermon Outline (Gen. 3:1–7 nasb)

A. Establish a Fire Wall—God's Word (Gen. 3:1–4)
   1. *God*—Satan recognized God's supremacy but offered Him no respect. Satan was cast down from heaven because of his pride (Isa. 14:14; Ezek. 28:13–19).
   2. *Satan said*—Satan knew what God said. He heard the conversation.

---

[18] V. H. Matthews, M. W. Chavalas, and J. H. Walton, *The IVP Bible Background Commentary: Old Testament* (Downers Grove, IL: InterVarsity Press, 2000), electronic ed., Gen. 3:7.

3. *Satan said*—Adam and Eve delayed picking from the tree of life (Gen. 2:9). Delayed obedience is the first step to disobedience.
4. *Woman*—He did not talk to her as Adam's wife.
5. *Woman*—He challenged the woman to function independent of God's structure.
   a) The Word of God establishes order, which empowers family life (1 Cor. 14:34, 40; Eph. 5:26; 1 Tim. 2:12).
   b) The focus of God's order is being "like-minded" (Phil. 2:1–2).
6. How do we recognized Satan?
   a) Facts—truth revealed is always denied (John 8:44).
   b) Satan quotes God with a twist—he always seems credible (2 Cor. 11:14).
   c) It is impossible for Satan to tell the whole truth (John 8:44).
   d) A destroyer (1 Pet. 5:8). He turns people against each other.
   e) Deceptive (Rev. 12:9)—twist the truth.
   f) He seeks to set things out of order—turn stone to bread (Luke 4:1–11).
   g) He likes to create doubt—kills faith and wisdom (James 1:5–8).
   h) He blinds the minds of people (2 Cor. 4:4).
   i) He takes the Word of God from their hearts (Luke 8:12).
   j) He does his best to hinder the work of the gospel (Acts 13:7–8).
   k) He will tempt Christians to lie (Eph. 4:25–27).
   l) He tempts us to immorality (1 Cor. 7:5).
   m) He tempts believers to cover up selfishness (Acts 5:1–11).
7. A virus will never be an asset to a computer. Its very nature is to destroy it.
8. *Satan said*—Eat from any tree—When the world is talking to your marriage, turn off the virus (Ps. 1).
9. *Eve said—God said*—Eve showed that Adam communicated God's message (Gen. 2:15–17). This is why a woman must keep what has been established (1 Tim. 5:14). When Eve spoke, it is in the perfect active means she is in a set condition. Eve's conviction did not drive Satan away.
10. *God's Word*—once God provides His Word to us, He allows us to obey or disobey (free will).
11. *God's Word*—once it is changed, it is no longer truth.

12. *Eve said—God said*—Eve functioned independent of her husband outside of God's structure.
13. *Eve said—God said*—Adam said nothing during the entire conversation.
14. *Eve said—God said not to touch it*—God never said this. Eve added to God's Word (Deut. 4:2; 12:32; Prov. 30:6).
    a) The word *said* as it relates to God is in the perfect active, meaning that Eve understands what is the past action and what must take place in the present. She clearly understands the intent of God's message was a completed action. There was nothing to change.
    b) *You will die*—This is in the imperfect active, meaning that Eve clearly understood that this death is a continuous separation from God.
15. *You will not surely die*—Satan acted as if this would lead to a better relationship with God; he is a deceiver.

B. Don't Click on Unknown Mail (vv. 5–6)

1. *Satan says*—Satan stimulates independence and then drives Eve to self-confidence.
2. *Satan says*—Gets Eve to drop God's Word and relies on her own understanding (Prov. 3:5–6; Eph. 4:17–21).
3. Up until verse 6, God is mentioned several times, but from Genesis 3:6 to verse 7 God is not mentioned once. Common sense reigns. His Word is no longer a part of the process. Satan has succeeded.
4. Once Satan had Eve moving in the wrong direction, he had nothing else to say.
5. *Woman saw*—Inspected the fruit based on how Satan convinced her to view it.
    a) *Delightful*—It pleased her when she looked at it.
    b) *Desirable*—Selfish desire; to wish for something that does not belong to us (Deut. 5:21); covet.
    c) *Took the fruit*—Eve taking the fruit is decisive act (imperfect active). There was no hesitation or pause. Once she decided to take the fruit, she was going all the way through with it.
6. *She/he ate*—Delayed obedience leads to disobedience.

C. Virus-Infected Hard Drive Must Be Reformatted (v. 7)

1. *Eyes were opened*—Evil kills innocence. Imperfect active—their eyes will now always be open to sin and death.

2. *Knew*—They came to an understanding of where their relationship now stands with God.
3. *Knew*—Experiencing evil makes them feel weak toward doing good. Imperfect active means that this is always going to be this way.
4. *Were naked*—Different from Genesis 2:25. Hard drive is now polluted.
   a) *Naked* means to recognize guilt.
   b) When sin is fully exposed (Ezek. 23:29).
   c) Weakness—No longer can rule with the same physical and mental strength.
5. *Sewed fig leaves*—When they became conscious of their sin.
6. The need for Christ is now apparent (Gen. 3:15). He comes to make us into a new creation.

Author's Comments

Comments

I was working on my computer one day when all of a sudden it began to slow down. I did a restart only for it to do the same thing. Apparently, since I get emails from various parts of the world, I had about seventy viruses attacking my computer. I asked the technician how long it would take. He said to do a good job it will take all night. I could not believe it!

Marriages are exposed to a virus name Satan. Always remember he is going all over the earth day and night seeking whom he may devour (1 Pet. 5:8; Rev. 12:10). When we let our guards down and get busy so that we are not praying, reading our Bible, or going to church as often as needed, we have opened ourselves to this virus called Satan. This is what Eve did.

A husband and wife can simply become so busy that they are not intimate for long periods of time, and soon Satan gets involved in their marriage. "Do not deprive one another except with consent for a time, that you may give yourselves to fasting and prayer; and come together again so that Satan does not tempt you because of your lack of self-control" (1 Cor. 7:5). The same can take place with just the stress of life overwhelming believers, leading them to not turn their troubles over to God. Satan can get a foothold in their lives. "Casting all your care upon Him, for He cares for you. Be sober, be vigilant; because your adversary the devil walks about like a roaring lion, seeking whom he may devour" (1 Pet. 5:7–8). Satan can do the same as it relates to anger (Eph. 4:26–27) or lack of forgiveness (2 Cor. 2:8–11). He can send us fiery darts if we do not keep our armor on (Eph. 6:11). Pride will allow him to influence us (Matt. 16:23). Lying can cause him to influence us (John 8:44; Acts 5:1–6). The same can take place if we do not hold to sound doctrine (2 Cor. 11:14; 1 Tim. 4:1–5), Satan can find ways to seek to interrupt the spread of the gospel (1 Thess. 2:18) or just simply influence us to decide to live a sinful life.

Satan has a variety of viruses. If we are not aware of his schemes, like Adam and Eve, we can become susceptible and ruin our marriages and families. We must function as Peter says:

> Therefore gird up the loins of your mind, be sober, and rest your hope fully upon the grace that is to be brought to you at the revelation of Jesus Christ; as obedient children, not conforming yourselves to the former lusts, as in your ignorance; but as He who called you is holy, you also be holy in all your conduct, because it is written, "Be holy, for I am holy." (1 Pet. 1:13–16)

God's sanctifying process protects us all. Our involvement in church is a great way to experience God's protection. We must virus-protect our marriages. Satan has no new schemes; just new victims.

Application

Commit to turn off viruses by not walking "in the counsel of the ungodly nor stand[ing] in the path of sinners . . ." (Ps. 1:1). Remaining in God's structure is safer than doing what makes sense. For instance, if a wife has a biblical question and has a believing husband, she should remain within God's order and ask her husband (1 Cor. 14:34–35). If her husband is unsaved, the believing wife should use God's back-up system and share her questions or concerns with a righteous woman (Titus 2:3; James 5:16) or her pastor. Even if everything does not work out perfectly, there is greater blessing because God's Word does not turn out void (Isa. 55:11), and when we obey Him, God promises "that all things work together for good to those who love God, to those who are the called according to His purpose" (Rom. 8:28). Those who love God are those who keep His commandments (John 14:15).

When Sarah's frustration got the best of her and she influenced her husband to have a surrogate child through Hagar, things went very wrong. When Job's wife sought to influence him, Job chose to challenge his wife to remain in God's structure. It did not mean things got better immediately, but in the long run God doubled his blessing.

Illustrate It

How many times have we seen baseball players hit the ball out of the park over and over again? They make tons of money, and people cheer and pour into stadiums to see them break records. Some of the players were Mark McGwire, Barry Bonds, and Alex Rodriquez. In 2016, the stadium was packed to say farewell to Alex Rodriquez.

With all the media announcers singing their praises, allegations of performance-enhancing drugs reared up. If these allegations are true, then what the people saw was not a player whose ability was at its natural best. What they actually saw were players pretending to be at their natural best. The players who did not receive all the attention from the media and fans and did not get the really big contracts were the true heroes. This emphasizes the old adage, "Not everything that glitters is gold."

We must keep things out of our lives that can pollute them. Instead of trying the newest principles from most popular books or advice from people who seem to have it all together, it is wiser to remain committed to the Word of God, whether it is out of season or in season (2 Tim. 4:2). The results over the long haul glorify God and bless those who trust Him.

Purposeful Parenting

Exodus 2:7–11

General Overview of the Passage

Moses was saved from the Nile River as a result of his mother's plan. This is because Pharaoh decided to kill, by way of the midwives, all baby boys born to Israelite families. God allowed Moses to be given back to his mother in the most formative years of his life, so that when he grew old he would not depart from the commitment God wanted him to have for his people (Prov. 22:6; Heb. 11:22–26).

No matter the obstacles that Moses' mother experienced, she was determined to save her son. She put a lot of work into hiding Moses, as well as in making the wicker basket. She positioned Moses so that he could be found and set her daughter in place so that she could remain in his life.

It is obvious that Moses' mother established a strong influence in his life that would cause him to want to rescue his people. Her teaching that was passed down through oral traditions established the Word of God in Moses' mind and heart. This is what, based on Hebrews 11:24–26 caused Moses to take a great step of faith. He was now fully prepared to provide leadership in Egypt. Moses made a decision to trust the Word of God taught by his mother and gave up everything for the sake of his people. The Bible says that when Moses went out, he intently looked at what was taking place with his people. It troubled him.

The influence of a parent, in part, led to the development one of the Lord's greatest leaders.

Historical Background

Establishing Context

Moses was born as a Levite to Amram and Jochebed (Exod. 2:1–2; 6:20). He had a brother, Aaron, who was three at the time Moses was born, and a sister

Miriam, who was seven years old. Moses' mother remained in his life nursing him (Exod. 2:7–9), even though Moses was trained to be an Egyptian (Acts 7:22).

> The Exodus account does not dwell on Moses' childhood but moves directly from his being drawn out of the Nile to his act of murder at about the age of forty and his subsequent flight to the desert. The structure of this section shows how Moses was preserved twice from death—from drowning as an infant and then from death by execution near the age of forty.[19]

> In Hebrew, 'Moses' means 'He Who Draws Out' (Heb. *mosheh*). In this manner, Moses' name can refer the reader to the living God, who is the true Deliverer, and also to Moses, who would deliver the Israelites from the Red Sea (chapters 14, 15). The one who was drawn out of water would be the means of drawing the Israelite nation out of water (1:22).[20]

Moses' mother still seemed to maintain influence upon his life because when he grew up, according to Hebrews 11:23–27, Moses decided to rescue his people rather than take on the position of an Egyptian leader. He could have easily taken on this role. According to "Diaspora[21] Jewish stories, Moses was an Egyptian military hero and stressed his great learning and knowledge (see comment on Acts 7:22). Yet the writer of Hebrews may allow the view affirmed by Philo—that Moses as son of Pharaoh's daughter was his heir."[22]

Moses learned about diplomacy from being so well educated and from being exposed to the Egyptian courts. This contributed to the leadership he provided when negotiating the release of the people and resolving issues among the people as they wandered through the wilderness.

---

[19] Walton, *Genesis, Exodus, Leviticus, Numbers, Deuteronomy*, 171.

[20] Radmacher, Allen, and House, *Nelson's New Illustrated Bible Commentary*, 89.

[21] **Diaspora:** The Jewish dispersion outside Palestine. The technical term "Diaspora Judaism" is thus used interchangeably with "non-Palestinian Judaism" in this commentary. (Glossary terms are from C. S. Keener's *IVP Bible Background Commentary: New Testament.*)

[22] H. D. M. Spence-Jones, *The Pulpit Commentary: Exodus*, vol. 1 (Bellingham, WA: Logos Research Systems, Inc., 2004), S. 35.

Moses spent forty years in Egypt, forty years as a shepherd, and forty years as a leader of the newly formed nation Israel. At forty years old, he had to decide whether he was going to permanently be a part of Pharaoh's family legacy or not. Because of the influence of his mother, he decided to identify, not with Egypt, but with his people.

What Does the Context Mean?

Because Moses' parents (Exod. 6:20; Num. 26:58–59) had complete confidence and trust in the divine truths of God when he was born, they hid him for three months, knowing and believing that he was no ordinary child because he was fair in the sight of God. Moses' parents did not give Pharaoh reverential respect, nor did they try to run from him.

Like his parents, especially his mother, Moses had complete confidence and trust in the divine truths of God. Even when he rejected God's statutes (such as deciding to kill the Egyptian in his anger), his relationship with Pharaoh suffered. Moses recognized that his people were God's people. It was this that illustrated his faith. He believed that God would fulfill His promise to His people. The influence of Moses' parents led him to turn down luxury, power, and a sinful lifestyle for forty years in the wilderness as a sheepherder. He made this decision because he was keeping his attention concentrated on the reward. Moses believed that the worst he could endure for Christ would be more valuable than the best of the world (John 8:56; Acts 5:41; Rom. 8:18; 2 Cor. 4:27; 1 Pet. 4:14). His parents exercised "purposeful parenting."

Sermon Subject and Title

Sermon Title: Purposeful Parenting
Big Idea: Preserving the life of a child both physically and spiritually is to parent with purpose.

Sermon Outline (Exod. 2:7–11 nasb)

A. Protect the Life of Your Child (Exod. 2:1–6)

1. No matter how impossible the circumstances, never stop thinking how to care for your child.
2. No matter how powerless you may feel, keep praying and trying different methods to save your child's life—spiritually and physically.

3. Moses was saved as a result of his mother's carefully designed plan.
4. Never compromise safety:
   a) The wicker basket was developed securely.
   b) The child was set among the reeds.
   c) His sister remained.
5. The baby was in a position to be found.
6. She set her daughter there to talk Pharaoh's daughter into allowing the mother to nurse Moses. She strategically allowed Miriam, a young girl, to ask Pharaoh's daughter to get a nurse.

B. Maximize Your Child's Potential (Exod. 2:7–10; Acts 7:22–25)

1. God allows Moses to be put back into his mother's care in the most formative years of his life so that when he grows old he will not depart from his commitment to God's people (Prov. 22:6; Exod. 2:11–15; Heb. 11:24–26).
2. Her Training (Exod. 2:8–10):
   a) Moses was taken to his mother's house.
   b) Jochebed was paid for training up her own son. She could have become bitter for having to give up her son, but she stuck to the plan.

C. Stimulate Faith (Exod. 2:11; Heb. 11:23–27)

1. A mother's influence led to Moses making a decision to be about the things of God (Exod. 2:11; Heb. 11:24–25):
   a) *Those days*—In the days of a cruel ruler, murder, slavery, and wars.
   b) *Grown*—Moses at forty years old was considered great (he had shown full development in all his training and learning; his mother had developed him from a young age). "Moses was learned in all the wisdom of the Egyptians and was mighty in words and deeds" (Acts 7:22). The training of Moses was the best education in the world at that time. Moses would have been trained in three languages: Egyptian, Akkadian, and Hebrew.
   c) *Looked*—Moses was very concerned for his people so he intently looked, like a person with a microscope inspecting a fruit fly.
      - Moses went out particularly to intelligently inspect what was his brothers were doing. He did this, the book of Hebrews tells us, because he "refused to be called the son of Pharaoh's daughter, choosing rather to suffer affliction with the people of God than to enjoy the passing pleasures of sin" (Heb. 11:24–25).

d) *Hard labors*—He saw that their labor was compulsory and burdensome.

2. Moses chose to be an Israelite rather than an Egyptian because of the influence of his loving mother.

Author's Comments

Comments

Parenting can be one of the most difficult tasks God gives us. It can be difficult because children are born in sin, shaped in iniquity (Ps. 51:5), and have foolishness bound up in their hearts (Prov. 22:15). Foolishness is not just in a child's actions; it is in their hearts. It is a natural part of their character at birth and can become a lifestyle. This can be compounded by the depravity both outside the home and that which comes into the home through television, radio, games, laptops, and smart phones. None of this is foreign to God. He knew this before the beginning of time. Despite the fact that parenting is a God-blessed process, it is a challenge and we must learn to "parent with purpose" as we "train up a child in the way he should go" (Prov. 22:6).

Moses' mother did not just pray and hope her child would not be found and slaughtered by Egyptian soldiers. She planned, worked hard, and organized saving her son's life. It was not just Moses' mother who planned this; it was God who knew her heart, so that this child was a gift from God (Ps. 127:3). He was born at the right time, to the right parent, and in the right place. God organized for Pharaoh's daughter to take baths in the Nile. God allowed for Miriam to be born years earlier so that she would be old enough to do what her mother requested. God knew that Moses would be placed in the house of Pharaoh. When we plan for the lives of our children, we must remember that the Lord is ultimately in control. "The lot is cast into the lap, but its every decision is from the LORD" (Prov. 16:33).

"Like arrows in the hand of a warrior, so are the children of one's youth. Happy is the man who has his quiver full of them; they shall not be ashamed, but shall speak with their enemies in the gate" (Ps. 127:4–5). Busy schedules, expensive tuitions, and broken marriages can cause children to seem like an encumbrance. Time can become so demanding that children grow up in their own strength. We must understand God's plan and become resolved to parent our children with purpose (Ps. 128).

Application

Abraham Lincoln's mom did her best to raise her son despite the poor conditions they grew up in. She did not know she raised a president that would change the course of the country. As parents, we must remember that our job is to train up a child, who God states is a gift, but is born in sin and shaped in iniquity with foolishness bound up in their hearts. We must nurture our children to become a gift back to God. This way, we create godly legacies. This focus should cause us to "parent with purpose."

Illustrate It

There was a father who had to get some chores completed. It was cold and snowing, so he delayed going outside to complete his work. In the meantime, he decided to spend time with his son. They had a great time together, but soon the father decided that he just needed to get those few items done. He told his son he was going outside for a few minutes and would be right back.

The father went to get his coat and head outside. As he was making his way outside, he heard his son's voice: "Dad, wait for me." Worried that his son may have come outside without the proper protection, he turned quickly only to find his son in his coat walking in his footprints.

How often when we build a relationship with our children does it stimulate them to follow our example?

Moses' mother did just that, and Moses led the nation of Israel from bondage to freedom, establishing God's nation forever.

Character Building Blocks

Hebrews 12:7–9; Ephesians 6:4

General Overview of the Passages

Discipline symbolizes the rule of God in shaping the life of a believer. The purpose is to develop wisdom and understanding. This is painful at first, but it brings the peaceful fruit of righteousness. This process seeks to train and educate believers by correcting, reproving, and instructing them. It produces a worshipful fear of God (as Paul tells Timothy in 2 Tim. 3:14–17). This fear creates an ongoing consciousness of God in the daily lives of believers, which in turn leads to godliness. It is this same system that the writer of Hebrews makes reference to as it relates to a father raising his children. God expects fathers to discipline their children. He does not include mothers in this command (Eph. 6:1–4). It is this process that exposes a father's heart to see his children develop great character traits. This is a unique relationship that takes place between a father and son. When there is no father-son relationship, the father does not invest the time or energy or make the sacrifices necessary, to see this process through.

Fathers must not be unreasonable with their children so as to purposefully arouse anger (provoke—over-protection, favoritism, discouragement, neglect, bitter words, outright physical cruelty). Correction is only as needed when their children continuously violate the principles being imparted by the father. The purpose of correction is to impart understanding concerning the issues the child has failed to respond to correctly. This also establishes the father as an influence in the life of the child. This creates an appetite for more instruction from that father.

Historical Background

Establishing Context

These passages of Scripture highlights the important place a father has in raising children that goes back to the beginning of time. "Hebrews 12:5–7 is a quotation from Proverbs 3:11–12 but has many biblical (e.g., Deut. 8:5; Ps. 94:12) and post-biblical (e.g., Song of Solomon 3:4; 7:3; 8:26; 10:1–3; 13:9–10; 14:1–2; 18:4) Jewish parallels; Philo[23] and some rabbis[24] used Proverbs 3 similarly."[25]

Being disciplined within this context has a different connotation than what we experience in our culture. Discipline in the minds of the Jews is to be willing to receive and apply instruction. "In the Greek world, the term translated 'discipline' (NIV, NASB) was the most basic term for 'education' (although this usually included corporal discipline)."[26] It is when the instruction is not consistently applied that punishment becomes a part of the equation. "In the context of Jewish wisdom literature, discipline was a sign of a father's love for his children, his concern that they would go in the right way."[27] This is how Jewish children demonstrate honor and respect toward their parents. When children accept their parents' teaching and live by it, they represent their parents well in society, bringing them respect. This was considered a very good child. Fathers were primarily responsible for their children's instruction and discipline (Eph. 6:4).

What Does the Context Mean?

Parents must be purposeful in raising their children. The home must have structure, an environment that would cause their children to want to accept

---

[23] **Philo:** A first-century Jewish philosopher committed to both Judaism and Greek thought; he lived in Alexandria, Egypt, and held a position of great influence and prestige in the Jewish community there.

[24] **Rabbi:** Jewish teacher. Sometime after AD 70 the term became a technical one for those ordained in the rabbinic movement, which probably consisted primarily of Pharisaic scribes. (To accommodate customary usage this commentary sometimes applies the term to Jewish teachers of the law in general, although such common usage may have technically been later; it also applies the term to the teachings of Jewish legal experts collected in rabbinic literature.) (Terms from Keener, *IVP Bible Background Commentary: New Testament*).

[25] Keener, *The IVP Bible Background Commentary: New Testament*, s.v. Heb. 12:5–7.

[26] Ibid.

[27] Ibid.

Christ, and a loving, nurturing atmosphere that disciples their child to love God with all their hearts. When a child is rebellious to the structure the parents set, guidelines for correction should be applied from the Word of God. When maintained, they should be consistent for every one of their children. This is how a father demonstrates a sincere love for his children and creates respect in the life of the child. The respect that is generated leads the child to develop a character that pleases God and blesses the parents.

Sermon Subject and Title

Sermon Title: Character Building Blocks
Text Idea: The discipline process for shaping the life of a child is a process that teaches, corrects, stimulates respect, instills faith, and punishes the child if the child persists in misbehaving.
Big Idea: Disciplining a child based on the Word of God shapes the life of the child because it instills faith in their hearts.

Sermon Outline (Heb. 12:7–9; Eph. 6:4)

A. Discipline Is Necessary (Pss. 51:5; 127:3; Prov. 22:15)

1. God's Description of Our Children:
    a) They are a gift from Him (Ps. 127:3).
    b) Born in sin and shaped in iniquity (Ps. 51:5).
    c) Foolishness is bound up in their hearts (Prov. 22:15).
2. A Foolish Person:
    a) Rejects knowledge (Prov. 13:16; 18:2; 23:9).
    b) Hates discipline (Prov. 15:5, 14; 17:10).
    c) Squanders money (Prov. 21:20).
    d) Is quick to quarrel (Prov. 20:3).
    e) When a foolish person is honored, they begin to believe they are the smartest person (Prov. 26:1, 5).

B. The Purpose of Discipline (Heb. 12:7–9)

1. The Nature of Discipline:
    a) *Deals*—It comes through many trials (Luke 4:1—Christ; Deut. 8:5).

b) It is to teach us endurance (James 1:2–4)—to bear up under trials. This is to be steadfast in our walk with the Lord despite the pressures that come from trials.
   - A parent must not save their child from going through difficult times. A parent should teach them how to make it through.
c) Discipline exposes God's love for us—demonstrates that we are truly saved (Prov. 3:12; Rom. 8:12–17).
   - When a parent disciplines a child based on an accurate interpretation of the Word of God, they are demonstrating love for God (John 14:15) and their child (Prov. 19:18; Heb. 12:7).
d) It provides instruction focused on instilling faith (2 Tim. 3:14–15; Moses, Hebrews 12:24–27).
e) Discipline is structuring a child's life by:
   - Seeking to lead them to Christ. The Holy Spirit is the best teacher (address the sin and iniquity in the child's life).
   - Teaching them to love the Word of God by the parents modeling the Word before them and giving the Word practical significance (this builds wisdom, removing foolishness).
   - Family structure—a time to eat, to sleep, to study for school, to go to church, to play, and to do chores. Structure teaches the child to manage their emotions and impulses and be responsible.
f) It is when a child does not respect the discipline structure that the rod of correction shapes character. The child clearly and quickly knows what they have done wrong. When we sin and are disciplined by the Lord, it is because He taught us what to do and we willfully chose not do it (James 4:17).
g) It is correction:
   - Correction is focused on teaching why someone is wrong (Prov. 29:17).
   - Correction shapes a person to submit their will to the Lord.
   - It establishes the rule of God (2 Tim. 3:16–17).
   - Spankings—forcefully moves a child to appropriate behavior (Prov. 13:24; 19:18; 22:15; 23:13; 29:15).
   - Creates a fear of God and respect for the parent.
   - Reverent fear creates wisdom and understanding—the child hears better (Prov. 29:17).

2. Discipline leads to a real experience of the life of God in a person.

a) A life controlled by the Holy Spirit breathes wisdom (Eph. 5:15–18).
b) Remains fixed on doing right no matter what occurs in their lives.

C. The Training Process that Leads to a Discipline Life (Eph. 6:4)

1. *Instruction*—A father must provide instruction for his child:
    a) Correct them by teaching appropriate behavior.
    b) Provides encouragement when the child behaves appropriately.
    c) Develops a good relationship with the child so they can be taught by influence.
    d) Create an appetite for knowledge and understanding (1 Thess. 2:11).

Author's Comments

Comments

With all the information available in the field of psychology and the many child-rearing self-help books that are available, many people—even believers—view the Bible as brutal and old-fashioned in the rearing of children. It is interesting, however, that the more "knowledge" we have, the more school shootings, gang activity, and drugs there are. With more psychology, there are more problems, and with how some Christians have interpreted discipline there has been some abuse. The challenge is growing a child from being born in sin to becoming a person of godly character. It is a challenge, but a challenge that God has addressed. He knew every child that comes from Adam and Eve is born with this problem. Let us take a look to see how God addresses this issue of disciplining our children.

Application

Set up a structure for the home that involves a time for breakfast, lunch (if not in school), and dinner, when chores are done, when the family will have devotions and who leads it, what chores each child is responsible to do, when is family time, and when mom and dad have date night. This structure keeps the child in a stable environment that in turn teaches them when they are wrong before the parent has to say anything. The same is true when it comes to spanking the child. Here is an example when parents set up rules that are equal, and guided by the Word of God, so that when the child is corrected, they are being oriented to the ultimate parent—God. If the child violates the rules, they can first receive a warning. Second, they can be punished by having something taken away, or doing the dishes for a week, etc. Punishment must of course be age sensitive: the younger the child, the shorter the time of each punishment. When they persist in doing what they know violates the rules, then they are spanked. Spanking a child is to get rid of foolishness, so it should only take place when the child is rebellious. Rebellion is sin on blast: Ephesians 2:1–3. The focus is to teach the child that they brought the spanking on themselves, thereby instilling in the child responsibility for their actions.

Illustrate It

A father, after giving out a list of chores to his children, told them that he expected all of them to complete their chores by the time he returned from running errands. The children looked at the list and asked all the questions they needed answered. Once everyone had a clear understanding, the father left.

Upon return, one of the children stated that he could not do the chores because it was not enough time. The father asked the child if he got any of the chores done. The child said there was no point trying to start because he knew he could not finish. The father asked the child why he didn't call him. The child said he did not think to do this.

The father immediately realized—especially after seeing the video game on the floor—that the child was making excuses. The father gave the child more chores than he had the first time and told him to finish within the time provided. The child dragged at doing what was expected and gave more excuses. The father, who was now becoming upset, told the child that he was going to give him more chores until his attitude changed. The child became rude to the father, leading the father to discipline the child.

The father disciplined this child because it was obvious that the child would rather play video games than do his chores. The father was forced to discipline the child because he knew that if he did not, the child would grow up to be irresponsible.

Beauty and the Beast

Judges 13:4, 10–11; 14:2–3, 10; 15:3, 7; 16:28–31

General Overview of the Passages

This story is about Samson, one of the "super-men" of the Bible. His mother was barren, and the Angel of the Lord came to her and told her she would have a son. The Angel of the Lord instructed her to make sure, by keeping a careful watch, that her son, Samson, does not drink any wine or strong drink or eat anything that violates God's law. As a Nazirite, he was to be set apart from anything offered to idols or any unclean animals. Samson's mother, with excitement and in a great hurry, told her husband about the message she received from the Angel of the Lord.

> Manoah got up and followed his wife. Manoah's intense desire for the repetition of the angel's visit was prompted not by doubts or anxieties of any kind, but was the fruit of lively faith, and of his great excitement to follow out the instructions given. Blessed was he who had not seen, yet had believed.[28]

As a young man, Samson went down to a Philistine village and inspected it and came to a full intellectual understanding of who Delilah was and decided that he wanted her. He told his parents to go and select her by summoning her and paying the dowry so that he could have her as his wife. "Samson's request for a wife defied the tradition that allowed the parents to arrange the marriage (14:2, 3). Despite Samson's disobedient and careless life, God intended to use him for His own purposes against the Philistines (v. 4), who were ruling over Israel at that time."[29] This decision led to Samson's demise. Samson ended up imprisoned by the Philistines, who also blinded him by plucking out his eyes.

---

[28] Jamieson, Fausset, and Brown, *A Commentary, Critical and Explanatory on the Old and New Testaments*, s.v. Judg. 13:11.

[29] Radmacher, Allen, and House, *Nelson's New Illustrated Bible Commentary*, s.v. Judg. 14:1–15.

Samson always believed God, although he didn't always act like it. Now, standing and acting on his convictions, he stood between the pillars that the house rested on and pushed the pillars down so that the walls of the temple crumbled and killed everyone. Samson called unto the Lord—"His penitent and prayerful spirit seems clearly to indicate that this meditated act was not that of a vindictive suicide, and that he regarded himself as putting forth his strength in his capacity of a public magistrate."[30] Samson must have prayed truly because it accomplished God's purposes, and God answered his prayer.

Samson died a hero because, despite his mistakes, he understood his role and was willing to take it to the grave. A person may not live a perfect life, but God is faithful to bless them whenever they submit to Him (Heb. 11:32).

Historical Background

Establishing Context

At significant times in biblical history the Angel of the Lord appears. Some people believe that the Angel of the Lord is a theophany of Christ. When the Angel of the Lord visited with Manoah's wife, he found a godly woman who was unable to have a child. She was given specific instructions on what not to do because the child was a Nazirite.

Long hair, in the time of Samson, was related to the person's life existence. Some cultures would check a prophet's hair to see if his messages were true. "This is evident, for instance, in the practice of sending along a lock of the presumed prophet's hair when the prophecies were sent to the king of Mari. The hair would be used in divination to determine whether the prophet's message would be accepted as valid."[31]

Also note that Samson was a defiant child and brought his potential wife home, which was unheard of in those days. He told his parents to negotiate all the arrangements, including making sure the dowry was paid. Even though they disagreed, they still did it.

Samson's disobedience cost him his life and brought disgrace to his family. "Every baby born into a godly home carries the responsibility of honoring the

---

[30] Jamieson, Fausset, and Brown, *A Commentary, Critical and Explanatory, on the Old and New Testaments*, S. Judg. 16:27.

[31] Radmacher, Allen, and House, *Nelson's New Illustrated Bible Commentary*, s.v. Judg. 16:23–27.

family name. Samson's inconsistent life brought shame to his father's house just as it brought shame to the name of the Lord."[32]

What Does the Context Mean?

The purpose is to demonstrate that even with godly parents who care for their child and desire to lead him to God, the child must still surrender his life to God. Despite Samson's sinful ways, God in His sovereign will used him. Since everyone seemed afraid of the Philistines, Samson was used as a catalyst who would eventually destroy the leaders of the Philistines, thereby subduing their power over God's people until Samuel and David came along to finish the job.

Samson lived with a consciousness of God because of the influence of his parents. Samson came back to God because his consciousness of God was always within him.

Sermon Subject and Title

Sermon Title: Beauty and the Beast
Big Idea: The teaching of godly parents will eventually impact the heart of our children because God's Word does not return void.

Sermon Outline (Judg. 13:4, 10–11; 14:2–3, 10; 15:3, 7; 16:28–31)

A. Excited Parents Devoted to God (13:3–5, 10–11; 14:1–3)

1. They were excited to have a child (Judg. 13:6, 10).
2. Samson's parents were God-fearing people ((Judg. 13:3–23):
    a) They were quick to obey the Angel of the Lord.
    b) Seemed to have a good prayer life ((Judg. 13:8).
    c) They were willing to learn how to parent Samson ((Judg. 13:8, 12; 16:17).
    d) Samson was born with a purpose and they were committed to fulfill it.
    e) They were quick to worship God ((Judg. 13:15–20).

[32] Warren Wiersbe, *The Bible Exposition Commentary: Old Testament* (Wheaton, IL: Victor Publishing, 2001–2004).

3. They seemed to have a good marriage ((Judg. 13:6, 10–11, 13, 22–23; 14:3).
4. They were godly people ((Judg. 13:21–23).

B. The Heart of Their Child, Samson (14:1–10, 19; 15:3–8; 16:1–3)

1. Samson was unwilling to submit to the will of God ((Judg. 14:2–3):
   a) By law, he was not allowed to marry a Gentile ((Judg. 14:3c).
   b) *Nazirite*—was not allowed to touch anything dead—(the lion (Judg. 14:8–9); was not allowed to drink strong drink (he probably did—v. 10); was not allowed to cut his hair—Delilah ((Judg. 16:17).
2. Samson did whatever pleased him ((Judg. 14:3c)
3. Samson had an immoral lifestyle ((Judg. 16:1–4).
4. Samson did not imitate a life of worship like his parents.
5. Samson's spiritual life was limited—two times he is recorded as praying ((Judg. 15:18–20; 16:28).
6. God incorporated all of Samson's bad decisions to fulfill His good purposes for His people ((Judg. 13:25; 14:6, 19; 15:14).
   a) God was busy working in Samson's life even when he was being disobedient ((Judg. 13:3–5).
      - We must do our best to lead a child to their bent (Prov. 22:6). When they are older, God will lead them back.

C. Godly Parenting Wins (16:28–31; Prov. 22:6):

1. Samson's disobedience leads to a humbled position (Judg. (16:21, 27).
2. Samson realized his need for God ((Judg. 16:28). Samson realized that without God he is nothing (John 15:5).
3. Samson humbly trusted God ((Judg. 16:28; Heb. 11:32).
4. A person may not live a perfect life, but God is faithful to bless them whenever they submit to Him (Heb. 11:32; His grace is sufficient).

Author's Comments

Comments

Have you ever raised a child who keeps giving you trouble? No matter what schools you enroll them in or how you discipline them, they just keep making bad decisions. You have prayed and fasted, read books on strong-willed children, and sought counsel. Yet your child keeps making bad decisions. In this story, you find good parents with a child that keeps making bad decisions.

It is obvious from the time God spoke to them to the time they disagreed with Samson on whom he chose to marry, that these parents sincerely loved God.

> Samson was born into a godly home, to parents who believed in prayer. He was God's special gift to them and to the nation. He had a father who prayed, "Teach us what we shall do unto the child" (Judg. 13:8; and see v. 12). His parents had a fear of God and tried to instill this same fear in their son. They brought offerings to God and dared to believe His wonderful promises.[33]

Samson's parents did their very best to raise Samson to be obedient to God. This was especially critical because Samson, a Nazirite, was chosen by God:

> A Nazirite who became unclean went through elaborate cleansing rituals (Num. 6:9–21). Note that both Samson's mother and Samson himself were to follow the regulations (13:4–5, 7). Samson's Nazirite service was remarkable in three ways. First, he did not take his vow voluntarily; it was his before birth (vv. 5, 7). Second, his service was to be lifelong, not temporary (vv. 5, 7). Third, he eventually broke every one of its stipulations: his head was sheared (16:17, 19); he associated with the dead (14:6–9; 15:15); and he drank at his wedding feast (14:10–20).[34]

Samson was self-centered and impulsive. His desire for Delilah destroyed him. Despite all that Samson put his family through, God continually worked with him. God empowered and rescued him several times.

Samson's defiance of God's Word did not just humiliate his parents; it put a nation in jeopardy. It led to the people having to turn against him in order to save their own necks. Samson's behavior ended up isolating him and costing him his life. "Rejoice, O young man, in your youth, And let your heart cheer you in the days of your youth; walk in the ways of your heart, and in the sight of your eyes; but know that for all these God will bring you into judgment" (Eccles. 11:9). Despite all of this, God accomplished His purposes.

---

[33] Jamieson, Fausset, and Brown, *A Commentary, Critical and Explanatory, on the Old and New Testaments*, s.v. Judg. 13:11.

[34] Radmacher, Allen, and House, *Nelson's New Illustrated Bible Commentary*, s.v. Judg. 13:4–5.

Godly parents loving their only son eventually influenced him to turn from a wayward life back to God: "Beauty and the Beast."

Application

When raising children, the temperament of the parents toward God will leave a mark in the child's heart and mind. When parents see the tendency of their child is leaning toward the world, they should do their best to try to live in a neighborhood that does not have a lot of bad elements. They should evaluate the child's friends. Maybe try to get the child into a Christian school and very involved in church.

Illustrate It

Prince William and Prince Harry are two princes born to Princess Diana. It is obvious that she loved her boys and did a lot to make sure they were grounded. Prince William enjoyed his single life, but after serving his country, he settled down and married Kate Middleton and they now have several children. Prince Harry, however, is living life and is many times in the news for not acting much like a prince. It has been reported that he lives a scandalous lifestyle. Two children grew up with the same parents under the same circumstances, but had different results.

Prince William understands his purpose and still serves in the military. Like Samson, he did not forget who he was, even though he formerly did not "act the part." The parents and the family never gave up on him and that helped to keep him focused.

Not every time a child misbehaves does it predict that they will remain the wild child. It is imperative that the parents and family cover them in love because love can steer them back to their home training. As time passes, Prince Harry has begun to settle down and is more representative of the kingdom.

Family Chorus Versus Family Chaos

Genesis 25:19–28; 27:5–17

General Overview of the Passages

This is a story of two godly people, Isaac and Rebekah, who choose to love one son more than the other. Isaac truly had a personal relationship with God, as evidenced in the manner in which he prayed and listened to God (Gen. 25:21). Isaac probably learned this practice from his father, Abraham. He was also a family man and was truly in love with Rebekah. Rebekah also had a good relationship with the Lord (25:22–23), and the Lord heard her and answered her prayers. These two parents were godly people, but that did not mean they were without character flaws or parenting issues.

The parents Jacob and Rebekah favored one child above another (25:28; 33), and the actions they took stemming from this favoritism negatively affected the children's relationship.

It is not that Rebekah and Isaac did not know the will of God (25:23): she just chose to take matters into her own hands. They were controlled by their desire to love one child more than the other. This led to both sons having serious issues in their relationship (27:41). It caused both boys to be sent away, Esau permanently, and left their father a broken man.

With God, there is always hope for reconciliation. God preserved the boys' love for each other (33:4–16), even though it was twenty years before they saw each other again (31:41). God established forgiveness in their hearts (33:10–11) and renewed their peace (33:16–17). God heals a family and sustains His legacy.

Historical Background

Establishing Context

Twins, Esau and Jacob, were born to Rebekah and Isaac. Esau was a man of the field, or more accurately, of the desert. He loved to roam free and was impulsive and impatient. Jacob was a man who was "among the tents." He knew how to cook, was close to his mother, and rarely roamed the land like his brother.

The issue of birthright became a great divide between the two brothers. A birthright held a high level of importance in this culture and was the necessary piece in determining the next leader of the tribe. Determining birthright also determined the spiritual leader and most of the family possessions were given to him. It also meant that the father's blessing goes to this person. Jacob tricked his brother into giving up his birthright for a pot of stew. Jacob's nature seemed to be tied to getting his brother's birthright from the time of his birth (came out of the womb holding on to his brother's heel; Gen. 25:25–26). "According to the accounts in Genesis, Jacob continued to 'take hold of' the possessions of others—his brother's birthright (25:29–34), his father's blessing (27:1–29), and his father-in-law's flocks and herds (30:25–43; 31:1)."[35]

> The birthright consists of the material inheritance. The firstborn usually received a double share from the father because he was expected to become the paterfamilias, having ultimate responsibility for all of the members of the extended family (e.g., mother, unwed sisters) as well as for the continuing care of the deceased.[36]

Esau's attitude toward his birthright obviously demonstrated that he did not take it as seriously as he needed to, whereas the manner in which Jacob cared for it showed that he took the significance of it very seriously. This, in turn, leads to Jacob being blessed. "The blessing that Isaac bestows on Jacob (whom he mistakes for Esau) grants him fertility of the ground, dominion over other nations, including those descended from siblings, and a boomerang effect for curses and blessings."[37]

---

[35] Ronald F. Youngblood, ed., *Nelson's Illustrated Bible Dictionary* (Nashville, TN: Thomas Nelson, 1986, 2014), 563.

[36] Walton, *Genesis, Exodus, Leviticus, Deuteronomy,* 1:105.

[37] Matthews, Chavalas, and Walton, *The IVP Bible Background Commentary: Old Testament,* s.v. Gen. 27:29–40.

The issue of favoritism can be clearly seen when Rebekah taught her son to trick his dad, a characteristic that continued to be a practice of Jacob. They were successful at the ruse, yet it was Isaac who truly was the heartbroken one.

What Does the Context Mean?

When parents disobey God and use deceitful methods, it can lead to a major breakdown in the family. The same can be true when they do not communicate how to obey God's commands. When favoritism is openly practiced, it can divide children and leave them with painful memories. God will always achieve His plan, but the pain of these memories will leave scars.

Sermon Subject and Title

Sermon Title: Family Chorus Versus Family Chaos
Big Idea: Favoritism in a family leads to division and chaos that can last for generations.

Sermon Outline (Gen. 25:19–28; 27:5–17)

A. A Family God Establishes (25:19–27)

1. Isaac had a personal relationship with God; he prayed and God listened (Gen. 2:21).
2. Isaac was concerned for his marriage and his wife (Gen. 2:21).
3 Rebekah had a personal relationship with God (Gen. 2:22–23).
4. God established the family (Gen. 2:22–24):
   a) God blessed them with twins.
   b) God established their personality traits (Gen. 2:22, 27).
5. The family allowed God to have control.

B. A Family in Crisis (25:28; 27:5–17, 38, 41)

1. The family had a problem they left unaddressed—favoritism (Gen. 25:28).
2. When we take the working out of God's will into our own hands, we create chaos.
3. Rebekah knew the will of God (Gen. 25:23), and believed she needed to take control (Bathsheba and Solomon—1 Kings 1:11–40).
4. Anytime there is chaos in a family, someone has stepped outside the will of God.

5. Where there is unity, people allowed themselves to be sustained by God (Eph. 4:12–13).
6. Where there is chaos, believers are in the flesh (Gal. 5:19–21).
7. It is better when something is wrong to allow God to make it right than for someone to try to be God and make it right (Samson and the Philistines; Saul and David).

C. God Restores a Broken Relationship (33:4–9)

1. Isaac submitted to the will of God, once again (Gen. 27:38–40; 28:3–4).
2. Parents began communicating again (Gen. 27:46).
3. God preserved the boys' love for each other (Gen. 33:4–16).
   a) God established forgiveness (vv. 10–11).
   b) God established mutual respect (vv. 13, 15).
   c) God renewed peace (vv. 16–17).
4. Restoration takes place when personal agendas are removed and God's will take preeminence.

Author's Comments

Comments

Sometimes the problems in a home are created by the parents. When this occurs, it tends to lead to sibling rivalry and pain. One of the major mistakes than can be made is favoritism. This can leave children as enemies rather than best friends. Here you have two godly parents who love one child better than the other. This led to trouble that continues today. What can be done when a "family chorus leads to family chaos" (see Gen. 27:38–45)?

God was clear from the beginning that the oldest child would serve the youngest. Both parents knew what God said but chose to do what was natural for them (Gen. 25:22–24). Isaac loved eating wild game and Esau was an outdoorsman. Isaac was outdoors a lot and then he became blind. He found a way to enjoy what he so missed. Rebekah, based on the custom of her day, was a housewife, and since Jacob liked being among the tents, she ended up being close to him. What was natural for the parents is what they did even though their lives demonstrate they both loved God. Rebekah cared for Esau and Isaac cared for Jacob, but when parents do what is natural rather than what is best, it can take a family chorus and make it a family crisis.

God's Word must always override our feelings. The first step to discipleship is to deny yourself (Luke 14:26) no matter the cost (Luke 14:27–28) or the cross to bear. We must always center our lives on God's purposes. The purpose was for God to create a nation unto Himself that would serve Him. I am sure Abraham relayed all of this to his son Isaac. So when God chose to provide two children and then specifically explain which child would serve the other, the parents should have been committed to see God's plan through. This would have led to a smoother process that would have probably not put two brothers at odds with each other; of would have probably also preserved the character of Jacob. This deceptive character remained with him throughout his life.

A child is ordered by God to be trained in the direction that God has prepared for them (Prov. 22:6). When God blesses a parent with a child (Ps. 127:3; especially here in the case of Rebekah), it is to "fill the earth and subdue it; have dominion over the fish of the sea, over the birds of the air, and over every living thing that moves on the earth" (Gen. 1:28). This nation was God's movement forward (Gen. 12:1–3) to continue to achieve His purposes. Parents must be focused on God's purposes.

Application

When a parent goes to buy something for one child, they should do something similar for the other. The manner in which a parent disciplines one child versus the other should be the same. Parents can teach their children to be deceptive in simple ways such as telling the children to lie when they answer the phone or receiving more change than they deserve and not returning it. Parents should not do this! Because a child is born in sin, the child will have a natural appetite for sin. The parent needs to be a godly example to shape the character of Christ into the life of the child.

Parents must learn the bent of their children so that it benefits the child's life. This can allow their child to better find a career they enjoy. The Scriptures say when they find a job they enjoy (Eccles. 3:12–13), this is a gift from God. Once saved, God provides them spiritual gifts (1 Pet. 4:10). They are either male or female. So they would be husbands or wives, fathers or mothers. Their race is set, and it is our job as parents to teach them how to run it (Heb. 12:1–2). Therefore, parents must be purposeful when they are raising their children.

Illustrate It

Arian Foster was the running back for the Houston Texans football team. He was undrafted and did not even make the starting squad in his first year. Other players were liked more and were given greater opportunities on the team. It was not that he did not do well. He just never got the chance to shine, for whatever reason. For the most part, it looked like the extent of his career was a benchwarmer until he was used on the practice squad. He was the opponent that the first team trained against. Not even at home games was he given the chance to dress out because of league rules. But he never gave up. He kept applying himself and he did not create problems on the team.

One day, one of the starters got hurt and he was given the chance to play. Young Arian never looked back. He became the starting running back and eventually earned a large contract that placed him among the top running backs in the NFL.

When we are treated unfairly by those in charge, we must not allow their actions to define us or determine our attitude toward others.

Counsel You Can Count On

Ecclesiastes 12:1, 13–14

General Overview of the Passages

In this passage, Solomon commands young men to make an inner decision to pay attention to God. This must be done before mischievousness sets in, leading to an inability to consistently measure up to God's good standards. This can take place when young men become more powerfully influenced by their sin nature. This nature inflicts powerful blows on the youth's desire to do evil. When this takes place, young men's inner desires drive them to no longer delight in their Creator. This is a serious issue because God is the one who has the power to create everything out of nothing and establishes all things by His sovereign power.

Solomon also warns the young men to be prepared for old age, when all the joys of youth (see Eccles. 12:1) would be just a memory. The best way to prepare for that difficult time is to love God and live for Him each day (12:1). Without such a commitment of faith, life would end as it began, without meaning or purpose (12:8; see 1:2). To forget the Creator while a youth is to invite bitter regrets and an empty existence in old age. To remember the Creator is to follow the path of wisdom and extend the joy of life.

When everything has been given full attention, since all that has been said is prophetic revelation, and the person has gained a full knowledge and understanding of everything, the youth develops a reverence of God. Reverencing God takes place when they are in complete awe of God, worshipping Him; this will then lead to righteous behavior as a devoted follower for God (Heb. 12:28–29). They must also pay careful attention and put a hedge around God's Word (David; Ps. 119:9–11) by guarding what they have learned from negative influences. By submitting to God, you will establish clear-cut directives of His moral law. One of the best ways to do this is to fear God by reverencing Him and by remaining continually conscious of His presence.

God's will continually brings the work of everyone's hands under His governing structure. God will judge whether or not these young men demonstrated an inability to come up to His standards. This is what should characterize everyone's life.

Historical Background

Establishing Context

Solomon has a group of young men gathered before him; as the teacher, he is focused on providing them wisdom. Solomon is highly respected as being given wisdom from God. "The Septuagint word for *Teacher* is *ekklesiastes*, from which most English titles of the book are taken, and from which such English words as 'ecclesiastical' are derived."[38] After spending most of the book on day-to-day, real-life issues, Solomon engages young men on how to remain focused in the days of their youth, since God judges every act.

This focus matches the development of the book well, because the first part of the book looks at man's activities being futile when done apart from the purposes of God. The second part of the book focuses on a person living their lives with a conscious awareness of God's purposes. So when Solomon ends the book challenging his listeners to fear God, it fits the context for young men to enjoy their lives but to remember that God judges all things. "To *fear God* is one of the major themes of this book and of wisdom literature in the OT. To fear God is to respond to Him in awe, reverence, and wonder, to serve Him in purity of action, and to shun evil and any worship of anything else in His universe."[39]

What Does the Context Mean?

We must instruct our youth to not take their younger years for granted. A person's actions will be judged because nothing escapes God's justice. They must remember God by fearing Him, by guarding their lives like David did during his youth. When a young man does this, he will preserve his life against the attacks of evil, which can damage his life and cause God to judge him. For these reasons, they must take the days of youth seriously so that there is little regret and less pain in adult life.

---

[38] Matthews, Chavalas, and Walton, *The IVP Bible Background Commentary: Old Testament,* s.v. Eccles. 12:1–8.

[39] Radmacher, Allen, and House, *Nelson's New Illustrated Bible Commentary*, 792.

Sermon Subject and Title

Sermon Title: Counsel You Can Count On
Big Idea: "Live footloose and fancy free" while remaining in submission and reverence toward God.

Sermon Outline (Eccles. 12:1, 13–14 NASB)

A. Teach Them to Remember God (12:1, 13a; John 14:6)

1. *Remember*—We must develop a determined inner commitment to pay attention to God (Dan. 1:8). This is an imperative; Solomon is commanding them to remember. This is important for everything else he is going to say.
2. *Remember*—Live life God-conscious (Col. 3:17; Matt. 22:36–40; Prov. 3:5).
3. *Remember*—Question to ponder: "Is God pleased with what I am doing?"
4. *Creator*—Definition: to establish everything out of nothing and regulate what has been established by His sovereign will.
5. *Creator*—Christ upholds everything by His Word (Col. 1:17; Heb. 1:3).
6. *Creator*—We can depend on God because everything depends on Him. No matter what happens in life, depend on His Word to work it out (Prov. 3:5; 2 Tim. 1:5; 3:14–16).
7. *Evil days*—Means the growing child becomes more conscious of the way it feels.
8. *Evil days*—Man's depravity becomes perpetually more evil. This is an imperfect, meaning evil continually proliferates.
9. *Draw near*—Inflects powerful blows on the youth's desire to do evil.
10. *Draw near*—Aware of strong feelings that conflict with obeying God.
11. *I have no delight in them*—When a youth does not live with a consciousness to please God, they lose the desire for godly things (Matt. 6:24; Rom. 6:12–19; 8:5–8; Heb. 6:1–6). When earthly passions dominate their decisions, their ability to please God is diminished (1 John 2:15–17).
12. *Heard*—What they are hearing is never going to stop being heard. This is in the imperfect—a past act that continues in the present and will continue into the future.

13. *Heard*—They do not lack knowledge or understanding, but desire (considered in the context of Eccles. 12:1).
14. *Heard*—This is a person who, because of life's attractions, willfully chooses to forget (Matt. 16:26; Dan. 1:10—other youths).

B. Teach Them How to Preserve Their Hearts (12:13)

1. If this is not preserved, a person will forget God and miss point A.
2. *Fear God*—Teach the children to fear God because that leads to wisdom and understanding (Prov. 9:10).
3. *Fear God*—Living conscious of how God blesses; He protects, He provides long life (Prov. 3:12–16). This is because He is the powerful and awesome One.
4. *Fear God*—Once this is established, it leads to sincere worship (Heb. 12:28–29).
5. *Guard*—They must protect what they know about God's Word so others cannot pollute it—means to put a hedge around God's Word (Ps. 119:9–11).
6. *Guard*—Do not allow trials or passions to cause them to drift away from God (Heb. 2:1–4).
7. *Guard*—Leads a person to forsake friends who seek to lead them astray (Ps. 1); determined to remember God; a life constantly being sanctified through the ministry of the Holy Spirit (Rom. 8:12–17).

C. They Must Live with No Regrets (12:14; 11:9)

1. Nothing is hidden (no secrets) from God (Matt. 12:25; Heb. 4:12).
2. God is gracious and just (Jonah 4:9–11).
3. His justice is for every act, whether good or bad.
4. *God will bring*—God, the most powerful person, perpetually executes judgment. This is an imperfect, meaning this action never stops.
5. It is best to live life in faith by God's grace (Hab. 2:4).

Author's Comments

Comments

Life Savers are a well-loved candy by many. But most people do not know that the Life Saver was developed because the person who made it lost his daughter to a candy being stuck in her throat. He made candy with a hole in it so that if it got stuck, the child or person could still breathe. We need to put principles together that would save our children's lives when they become stuck in the muck that this depraved world can lead them to. There is so much being thrown down their throats on the Internet, television, phones, music, as well as pressure at school, the natural changes taking place in their bodies, and, let's not forget, pressure from their peers. It is like a person who is playing dodgeball when all of a sudden everyone starts throwing all the balls at them at one time. Someone has to step in to be a lifesaver.

Solomon wants these young people to know that life away from God is empty. It may start off well, but it will soon crumble and become useless. Life is only productive for a long time when it is directed by God as His Word is applied to real-life circumstances. This application of the Word of God requires wisdom. When these young people remember what God says and apply wisdom when the time of God's judgment comes, they will be blessed because they feared God. This is critical, since God judges every act of man and every word that we speak (Matt. 12:36–37). It is not that Solomon is suggesting that young people should not enjoy their youth; rather, it is that when they do, they must remember they will one day grow old, and then stand before God.

Application

Young people should enjoy the days of their youth. They should enjoy sports, games, friends, and family. These days of not having to pay bills, free food at the house, and using cars that they do not have to up keep will never come again. But if they do not live with a consciousness of God, they can become sexually active, alcoholics, irresponsible, and non-productive. Their adult life can be filled with trying to kick bad habits, paying debts, a criminal record that makes getting a job and even an apartment difficult, and struggling to gain the trust of family members. Worst of all, living in sin can bring an early death (1 John 5:16). There is nothing wrong with enjoying one's life as a youth, but they must remember it is the laying of a foundation.

Illustrate It

Years ago while in seminary I worked as a juvenile probation officer. I had to go to the home of a teenager who had gotten into trouble. As I got to know the young man, no matter how many times I talked with him, I could not get him to become serious about school and developing his life productively. All he wanted to do was to have fun with his friends, even if it meant skipping school.

One day I came to his home because I had to arrest him. When I got to the house, he took off running. After chasing him down and getting some help from some police officers, I took him back to jail.

I sat with him several times in jail because I knew he would eventually get out. Well, he did not change his attitude: parties, girls, drinking, drugs, no school, just "fun, fun, and more fun." One day later, as I approached the door, his mother met me with tears in her eyes and sadly told me that he and his friends were driving really fast, lost control, and he was killed instantly.

Life is a gift from God. It is only productive when the life (God) is developed in the hearts and minds of each person. To take the gift and not develop it is to automatically move in the direction of death. Electricity produces light. To ignore electricity is to decide to walk around in darkness. It is not that the electric current is not available to the person; it is just being ignored by him or her.

Sermon Series 6
Evidence of True Faith

Game Plan for Victorious Living

James 4:7–10

General Overview of the Passage

In the midst of quarrels and believers living worldly lives, James challenges them to develop a game plan for victory. He has already stated how they need to accept trials as God's refining process (James 1:2–4) because there is a crown for those who endure (1:12). They must manage their anger and live by faith and true wisdom because they now must focus on developing a productive relationship with God.

They must decide to come under the authority of God, like a soldier following orders, and make it an urgent matter to resist Satan's attacks without being double minded. It is this kind of decisive behavior under the authority of God that causes God to fight for them. As a result, these believers make their spiritual growth their complete focus. This is because when you "draw near to God, . . . He will draw near to you" (4:8). A person draws near by keeping their lives holy before God. They cannot be double-minded because, as chapter 1:8 describes, this will lead to them being unstable. All of the above will work if believers commit to live totally dependent upon God with a willing heart to obey what God says. When believers live like this, they maintain a constant awareness that it is "in Him we live and move and exist" (Acts 17:28 NASB). When a believer is committed to draw near to God, James states, God will honor him.

Historical Background

Establishing Context

While a person is resisting the devil, they are told to submit to God and draw near to God. "The idea of submission suggested by *ὑποτάσσεσθαι* is usually directed to human authority (Luke 2:51; Rom. 13:1; Eph. 5:22; Titus 2:9; 1 Pet. 2:13) and not God (as here and at Heb. 12:9; see Adamson, 174). The thought of submitting to God is rounded off in v. 10 by the command to become humble before the Lord (an *inclusio*? See Davids, 165).[1] They were expected, especially since they were quarreling and gaining a love for the world, to bring themselves under the authority of God.

To draw near to God comes through faith that is lived by way of wisdom and understanding (James 1:5–9). It is a process just like in the case of a priest. "'Cleanse your hands' seems odd in the passage but it is a reference to 'washing' and 'purifying'; it stems from Old Testament requirements for priestly purity when administering the things of the Lord."[2] This process seems to also take a strange turn when James says to "lament and mourn and weep! Let your laughter be turned to mourning and your joy to gloom" (James 4:9). "Old Testament texts often connected mourning and self-humiliation with repentance (Lev. 23:29; 26:41), especially when confronted by divine judgment (2 Kings. 22:11; Joel 1:13–14; 2:12–13). The exaltation of the humble was also a teaching of the prophets (Matt. 23:12). James is no killjoy, wanting Christians to walk around with long faces and somber expressions. Key to understanding his exhortation here is to recognize that 'laughter' is often associated with the 'fool' in biblical wisdom."[3]

What Does the Context Mean?

We must force ourselves to come under God's authority. When Satan sees this consistently being done, he will flee from us. In doing this, we must seek God out by making every attempt to draw near to Him, to live a pure life, and to not be double-minded, because a double-minded man will not receive anything from God. We must not use earthly wisdom, because it is demonic leading us directly into the hands of Satan.

It is this focus that should cause us to be willing to be miserable, mourn, and weep, and even turn laughter to gloom, so that our submission is complete and Satan does not cause us to change our minds when things are difficult. This process requires a humble spirit, always remembering to live life in the sight of

---

[1] Ralph P. Martin, *James,* vol. 48 in the Word Biblical Commentary series (Dallas, TX: Word, Incorporated, 1988), 152.

[2] Ibid.

[3] Ibid., 110.

God. When this is complete, God will take our gloom and turn it to a joy. This joy is supplied by Him because He will exalt us.

Sermon Subject and Title

Sermon Title: Game Plan for Victorious Living
Big Idea: The devil is not intimidated when someone rebukes him, but he is resisted by a believer's godly character and acts of faith.

Sermon Outline (James 4:7–10 NASB)

A. Resist the Devil (v. 7)

1. *Submit*—James commands us to come under God's authority for guaranteed victories (Isa. 55:11; Heb. 4:12). We are commanded to make this decision once and for all (aorist tense).
2. *Submit*—A military term for following orders. Recognize God's supreme power and authority over all (Rom. 8:37; Phil. 4:13).
3. *Resist*—It is an urgent matter to withstand the attacks of Satan. He came to "steal and kill and destroy" (John 10:10 NASB). This is another command (imperative mood) but a decisive decision (aorist)—a once-and-for-all action.
4. *Resist*—Failing to resist the devil is to act like the double-minded person (James 1:5–8).
5. *Resist*—We must urgently fight against the attacks of Satan (Eph. 6:12–18; the armor of God). James provides a game plan in this passage.
6. *Devil or Satan*—He attacks with accusations and slander (Rev. 12:10). He wants to separate people from God. He can influence believers who desire to depend on their common sense (James 3:15), who are selfishly ambitious (3:16), hate people (4:2), love the things of the world (4:4), or use earthly wisdom (3:13–18; 2 Cor. 10:3–6).
7. *Flee*—The devil views a believer as dangerous who lives a submissive life before God.

B. Draw Near to God (vv. 8–9; Matt. 4:4–10; this is how Satan is resisted)

1. *Draw near*—When we do come under the authority of God, we are commanded to make spiritual growth our complete focus. This needs to be a decisive act (aorist tense).

2. *Draw near*—Resisting the devil means we must also run toward God (1 Tim. 6:11; 2 Tim. 2:22).
3. *Draw near*—We must take growing in our service, worship, and knowledge of God seriously. We also must:
   a) *Cleanse your hands*—Keep anything that is under our control acceptable in the sight of God. This is another aorist imperative. James commands us in the sense of making up our minds and deciding once and for all to carry out these actions, because of the relentless actions of Satan (1 Pet. 5:8–9).
   b) *Purify*—We must live consecrated lives to God. Again, this is an aorist imperative.
   c) *Purify your hearts*—Keep Satan's battleground, our minds, consecrated to God (2 Cor. 10:3–6).
   d) *Double-minded*—We must not doubt (James 1:8) or waver (Rom. 4:18–19).
   e) *Double-minded*—We cannot have a double allegiance to God and the world (James 3:9–12).
   f) *Be miserable, mourn, and weep—turn laughter to gloom*—Whatever pain, difficulty, or suffering drawing near creates, we must remain focused (Rom. 8:18; Phil. 3:7–11; 2 Tim. 4:6–8). If we do not, the pain will hamper our spiritual growth (Luke 8:14). James uses the aorist imperative consistently because as believers we must be determined and steadfast in our focus. "Blessed are the poor in spirit, for theirs is the kingdom of heaven" (Matt. 5:3).

C. Depend on God to Supply the Victory (v. 10)

1. *Humble*—Accept our limitations and totally depend on God (Phil. 4:13). This is another aorist imperative, but this verb is passive. This is something the believer must receive from the Holy Spirit.
2. *Humble vs. Submit*—Submit is to come under God; humility is a disposition, a way of life.
3. *Humble*—Those who bring themselves under God's authority will sometimes be miserable, mourn, weep, and have their laughter turned to gloom, so they must be willing to bring themselves low (John 12:23–26).
4. *Humble*—God gives grace (God bestows spontaneous, free-hearted gifts) to the humble (James 4:6).

5. *Humble*—A characteristic that positions God to fight for us (1 Pet. 5:5–11).
6. *Presence of the Lord*—Live constantly aware of who God is.
7. *Lord*—All authority to take me from suffering to complete exaltation (Joseph, Daniel; Gal. 6:9–10). "The Lord" is in the genitive, meaning the Lord takes possession of this moment to exalt the believer.
8. *He will exalt you*—God, who has all authority, guarantees honor for a humble person.

Author's Comments

Comments

Perhaps James feels that the believers were merely playing church; for example, they complained about being in trials, but they were double-minded and were getting caught up in temptation. Or perhaps it was anger, because of their oppression, turning them into hearers of the Word who failed to live it, and responding to people based on their financial status. They demonstrated intellectual and static faith but not dynamic faith. Instead of being overcomers, they remained stuck in the same struggle every day, which even caused them to fight each other. To not commit to a game plan for victory can lead to a stagnant life of misery day after day. It is not just going to church; it is developing a dynamic game plan after church so that we experience Christ powerfully each day.

There are reasons why we may shun the game plan. It takes a certain mindset to count trials all joy (James 1:2). A person must keep "the crown of life" (1:12) ahead of them. They have to live by faith and not by sight and constantly ask for wisdom from God. James goes to another level when he says, "Lament and mourn and weep! Let your laughter be turned to mourning and your joy to gloom" (4:9). Who would desire this experience? Not me! However, as my faith deepens, so does my burden for the lost, my passion to see people desire to know God, my pain when people are hurt by their children's choices, my frustration when missionaries are overwhelmed with zeal but cannot find financial support. Faith has a habit of taking me to the cross and forcing me to bring myself under His authority. It requires complete trust and total surrender, so sometimes it takes my laughter and turns it to mourning and my joy can become gloom. But then I remember Paul saying: "Yet in all these things we are more than conquerors through Him who loved us. For I am persuaded that neither death nor life, nor angels nor principalities nor powers, nor things present nor things to come, nor height nor depth, nor any other created thing, shall be able to separate us from the love of God which is in Christ Jesus our Lord" (Rom. 8:37–39).

Living focused (Heb. 12:2) is the only challenge this life brings because we only have one fight to fight, and that is whether or not we will keep the faith (1 Tim. 6:12).

Application

The devil is always on the attack (Rev. 12:10). We must remain alert by maintaining a submissive spirit to the Word of God. The Word does not come back empty (Isa. 55:11). Keeping the Word of God during struggles is our main fight (Eph. 6:17; 1 Tim. 6:12) because it requires godly wisdom, so that we bring ourselves completely under the authority of God. When we are willing to take refuge in God, Satan is automatically resisted. This commitment is necessary because it may cause us to mourn and weep and this pain can drive us to forsake God rather than draw near. Imagine miscarriages, loss of a loving parent, repeated layoffs, health issues that just won't go away, a marriage that is in constant conflict or even abuse. How do we draw near?

Illustrate It

While I was driving through the streets of Rwanda with Dr. Faustin Ntamushobora, I asked him a loaded question. You see, these are the streets he had to use to escape the soldiers who wanted to kill his entire family. Streets where his wife lost seventeen family members. Streets with dead bodies in them. Streets with people you're not sure you can trust. How does he feel when he drives through these streets years later?

He said to me without taking much of a breath: "Dr. Cannings, we need to transform the lives of people to sincerely have a love for Christ. We need to disciple leaders so that they are not given to such sinful deeds because they love God and want to help others." You see, Dr. Ntamushobora did not see defeat when he looked down these alleyways; he saw a greater reason and need to challenge people to live victorious in Christ Jesus. This is why he is back in the same city, bringing leaders from various parts of the world to strengthen churches by training their leaders and pastors, teaching on marriage and parenting to strengthen homes, and risking his life by still taking trips into Uganda to make a difference for the kingdom of God. Satan is busy, but he cannot defeat us when we are committed to drawing near to God.

Wisdom . . . the Good, the Bad, the Ugly

James 3:13–18

General Overview of the Passage

The Jerusalem church, because of Paul's persecution, had scattered into various cities. Believers were reestablishing the church in the midst of a society that did not warmly welcome these relocated Jews. Their former pastor (James) writes them because there is a need for wisdom. He teaches that true wisdom comes directly from God. God is the only person who can impact a believer's life (Col. 1:9–10) to provide the spiritual guidance to influence him and to skillfully apply the knowledge of God into real-life situations. It is this process that leads to the balancing of biblical knowledge with the facts of a situation and provides direction on how to live godly in difficult circumstances.

Anyone who continuously demonstrates sinful characteristics so that it becomes a habit exposes their true nature. These individuals boast about what they are doing even though the negative effects are visible. This causes confusion to erupt, leading to believers fighting for their rights. This can become violent in the church. This kind of "wisdom" did not descend from heaven and therefore it is inferior and based on a person's feelings and way of thinking. "You can always tell when a church or a family follows false wisdom: you will find jealousy, division, and confusion. Instead of humbly depending on the Spirit and the Word, they look to the world for ideas and to the flesh for strength, and by so doing play right into the hands of the devil."[4]

Wisdom from above is vastly different than earthly knowledge. Wisdom from above displays attributes that are representative of the nature of Christ. It is unmistakably beneficial, especially since it resolves issues and makes

[4] W. W. Wiersbe, *Wiersbe's Expository Outlines on the New Testament* (Wheaton, IL: Victor Books, 1992), 728.

relationships harmonious. Relationships are harmonious because there is no selfish ambition, no strife, and people are willing to come to compromise, not being quick to punish each other for what was done wrong. They are unshakable about their biblical convictions because they are deeply committed to the standards of God. As a result, these attributes create a powerful influence among believers leading to peace. "Those who make peace, who do their just acts in a peaceful way. The phrase aptly recalls Jesus' words in Matthew 5:9 to the reader: 'Blessed are the peacemakers . . .'"[5]

Historical Background

Establishing Context

James is writing to a congregation he once pastored. There are a lot of dynamics in this church that James needs to address. One of the fundamental concepts James is trying to teach is obedience to the Word of God rather than only being a "hearer." Since he is writing in this section of the letter to teachers, wisdom fits well. "James's insistence that wisdom is revealed in a godly lifestyle picks up a key theme of the letter (see 2:14–26) and reflects the common Jewish focus on the practical dimensions of wisdom. Wisdom, Proverbs reminds us, leads us to 'walk in the ways of good men and keep to the paths of the righteous' (Prov. 2:20)."[6]

There was a Jewish revolt in this city, and the Zealots' violent retaliation that took place in Jerusalem against the Romans began to take root in this church. This is why James addresses anger and faith in God before he discusses the results of true wisdom. "The term for 'zeal' used by the Zealots, who fancied themselves successors of Phinehas (Num. 25:11; Ps. 106:30–31) and the Maccabees and sought to liberate Jewish Palestine from Rome by force of arms. "Strife" (KJV; 'selfish ambition'—NASB, NIV, NRSV) also was related to disharmony and had been known to provoke wars."[7]

Therefore, if a person is a teacher guided by the Holy Spirit, their wisdom (James 1:5–9) would lead to good behavior that is "peaceable, gentle, willing to

---

[5] P. H. Davids, *The Epistle of James: A Commentary on the Greek Text* (Grand Rapids, MI: Eerdmans, 1982), 155.

[6] C. E. Arnold, *Zondervan Illustrated Bible Backgrounds Commentary: Hebrews to Revelation* (Grand Rapids, MI: Zondervan, 2002), 4:106.

[7] C. S. Keener, *The IVP Bible Background Commentary: New Testament* (Downers Grove, IL: InterVarsity Press, 1993), s.v. James 3:14.

yield, full of mercy and good fruits, without partiality and without hypocrisy. Now the fruit of righteousness is sown in peace by those who make peace" (James 3:17–18). "This is the antithesis of the advocates of revolution, who were gaining popularity in the tensions stirred by poverty and oppression in the land."[8] These are the dynamics in this church that lead James to have a powerful discussion about the evidence of true faith and wisdom.

What Does the Context Mean?

If a person actually has a spiritual, skillful, practical knowledge of God, it should be obvious to those who see their lifestyle. It will benefit those around them. This is because their Christian walk, which is energized by faith, would be free from malice and revenge. But if on a continual basis this person demonstrates resentfulness that is self-seeking, James commands this church to accept what they see as truly what is going on in the person's heart. This lifestyle is associated with emptiness and sinfulness that come from the human nature that is not controlled by God and is influenced by demons. The evidence of this kind of wisdom is a fierce desire to promote one's own opinion, a self-seeking attitude to gain an advantage over someone like a politician, creating confusion, anarchy, and violent opposition that is not representative of godly wisdom. This kind of earthly wisdom does not benefit anyone.

Wisdom that is constantly flowing from above is free from contamination from the world. It makes peace with others, demonstrates steadfastness in the midst of trouble constantly trusting God, listens in an effort to come to productive conclusions, and withholds punishment from those who deserve it. This is a wisdom that benefits others because it comes from God. It is unshakable without any pretense, producing powerful internal growth that leads to external conformity to God's standards. This lifestyle does not create strife because it is controlled by God and not demons.

Sermon Subject and Title

Sermon Title: Wisdom . . . the Good, the Bad, the Ugly
Big Idea: When godly wisdom and earthly wisdom are compared, godly wisdom proves more beneficial in stimulating spiritual growth in a believer's life.

[8] Ibid.

SERMON OUTLINE (JAMES 3:13–18 NASB)

A. Wisdom: The Real Deal (v. 13a)

1. What is wisdom?
   a) It comes directly from heaven (James 1:5).
   b) It is a skillful, practical application of the knowledge of God to everyday situations. This is why it requires a believer who is a doer, not just a hearer. It requires a person who lives by a faith that works.
   c) Wisdom is in the nominative, demonstrating that it is the objective of James's letter in this section of Scripture.
2. What is understanding? It is balancing biblical knowledge with a particular situation for effective application (Col. 1:9–12).
   a) "Understanding" is in the nominative, demonstrating that it is another objective of James's letter in this section of Scripture.

B. Wisdom: The Bad and the Ugly (vv. 14–16)

1. To *have*—Means to continuously demonstrate sinful attributes while claiming to have wisdom. This is a present active verb, which means these behavior characteristics are continuous. This is who the person is because it is habitual.
2. When wisdom is forsaken, there is:
   a) *Jealousy*—To be upset about the good one person sees in another. To be upset that one teacher receives more recognition than another.
   b) *Selfish ambition*—They were seeking to win followers for themselves and their own purposes.
   c) *Heart*—This person is jealous and desires to fulfill their selfish ambition.
3. *Truth*—It is the reality before everyone's eyes. It is also the divine will of God.
4. *Arrogant about the truth*—They looked at the facts that their teaching created problems, yet they boasted about their teachings. They boasted in what they believed, because they wanted to advance themselves (selfish ambition).
   a) James commands (imperative) not to continually do this (present active) because they are being deceived by lies against what is actually taking place before their eyes (Rom. 16:17–18).
5. A person's level of spiritual growth is reflected in how they treat others (Matt. 22:36–40; Col. 1:9–12; 1 John 4:7–8).
6. Traits of wisdom that is not from above:

a) *Is*—James instructs us to understand that the wisdom he describes in this section of Scripture does not come down from above.
b) *Wisdom*—Mental excellence in its highest and fullest sense, as a person seeks to make decisions. Again, this is in the nominative because it is the direct focus of this passage.
c) *Comes down*—Wisdom that displays selfish and arrogant behavior does not come down from above. We must pray for it (James 1:5). This is a present active verb, meaning it is always this way.
d) *Earthly*—It is empty and inferior to wisdom provided by God (1 Cor. 2:1–9). It does not positively impact a person's life forever because it fades away.
e) *Earthly*—Can find it in a book, on the radio, blogs, TV. (Example: some people use to develop their relationships based on the television series *Days of Our Lives*.)
f) *Natural*—It is based on how a person feels or thinks. It springs up from their own desires, which can be influenced by the way they were raised or from influences from the world.
g) *Demonic*—It is divisive and destructive—the nature of demons.
h) *Disorderly*—It creates confusion; people fight for their rights and can become violent (James 4:1–10).
i) There is *jealousy*—People become fierce in promoting their own thoughts trying to outdo the other person.
j) *Selfish ambition*—Believers in the church working to gain an advantage on another believer. They may even withdraw from the church to start their own ministry (Phil. 1:15–17; 2:3).
k) *Disorder and every kind of evil*—This leads the church to confusion, anarchy, and even violence because these people demand their own rights, which makes circumstances in the church go from bad to worse.

C. Wisdom: The Good (vv. 13b, 17–18)

1. *Is*—James commands us that this wisdom comes down from above.
2. Traits of wisdom that is from above:
   a) *Good behavior*—James commands (imperative) believers who claim to have wisdom and understanding to make a decisive decision (aorist) to demonstrate a lifestyle that is in conformity to God's standards. This behavior proves itself to come from God when it in turn benefits the lives of others (James 1:26–27).

- *Good* is a genitive which means it is the kind of behavior a wise person possesses.

b) *Good*—It benefits people around us.

c) *Good*—Problems are resolved in a productive manner.

d) *Good*—Relationships are harmonious leading to spiritual growth.

e) *Behavior*—A life that embraces the whole of the Christian walk.

f) *Behavior*—This Christian lifestyle:

- *His deeds*—Believers are energized about their faith and service to God.
- *Gentleness of wisdom*—Believers do not act maliciously or vengefully in difficult times; they wait on God because He is a just Judge.
- *Gentleness of wisdom*—This attribute demonstrates strength because the believer is under the control of the Holy Spirit. If they become angry, it is at the right time and it is anger under control.
- *Pure*—Is free from jealous and selfish ambitions; the motives are pure (James 3:16–17).
- *Peaceable*—These believers do not seek to create strife.
- *Reasonable*—They listen to the facts, compromise, and are compliant.
- *Full of mercy*—They are quick to not punish other believers for the wrong they have done. It is not vengeful.
- *Unwavering*—They are unshakable because they have a deep conviction of God's Word. They are free from prejudice because their allegiance is to God.
- *Fruit of righteousness*—These believers faithfully maintain the standards of God's Word.
- *Makes peace*—This wisdom creates a powerful spiritual influence which leads to peace.

3. Knowledge puffs up (1 Cor. 8:1), but spiritual wisdom humbles us. While the false wisdom has its origin in the world, the flesh, and the devil, the true wisdom "comes down from above" (see James 1:17).

Author's Comments

Comments

Far too many people have the idea that to be "spiritual" means to be impractical; nothing is farther from the truth. One of things that James is dealing with here is that the believers were playing church, they complained about being in trials, they were double-minded, getting caught up in temptation and anger, hearing the Word but not living it, and responding to people based on their financial status. They demonstrated intellectual and static faith but not dynamic faith, because they were more religious than true to God's Word. They lacked wisdom.

When a person obeys God, they practice true religion by caring for widows; they endure trials, manage anger, and treat the poor the same way they treat the rich. As a result, the application of the Word of God leads to acts of faith, which demonstrate wise behavioral characteristics that benefit others.

Therefore, those who claim to be teachers and exercise wisdom that they believe is from God should produce a behavior that blesses the people of God. Those who claim to have wisdom but only make matters worse are not applying the Word of God and are "earthly, sensual, demonic. For where envy and self-seeking exist, confusion and every evil thing are there" (James 3:15–17). "God's genuine wisdom is nonviolent rather than given to lashing out: 'peaceable,' 'gentle,' 'open to reason,' 'full of mercy' (cf. 2:13); it was also 'unwavering' (NASB), better rendered 'impartial' (NIV), or 'without prejudice or favoritism' (cf. 2:1–9)."[9]

We certainly need godly wisdom (the practical application of God's Word in day-to-day living) because just like these believers we have struggles every day, problems to resolve, families to develop, and people we love seeking advice. Wisdom from God is essential to living productively so that we can distinguish the "good, bad, or ugly."

This is the kind of wisdom we need for our homes, jobs, communities, and churches, because it's only source is God. Believers who exercise this wisdom live by faith because they are not just hearers of God's Word, but doers.

---

[9] Keener, *The IVP Bible Background Commentary: New Testament*, s.v. James 3:17.

Application

Pray for wisdom and test it when we believe we have it by what comes from the decisions we make. The decisions we make for our homes should not produce division and promote selfish ambition. The advice provided to those in the church who respect us should not lead to "disorder and every kind of evil." Our decision should lead to peace and righteousness when it is influenced by God. We know we are empowered by God to make those decisions when we are committed to apply God's Word as we live by faith.

Illustrate It

Hitler influenced a nation to fight to develop itself, its military might and power. He was ambitious and wanted to rule the world and get rid of anyone who was feeble or threatening. In his march to conquer the world, he killed six million Jews, many innocent civilians who were only trying to live out their lives and enjoy their family and friends. Many Germans who opposed him were killed. His war led to starvation, thousands of soldiers losing their lives, and the atomic bomb killing thousands.

His selfish ambition was demonic.

Make Your Goal Gold

James 5:7–11

General Overview of the Passage

When we are suffering, endurance can be very challenging. When there is no timetable as to when the suffering will end, we often fall apart, questioning how we will make it. James understood and teaches us how to endure these trials. In the midst of trials, we must be determined to make it to the end. This determination is filled with anticipation, like a farmer waiting for the early and late rains, knowing that his crop and livelihood depends on it. "The verb used here for 'Be patient,' *makrothumesate*, together with its cognate noun, usually rendered 'long-suffering,' denotes not so much the brave endurance of afflictions and the refusal to give way before them even under pressure."[10]

Because our emotions can get the best of us during these times of endurance, James encourages us to firmly hold to the ministry of the Word. We are not just hearers; we are doers. We live out the wisdom of God with understanding. James repeats that the coming of the Lord is a set condition that nothing can change and it is compared to those in the Old Testament. Because we need to keep our hearts firm in the Word, we must make sure there is no space between God and us (Col. 3:1–4). We need to resist the devil, encourage the weak, and live in godly wisdom. "The reason for this hope is clear: God is not vicious; he does not love watching people suffer. Rather he is compassionate."[11] Whether it is the prophets, Job, or our Lord, we see that because they endured to the end, they were blessed.

---

[10] Davids, *The Epistle of James*, 181–82.

[11] Ibid., 188.

Historical Background

Establishing Context

James calls for patience in the midst of ongoing trials because he knows that this is something many people who were farmers would understand.

> In Palestine, the growth of crops was particularly dependent on the rain that came in late autumn and early spring. Note, for example, Deuteronomy 11:14, where God, in response to his people's obedience, promises: "Then I will send rain on your land in its season, both autumn and spring rains, so that you may gather in your grain, new wine and oil." Every passage in which the language of "early and late rains" appears in the Old Testament affirms God's faithfulness to his people.[12]

The rains were not just important for growing their crops; they also represented food for their very existence.

Because some of the members in the church were poor, it is possible that they worked the fields. Some of the rich in the church could have been landowners when they came to church. "In this section of scripture believers were suffering at the hands of the rich, so James wants to encourage them. The rich in the church were exploiting them by taking the best seats and by eating the Lord's Supper before the poor can get to church. The poor may have become angry, and this created the fighting and quarreling with the rich being too proud to respond appropriately."[13] The rich were not only landowners; they were also functioning in the church and controlling how things worked. They took the best seats (James 2:1–7), ate the Lord's Supper before the poor could get out of the fields, and expected special treatment. On top of all of this, Satan was aggressively attacking the poor. This behavior led to anger (1:19–20). This is why James challenges them to endure by keeping in mind that the Lord's return is imminent, and that He is an impartial judge. The examples of the Old Testament exemplify for us that God blesses those who endure to the end.

James uses the word *grumble* in this passage because it would resonate with the Jewish people. "How long shall I bear with this evil congregation who complain against Me? I have heard the complaints which the children of Israel make

---

[12] Arnold, *Zondervan Illustrated Bible Backgrounds Commentary*, 4:114.

[13] Keener, *IVP Bible Background Commentary*, s.v. James 5:7.

against Me. Say to them, 'As I live,' says the LORD, 'just as you have spoken in My hearing, so I will do to you: The carcasses of you who have complained against Me shall fall in this wilderness, all of you who were numbered, according to your entire number, from twenty years old and above'" (Num. 14:27–30; see also Exod. 16:7; Num. 14:36; 16:11). This history may cause them to quickly focus on their walk of faith. This would explain why James goes on to cite very familiar Old Testament references.

What Does the Context Mean?

James challenges these believers to be continuously determined to face their trials like a long-distance runner focused on giving their very best, since Christ's return is imminent. They must have the mind-set of a farmer who continuously, with great expectation, waits for the rains. This is the mind-set that would aid them in enduring difficulties without becoming angry or giving up. They must not allow the heart to distract them in these stressful times since it tends to vacillate when circumstances are stressful. A farmer would clearly understand the role and importance of having an enduring heart.

In the midst of enduring their many trials, James instructs them to not groan against one another because Christ is the judge and His judgment is imminent. They need to remember the examples of the afflictions the prophets experienced. These prophets suffered with self-restraint even though they had the power to avenge themselves. They faced misfortune, endured it without complaining against anyone, and never gave up. The fond memory of these prophets speaks of how fortunate they became. The same occurred with Job, who was doubly blessed because he maintained his faith in the midst of persecution.

Sermon Subject and Title

Sermon Title: Make Your Goal Gold
Big Idea: Enduring suffering to the end without complaining is for our benefit.

SERMON OUTLINE (JAMES 5:7–11 NASB)

A. Trust that the Lord Has Your Back (James 5:7–8)
   1. *Therefore*—Despite the abuse of the rich (5:1–6), a believer must not take things into their own hands.

2. *Patient*—Believers must remain determined to please the Lord in the midst of difficulty. They were commanded to have this mind-set and must make this decision once and for all.
3. *Patient*—Like a long-distance runner, believers must focus on finishing the race (Heb. 12:1).
4. *Brethren*—They must work hard to remain cohesive (Matt. 24:12; James 4:1–12).
5. *Coming of the Lord*—Keep hope alive (James 4:13–16; 1 John 3:1–3).
6. *Lord*—Trust that Christ is in control and has all power and authority (1 Cor. 10:13).
7. *Farmer*—A farmer works hard but is still forced to trust God to send rain.
8. *Waits*—The farmer waiting for crops to grow is a continuous, habitual process. This is the mind-set they must have.
9. *Patient*—We must remain steadfast under trials, waiting for God to act. Patience is a continuous, habitual action (present active).
10. *Strengthen your hearts*—In the midst of difficulty, the heart sometimes becomes overwhelmed with anxiety, fear, hopelessness, or even a sense of despair (2 Cor. 4:7–12).
11. *Coming of the Lord is near*—Always keep in mind that the Lord's coming is sure.

B. Remain Focused on the Goal (v. 9)

1. *Complain*—Believers must not hold grudges that lead us to groan or sigh.
2. *Brethren*—We are the body of Christ (Eph. 4:1–7); we cannot win this fight without one another (Eph. 4:11–16).
3. *Brethren*—If Satan divides us, no one will stand (Matt. 24:12; Luke 11:17; James 4:6–10). This is the group that James is most concerned about addressing (vocative).
4. *Judge*—We are not allowed to judge another person's motives; we can only confront their actions that are sinful. A healthy church body restrains Satan (Matt. 16:16–20; 18:15–20; Eph. 3:10).
5. *Judge standing at the door*—Christ is a perfect Judge and is now ready to judge. This is a position that will never change (perfect tense).
6. *Judge standing at the door*—No need to fight our own battles; God will fight them for us (Rom. 12:19; 1 Thess. 2:16).

C. Go for Gold (vv. 10–11; James 1:12)

C. Go for Gold (vv. 10–11; James 1:12)

1. *Prophets/Job*—Remember the crowd of witnesses (Heb. 12:1–3; 1 Pet. 2:21–25).
2. *Suffering and patience*—Their trials became suffering for the sake of God (1 Pet. 3:13–16).
3. *We count those blessed who endured*—Those who endure this process have a guaranteed victory (James 1:12). It is reckoned to them—put in their account.
4. *Compassion and mercy*—It does not matter how bad things look; God deeply cares for us.
5. *Compassion and mercy*—No need to give up in trials. The Lord feels and has a deep sense of grief and sorrow when we suffer (Heb. 3:14; 4:14–16).
6. *Compassion and mercy*—The Lord cares with a steadfast love (1 Pet. 5:7–9).

Author's Comments

Comments

One of the hardest things to do when you are experiencing many obstacles is to wait on God. He sometimes seems to take forever to resolve the issues we may be experiencing. A hundred-yard dash may take less than ten seconds, but it takes years to train for. A football game may take three hours one day a week, but college players practice all year for it. The more effort they put into practicing, the more their skills are fine-tuned and the more effective they are come game time.

Like these believers in the book of James, we may have a lot to complain about, but Christ would rather us focus on His preparation so that we grow closer to Him and stronger through whatever trials we experience. This must be our focus as it was with all the great men in the Bible. The more difficult the problems they faced, the more they sought God, and the more refined they became. Moses would even say to God he would not move forward unless God went with him. It took Moses forty years to be ready to lead God's people, but when he was fine-tuned and ready, there were no obstacles he could not, with the help of God, overcome.

Application

A believer may be faced with an unfair boss or difficult employment situation. Dealing with this boss can develop character flaws if handled well, or create discouragement, if handled poorly. Like a runner working to win gold at the Olympics, the believer must focus on the discipline process that God has called them to, knowing that even though He may seem late, He is always on time. If nothing changes, we can live with the hope that Christ's return is sure and He will judge people for the work they have done (1 Cor. 3:15).

Illustrate It

Abraham Lincoln was honored primarily because he played a key role in abolishing slavery. He was a man who did not know the words "give up." He led the country through the Civil War to the other side. He was mostly self-educated. He ran several times for government office and failed. President Lincoln even had a nervous breakdown in 1836. He was fired from one of his jobs as a young man and his sweetheart died in 1835. He did not grow up rich but as a self-taught lawyer who developed a successful practice.

Success is not in the number of things we achieve. Success is built into the fact that, despite the number of failures we may have, our faith keeps us trying again and again.

Character Traits for Godly Living

Ephesians 4:25–29

General Overview of the Passage

In order to develop the character traits that represent the nature of Christ, we must decide once and for all to no longer deliberately communicate information that is false. This is a sin that can invite Satan's influence into a believer's life, just as it did into the lives of Ananias and Sapphira in Acts 5:1–11.

We must purpose in our hearts and minds to speak truth, not speculation. We must be committed to uphold what correctly represents the divine truths of God (2 Tim. 2:15). There are tremendous benefits for this. We experience spiritual growth, righteousness, and holiness as a result.

The Word of God allows us to be angry, but we must not allow our emotions to control what we do (James 1:19–21). This is important because, even though the Scriptures say we can be angry, we are not allowed to sin. We cannot slander a person when we are angry, or hold on to what made us mad for long periods of time. We must be committed to speak the truth.

Another character building block for godly living is that we must work hard with our hands because this is beneficial to everyone. The reason it is beneficial is that once we reap what we worked for we can share what we have with those in need. This leads to acceptable hands for worship (1 Tim. 2:8).

We can tear down all these building blocks if we do not control the tongue (James 3:1–12). God does not allow us to use abusive words or words that are poisonous to other people's souls. We must use our tongue for the purpose of helping others in the church to be built up for Christ (Matt. 12:36–37; Col. 4:6). This allows us to be a part of making the church productive, as described in Ephesians 4:11–13.

These character building blocks are not mainly focused on "acquiring" attributes. Rather, they are more focused on growing up in Christ and allowing the Holy Spirit to mature from the inside out. Being spiritually controlled empowers us to exemplify these traits in our lives daily (Eph. 5:15–21).

Historical Background

Establishing Context

This letter was not written to correct a problem in the church but to further develop the character of the saints. Similar to the moralists of his day who fought against the wrong people in their society, Paul addresses the character of the true believer. Unlike the moralists, Paul viewed this issue through the lens of the Old Testament and as the work of the Holy Spirit in the life of the believer (as they are established in and through the local church: Eph. 4:11–13). "The exhortation to avoid sinning while angry is from Psalm 4:4; on the wickedness of those who hold anger overnight, cf. Hosea 7:6."[14]

The reference about grieving the Holy Spirit could be a reference back to the time when Israel rebelled against God. "'Grieving' the Spirit reflects a serious offense; in Isaiah 63:10 (one of the only two Old Testament texts to use the title 'Holy Spirit'), it refers to Israel's rebellion in the wilderness, which led to their rejection by God. Similarly, Israel's rebellion against the Spirit led Moses to sin with his mouth according to Psalm 106:33 (Num. 20:10; Deut. 3:26)."[15]

The Holy Spirit is a deposit. "This is a term used in ancient business documents to mean a 'down payment.' Those who had tasted the Spirit had begun to taste the life of the future world that God had promised his people."[16]

The word *seal* came from the seals of kings or governors who would seal documents by pressing their seal on some wax, which was placed on a letter or a package. It provided a sign of ownership as well as preserved the confidentiality of the document, so that it gets to the correct people upon delivery.

What Does the Context Mean?

Paul is seeking to focus this church on developing a unified body. This body is made up of individuals of various backgrounds. It is imperative for them to live the Christian life as new creatures, actively taking off the "old man." In

---

[14] Keener, *IVP Bible Background Commentary*, s.v. Eph. 4:26.

[15] Ibid., s.v. Eph. 4:31–5:2.

[16] Andrew T. Lincoln, *Ephesians,* vol. 42 of the Word Biblical Commentary series (Dallas: Word Inc., 1990), 303–4.

the process of doing so, they must lay aside falsehood and speak truth. If they become angry, they must not allow the devil to get a foothold in their lives. It is best that they work rather than steal, and they must share their gain with those who are poor in an effort to strengthen everyone in the church. They must also watch their words so that what they say serves to build up the believers around them. As the church, they should work to mature believers (Eph. 4:11–13), and in turn, these believers must be committed to "work out your own salvation with fear and trembling" (Phil. 2:12). This is important because, "it is God who works in you both to will and to do for His good pleasure" (Phil. 2:13).

Sermon Subject and Title

Sermon Title: Character Traits for Godly Living
Big Idea: Godly living instills character building blocks that prevent the old life of a believer from returning.

Sermon Outline (Eph. 4:25–29 nasb)

A. Character Traits that Preserve Us from Satan (vv. 25–27; Col. 3:9)

1. *Lay aside falsehood*—Make a purposeful decision to not make statements that are deliberately false (Prov. 19:5, 9; 21:28).
   a) This is in the aorist tense, meaning that once this decision is made, there is no turning back. It is in the middle voice, meaning that this is something one must determine on one's own to do.
2. *Lay aside falsehood*—Falsehood is a sin that can easily cause Satan to influence a believer's life (Acts 5:1–11).
3. *Speak the truth*—Giving up lying is followed immediately by a command to speak based on facts.
   a) This is in the present active imperative, meaning that speaking the truth is a command that a believer must make a practice in their lives. This is something the Holy Spirit empowers (John 14:16–17) us to do, once we are determined to lay aside falsehood and put on the new man (Eph. 4:22–24).
4. *Speak the truth*—We must not speculate; it leads to quarrels (2 Tim. 2:23–26).
5. *Speak the truth*—Paul commands us to speak God's divine will (truth) accurately (2 Pet. 1:2–4) because:

a) It preserves us from being controlled by false doctrine, which is demonic (Eph. 4:14–15; 1 Tim. 4:1–4).
b) Our lives do not become unstable (Prov. 3:5; Eph. 4:14–15).
c) It stimulates spiritual growth (Eph. 4:15).
d) We experience the life of Christ (4:21).
e) It leads to righteousness and holiness (4:24).

6. *Neighbor*—Whatever we do, it must be for the building up of the body (4:3–7, 12–13). This is because "we are" (present active verb—meaning we will always be) a part of the body of Christ.
7. *Angry*—If falsehood exists because the truth is purposefully being ignored, it should create righteous indignation (John 2:13–17). Paul commands us to make it a habit to be angry in these circumstances. However, it comes with admonishments:
   a) *Do not sin*—We cannot allow our emotions to cause us to violate the very truth we stand for (James 4:17).
   b) *Do not sin*—We must not allow ourselves to become a slave to our emotions (Rom. 6:6–7).
   c) *Do not give the devil an opportunity*—To put things in our lives that allows the devil the opportunity to position himself to influence us (Acts 5:1–11). "Do not give" is in the present tense imperative, meaning Paul commands us to make this a continuous action.
      - False doctrine (1 Tim. 4:1).
      - Lying—Satan is the father of all lies (John 8:44).
      - Sin (Gen. 4:5–7).

B. Character Traits that Help Those in Need (v. 28)

1. *Do not steal*—Paul commands us to repeatedly not steal (present imperative).
2. *Labor*—A believer needs to commit to a hard day's work, even if it makes them weary (Prov. 6:6–11; 10:4; 13:4). This is something we are commanded to do on a continual basis (present imperative).
3. *Performing with our own hands*—A believer must be habitually committed to work (this is an agrarian group of people). The nominative guides us to understand that working hard with our hands is what we should be focused on doing.
4. *Good*—What we have in our control to do must be for the benefit of others. This is a genitive, which means that this is the objective.

5. *Good*—What we have in our control to do we must do to please God (Col. 3:17).
6. *Something to share with those in need*—When we are paid, we must think of how we can supply the lack that other believers have (Acts 2:44–46). A present tense subjunctive, meaning this is what must continuously take place, and it must be intentional.
7. A strong church is where believers think for the common good first (Phil. 2:1–5).

C. The Tongue that Builds Up Godly Character (v. 29; James 3:2–12)

1. *Let no unwholesome words*—These are curse words, words that are of no benefit to anyone (Eph. 5:3–5). We shouldn't use words that poison people's hearts or corrupt relationships (Col. 4:5–6).
2. *Proceed*—We are responsible for what comes out of our mouths (Matt. 12:36). Paul commands us to stop these words from coming out of our mouths on a continual basis.
3. *Edification*—What we say must stimulate spiritual growth. Edification builds up what lies tear down (Eph. 4:12–13).
4. *Need of the moment*—Our conversation needs to be focused on what someone lacks, so that they are built up.
5. *Grace to those who hear*—Words that build up encourage those who hear and provide them hope.
6. *Grace to those who hear*—This stimulates spiritual growth for those who are constantly listening and have a heart to do God's will.

Author's Comments

Comments

We all have a common enemy, and he has no desire to be our friend. His only passion is to destroy us, but Christ will use his attacks to grow us (the story of Job; Rev. 12:10). So the question then becomes, *How does what Christ allows achieve His purposes and bless our lives?* A decision for Christ is a quest for a Christlike character.

To develop this character, we must first seek to maximize what God did for us when He saved us and made us into a new creation (2 Cor. 5:17). This explains why Paul writes about the transforming work of God (Eph. 1:3, 13–14; 2:8–22; 3:14–19; 4:11–16) before diving into this Scripture. However, the members of our flesh are still prone to sin, and progressively being sanctified

(Rom. 6:12–14). We see this with the eyes (Matt. 6:22–23), the tongue (James 3:1–12), the mind (Rom. 12:2; Eph. 4:17–20), and the devices of the flesh (Gal. 5:16–19). It is Paul who states:

> For what I am doing, I do not understand. For what I will to do, that I do not practice; but what I hate, that I do. If, then, I do what I will not to do, I agree with the law that it is good. But now, it is no longer I who do it, but sin that dwells in me. For I know that in me (that is, in my flesh) nothing good dwells; for to will is present with me, but how to perform what is good I do not find. For the good that I will to do, I do not do; but the evil I will not to do, that I practice. Now if I do what I will not to do, it is no longer I who do it, but sin that dwells in me. (Rom. 7:15–20).

"O wretched man that I am! Who will deliver me from this body of death? I thank God—through Jesus Christ our Lord!" (Rom. 7:24–25). This is why Paul is saying "that you put off, concerning your former conduct, the old man which grows corrupt according to the deceitful lusts, and be renewed in the spirit of your mind, and that you put on the new man which was created according to God, in true righteousness and holiness" (Eph. 4:22–24). This practice leads to the development of Christian character.

When we are deeply committed to this process, we prove to be true "saints" (Eph. 4:12) of God, not just churchgoers (James 1:22–25). This determination to "work out our salvation" allows the church to accomplish its work and God to get the glory (Eph. 3:20–21).

Application

It is one thing to say that we are saved; it is another for our lives to represent the character of Christ. It is one thing to attend church; it is a whole other thing to apply oneself to building up those around us. Do any of these sinful traits represent our actions and thoughts? If so, we need to practice ridding ourselves of these vices. It will prevent Satan from corrupting us and will bless those around us. How do people close to us describe us? Could our lives, just by what they represent, win someone to Christ?

Paul states in Ephesians that believers have the fullness of God (3:19), and the church, being led by the pastor teacher, stimulates this work in those who are saints (4:11–13). Thus, if believers do not focus on removing the old man, the church is going to be ineffective in maturing them to the fullness of God from the inside out.

Illustrate It

A young man who was on a college football team was very frustrated with the head coach because he felt that the coach was picking on him. He said that during the practice the coach seemed to focus on his every move. The coach would demand he come to his office often to review.

One day he asked the defensive backs coach why it seemed like the head coach gave him, and a few other players, so much attention. The defensive backs coach replied, "He sees a lot of potential in you and believes that you can be a great player one day. He doesn't want to tell you that because he doesn't want you to get a big head and stop listening!" The player did do well and went on to do well as a great individual.

Sometimes believers come to church and believe that God is picking on them. However, if they shift their perspective a little, they might see what God sees and be equipped to grow into the fullness of Christ. Christ knows He has deposited the Holy Spirit in them, so their potential is limitless. Like this player, we need to trust the coach, listen to His direction, and trust the discipline process He takes us through so we can develop character traits that bless us to experience God's goodness.

Sermon Series 7

Experiencing God

When Life Does Not Make Sense

Exodus 2:11–15; Acts 7:22–25; Hebrews 7:24–25

General Overview of the Passages

In the days of a cruel ruler, murder, brutal labor practices, and wars, Moses, at forty years old, was considered great. He had shown full development in all his training and learning. "And Moses was learned in all the wisdom of the Egyptians, and was mighty in words and deeds" (Acts 7:22). Moses most likely received the best education the world had to offer at this time. He was likely trained in three languages: Egyptian, Akkadian, and Hebrew. Moses was, in fact, the perfect ambassador to deliver God's message, since he was no stranger to royal proceedings when he was demanding the Israelites freedom.

One day, Moses went out to inspect what his fellow brothers were doing. He did this because, the book of Hebrews tells us, he had decided not "to be called the son of Pharaoh's daughter, choosing rather to suffer affliction with the people of God than to enjoy the passing pleasures of sin, esteeming the reproach of Christ greater riches than the treasures in Egypt; for he looked to the reward" (Heb. 11:24–26).

As he carefully inspected his brethren, he witnessed the compulsory and burdensome labor they were under. Moses was in a life of luxury while his family was being abused. At one point, Moses became so enraged at the unjustified ill treatment of his brethren, that he killed an Egyptian who was striking his brethren.

Moses looked around to see if anyone would see him breaking the law. After careful observation, Moses struck down the Egyptian. He was moved by the injustice he beheld, and thus killed the taskmaster. Stephen in Acts says: "And seeing one of them suffer wrong, he defended and avenged him who was oppressed, and struck down the Egyptian. For he supposed that his brethren would have understood that God would deliver them by his hand, but they did not understand" (Acts 7:24–25).

Moses went out the same direction the next day, and this time saw two Hebrews engaged in a hostile struggle (this could have been a Hebrew foreman and a Hebrew laborer). In this instance Moses speaks, because they were both Hebrews. One man responded by saying, "Who made you a prince or a judge over us?" (Exod. 2:14 NASB). This man unknowingly prophesied about Moses. The man then asked Moses if he was going to kill him, as he did the Egyptian. With this, Moses became afraid; he ran from Pharaoh, who tried to kill him. By running from Pharaoh, Moses shows that he was committed to his people and there would be no compromise with Pharaoh. Moses fully expected evil to be done against him because of his full knowledge of Egyptian law and custom.

Historical Background

Establishing Context

Even though Moses was being groomed to be a Pharaoh, he was still an Israelite, and the Egyptians viewed themselves as a superior race. We see the same thing with Joseph. The Egyptians never ate with him. So, for Moses to kill the Egyptian, even though he was in line to be a Pharaoh, would be viewed by the Egyptians as a punishable offense. "Egyptians maintained a substantial sense of ethnic pride that caused them to consider foreigners inferior. For a foreigner to kill an Egyptian was a great crime."[1]

Moses was well trained in all that he needed to know as a Pharaoh (Acts 7:22). Moreover, when an Egyptian turned forty years old, he was considered fully grown and ready to take on more responsibilities. It is at this time that Moses decides to follow the teaching of his mother (Heb. 11:24–27). "His first 40 years, in Egypt (7:17–28): God promoted him; his second 40 years, in the Sinai desert (7:29): God prepared him; his final 40 years, en route to Canaan (7:30–38): God empowered him."[2]

---

[1] V. H. Matthews, M. W. Chavalas, and J. H. Walton, *The IVP Bible Background Commentary: Old Testament* (Downers Grove, IL: InterVarsity Press, 2000), s.v. Exod. 2:12–15.

[2] H. L. Willmington, *The Outline Bible* (Wheaton, IL: Tyndale House Publishers, 1999), s.v. Acts 7:30–38.

When Moses leaves Egypt, he runs into Jethro's daughters. They must have been shepherdesses. By God's providence, this encounter leads Moses to Jethro, who later gives him counsel on how to organize the leaders so that Moses can effectively lead the nation of Israel. "In fact, the biblical text may be trying to depict Moses' eventual father-in-law, called a priest in 2:16, as a worshiper of Yahweh. That he lives in this region and has flocks that need shepherding certainly qualifies him and his family as *shasu* (Bedouin shepherds).[3]

What Does the Context Mean?

When Moses was fully grown, he decided to give up all the pleasures of being a prince and identify with his people. One day as he was investigating all that was taking place, he noticed an Egyptian cruelly beating an Israelite. Moses defended the Israelites by killing the Egyptian. The next day, Moses saw two Israelites fighting. When Moses sought to stop them, one asked him who made him judge, and whether he was going to kill him too. Moses became afraid because he believed that the issue was well-known and ran from Pharaoh, who was trying to kill him; he ran into the land of Midian.

Sermon Subject and Title

Sermon Title: When Life Does Not Make Sense
Big Idea: When our good intentions get ahead of God's timing, His timing and purposes still remain the perfect plan.

Sermon Outline (Exod. 2:11–15; Acts 7:22–25; Heb. 7:24–25 NASB)

A. Make Decisions for the Things of God (Exod. 2:11; Col. 3:1–4; Heb. 11:24–25)

1. *Those days*—These are the days of a cruel ruler, murder, brutal labor practices, and wars. Moses saw that their labor was compulsory, cruel, and burdensome. This is in the imperfect; things were not going to change.

[3] J. H. Walton, *Genesis, Exodus, Leviticus, Numbers, Deuteronomy,* vol. 1 in the Zondervan Illustrated Bible Backgrounds Commentary series (Grand Rapids, MI: Zondervan, 2009), 172.

2. *Full grown*—Moses at forty years old was considered great (he had shown full development in all his training and learning; his mother had developed him from a young age). This is in the Qal, imperfect active—meaning who Moses was in the past is what he was going to be in the present (a well-trained Egyptian; an Israelite influenced by his mother) and in the future.
   a) "Moses was educated in all the learning of the Egyptians, and he was a man of power in words and deeds" (Acts 7:22 NASB). The training of Moses was the best education in the world at that time.

B. Trust God's Timing as Perfect (Exod. 2:12–14; Acts 7:25)

1. *Moses saw the Egyptian beating a Hebrew:*
   a) *Beating*—Severely and intentionally striking.
   b) He was beating Moses' people so severely that it could have caused death.
   c) Moses was in a life of luxury while his family was being abused.
   d) *Looked*—Moses looked around to see if anyone would see him breaking the law because he knew he had no jurisdiction in this area. After careful observation, Moses struck down—which could mean he used a sword, his hands, or any object—with the specific focus to kill the Egyptian. He was moved by the injustice he beheld, and thus he killed the taskmaster. Stephen in Acts says: "And when he saw one of them being treated unjustly, he defended him and took vengeance for the oppressed by striking down the Egyptian" (Acts 7:24–25 NASB).
2. *Moses went out the next day*—It seems like Moses' immediate success led him to believe that this was the time to be the deliverer. This is highlighted by how and for what purpose he approached the two Hebrews who were fighting.
3. *Moses went out the next day*—Moses did not plan to stop going out. This, again, was in the imperfect tense.

C. Accept God's Results (Exod. 2:14–15)

1. *Who made you a prince or a judge?*—Who made you deliverer and one who arbitrates between two people and administers rights for the poor and oppressed? Moses is ahead of God's timing.
2. *Who made you a prince or a judge?*—This is in the perfect active, which means that they were asserting that Moses believed that he was permanently in a position of authority.

3. *Afraid*—Moses became afraid, but the passage does not say of whom. We do know from Hebrews 11:27 he was not afraid of the Pharaoh. It seems from Hebrews 11:26 that he had a reverent fear of the promised Messiah.
4. *Moses fled and settled*—God allowed Jethro's daughters to come by and establish for Moses a new job and family.

Author's Comments

Comments

This incident took place when Moses was fully grown. God brought him to a point where he had to decide what he wanted to do with his life. Moses specifically went out "to his brethren." It seems like Moses had already made the decision before going out due to the language of the text. He knew their circumstances and decided to do something about it. There was no prayer, no seeking wise counsel—just passion and action. This passion and action cost Moses years later (Num. 20:6–12).

Moses, with his decision firm, looked at the hard labor and abusive work environment his people constantly experienced. He looked left and right. Moses knew that what he was about to do was not within the law or his authority. He understood clearly what his actions meant.

After killing the Egyptian, he went back out the next day. It seems like Moses' decision for his brethren had become a passion. Being passionate about serving God is great, but learning God's steps and experiencing God's timing is everything.

Moses' passion for his people put him ahead of God's timing. This is interesting because Moses at forty years old had to make up his mind regarding which direction he would take in his life (Heb. 11:23–26). Since every child is a gift from God (Ps. 127:3), the timing of his birth and having to make up his mind at forty years old were all within the will of God. So the time of Moses' birth was perfect, especially since we see how it works well to get him into the palace of Pharaoh so he can be prepared to come back to Egypt to deliver God's people (Acts 7:22–25). When Moses decided to deliver his people, this was all within God's control. God knew Moses needed to spend forty years in the wilderness taking care of sheep so that he would be ready to lead God's people for forty years to the very place he experienced God: Mount Sinai. This is why when life does not seem to make sense we must trust God. We must remain faithful to be exposed to all He has in store for us.

Application

Some of the trials we experience seem to go on forever. Often, the longer it takes for God to resolve the trial, the greater our desire to take things into our own hands. When we get ahead of God like Peter did, cutting the soldier's ear off, we end up outside of the will of God. This can cause our circumstances to become even more difficult. We must remain in God's will and trust His timing to be perfect (Eccles. 3:1–8).

Illustrate It

When things are at their worst but a believer trusts God through it all, his or her faith exposes God at His best.

There are so many examples of this throughout Scripture. David running from Saul is one of the many examples. Because of God's Word—"don't touch my anointed"—David ran from Saul for years. It could have seemed like a never-ending process, but David did as God would have him to do. In the midst of his running, David built an army of mighty men and won the favor of a nation. Thus, when it was time for David to become king, he was welcomed by a nation that loved him (2 Sam. 5).

The same is true with Joseph. Things seemed to go from bad to worse. He was once leading Potiphar's house only for Potiphar's wife to lie against Joseph, putting him back in jail. Joseph kept his faith in God and became the best prisoner. This led him to be exposed to the chief baker and chief cupbearer. Because Joseph remained faithful interpreting dreams by God's grace, the chief cupbearer was able to speak to Pharaoh. Ultimately, Pharaoh came to believe in Joseph. Pharaoh, once his dream was interpreted, elevated Joseph to be ruler of his nation within days.

When things seem to be at their worst but a person keeps their faith, they experience God moving at His best.

Called to Be the Difference

Exodus 3:10–15

General Overview of the Passage

Because God heard the cries of His people in Egypt, due to the oppression by the Egyptians, God commanded Moses to take the initiative and go back to Egypt. That meant leaving all that was familiar and all that he loved, from his extended family and even his father-in-law's sheep. Moses' mission was specifically outlined by God; God was clear in telling him where to go, his purpose in going, and who he would represent. Yet God did not supply Moses a chariot or army. He gave him a stick to lead the people. Notice that even in the midst of all this, God calls them "My people." They don't belong to Moses even though God has chosen him to lead his people out of Egypt.

Moses' answer to God provides the stark difference between the man who fought the Egyptian and this new Moses. Moses does not see himself as being fit to stand before the leader of the most powerful nation in the world. He is ill-equipped to return to Egypt and go directly to Pharaoh. It is also difficult to bring the people out of Egypt; after all, the first time he tried, the Hebrew slave asked Moses who appointed him as judge or prince over Israel. So to return with only a stick is a challenge for Moses, but he listens to God.

God promises to be with Moses because it is not Moses' fight. Moses understands the governmental structure of Egypt and, having served as a general, asked God to explain how he will now approach Pharaoh as God's ambassador. Moses even asked God for a name to reference because he is thinking as a government representative (this is his training; Acts 7:22). God instructs him to tell Pharaoh his name is "I AM WHO I AM."

> In the Old Testament, it appears in the sense of "I am the Absolute" or the like, and this application certainly prepared the ground for the *ego eimi* of the Messianic Presence. He is sovereign, uncreated, unimaginable, personal, matter of history, holy, and the universal monarch whose

purposes cannot ultimately be thwarted. God is the one independent, entirely self-subsistent Being in the universe.[4]

God then told Moses what he should say to Israel. The one who has all authority over His chosen people is God; all divine activity is subject to Him and He is over the land, the sea, and the heavens, and is clearly the highest authority to be trusted. He has been the God of Abraham, Isaac, and Jacob. This name that He has given to Himself will be His name forever and will be His name for all generations.

Moses, under the authority of God, now returns to deliver the people of God. This is done under God's direction and by God's power.

Historical Background

Establishing Context

Moses was born to Amram and Jochebed and lived in a slave hut in Goshen. Moses was soon to be a Pharaoh because he had come of age (Heb. 11:24) and was well prepared by the Egyptians to become Pharaoh (Acts 7:22). He learned three languages, and become a general in Pharaoh's army. "Moses' objection carried little persuasiveness, given the training provided for him in the household of Pharaoh."[5]

After Moses left Egypt, he lived in Midian for forty years, where he cared for his father-in-law's sheep. He married Jethro's daughter, Zipporah, and at the end of this forty-year period, God met him and redirected his life. Moses was sent back to Egypt to deliver Israel, God's chosen nation. Returning to the most powerful nation in the known world was a challenge that Moses did not willingly accept (especially with the knowledge and experience Moses brought to the process, with just a stick in his hand was a major challenge for him). "God promised to be with Moses. Not only had God 'come down' to deliver (v. 8), but now He promised to be present. This prefigures the Incarnation: Jesus would come down to deliver us from our sins and be with us. God gave Moses a sign, a final proof that this experience was a divine manifestation and not a dream. Here the sign is a reminder, memorial, or symbol (Exod. 8:23; 12:13). But the

---

[4] Matthews, Chavalas, and Walton, *IVP Bible Background Commentary: Old Testament*, s.v. Exod. 3:10–17.

[5] Ibid., s.v. Exod. 3:11.

word can also mean a miracle of God, a wonder that demonstrates His power and presence (7:3)."[6]

What Does the Context Mean?

God had heard the cries of His people all along, but it was not the right time. God now has Moses ready and challenges him to return to bring His people out of captivity. God promises to be with him. The powerful experience that Moses had on Mount Sinai served as a supernatural event to demonstrate to Moses God's power, increasing Moses' confidence in God's ability to deliver His people. As a result, there is no possibility for failure. Moses' desire to know God reveals the nature and supremacy of God. Despite the bondage the people of Israel had experienced, God was still able to free them—it was just not God's timing. God is the Lord God who has authority to do all things just as He did for Abraham, Isaac, and Jacob, and this name shall be His name forever.

Sermon Subject and Title

Sermon Title: Called to Be the Difference
Big Idea: Obedience to execute God's plans leads to accomplishing things that only God's sovereign will and empowerment can achieve.

Sermon Outline (Exod. 3:10–15)

A. The Challenge (v. 10)

1. *Come now*—God commands Moses to make preparations to go to Pharaoh.
2. *Go*—The command to go carries with it the reference to a new righteous lifestyle that must now dominate how Moses lives. Moses' life as a shepherd is over, and what he does from this point forward needs to be totally directed by God.
3. *Send*—Moses has a specific purpose for going to Egypt and he is guaranteed success. It is in the imperfect, which means this is the direction for Moses for the rest of his life.

---

[6] E. D. Radmacher, R. B. Allen, and H. W. House, *Nelson's New Illustrated Bible Commentary* (Nashville, TN: Thomas Nelson Publishers, 1999), 92.

4. *Bring*—God defines Moses' purpose and then commands him, no matter what Pharaoh or the people say, to move God's people from Egypt to Mount Sinai.

B. God's Plans Are Perfect (vv. 11–13)

1. *Moses said to God*—The imperfect active explains that when Moses spoke he had no intent to stop saying what is on his mind.
2. *Moses said to God*—Moses was intimidated by Egypt.
   a) God needs our availability. Moses had found a life, but God had a different purpose.
   b) When God gets ready to use us, it is better to do His will than become a stumbling block to yourself. Moses left Egypt a warrior, now he is a shepherd and a lot older.
   c) God's purposes are specific—to whom he is going, where he is going, for whom he is going, and for what purpose—"My people." Moses understood God (Exod. 3:13).
3. *Who am I*—Moses evaluated himself based on how life defined him, not based on how God viewed him (Acts 7:22–25). He compared himself with how he viewed the mighty nation of Israel.
   a) God uses people who humbly serve Him (Exod. 3:11; 2 Cor. 3:4–5). *Who am I*—This allows us to be:
      - Teachable, we remain dependent on the power of God rather than our ability (2 Tim. 2:2).
      - God fights the proud (1 Pet. 5:6).
      - Humility allows a person to look out for the best interests of others (Phil. 2:1–5).
4. *God said*—God responded to Moses, explaining what He was thinking. God did not intend to stop saying this to Moses because it is a command and Moses is His choice for leadership. Another imperfect—what God is saying remains forever.
5. *I will be*—God's commitment to be with Moses is forever. He will never walk alone (Matt. 10:30; 28:20).
   a) Never forget that it is God's fight, not ours (Exod. 3:8 compared to v. 11b—e.g., David and Goliath, 1 Sam. 17:47).
   b) God will remove all your excuses when He purposes to use you (Exod. 6:10–13, 28–30).

c) God promises to be with Moses (Exod. 3:12). Hairs are numbered (Matt. 10:30); eyes upon us (1 Pet. 3:12); He will never leave nor forsake (Heb. 13:5).
d) *When you have brought the people out*—When God is working for us, there is no possibility for failure. When Moses is in the business of constantly, endlessly bringing God's people out of Egypt, God is with him. This is God's battle.

6. *Worship*—God wants His people to continuously serve in a worshipful manner at Mount Sinai.

C. We Must Place Our Trust in the Ability of God (vv. 14–15)

1. *Moses said*—Moses, recognizing his insufficiency, expresses a need for God to reveal Himself.
2. *I AM WHO I AM*—The One who is always present; He has all authority and all divine activity is subject to Him; He has a covenant relationship with His people, independent of everything and complete (Acts 17:28).
   a) *To be*—God will never stop being God.
   b) God is the one independent, entirely self-subsistent Being in the universe. All that is depends upon Him (Gen. 1:1; Col. 1:17; Heb. 1:3, 10).
3. *I AM has sent me to you*—We must trust Him for who He is in order to experience what He will do (perfect, meaning a set state or condition). God's nature is always going to be what it is. He is the Creator of all things and every creature is in debt to Him.
4. *I AM has sent me to you*—God was not entertaining a discussion about who He is.
5. Remember God's history (Exod. 3:15); it allows us to find strength to trust Him in the present and for the future.
   a) The history God has with Israel exposes His dependability and faithfulness.
   b) His history demonstrates His power, authority, and independence, because He is self-subsistent and committed to the covenant He made with Abraham.
   c) We must trust Him in order to be exposed to His power.
6. *This is My name forever*—What God is going to do will remain forever.

Author's Comments

Comments

Experiencing God is an intimate process because it requires total reliance on Him. When we live with total reliance on God, He may place before us issues that only He can resolve. When we rely on His promises, trust His power and ability, and commit to obey Him, we experience His plans. Under these circumstances the problems we experience are going to be bigger than our ability and perplexing, because they require His wisdom. They will be humbling because they require reliance on His strength. This causes our lives to become purposeful while God strips us of ourselves.

Moses spent forty years being groomed to be a Pharaoh. He was trained to rely on his mental capacities, physical abilities, his political power, and the wealth of Pharaoh's kingdom (Heb. 11:23–29). God stripped him of everything and called on him to return with the one thing he had: a staff. He had no sword, horse, or battalion of trained warriors. He had to contend against the most powerful military in the known world, and God sent him with a staff and a burning bush experience. It is obvious that God did not need Moses, but the people did. Since they had no army and their placement in Egypt was directed by God, the only person who could release them is God. It is His plan that is being worked out based on His covenant with Abraham that He on His own initiative established (Gen. 15).

One of the things that is clear in this passage is that God does not share glory because it is not possible since only He and the rest of the Trinity can actually be glorified.

Application

Trusting God means that we rely on His ability for the challenges we encounter. Like Moses, when God calls upon us—whether to use our spiritual gifts or function based on our call to ministry—in obedience to Him we must press forward. The obstacles must not determine whether or not we do what He says. Schoolteachers may have the gift of evangelism; how do they use it in an environment where it may not be permissible? A missionary may be called to spread the gospel to a country that is mostly made up of another religion. How does he/she do that? A person marries into a blended family and God calls her to nurture the children, even if they are teenagers. Is she equipped? When God places a call on our lives, the issue is obedience and trust in God, not if what God is calling us to do is possible or impossible. This is how our trust in God deepens.

Illustrate It

Until a person is fully emptied of themselves, they will not see God for all that He is. This is the story of all great leaders who trusted God.

Abraham trusted God and left everything; Ruth trusted in the God of Naomi and forsook her own family; Nehemiah trusted God and risked his life to rebuild a wall in a forsaken city; Peter had to be in doubt and despair at Pentecost only to be stripped of everything and placed in the back of a jail before the determination to serve God possessed him; Paul came to the point where he realized that he no longer lived, so now he could count all things lost to experience one person—Christ.

The people that allow faith to take them where faith directs are the people that experience God for who He is.

It's All about God!

Exodus 9:13–17, 27, 30

General Overview of the Passage

The Lord summons Moses and instructed him to go to Pharaoh at daybreak (kings normally attend to their work early in the morning) and confront him. Understand the meaning behind the positioning: Moses is expected to stand before and in the face of Pharaoh, meaning he is to position himself to be in direct opposition to Pharaoh. This stance clearly indicates that it will not be a friendly encounter. This is something that God has commanded Moses to do. Notice that Moses no longer has an independent life—it is totally consumed with the mission God has given him.

God told Pharaoh that He will stretch out His hands so that plagues will only come upon Pharaoh's house and his people; God's people would be spared. The purpose is so that in the present and in the future, people will have the ability to distinguish from all other gods an intimate, experiential knowledge of the one true God (Rahab; Josh. 2:1–3).

It is for the reason of God's kingdom plan that the Egyptians are allowed to dwell in the land of Egypt permanently. This is because God wanted everyone to clearly and fully understand His strength, power, and capability. Despite God's display of mercy, the Egyptians defied God and God's people by not allowing them to leave.

Now Moses had been sent by God to deliver His people by the very power that God made Egypt a great nation. This power was provided only to incubate God's people. Now that they are many (fulfilling God's covenant with Abraham), it is time for God to bring them to Himself.

Historical Background

Establishing Context

After forty years in Meidian, God's timetable that He gave to Abram in Exodus 15:13 was being fulfilled: "You in Your mercy have led forth the people whom You have redeemed; You have guided them in Your strength to Your holy habitation." Moses was now a general and a shepherd. Moses had spent forty years not just in Meidian but probably taking his sheep to various places in the wilderness. When God spoke to Moses, he was at the mountain God wanted Israel to come to for their first worship service as a nation. Moses was totally oriented to God's plan. It was now time for an old warrior and shepherd to return to a nation that trained him. God established this government for a purpose He was now going to reveal. "God used Pharaoh's stubbornness (Exod. 4:21): (1) to demonstrate His *power*; and (2) to make known His *name* (10:2; Rom. 9:17–18). Pharaoh was not only an evil ruler in a powerful state; he was an evil man, ungodly, unrighteous, and anti-God. Pharaoh set himself up as a god who maintained the stability of his kingdom. The Lord's judgment on him was an appropriate response to this fraud."[7]

God uses Moses to create a number of plagues. Each plague is a direct attack against all the Egyptian gods. Moses' rod eating the rod of the wise men, sorcerers, and magicians of Egypt was another demonstration that there was no leader greater than the one sent by the God who is the true and only God. There is no other god. "God is beyond comparison (8:10). He is distinct from all the supposed gods of Egypt, who were now under His direct attack."[8]

Pharaoh's heart was not right (Exod. 9:27–30). God, who is holy, goes against a man who is wicked, exposing the depth of his wickedness and the power of God's holiness.

What Does the Context Mean?

God ordered Moses to confront Pharaoh and demand that God's people be released. This was done for the purpose that they can worship God by offering sacrifices (Exod. 3:12). God tells Moses to let Pharaoh know that he is being spared because if God wanted to destroy all the Egyptians He could do so, including Pharaoh himself. God is demonstrating to the Egyptians, His people,

---

[7] Radmacher, Allen, and House, *Nelson's New Illustrated Bible Commentary*, 103.
[8] Ibid.

and us today, that He is God before all the earth. God is the only one who has authority and power to produce these effects. It is God who allowed him to remain so that His nature is declared before the earth. Despite God's mercy, Pharaoh operated in pride and arrogance and did not allow God's people to go. Pharaoh's resistance only clarifies God's mighty ability as God uses Moses to overcome one obstacle after another.

Sermon Subject and Title

Sermon Title: It's All About God!
Big Idea: When obstacles are before us, our trust and obedience in God expose God's power and accomplish His purposes for His glory.

SERMON OUTLINE (EXOD. 9:13–17, 27, 30 NASB)

A. God's Will (v. 13)

1. *The LORD said*—In order for God's will to be revealed, obedience is everything. What God is saying to Moses is perpetual. It is in the imperfect active voice.
2. His Word, done His way. God's will is always done based on His Word (Rom. 12:2; 2 Tim. 3:17; 2 Pet. 1:3).
3. *Rise early*—Moses is commanded by God (imperative) to rise early. Moses no longer has his own life; it is totally consumed (Col. 3:1–3) with the mission of God (Acts 17:28).
4. *Stand*—Moses is commanded to confront the most powerful man in the known world. God expected obedience.
5. *Say*—What Moses is told by God to say is a message that is permanent (perfect tense). God's promise to Abraham in Genesis 15:13 must be fulfilled.
6. *Serve*—Fulfilling God's will always leads to worship. This is in the perfect tense.
7. *Serve*—God's will is purposeful.

B. God's Way (vv. 14–15)

1. *Send all My plagues*—God is going to cause His presence to be known, especially since Pharaoh acts arrogantly toward His people.
2. *Know*—Pharaoh and all Egypt came to a full, intimate experience that there is no other God.

3. *Know*—Their newly found knowledge that God is the only true God was continually made known (this story changed Rahab's life; Josh. 2:1–3).
4. *Hand*—God's way always functions under His authority and power. He is always in control even when it seems like He does not care. He only allows Pharaoh to rule His people for a purpose (Gen. 15:12–16; Exod. 9:17).
5. God's way is always full of mercy and grace.

C. **God's Plan (vv. 16–17)**

1. *For this reason*—All of this was preserved for God to fulfill His purposes (Gen. 15:13).
2. *Remain*—God has allowed Pharaoh to have a permanent presence in the land. He did not remain Pharaoh because of his power or might. It was only by God's mercy.
3. *Show*—Pharaoh now has to reckon with God's power.
4. *My power*—God's ability is now manifested before the world because it is time for His people to be removed from their host.
5. *Proclaim my name*—God's reputation was made known throughout the earth because of how He liberated His people from the most powerful nation in the known world.
6. *Still you exalt yourself*—Pharaoh became arrogant and defiant because God allowed him to rule over His people. The Egyptians lifted up themselves over God's people and did evil.
7. *My, I, and Me*—God use personal pronouns nine times in these passages. It was very personal to God for Pharaoh to no longer harm or control God's people. God must keep His Word He gave to Abraham. This is not about Moses or Aaron; it is about God letting Pharaoh know that he was only a great leader in a great kingdom to fulfill God's plans to create for Himself a people. Now it was God's time.

Author's Comments

Comments

When things may have seemed out of control for Moses, God was always in control. Let's check the record. God's providence allowed Moses to be found by one of the sixty daughters of Pharaoh; a daughter who would love him, teaching him everything he would need to know that would later be used to combat

Pharaoh. Jethro's daughters coming to the well and Moses being there to defend them, only to be brought to Jethro's house, who was a descendent of Abraham from his second wife, Keturah, who happens to be a worshipper of the Most High God—God ordered Moses' life to be full of humanly insurmountable obstacles so that Moses' history would become an experience of God's providence and sovereign, unlimited power.

All that has taken place in our lives is a manifestation of all that God is. A person may say that our lives are not like Moses' because they are full of sin. God's response would be that there is no sin that grace cannot overcome. It's all about God—"for in Him we live and move and exist" (Acts 17:28 NASB).

We can experience God more intimately when we surrender to His will, like Moses, and become all that God has lovingly created us to be. This is how we move from our ability to His.

Application

Obeying God has nothing to do with common sense (Prov. 3:5). It is about trusting His Word and believing in His promises. God doing the impossible is normal. This is why "without faith it is impossible to please Him" (Heb. 11:6).

If God does not change the circumstances in your life, you must remain focused on obeying His Word. He will deepen your faith and strengthen your convictions. When God does not change circumstances, He is changing the people involved so that He can use them to be change agents.

Illustrate It

Life is an uphill battle when God is directing our path because He is always functioning on His ability, not ours.

If I went out to play a basketball game I probably would not invite a NBA player in his prime on the court. Maybe I would ask for a person my age who has sprinkles of gray and some struggles with his knees. If I am playing to just get exercise, I would probably pick a winning team where I am the weak link so I can relax when I shoot an air ball. It is different when I play to win because then whom I play against or whom I play with is important. When God plans anything in order to teach us to trust Him, He picks the hardest thing and will sometimes make things look very bleak to expose our level of faith (Rom. 10:17) and then test us to trust Him at His ability.

Moses once carried a sword; now he carried a stick. Moses was once a general in the most powerful army in the known world; now he is a shepherd. The skills he needed at first would be necessary if he were delivering the people; but he is called to guide them for forty years, as a shepherd. God needed to take him on a forty-year journey so that he could endure forty years with a "stiff-necked" people. God did this in the midst of everyone having freedom to act as they wished. Keep in mind that Moses did not provide the deliverance. What God wanted from Moses was his faith. Everything else was all God.

It is all about God.

No Fear . . . God Is Always Near

Exodus 14:10–20, 25, 28–31

General Overview of the Passage

God instructed the Israelites how to proceed as they traveled. Pharaoh interpreted their movement as wandering aimlessly (Exod. 14:3). When he saw this and evaluated that he had no one to serve him (he lost his entire workforce), he decided to make Israel pay for their disobedience. When he made this decision, God hardened his heart again (v. 8) and Pharaoh gathered his army together and went after Israel.

> "And I indeed will harden the hearts of the Egyptians, and they shall follow them. So I will gain honor over Pharaoh and over all his army, his chariots, and his horsemen. Then the Egyptians shall know that I am the Lord, when I have gained honor for Myself over Pharaoh, his chariots, and his horsemen." And the Angel of God, who went before the camp of Israel, moved and went behind them; and the pillar of cloud went from before them and stood behind them. (Exod. 14:17–19)

When the Israelites lifted their faces and saw the advancing army of horsemen, chariots, and foot soldiers, they became very terrified. They cried to God making a sound like thunder. They were in great distress especially since they had personally experienced the might and brutality of the Egyptian army. The Egyptians were already in battle array and in attack formation.

The Israelites then accused Moses of moving them from their old existence in the safety of slavery and now leading them to their death. They wanted Moses to leave them alone, and made it clear that they would rather have gone on as slaves.[9]

[9] Noel D. Osborn and Howard Hatton, *A Handbook on Exodus* (New York, NY: United Bible Societies, 1999), 337.

Moses responded in the midst of the advancing army, and in the midst of angry, fearful Israelites. When Moses responded, he demonstrated trust in God because he was yet to receive a word from God. Despite all that was before Moses, he made a decision not to let the power and might of the Egyptian army intimidate him. Moses told the people to oppose the army in defiance because God is their help in the time of trouble. He is their deliverer because He is the one who has all authority and power and is always near. He reminded them that God only has a covenant with Israel—not the Egyptians. Moses somehow knew that God would utterly destroy the Egyptians. He cried out to the Lord (v. 15), and the Lord responded. The most important thing is to be on the Lord's side. Moses was confident that the Almighty, most powerful God who has all authority would go to battle for Israel.

God decided to let an obstinate sinner, Pharaoh, become even more steadfast in his decision to not listen to God. God hardened his heart, which in turn hardened his mind, and he became even more stubborn. God wanted the Egyptian people to come to a full understanding of His impressive power. His plan was to display His power over all of the Egyptians, the most powerful army in the known world. God knew this would cause them to respect Him.

The Angel of God—which could be the incarnate Christ—was in front of the camp. The Angel of God then moved to the back of the camp in the form of a pillar of cloud. Once the pillar got to the back of the camp it "stood," meaning it became still, immovable, and upright between the Egyptian army and the Israelites. For Pharaoh to still advance against Israel only demonstrated further the hardness of his heart. As the Egyptians approached, the pillar of cloud hid Israel from them, becoming darkness to the Egyptians but lighting the Israelite camp (14:20). "This light marks the first appearance of what would come to be known as the 'Shekinah,' the visible indication of God's presence. This is usually referred to as "the glorious presence of the Lord" (see 16:7, 10; 24:16; 2 Chron. 5:14; 7:1; exposition on Ezek. 11:22–25; 43:1–5; Rev. 15:8). The Hebrew root of the word *Shekinah* actually means "dwelling," and describes God's choosing to dwell among his people, as he did in the Tabernacle (29:43–46)."[10]

When the water opened, allowing the people of Israel to walk on dry land to the other side, the soldiers were commanded to follow them. The soldiers' chariots became stuck in the mud and they realized that the Lord was battling

---

[10] H. L. Willmington, *Willmington's Bible Handbook* (Wheaton, IL: Tyndale House Publishers, 1997), 51.

against them. The land was dry for Israel as they moved through the sea but muddy for the Egyptians as they tried to get their chariots through.

The Almighty Lord who has all power and authority is compared to the hand (meaning power and authority) of the Egyptians, and the Lord is the one who provided deliverance. The Lord is the one who preserved them as a nation. The evidence of God's power washed up on the seashore so that Israel understood and accepted that the Lord is their deliverer. When the Israelites understood and accepted what God had done as a result of His innate ability, the Israelites reverently trusted in God and became committed to His will (fear—they stood in reverent awe of God). They became convinced that God could be trusted.

Historical Background

Establishing Context

The unit of chariots assigned to Pharaoh is about 600 chariots. There could be another 10 to 150 chariots in addition to that. The roads traveled by the military were not concrete roads. They were dirt roads. This is why there were seasons of war. They could not go out to war when it was raining or wet. Having approximately 700 chariots and several thousand foot soldiers coming toward you would be threatening. Sometimes the soldiers would stand on an elevation and let the sun shine off their armor so that they looked as intimidating as possible.

With all the above taking place, only soldiers were allowed to carry weapons. So the 600,000 men that are a part of all who left Egypt may not have sufficient weapons.

Pharaoh came after Israel because it seemed like they were boxed in by the sea. This was because when Moses went to the lowest side of the Red Sea to cross, God did not want them to go the way of the Philistines (Exod. 13:17–18). So Moses had to come back to another place with about 2 million people following him only for God to put the Red Sea at flood stage.

> "For Pharaoh will say of the children of Israel, 'They are bewildered by the land; the wilderness has closed them in.' Then I will harden Pharaoh's heart, so that he will pursue them; and I will gain honor over Pharaoh and over all his army, that the Egyptians may know that I am the LORD." And they did so. (Exod. 14:3–4)

What Does the Context Mean?

When fear becomes greater than faith, the past sometimes seems better than the future. Fear makes us seek security, whereas faith drives us forward, surrendered to the goodness and faithfulness of God. The people saw the soldiers coming and became afraid, but Moses showed leadership and cried to God for help rather than looking at the army and feeling helpless. God responded by instructing Moses to move the people forward. Before the Red Sea could open, the people must begin moving forward. Moses believed God and did as God commanded. Moses placed his complete trust in God. After the opening of the sea and the destruction of the army, the people reverenced God and believed in God. Their belief in God is the first mention of its kind.

Sermon Subject and Title

Sermon Title: No Fear . . . God Is Always Near
Big Idea: When obedience to God's will puts us in "Red Sea situations," God is there. He never leaves us nor forsakes us, no matter how mighty the enemy may seem.

Sermon Outline (Exod. 14:10–20, 25,28–31 NASB)

A. A Battle to Experience; a War to Avoid (13:17; 14:5–9)

1. *The way of the Philistines*—This was a shortcut that could have put them back into slavery. God's way may seem long and cumbersome, but it produces the best results.
2. *The way of the Philistines*—This battle would have cost them their heart (Exod. 14:17); they were fresh out of their incubator—Egypt.
3. They must go in the direction where the battle belongs to the Lord (14:3–9; 1 Cor. 10:13).

B. The Attitude that Leads to Victory (14:10–14)

1. The power of dreadful fear (Exod. 14:10–13).
   a) *Do not fear*—They were terrified. They were totally overwhelmed with fear.
   b) Their cry was like the sound of thunder—two million people wailing at the same time. They were in great distress because they knew by experience the kind of people these soldiers were.
   c) They accused Moses of putting them in a set condition to die.

   d) It was a cry of disbelief (vv. 10–13). This should not have been because God just manifested powerful, miraculous acts before them.
2. Moses cried to God (v. 15) and trusted God for His Word.
3. *Stand still*—It was not their fight; they do not have to do a thing.
4. *The Lord will fight*—The one who is always near, who has all authority, power, and might fights for them.

C. A Commitment to Faith (vv. 15–20)

1. *Why are you crying?*—God promised to deliver Israel from Egypt at a specified time, and it was that time. God just gave them a glimpse of His mighty power and told them through Moses that He will deliver them to Mount Sinai, but here they are crying at their first obstacle.
2. *Go forward*—When God's Word is clear, crying out is unnecessary (vv. 15–17, 19–20).
3. Moses must follow God's instructions even though it makes no sense. "The Lord said . . ." (vv. 15–16).
4. *Lift up; stretch out*—Two specific commands in front of all the people crying and wailing. This is an action that everyone would know did not make the sea roll back. It was God, responding to Moses' obedience, who parted the sea.
5. *The Egyptians will know*—The Egyptians had a vivid experience of God's power so that they would know without a shadow of a doubt that there is no other God but the Lord God of Israel. They came to a full knowledge of God's power.

D. "Victory Is Mine"—Allow God to Fight for You (vv. 19–31)

1. The Angel of God moved from the front to the fear (from leading to protecting) (v. 19a):
   a) *Been going*—This represents, possibly, the eternal existence of the Angel of the Lord (if the angel is indeed Christ).
   b) *Stood*—The obedience of Moses caused the Angel of the Lord to move in front of the people. This word means to be immovable. All the Egyptians' powerful could not move this one angel.
   c) *Who had been*—Means to be ready to fight.
   d) God placed a wall between the Israelites and the Egyptians. Shekinah glory for Israel and soon coming judgment for Egypt:

- The light marks the first appearance of what would come to be known as the Shekinah, the visible indication of God's presence—the glorious presence of God.
- The Hebrew root of *Shekinah* means "dwelling." It describes God's choosing to dwell among His people, as He did in the tabernacle (Exod. 29:43–46).

2. When the Egyptians realized that God was fighting for the Israelites, they fled. Because of the obedience of a leader, Moses, to trust God and lift one staff, God brought a military power to its knees.
3. When God is able to fight for you, His purposes are accomplished and true victory is established (14:28–31):
   a) Israel saw the power of God revealed (v. 31a).
   b) Israel now reverenced God. They were in awe.
   c) Israel finally believed God. They finally chose to reverently trust Him and His leader Moses.
   d) They became convinced that God can be trusted, that He is faithful, true, and able to defeat any powers raised before them.

Author's Comments

Comments

Picture the scene. There were God's people confronted by a raging sea in front of them and a raging army behind them. Thousands and thousands of soldiers, horsemen, and chariots were marching toward them, and there was no place to flee. They were hemmed in. How could they not fear? A terrifying fear would be a normal reaction in such an impossible situation. But there was God's messenger shouting out, "Do not fear!"

There are four motives that move men to action: Fear, hope, faith, and love—these four, but the greatest of these is fear. People are afraid of losing their health, their wealth, and their loved ones. People are afraid of life itself. When God forces us to trust Him in the face of overwhelming difficulties, will we put our trust in His Word?

This is the issue facing the Israelites. God told them, through Moses, that He would deliver them. Moses' mother knew this and trained Moses on the hope of the deliverance. Moses told them that God would deliver them to Mount Sinai to worship Him. They saw one powerful act of God after another harm the Egyptians, but not one plague touch them in any way. Despite God's powerful protection, when they were stuck between these two terrors, they said they would rather go back to Egypt and serve Pharaoh. The issue was actually not the army. The real issue depended on whatever emotion the surrounding circumstances stirred up within them that caused them to turn against the Word of God. This is repeated over and over again in the wilderness.

This was never their fight. God made a promise that He was going to keep no matter what. The Egyptian army was only powerful because God allowed it to be. This was to protect the Israelites from outsiders going into Egypt and taking His people captive (Exod. 9:16–17). When God had fully developed His nation, He did what He told Abraham He would do (Gen. 15). If they had trusted God, there would have been less stress and they would have seen the Promised Land they wanted to see from generation to generation.

The greatest battle we all face is whether or not we will believe God for His Word. When Paul was writing to Timothy, a young Christian facing trouble, Paul said: "Fight the good fight of faith, lay hold on eternal life, to which you were also called and have confessed the good confession in the presence of many witnesses" (1 Tim. 6:12).

Application

The only fight we face in this life is the fight of faith (1 Tim. 6:12). It does not matter how impossible a marriage may seem to fix, how difficult it may seem for our children to be healed, or how impossible financial struggles may become. The greatest struggle is to deny ourselves and place our faith in God by believing Him for His Word.

Illustrate It

A young man decided he wanted to serve God on the mission field. He wanted to go to a remote part of the earth and reach people who had never heard the gospel. After settling on a particular tribe of people in South America, raising funds, going through training, learning about the tribe, and spending time with family and friends, he headed out. He found some guides who would take him to these people. When he arrived, the people soon learned who he was, and being a friendly group of people, they got to know him.

One day he found out that a very special person in his family was ill and near death. He wanted to minister to them because he knew they were not saved, so he rounded up the guides and started out. He soon learned that the guides were terribly lost. Because he was afraid the person would die before he got there, he started to panic. Then, he remembered that his guides were looking at him and that would not be a good testimony. So he stopped and prayed. Within a few minutes the guides got their bearings and found their way out, and he was able to leave the island in time to share Christ and lead the person to a personal relationship with the Lord.

Sometimes we come to Red Seas and our backs are against the wall, and we must decide how to react; we can panic, or we can pray and trust God to do the impossible.

Leadership that Leads to Peace

Exodus 18:17–23

General Overview of the Passage

In an effort to address and resolve all the issues Moses had to manage, Moses had to work day and night. What he was doing was not good for him or the people. After a period of observation (Exod. 18:13–16), Jethro instructed Moses to do what God has designed for a person in his position to do. Jethro directed him to select able men to assist him in resolving minor disputes. This process, Jethro advised, would lead to peace among the people, and stop the people from taking the law into their hands. With the assistance of these leaders, Moses improved the well-being of the community and lessened his load.

Moses' lack of structure placed him in a state of being dried up like dry grass. As a result, he became nonproductive. Jethro provided Moses with good advice for decision making, like a general being given military intelligence in order to manage the battle. "The word 'capable' here can mean 'brave,' 'heroic,' or even 'upper class.' In light of the qualifications that follow this one, though, 'capable' or 'competent' is probably better. The other qualifications literally read, 'fearers of God, men of truth, haters of unjust gain.'"[11]

The men whom Moses selected were required to reverence God and respect His holy nature. They must be men who do not waver in doing things faithfully for God and only stand for truth. They are competent men, men of power who can deal with issues like soldiers of war. They must be men who despise dishonest gain. The amount of people these men managed (thousands, hundreds, fifties, and tens) must have correlated to their ability. These men would have served as arbitrators for the small issues and brought the major issues to Moses.

---

[11] Walton, *Zondervan Illustrated Bible Backgrounds Commentary*, Vol. 1, 224.

Moses was responsible for making sure they knew what their responsibilities were before God. These were the specific enactments or regulations God gave, as well as the ceremonial, civil, and moral laws God provided. He must also teach them right and wrong, leading them to learn by application the divine will of God (discipleship; Matt. 28:19; 2 Tim. 2:2).

Historical Background

Establishing Context

Moses' father-in-law was from Midian (a name that means contention and strife). Jethro is actually a distant relative of Moses because his forefather was born from the second wife of Abraham, Keturah (Gen. 25:1). She along with his concubines was sent away with gifts into the wilderness to prevent a contest over the inheritance of Isaac (Gen. 25:1–6). He was the person whose sheep Moses took care of for forty years. They were desert people who lived in tents like nomads (Exod. 3:1; Num. 10:29–31). It is very possible that they had some consciousness of God because of their heritage with Abraham or any influence Moses may have had.

Jethro gave Moses advice to help him manage the people of God. In Jethro's day, the seat of authority was that of a judge. This seat, in most cities, was at the gate of the city. Moses was advised to set up a hierarchical system with Moses being at the top and other judiciaries settling the lesser disputes in lower levels. "There were no lawyers, so most people represented themselves in court. Witnesses could be called, and oaths played very significant roles since most of our scientific means of gathering evidence were not available."[12] This was Jethro's frame of reference that may have influenced his advice to Moses.

What Does the Context Mean?

This passage vividly portrays what God has done to make sure His people are cared for in a dangerous and difficult time. Moses working all day and night, neglecting his family (Exod. 18:13), and having the people wait for a long time to meet with him was not good for him or the people.

---

[12] Matthews, Chavalas, and Walton, *IVP Bible Background Commentary*, s.v. Deut. 1:16; Exod. 18:27.

Moses needed to select godly men to care for the people so he could remain focused on what God wanted him to do and so the people could experience peace.

Sermon Subject and Title

Sermon Title: Leadership that Leads to Peace
Big Idea: When leading becomes overwhelming, God's plans to lead His people can perfect the leader and the people being led.

SERMON OUTLINE (EXOD. 18:17–23 NASB)

A. God-Directed Leadership Demonstrates that God Cares (vv. 17–22)

1. Because they recognized God as the leader of their souls, they sought advice from Him.
2. *Not good*—It is not the wise, excellent, or the practical way; it is not beneficial for the community.
3. *Wear out*—Moses will continuously (imperfect) dry up like grass (could be physically, emotionally, and spiritually); Moses would become nonproductive.
4. *Listen*—Jethro commands (imperative) Moses to give him his undivided attention (active verb) to gain intellectual and spiritual knowledge as God leads him.
5. *Counsel*—This word carries the meaning of decision making like a general being given military intelligence in order to manage the battle. This counsel is going to be unfolding, which is why Moses needs to give his undivided attention.
6. *Teach*—To communicate information that has a legal prescription of something that must be done. Moses must remain in this state of action.
7. *Statutes*—The commands of God.
8. *Laws*—These were the specific enactments or regulations God gave, as well as the ceremonial, civil, and moral laws God provided.
9. *Make*—Cause them to . . .
10. *Known*—They must experience by observation (Matt. 28:19) and follow the leaders' conduct (Heb. 13:7).
11. *Way*—The divine will of God.

12. *Walk*—He must also cause them to experience what is right and wrong to develop character in the people (New Testament discipleship concept). This is accomplished by causing them to learn the divine will of God (Matt. 28:19; Eph. 4:12–13; 2 Tim. 2:2).
13. *Work*—Moses must also teach them to become skillful in their faithful service to God (In the New Testament, this would be the development of spiritual gifts to work itself out through spiritual growth; Eph. 4:12–13, 16; 1 Pet. 4:10).
14. *Able men*—Men of power, capable, competent; men of strength who can deal with warlike issues.
15. *Fear God*—These men stand in awe of God; they understand and recognize the power and the position of God and respect His holy character.
16. *Truth*—Who do what is right. The church is the "pillar and support of the truth" (1 Tim 3:15 NASB).
17. *Judge*—Moses must allow them to designate the function of government and arbitrate between the people regularly so that it is a recurring incident. These are not the major issues.

B. Godly Leadership Produces God-Given Results (v. 23)

1. *Easier*—This would not only make Moses' responsibilities lighter; it would also make this a ministry in which he can stand upright. Jethro commands Moses to implement this structure.
2. *This thing God commands you*—Knowing that in all things Jethro was acting under the immediate direction of God. The counsel was doubtless inspired by the Holy Spirit, for Moses acted in every respect according to the advice he had received.
3. *Able*—Men of power who are capable and competent to deal with warlike situations. Moses' ability to manage the people's struggles remains strong (the verb is in the perfect, so it is in a set condition).
4. *Endure*—You can stand upright in one spot. Bear up under a load. Moses would be in the state of strength to bear the load.
5. *Peace*—This also causes the people to leave in a satisfied condition (carries the meaning of harmony and well-being within the community) with a sense of well-being and with an absence of strife, since their issues are being addressed. This condition is a perpetual state of being.

Author's Comments

Comments

Let us evaluate some of the things people may have experienced during the week. Someone's husband was in the hospital; someone's boss is giving them a hard time; loneliness and the burden of raising kids as a single parent have made for an overwhelming week; a family member passed away; elderly parents may have needs. The list can go on and on. Any given week can stress anyone out. Knowing God cares and experiencing that He cares are two different things. God desires that we be cared for. He knows we have trials, struggles with the hardships in life. God also wants us to know His will and how we must manage our lives through the many issues we experience daily.

It was not any different for the people who had left Egypt and were now in the wilderness with no restroom facilities, no doctors when babies were born, and no civil courts when there were disputes to resolve. These people were not just traveling together; they were going to the same Promised Land. This left Moses to manage every issue that arose in a brand-new nation of two million people. It was not just hard for the people; it was hard for the leader. If he did a bad job, the people would be miserable while they lived, traveled, and functioned together 24-7. These challenges have to be met with structure so that God's people live in peace. This structure is not merely so we can have a good time when we come together; it is designed so we can effectively become an assembly of the living God where people's needs are met. Structure does not hurt people; it shapes people.

These people, who had no Bible, no synagogues, no rabbis, and no temples, could better understand God, know how to implement His will (especially since they were slaves and maybe were unable to read), and learn to live at peace with each other under difficult circumstances.

Creating a leadership structure that serves the spiritual, physical, and sociological needs of the congregation didn't just help the people, it allowed Moses to better serve his family and have more time with God. Moses having more time with God served to better God's influence on the people's lives. This is why this kind of leadership leads to peace.

Application

The church is designed so that as leaders we can give an account for all the people (Col. 1:28–29). The job of leaders is to present them complete just like a husband is to present his wife complete in Christ (Eph. 5:32). A tired and worn-out leader may be getting a lot done, but the ultimate responsibility will go neglected, and that is to consistently teach God's people the way they are to walk before God. To accomplish this task, a pastor must gather able men who hate dishonest gain. The same takes place for each ministry leader within the church. This allows members to grow and experience God intimately.

Illustrate It

At the conclusion of the Iraq war with Saddam Hussein, the issue to be solved was who would now run the country. What kind of government will it be? There was a need for a constitution, new military leaders, and a voting system. This took time to implement, and the nagging question was which religious group would have control.

President Obama made it a point to push for a mixture of religious groups in government so all the people would have a voice. This was eventually instituted and led to more harmony in the country and greater strength to defeat terrorists.

No matter how great the leader, if he has a broken structure around him, leadership will be challenging. The leadership structure is critical for the needs of the people to be met. This principle is also provided for the church when Timothy is sent to Ephesus to pastor. Apparently, the people Paul put in leadership (Acts 20:25–31) had died and Timothy needed to reorganize the church. Once the leadership was put in place, Paul told Timothy that everything was now in order (1 Tim. 3:15). He never talked about a choir, building, ushers, or a missionary society, but the church was settled and in order.

Desire His Presence

Exodus 33:12–16

General Overview of the Passage

In the midst of organizing the Israelites to function smoothly, Moses went to Mount Sinai to listen to God. During this time of receiving God's law, the people turned to worship a golden calf. Moses, upon his return, became angry and threw the tables of the law so that they shattered. God's anger burned against the people and He told them that because they were obstinate and refused to submit to His will, He would no longer personally lead them. God said he would put an angel before them to lead them. Moses was not satisfied with God's decision to send an angel. Moses' desire was for God's presence to remain with His people. Moses repeated what God said about him earlier (Exod. 3:10–14)—that God knows Moses by name. Moses desired more from God; he sought God's favor, grace, kindness, and knowledge of His divine will. Moses deeply desired to know God. Looking at these two key words, *favor* and *know* God, it seems that Moses' greatest desire was to have an intimate interaction and relationship with God. Moses did not desire to go anywhere until God promised to go with them.

Yahweh reconciled with the people as a result of Moses' intercession and their own sincere repentance. "Things are now restored to the state in which they were at the establishment of the covenant, and consequently the presence of the Lord, which is promised here to go with them, is the same as the angel whom He pledged Himself to Moses to 'send before him' (Exod. 23:20–21: cf. Isa. 63:8–9)."[13]

Moses did not want to move unless the presence of God was with him. "Without supernatural assistance, and a most particular providence, he knew

---

[13] R. Jamieson, A. R. Fausset, and D. Brown, *A Commentary, Critical and Explanatory, on the Old and New Testaments* (Oak Harbor, WA: Logos Research Systems, Inc., 1997), s.v. Exod. 33:14.

that it would be impossible either to govern such a people or support them in the desert; and therefore he wishes to be well assured so that he may lead them up with confidence and be able to give them the most explicit assurances of support and protection."[14] God's presence with this large group of people must cause the world to recognize that there is something unique about this nation.

Historical Background

Establishing Context

The Tent of Meeting was a place where Moses had personal meetings with God. He once had the tent in the midst of the congregation, but because of the sin of the people, he moved it outside the camp. Joshua would stand guard at the tent of meeting. "There are no sacrifices offered there, and it contains no altar. It is a place for prophetic, not priestly, activity. Once the tabernacle is constructed and takes its place in the middle of the camp, it also serves as a Tent of Meeting."[15] God would come upon the tent as a "pillar of cloud would descend and stand at the entrance of the tent" (33:9 NASB). "Speaking face to face is an idiom suggesting an honest and open relationship. It does not contradict 33:20–23. Numbers 12:8 uses a different expression with the same meaning, 'mouth to mouth.'"[16]

Because of the people's sin, God said He could no longer go with the people and would send an angel. "Moses' request to see the glory of God is not a request for God to do what he has never done before."[17] God granted Moses his request. "My Presence means literally in Hebrew 'My Face.' This extraordinary promise of God's Presence with His people was ultimately fulfilled in Jesus, God made man."[18]

What Does the Context Mean?

God is a jealous God. He had just released the nation of Israel from Egypt—a nation that was polytheistic. The Egyptians worshipped just about

---

[14] Osborn and Hatton, *A Handbook on Exodus*, 789.

[15] Matthews, Chavalas, and Walton, *IVP Bible Background Commentary*, s.v. Exod. 33:7–10.

[16] Ibid., s.v. Exod. 33:11–23.

[17] Ibid., s.v. Exod. 33:23.

[18] Radmacher, Allen, and House, *Nelson's New Illustrated Bible Commentary*, 143.

everything that moved. This is why God ordered so many plagues. God was seeking to show the Egyptians and the Israelites that He was the only God. Pharaoh viewed himself as a god, so God took him on at the Red Sea and destroyed his army. After vividly seeing the power of God, the people, just a few days out of Egypt, worshipped one of the very gods that God destroyed before they left. This made God angry and He decided that the people were so sinful that he could no longer be in their midst. Moses did not want to go on the journey with the people without God leading them, so Moses pleaded with God to go with them.

Moses wanted God's complete presence, so he asked God to bless him with His favor (something he requested about four times in this short passage), to know God's will (God did answer this in 34:4–9), and to have God's presence go with them. Moses pleaded with God not to have them move from in front of Mount Sinai with His presence. Moses wanted God to so identify with His people that His people would be distinct from all the people on the earth.

Sermon Subject and Title

Sermon Title: Desire His Presence
Big Idea: Being empowered by the presence of God is of greater importance than anything we can desire to do for God.

SERMON OUTLINE (EXOD. 33:12–16 NASB)

A. A Cry for God (v. 12; Rom. 8:26–28)

1. *Moses' request*—This is because God planned to send an angel to move in front of the people rather than Himself (Exod. 33:1–2). This being in the imperfect means that what Moses is saying to God he has no intentions to ever stop saying. Moses is very persistent.
2. *See*—God's command (an imperative) does not leave Moses understanding why He would not go with him.
3. Moses understood God's request and the help God planned to provide, but without the Lord, he does not want to go forward. *Send* is a set condition, meaning that once God put this in place it will not change (perfect active).
4. Even if the people act up, the Lord knows Moses intimately.

a) *Know*—God desires to have a relationship with Moses by name, meaning it is very personal and it is a set condition that does not change (perfect active).
b) *Name*—He knows Moses' origin, history, and has had frequent communion with him. God has created a greater interest in experiencing God.
c) *In knowing Moses*—God has extended acts of kindness showing that He desires to know Moses.
d) *Sight*—All of this takes place in the very presence of God.

B. A Desire to Covet God's Presence (v. 13)

1. *I have found favor*—Because Moses has this kind of intimate relationship with God, he urgently seeks God's favor (God's kindness and blessings, which display God's desire to continue the relationship). What is powerful to note is that the favor Moses has experienced continues in the same manner and does not change (perfect active).
2. To come into the presence of God and leave alive (for one sin a high priest died) is a challenge Moses is willing to address.
3. Because of the relationship he has with God, Moses would like to:
   a) *Let me know*—Moses actively commands God (imperative) to allow an intimate experience with him. Not just meeting in the Tent of Meeting but a constant movement of God upon his life each moment of each day.
   b) *Ways*—Experience God's customs—manner of dealing with men. To fully know God's manner of operating.
   c) *Find*—To continuously look with purpose for something that was lost.
   d) *Sight*—To be in God's face or presence.
   e) *Consider too*—Moses commands God (imperative) to recognize that this is God's nation. It seems as if Moses is seeking to convince God that He could not leave a people that belong to Him.

C. God's Company to Keep (vv. 14–15; John 15:7–11)

1. God's Answer to Moses' Desire:
   a) *My presence*—God is now reconciled with His people as a result of Moses' intercession.
   b) *Shall go*—His presence will continuously go with His people (imperfect active).

c) *Rest*—Provide peace and understanding; be in a state of favorable circumstances.
d) *Lead*—Without supernatural assistance and a most particular providence, he knew that it would be impossible either to govern such a people or support them in the desert.

D. His Blessings to Experience (v. 16)

1. The world should see that you have a personal interest in your people.
2. *Found*—The favor that Moses has achieved is continuous (imperfect active).
3. *Favor*—God's attitude toward Israel needs to be public.
4. *Sight*—God's grace displayed in His kindness needs to be public.
5. *Distinguish*—God's work needs to be a testimony to the world. They would be a unique nation with a unique God.

Author's Comments

Comments

It seems like in the Christian community, we covet more of God's blessings than His presence.

Moses remained on Mount Sinai for an extended period of time, and this caused the people to make a calf god to worship. God wanted to destroy them, but decided against it and allowed Moses to go down and work with the people. After Moses killed people who were worshippers of the gilded calf god, he went to the Tent of Meeting to present himself before God. The people followed him there.

When trouble is on every side of our lives, do we run to or from God? One of the most crucial things about this passage is Moses' desire to know God's heart, His ways, and to experience God's presence. Experiencing God's presence is not a science, but it is a process we must all learn. It is an important lesson and is one of the main reasons Christ died for our sins. Christ came for us to experience life and life abundantly (John 10:10). His focus for dying for us is to be our friend (John 15:13–14) so that we have an intimate relationship with Him from the inside out (Eph. 3:14–19; 1 John 4:4). Our passion should be to walk in the Spirit and not in the flesh (Gal. 5:16–25; Eph. 5:15–18). Paul puts it this way: "If then you were raised with Christ, seek those things which are above, where Christ is, sitting at the right hand of God. Set your mind on things above, not on things on the earth. For you died, and your life is hidden with Christ in God. When Christ who is our life appears, then you also will appear with Him in glory" (Col. 3:1–4).

The people of Israel were glad to be released from Egypt, but struggled to maintain a healthy and productive relationship with God. How many of us are excited about being saved and know we are going to heaven but don't show the same passion for experiencing heaven on earth (Eph. 1:3–4, 20; 2:6; 3:10; 6:12)? How many of us enjoy having a great time at church but are not interested in becoming a true representative of the church? If we are just excited about being saved and being in a great church experience, we are no different than the nation of Israel when they left Egypt.

Application

Our call to serve God is not enough; experiencing His presence is everything (John 15:1–11). How often when leading our homes, small groups, or churches do we seek to walk with God rather than just fulfill a task? How often do we fight for God to lead our homes, churches, or small groups so that His presence is among us? When experiencing God becomes everything, then everything is worth experiencing.

Illustrate It

After the movie *Angels in the Outfield* premiered, many people believed that they had a guardian angel watching over them. Made in 1994 with actors Danny Glover, Brenda Fricker, and Tony Danza, it told the story about a boy praying that God would provide him a family. The only way he could get a family is if the California Angels won the pennant race. As an answer to his prayers, angels were assigned to him; thus "Angels in the Outfield" became one of the major focuses of the movie.

The popularity of the movie led to many discussions. People began to believe that they had guardian angels. In fact, many people began to even pray to angels rather than to God.

The writer of Hebrews in Hebrews 1:14 states, "Are they not all ministering spirits, sent out to render service for the sake of those who will inherit salvation?" (NASB). "The angel of the LORD encamps all around those who fear Him, and delivers them" (Ps. 34:7). There are angels with us, but not for us to pray to. Angels serve their purpose when we focus, like Moses, on experiencing the work of the Holy Spirit in our lives so that we live in the power of God.

Holiday Messages

Easter: Christ's Sacrifice

1 Peter 2:21–25

General Overview of the Passage

Peter's audience has a divine call to participate in the exercise that requires patient endurance of suffering because of the evil that exists around them. In this respect, Christ has given them a model of conduct because we see that although He did nothing wrong, He was accused, punished, and killed. Christ was affected by beatings and difficulties, and the physical effects of those who remained after His death (Thomas seeing and touching the marks of His crucifixion; John 20:26–29). This serves as a pattern for us (*follow*—to walk in the steps of another; these are footprints of suffering; to take the same road that someone else has taken). They are suffering for Jesus in the sense that by their patient endurance of unjust punishment they continue in the "living hope" (1 Pet. 1:3), trusting Christ as they anticipate the obtaining of "an inheritance which is imperishable and undefiled and will not fade away, reserved in heaven for you" (1:4 NASB). How they "held up" under suffering is a powerful testimony of Christ's saving grace.

Christ was a silent lamb (Matt. 27:12–14, 34–44). He remained silent while people heaped abuse and slander upon Him, continuously using vile and highly insulting language. Here the Greek present participles and imperfect tenses emphasize that under sustained and repeated provocation, never once did Christ break His silence. While experiencing pain from their abuse, He did not say to them anything suggesting He would cause them harm, whether at the time of the crucifixion or in the future. Instead, He asked God to forgive them (Luke 23:34). Christ gave Himself over to the control of God. Christ trusted God. He proved that a person could be in the will of God, be greatly loved by God, and still suffer unjustly. There are those who may claim that Christians will *not* suffer if they are in the will of God. Those who promote such ideas have not meditated much on the cross. "But the Lord said to him, 'Go, for he is a chosen vessel of Mine to bear My name before Gentiles, kings, and the children of Israel. For I will show him how many things he must suffer for My name's sake'" (Acts 9:15–16).

No one else made an offering for our willful and intentional acts against the will of God. God's will is that Christ must die so that the power of the sinful nature in mankind may be removed. Breaking the bondage of sin frees us to enjoy the spiritual and eternal quality of life. "This quality of life allows us to live in conformity with all that God commands or appoints (God's uprightness or standard which is imputed into man by the Holy Spirit). For by the bruises and wounds that Christ suffered from the scourging (the stroke of divine judgment administered vicariously to Him on the cross) we are made."[1] The purpose of Christ's passion is to provide separation from sin and a new life based on the ministry of the Holy Spirit imputing a new life of righteousness. Christ's suffering was not for Himself, but for us, to free us from the very sin that influenced people to nail an innocent man/God to the cross. In the same way, when we suffer for living holy (Ps. 34:19–22), it can pave the way for others who may travel the same path of life by providing encouragement. When others see those suffering do well, it will encourage them in the same situations. It can lead to providing godly wisdom when counseling with those individuals.

Peter tells them that they were continuously and habitually wandering away from Christ on their own initiative. They willfully turned their hearts toward God, which leads them to have a changed attitude for a positive and acceptable direction toward the Good Shepherd who tenderly and vigilantly cares for His sheep. He oversees them with a watchful, tender care, guarding them against Satan each and every day. They have a faithful Shepherd who tenderly loves them and nurtures them to spiritual maturity so that they do not fall into temptation because of all that the world has to offer.

Historical Background

Establishing Context

Although slaves and masters cooperated in many households as members of a common family, laws viewed slaves as property as well as people, and some owners abused them as property; nearly all owners treated them as socially inferior. In the midst of all their suffering, slaves needed a role model whose similar

---

[1] Timothy Friberg, Barbara Friberg, and Neva F. Miller, *Analytical Lexicon of the Greek New Testament* (Grand Rapids, MI: Baker Books, 2000), 201.

experiences encouraged them to accept, while trusting in God, the pain they experienced. A soldier who has been to war can better identify with another soldier who is at war. So Christ's suffering provided a perfect model that His power provides the ability to overcome. Peter chose to use Christ as the example of what this means and the benefits of remaining focused for God's glory. This is why Peter quotes Isaiah 53, instructing them that Christ is the suffering servant. "Here Peter reflects the language of Isaiah 53:4–5. In this context (1 Pet. 2:24–25), Peter takes the 'wounds' as the wounds of sin, as it often was intended in the prophets (e.g., Isa. 6:10; Jer. 6:14; 8:11) and sometimes in later Jewish literature (as probably in the eighth benediction of the Amidah, a regularly recited Jewish prayer)."[2]

Straying sheep (Jer. 50:6; Ezek. 34:6; cf. Ps. 119:176) are in a dangerous position because sheep cannot defend themselves and are not animals that can run fast. Each believer is blessed because they have a Shepherd, and He is their Guardian. "This verse echoes Isaiah 53:6. The image of Israel as sheep was common in the Old Testament[3] (e.g., Isa. 40:11), and the image of Israel as scattered sheep wandering from the shepherd also appears elsewhere (Jer. 50:6; Ezek. 34:6; cf. Ps. 119:176). An 'overseer' (NIV; 'guardian'—NASB, NRSV) was one who watched over, protected and had authority; Diaspora Judaism sometimes applied the term to God. In the Old Testament, God is the chief shepherd of his people (see comment on John 10:1–18)."[4]

What Does the Context Mean?

Peter's former misunderstanding of his call meant that he did not identify with Christ at His trial. He did not understand that his faith would be tested when he was told to walk on water. But now Peter understands that his call was not to follow Christ through good circumstances and then establish His throne in Jerusalem (Mark 10:35–40), but through difficulty so that the kingdom of God can be reestablished on earth (John 12:23–26). Because Satan is against God, this would lead to suffering. It was because Christ was committed to His

---

[2] C. S. Keener, *The IVP Bible Background Commentary: New Testament* (Downers Grove, IL: InterVarsity Press, 1993), s.v. 1 Pet. 2:22.

[3] **Old Testament:** The common modern term for the Hebrew Bible (including Aramaic portions) as defined by the Jewish and Protestant Christian canons; Jewish readers generally call this the Tanakh.

[4] Ibid., s.v. 1 Pet. 2:22.

Father's will that He suffered. Christ endured the suffering because it was the will of God. He was not going to forsake God's will, so the suffering intensified. This blesses all of us, because Christ's suffering was good for all of us.

It is this growth process and the revelation that Christ provided Peter as His leading apostle that allowed Peter to guide this congregation through a very difficult time. They were not neglected by Christ because their suffering was due to their commitment to obey Christ. They were suffering with the expectation to be refined for a great reward, which at the same time glorifies God (1 Pet. 1:3–9).

Sermon Subject and Title

Sermon Title: Christ's Sacrifice
Big Idea: Christ's suffering for the cause of God is a model to imitate when we suffer for the purposes of Christ.

Sermon Outline (1 Pet. 2:21–25 nasb)

A. The Footprints to Follow (vv. 21–22)

1. *You have been called*—This is an aorist tense, which means that this call has happened once and for all. To *call* means to cry out for a specific purpose.
2. *Purpose*—This is a model for Christian conduct. We have a divine purpose that finds favor with God (1 Pet. 2:20).
3. *Christ suffered*—Christ endured much affliction once and for all.
4. *Leaving us*—What Christ left us is a footprint, a pattern for suffering that would always be this way. This model is continuous, and gives us a footprint to copy in the midst of a wicked world (Phil. 2:15).
5. *His steps*—His life is our pattern. His footprint says:
    a) *Committed no sin*—Jesus never committed any offense against God, whether willful or unintentional.
    b) *Deceit*—No dishonesty.
    c) *Found*—After careful scrutiny (Isa. 53:5, 7, 9, 11–12). He did not suffer as an evildoer.
    d) Aorist passive indicative—meaning it took place in the past and it was not something He did but He willingly received what was done to Him.

B. An Attitude to Imitate (v. 23; reflects back to vv. 20; 3:13, 16–17)

1. While people were continuously (He was under sustained and repeated provocation) insulting Him using abusive language, He (having all power) did not insult or harm anyone (1 Thess. 5:15—do not pay back evil for evil). Present passive verb, meaning they continuously insulted Him with no end in sight and kept giving out insults.
2. *Did not revile in return*—(imperfect active indicative)—Christ did not, whether it was during the time they crucified Him or if they were to crucify Him today or in the future, return any insults. Jesus asked God to forgive them (Luke 23:34). The indicative means that this is a fact. There are eye-witnesses who would support this action.
3. *While suffering*—In the midst of His suffering—intense as it was—Christ never returned insults for insults.
4. Christ demonstrated for us that a person could be in the will of God, be greatly loved by God, and still suffer unjustly ("if God should will it so"; 1 Pet. 3:17 NASB).
5. *Christ entrusted Himself*—(imperfect active indicative)—Christ leaned on God (*entrusted*—to hand over Himself), to have matters continuously decided based on the standards of God. This action never stops. It is always active.
   a) "Who is there to harm you if you prove zealous for what is good? But even if you should suffer for the sake of righteousness, you are blessed. 'And do not fear their intimidation, and do not be troubled'" (1 Pet. 3:13–14 NASB).

C. His Model of Suffering Provides Victory (v. 24)

1. *He Himself bore our sins*—(aorist active indicative)—As a true sacrifice, He offered up ("snapshot" event in the past) our sin (intentional and willful acts against God) to God.
2. *That we might die to sin*—Aorist tense, meaning His death was a one-time act. He broke the power of the sin nature by giving us the power of the Holy Spirit that quickens our spirit that was once nonfunctional. He freed us to enjoy the spiritual and eternal quality of life (John 10:10).
3. *Live righteously*—Dative, meaning this is the direct purpose of His death. Righteousness was imputed to us as a gift from Him (Titus 3:4–8). It was not earned (work out; Phil. 2:12), and it establishes God's authority to direct our life based on His upright standards (Rom. 8:9–11).

4. *Wounds—healed*—Dative, meaning this is the direct purpose of His death. By His severe beating, which left many bruises and cuts, we were delivered from sin, made whole, and renewed (Matt. 13:15; 2 Cor. 5:17).

D. While Following, We Must Keep Our Eyes on Christ (v. 25)

1. *You were*—(imperfect active indicative)—We were continuously being provided false information and we habitually followed it. We abandoned the truth and followed error seeking to make it look like truth.
2. *Straying like sheep*—(present participle)—Straying like sheep is a continuous description of the nature we once had before we were saved.
3. *Returned*—(aorist passive indicative)—We once and for all received the influence provided through the Holy Spirit and changed directions back to right relationship with God. We have returned to a caring, tender Shepherd who is also a vigilant Caretaker.
4. Christ sits at the right hand of God with an all-seeing eye. He guards us against Satan's attacks (Job; 1 Cor. 10:13). We have angels around us (Heb. 1:14) and will not receive more than we can, in the power of the Spirit, endure.

Author's Comments

Comments

Today, we do not mourn the death of Christ; we celebrate the resurrection of Christ. This resurrection has been debated, but no one refutes this conclusion because of hundreds of eyewitness accounts (1 Cor. 15:3–11), and the lack of convincing evidence of His bones. To some, the resurrection is all about life after death; to others, Christ's place at the right hand to deal with forgiveness of sins; and to others it is exciting because they believe in someone who is not dead.

We are blessed with the inner power of the Holy Spirit because of Christ's resurrection. It is this power that Paul counted all things as loss to experience:

> But what things were gain to me, these I have counted loss for Christ. Yet indeed I also count all things loss for the excellence of the knowledge of Christ Jesus my Lord, for whom I have suffered the loss of all things, and count them as rubbish, that I may gain Christ and be found in Him, not having my own righteousness, which is from the

> law, but that which is through faith in Christ, the righteousness which is from God by faith; that I may know Him and the power of His resurrection, and the fellowship of His sufferings, being conformed to His death, if, by any means, I may attain to the resurrection from the dead. (Phil. 3:7–11)

It is this inner power that strengthens us (1 John 4:4), provides us wisdom, and guides us (Eph. 5:15–18) to walk with the Scriptures illuminated in our minds (John 14:26). Our suffering leads us to the greater experience of the Holy Spirit in us. This is why Peter begins by talking about salvation "through the resurrection of Jesus Christ" (1 Pet. 1:3) leading to "obtain[ing] an inheritance" (1:4 NASB). This inheritance Paul explains to us is the Holy Spirit (Eph. 1:13–14). This is why it is crucial that we remain sober, influenced by the Holy Spirit to "be holy yourselves also in all your behavior" (1 Pet. 1:13–16 NASB).

Even though we are called to suffer, with Christ being our example, we can do so with the power of the Holy Spirit working within us. Just as Christ can endure suffering, we can do the same because when we are spiritually mature, we can say: "I have been crucified with Christ; it is no longer I who live, but Christ lives in me; and the life which I now live in the flesh I live by faith in the Son of God, who loved me and gave Himself for me" (Gal. 2:20). The suffering of Christ becomes our suffering because we live for the same purpose: to do the Lord's will, and we are empowered by the same Spirit.

Application

Anyone who chooses to live right, the Bible teaches, will be persecuted (Ps. 34:19; 2 Tim. 3:12). Because of the example Christ left us, we must handle persecution as a badge of honor, especially since Hebrews 12:6 says God only disciplines those whom He loves and James 1:2–4 explains that this is God's classroom to make us "perfect and complete, lacking nothing." We tend to want to do anything to get out of trials when our focus should be to count it joy and work through the trials. This kind of suffering allows us to reign with him. "For I consider that the sufferings of this present time are not worthy to be compared with the glory which shall be revealed in us" (Rom. 8:18).

Illustrate It

Many times, people see athletes perform and assume they were blessed with an ability that has provided fame and fortune. What people don't know is that many of these athletes have heroes, trainers who work with them relentlessly on regiments for eating, running, and weight lifting. They push their bodies to give 100 percent. When we see them performing, we sometimes forget that it is a compilation of activity. We enjoy the entertainment and marvel at their talent, but many times forget their sacrifice.

We are blessed to have the Holy Spirit in our lives, to have God watch over us through the blood of Jesus Christ, and to have an Advocate who faithfully cares for us. There, however, has been a long journey that we have benefited from. A journey that called for much sacrifice and pain that many leaders of the Old Testament experienced, culminating in the sacrifice of Christ on Calvary (Gal. 4:4–5). Even if we suffer for righteousness we are blessed, because when we suffer, it is because we decided to get up off the pews and join the game. To play at this level calls for sacrifice and persistence. We are guaranteed success because we are empowered in our trials through the ministry of the Holy Spirit. We must accept the training, and when it is painful, remember Christ.

Mother's Day: Who's Who among Women

1 Timothy 5:3–10

General Overview of the Passage

Paul was delayed in getting to Timothy, who was in the city of Ephesus, so he sent him a letter to provide instruction on how to organize the church (1 Tim. 3:15). One of the action items he gave Timothy was how to give proper respect to widows. This is because widows were particularly vulnerable in ancient societies because they had no pensions, government assistance, or life insurance.

A widow is one who is without a family and is therefore left desolate (Mark 12:41–44). A widow who is truly a widow is also one who has fixed her desires with an attitude that is fully trusting in God. She continuously remains focused on maintaining a dependence on God. This is based on what is promised in the Scripture (Deut. 10:18; Pss. 68:5; 114:9). She does this like Anna in Luke 2:36–38, serving God day and night. These widows are irreproachable because they have a good reputation inside and outside the church. "Paul means not simply those bereaved of husband but those both committed to the church's ministry of prayer (1 Tim. 5:5) and experiencing the stereotypical Old Testament plight of widows: destitution (5:4)."[5]

Paul instructed Timothy that if widows had children or grandchildren, they must be taught to practice a devotion to their mother or grandmother, because this is true worship to God (notice the word *acceptable*—a divine act). It is a direct acknowledgment to God's nature, attributes, and ways. James calls this true religion (James 1:27). These children and grandchildren must create some payment back to their parents, because God finds pleasure in this. This process is continuous and it is something that is truly a desire of God.

---

[5] Keener, *IVP Bible Background Commentary*, s.v. 1 Tim. 5:3.

The widow, upon receiving assistance from the church, should not be self-indulgent. She must be a godly woman, conscious of God's presence, who fixes her hopes in God and serves in the church faithfully. Her service produces fruit in the lives of others. This is how Timothy would know it is empowered through the Holy Spirit.

The woman who seeks to satisfy her own appetites is continuously and habitually doing whatever makes her happy. This person is not a truly a widow, according to Paul in this letter of instruction. This is because her actions demonstrate that she is spiritually dead, even though she is physically alive. It is possible that those women had lived in luxury, often ignoring the needs of the poor and service to God. They demonstrated no deep commitment to worship God. These widows have no claims in the church.

If a child or grandchild ignores continuously their own mother or grandmother, especially if they are in the same house, they demonstrate that they have no respect for the Word of God. This person is worse than the person who is not saved.

Historical Background

Establishing Context

The plight of widows was a continual concern for God. The average age in the times of Christ for a man was about forty-five years old. It is addressed several times in Scripture: Deuteronomy 24:19–22; 26:12; Psalm 68:5; 146:9. This is probably why Job stated that he shared his food with widows (Job 31:16–17). James states in James 1:27 that "pure and undefiled religion in the sight of our God and Father is this: to visit orphans and widows in their distress, and to keep oneself unstained by the world" (NASB). God even mentions Himself as their defender (Pss. 68:5; 146:9).

God gets upset with anyone who takes advantage of them (Ps. 94:6; Ezek. 22:7; Mal. 3:5). "In the Mosaic legislation, special regard was paid to widows. It is true that no legal provision was made for their maintenance. But they were left dependent partly on the affection of relatives, especially the oldest son, whose birthright, or extra share of the property, imposed this duty upon him."[6]

---

[6] Merrill F. Unger, *The New Unger Bible Dictionary* (Chicago, IL: Moody Bible Institute, 1988), s.v. "widow."

When husbands passed, most of the widows were left dependent on relatives, as in the case of Naomi in the book of Ruth. "They also were dependent on the privileges provided for other distressed classes, such as participation in the triennial third tithe (Deut. 14:29; 26:12), in gleaning (24:19–21), and in religious feasts (16:11, 14)."[7] However, some of the widows may have been well off: "in like manner also, that the women adorn themselves in modest apparel, with propriety and moderation, not with braided hair or gold or pearls or costly clothing, but, which is proper for women professing godliness, with good works" (1 Tim. 2:9–10). This could have led some of them to have the means to chase after their own desires (1 Tim. 5:6). These widows were not those that Paul told Timothy to honor.

As a result of God's compassion and the continual needs of these widows, Paul writes providing Timothy instruction on how to manage this group of people within the church. The same issue took place at the very beginnings of the church in Acts 6:1–6.

What Does the Context Mean?

This passage provides direction to a young pastor to take care of widows who have no family and have been faithful servants of God, and who were once very committed to their husbands and children. They must be placed on the church list for the purpose of financial support.

Apparently, just as in the church of Jerusalem during the time of Pentecost (Acts 6:1–6), there were many widows in the church who had needs. Paul instructed Timothy how to care for the widows. If they had children or grandchildren, then these people must restore to the widows what is owed to them for the service they provided to their children and grandchildren when they could not help themselves. If the widows (like Naomi) do not have children and grandchildren to support them, the only way they can be put on the list is if they demonstrate a true commitment to their Christian faith. This is because they fixed their expectation of supply from God because the Word of God promises to take care of them. They also have demonstrated a serious commitment to obey God's Word in how they serve in the church, how they faithfully served their husbands and children, how they took care of strangers, washed the saints' feet, helped those in distress, and with a deep commitment did everything God

---

[7] Ibid.

called them to do. Widows who did not demonstrate these characteristics were not allowed to be on the church's list.

Sermon Subject and Title

Sermon Title: Who's Who among Women

Big Idea: Women of the faith who must be honored are those widows who continuously demonstrated a sincere faith in the Lord.

SERMON OUTLINE (1 TIM. 5:3–10 NASB)

A. Women of Honor (vv. 3–8)

1. Let us first take a look at what would cause a widow not to experience honor from God (1 Tim. 5:6):
    a) She whose desires are self-indulgent—continuously satisfying whatever she feels. It is a habitual act that is directly related to how she truly feels (nominative). Her husband is gone, so she does whatever she wants.
    b) She is dead—her faith has no works (James 2:14–26).
    c) She demonstrates no commitment to the things of God (1 Tim. 5:12–14).
2. A woman of honor (v. 5) is the total opposite (Luke 18:1–8)—a woman who is totally devoted to God (1 Tim. 5:10; Luke 2:36–37):
    a) *Honor*—It is a command (imperative) that is directly (genitive) related to continuously and habitually (present tense) providing proper recognition and respect to widows.
    b) Demonstrates an attitude of trust in God. God had a lot to say about widows. She trusts Him to do what He said (Deut. 10:18; Pss. 68:5; 146:9).
        - They should show evidence that they expect God to do what He said He would do.
        - She consistently cleaves to God's Word, demonstrated by her actions.
        - She always pleads with urgency for help from God.
        - Her prayers are concerning persistent specific needs.
        - Her prayers are for others—she shows concern for others.

3. God commands Timothy to make sure His "Who's Who among Women" are honored in the following manner:
   a) *Grandchildren must learn*—Paul commands Timothy to make sure that grandchildren continuously (present tense) give recognition (must become a habitual action) for what they have been taught by the way to take care of their grandmother.
   b) God finds pleasure (blesses them) with children and grandchildren who:
      - Demonstrate inner devotion to their parents (piety—a divine act of obedience); it demonstrates who God is in them.
      - *Practice piety*—This is a habit-forming attitude of inner devotion to caring for their grandparents. This attitude relates directly with God's attitude toward widows (Pss. 68:5; 146:9).
      - Their children work to restore strength to parents (some return).
      - Serving their grandparents is an action that God views as a form of worship (acceptable; James 1:27) because it gives God pleasure.
      - God oversees this very carefully (sight or presence of God).
   c) God blesses a church that cares for a widow who has no help—in their culture she could be desolate (Naomi):
      - *Alone*—This gives the sense of a person who is desolate, like the widow with the mite (Mark 12:41–44). Absolutely no one is caring for her.
4. A person who neglects to care for their family or parents is vividly demonstrating that he is in a set state of increasing neglect of the Word of God (apostasy; Heb. 6:4–6) and the convictions provided through the ministry of the Holy Spirit. God will hold this person accountable because they willfully turn away from God's direction. This is why they are worse than an unbeliever because at least an unbeliever does not know God's Word.
5. This is another way of saying the Word of God is not written on the person's heart.

B. The Who's Who List (vv. 9–10; Acts 9:36–42)

1. God's honor roll is based on:
   a) Must be a one-man woman—faithful to her husband.
      - This does not mean that she was not married twice since younger widows are told in verse 14 to remarry.

b) There are eyewitnesses of the things the widow has done for her family and the church.
c) She actively and consistently demonstrates service in the church.
d) She was a faithful mother.
e) She faithfully helped strangers in need of housing.
f) She faithfully served the needs of other believers.
g) She is faithful to help those who had a troubled life.
h) She is devoted to God. She faithfully and actively labors (to the point of weariness) and continued work for the Lord.

Author's Comments

Comments

Paul was delayed in getting to Timothy in Ephesus, so he sent him this letter to provide instruction on how to organize the church by putting everything in order (1 Tim. 3:15). Paul is looking at the end of his life and wanting to make sure that every element of the church he started is in order. It seems like the leaders he put in place, before his departure from Ephesus, had died (Acts 20:25–35). Since most men lived an average age of forty-five years, some of the members were widows. This means that some of the widows were very young since a lot of times the men married women who were several years younger. Timothy needed to know how to manage the widow population in the church. This is a serious issue because most of the women did not have a skill that they could use to make a living, as we see in the case of Naomi. So if they were not cared for, they would be like the widow with the mite in Mark 12:41–44, poor and destitute, vulnerable to abuse.

Since there were issues of how women functioned in the church, Paul wanted to highlight who are the "who's who" of women. His definition determines her value to the church when no one in her family cares for her. It builds upon her difficult circumstances and the role of women. Many times in our arguments in the church, we focus on 1 Timothy 2:11–14, which is a discussion about the woman's function in the church, whether the manner in which they adorn themselves or in what structure they can teach. However, what determines the level of respect they experienced is the character they display. The woman who received honor is the woman who is like the Proverbs 31 woman, or the woman described in 1 Timothy 5:9–10. It is the same for the man who is respected in the church (1 Tim. 3:2–10). This is why this passage provides a great example of the woman who is honored.

In our culture, success is determined by our accomplishments, not by what God has accomplished in shaping our character. It is determined by our ability to lead, rather than the humility we demonstrate in the manner in which we allow God to lead our lives. It is based on how we impress those around us, rather than the godly impression we place on their lives. We need to be countercultural to make our homes strong and our churches productive.

Application

It is the children's responsibility to take care of their mother. Parents, especially those who have been faithful in raising their children (1 Tim. 2:15), must receive support from children when they are older. A person who knows that their mother has a need and knows what the Scripture says to do about it should willfully decide to take care of their mother.

If a child decided not to take care of their mother, it shows a willful violation of God's Word. If the widow has no children, then it is the church's responsibility to take care of her. A person should organize their family budget in such a way that there are funds available when it is necessary to help their widowed mother. The church should have a line item in the budget to care for widows who meet the qualifications listed in this passage.

Illustrate It

There was a missionary, now with the Lord, who came home from the field to care for her sick and elderly parents. She was severely criticized by some of her associates ("We should love God more than father and mother!"), but she remained faithful to the end. Then she returned to the field for years of fruitful service, knowing she had obeyed God. After all, we love God by loving His people; and He has a special concern for the elderly, the widows, and the orphans. What she won (without this being her purpose) was the admiration of many people and a true appreciation from her mother, who truly needed her.

Even if we are serving God, He does not expect for us to neglect widows. There is no exemption in this text. Christ did not say they had to be perfect mothers who did everything right. This missionary listened to God and was blessed for her faithfulness.

Father's Day: A Model to Imitate

Genesis 35:1–7

General Overview of the Passage

After Jacob's sons had killed all the men in Shechem for the rape of their sister, God came to Jacob and told him to go to and remain at Bethel. This was no quick stop. God reminded him of the place by telling him it is the same place that he carefully inspected, accepted, and understood that God met him there (Gen. 28:22—Jacob made a vow to God thirty years earlier during a great crisis in his life and he did not keep it; God reminds him thirty years later). This is the first time in the Bible that God commanded an altar to be made for Him.

Jacob spoke to his household, appointing them to turn aside from their idols by making decisions to rid themselves of all foreign gods. He also commanded them to cleanse themselves from defilement, change their garments (probably outer garments), and get up and organize themselves to leave for Bethel. Obeying God's commands, Jacob said that he would create and fashion with tiresome effort an altar to the One who desires a relationship with him and seeks to draw near to him. He instructs them to continuously be in a state of movement that suggests a lifestyle change of going to Bethel so that they live in a responsible manner before God. These foreign gods were gods of other people, not of Jacob. Jacob recalled God's constant protection (Gen. 32) and His fulfillment of His promises (Gen. 28:13–15) as a reason to obey and worship God. Worship, which brings one into the presence of a holy God, demands inward and outward purity, the latter being seen as an expression of the former. "Purification usually took the form of bathing the body, washing the clothes and shaving (Lev. 14:8–9; Num. 8:7)."[8]

[8] Gordon J. Wenham, *Word Biblical Commentary, Volume 2: Genesis 16–50* (Dallas, TX: Word Inc., 2002), 323.

Jacob's household put away their idols into the custody of Jacob. Jacob then buried the idols under the oak tree. This demonstrates Jacob's complete determination to dispose of the idols and also any material that could be used to replace them.

As they journeyed to Bethel, the terror on Shechem was continuous, as if it would not end. As a result of this, the people were in a set state of hunting them to kill them. "The family's readiness to dedicate themselves solely to their father's God is rewarded, and the divine promise of protection cited in verse 2 is again vindicated."[9]

Jacob and his group of people are now larger than a tribe, and by God's grace they are placed in a sustained relationship of fellowship with God at Bethel. After constructing an altar in obedience to God, Jacob shouted with a specific message desiring a specific response calling the place El-Bethel, because it is there God clearly presented Himself to Jacob's face. "Here, the narrative is emphasizing that the changed name of Bethel shows that God had revealed himself or spoken there (vv. 7, 13–15)."[10]

Historical Background

Establishing Context

Jacob was called to return to Bethel, a place he had neglected but God had not forgotten. This is a place where, "Abram built altars during his journeys (12:6–8), it was not for the purpose of sacrifice but for calling on the name of the Lord."[11] This was a place where Jacob met with God earlier:

> Then Jacob made a vow, saying, "If God will be with me, and keep me in this way that I am going, and give me bread to eat and clothing to put on, so that I come back to my father's house in peace, then the LORD shall be my God. And this stone which I have set as a pillar shall be God's house, and of all that You give me I will surely give a tenth to You." (Gen. 28:20–22)

---

[9] Ibid., 324.

[10] Ibid.

[11] V. H. Matthews, M. W. Chavalas, and J. H. Walton, *The IVP Bible Background Commentary: Old Testament* (Downers Grove, IL: InterVarsity Press., 2000), s.v. Gen. 35:1–5.

It seems like Jacob made this a place of meeting that he then neglected. God preserved and kept Jacob, but Jacob forgot the vow he made to God. His neglect of this place of worship seems to have created the worship of many false gods among those who lived with him (Gen. 35:2).

Jacob's household had much jewelry and household gods: "These earrings probably represented some form of idolatry. In two other passages, earrings are mentioned in connection with idolatry (Judg. 8:22–28; Hos. 2:13)."[12] This is why it became imperative that they purify themselves. The purification process also included changing their clothes to clean clothes. This is probably because they were shepherds whose garments became soiled from caring for the sheep and from their journey to Bethel.

The building of an altar was something Jacob's grandfather did at this very place. Jacob, who had been at this altar, Bethel, many years earlier, now builds an altar. This is the first time that God told someone to do so.

What Does the Context Mean?

God instructs Jacob to leave Shechem and go thirty miles away to Bethel, a place where God in Genesis 28 renewed the covenant He made with Issac (Jacob's father) and Abraham. Jacob vowed to God that he would make Bethel a place of worship and bring to God a tithe. Jacob soon got busy and forgot his promise. After Dinah was raped and Jacob's sons killed the men of Shechem, Jacob was reminded of his promise and was told to go to Bethel and worship God there. Jacob now had a large group of people with him (probably because his brother gave him some of his people; Gen. 33:15), so he gathered them up and went on to Bethel. This is a place of worship where they must now spend a significant amount of time before God.

This place of worship was forgotten and that led Jacob and his family to stray from God. Their absence created a need for God, and God provided leadership in directing him back. This place of worship has been a family legacy.

Sermon Subject and Title

Sermon Title: A Model to Imitate
Big Idea: God's call to worship must be respected, leading to reverent service, especially by the head of the home.

---

[12] Ibid.

Sermon Outline (Gen. 35:1–7 NASB)

A. The Call to Worship Is Not an Option (v. 1)

1. The call to worship was a thirty-mile walk to Bethel.
2. The call is the same for us today (Heb. 10:23–26).
3. It was not a suggestion, but a commandment.
4. God did not want a quick stop. God commanded him to dwell at Bethel. The word for *live* means to remain or have a lengthy stay there.
5. God spoke to him at Shechem, but exposed himself to him at Bethel. In Psalm 128, God said He will bless us from Zion.
6. God reminded Jacob that this is a place he promised to come worship God thirty years ago.
7. Jacob's walk with God is not just because of Abraham and Isaac. It has become personal between God and him.
8. Abraham's legacy lives on. Abraham's worship becomes the lifestyle of his grandson.
9. We seem to have to wait until there is a crisis before we take worship seriously.
10. This is the first time in the Bible when God commanded an altar to be made for Him.

B. Preparation that Leads to Worship (vv. 2–6)

1. Jacob had allowed his household to sin against God and now his life is in crisis (false gods, murder in Shechem).
2. Jacob took leadership in the matter as the head of his household.
3. Jacob commanded his house to forsake all their other gods. He commanded his household to purify themselves to the point of bathing and putting on new garments (Lev. 14:8–9; Num. 8:7). No one in his household was allowed to not clean themselves up (1 Cor. 10:14–22; Heb. 10:22).
4. It was not an option for his family to attend worship. He commanded them to get up and go to Bethel.
5. Jacob was not just coming to worship; he was going to give leadership in building a place of worship.
6. Jacob was going to make his household become engaged in active labor to establish this altar.
7. *Go up*—Worship to God is a constant state of living so that it is the lifestyle of the worshipper.
8. Respect and love for God makes worship the center of a person's life.

9. One of the reasons Jacob is protected and blessed is because of his previous worship experience with God (Gen. 28:13–15; 32; Ps. 128).
10. *Give*—Jacob leads his household in ridding themselves of all their gods. The gods do not make the trip to Bethel.
11. If you are a single parent or married to an unsaved person, don't forget Lois and Eunice's impact on Timothy's life (2 Tim. 1:5). Hagar's commitment led Ishmael to become great (Gen. 21:20–21).
12. *To be*—Jacob's commitment led to God's protection of his household.
13. The family's readiness to dedicate themselves solely to God brings a reward of protection.

C. **Obedience and Preparation Led to Sincere Worship (v. 7)**
   1. *He built*—Jacob gave leadership in establishing a place of worship.
   2. His worship called for sacrifice. They had to sacrifice their gods, walk a long way, and build a place of worship (Rom. 12:1).
   3. Jacob made the place personal for God and himself, calling it Beth-El.
   4. *Revealed*—God clearly presented Himself to Jacob. God desired an open relationship with Jacob.
   5. Jacob delayed his relationship experience with God. God was ready and waiting.

Author's Comments

Comments

After their sister Dinah was raped, Jacob's sons became angry and tricked the people by having all their men circumcised. While they recovered, they came in and killed them all for raping their sister. The people wanted to come after Jacob's sons, but God allowed a great terror to fall upon the cities so that they did not follow Jacob. In the midst of this family turmoil, God speaks to Jacob, instructing him where to go and how to keep his family before God.

This story provides a model to follow. Many families experience tremendous difficulties that overwhelm everyone involved. Having a model to follow can reduce mistakes and allow families to recover most productively and protect the family from harm and danger. Here is an imperfect family that grows to become a model we can imitate.

Jacob had not been to Bethel in thirty years. This thirty-year absence teaches us how sin creeps in and idols become dominant. The rings and earrings are symbols that show Jacob's family and servants had become associated with foreign gods. The surrounding cities influenced them during Jacob's thirty-year absence from the true worship of God. Bethel was only thirty miles away. This was a long way when transportation was donkeys and horses. It is not that Jacob missed worshipping God and told everyone to go. God demanded that he return to Bethel. God made sure that he would come to Bethel; He allowed Jacob's enemies to chase him, thereby ensuring that that there was no way he could change his mind. He needs God's protection again. The last time, it was for running from his brother. This time, he is running from the angry citizens of the city of Shechem.

This is how easy it is for a family to forget God. Idols come in many forms, such as sports, house maintenance, car shows, pets, and jobs. These can soon become so important that God is no longer a priority. Next, going to church becomes a challenge because of all these idols.

This story serves as a great example of why serving God must be consistent and must be led by the person God has put in place to lead his home—a father.

Application

Busy schedules, demanding jobs, and the energy it takes to raise a family can create so much pressure that a family strays from worship. Often, families come out of commitment, rather than worship being an outgrowth of a relationship with God. This can lead to reduced spiritual growth, leaving us in the flesh, which according to Galatians 5:19–21 can lead to strife, dissension, and many other things. Keeping Christ first may be a challenge, but when He is first, the Spirit's influence leads to family unity because the fruit of the Spirit is joy, peace, love, kindness, and strength for long-suffering situations so that when crisis comes, families grow rather than become more stressed or dysfunctional.

Illustrate It

Four of my seven grandkids were at my house playing and having a great time together. There is a certain part of the house that is all tiled. Because their bicycles were not making any marks on the floor and the weather was not good outside, I allowed riding their bikes on that part of the floor, which took them through the kitchen. I told them they couldn't go through the kitchen. After I thought about it, I realized what I said was not clear.

However, they all took off in total excitement, glad to finally ride their bikes. All of a sudden, my oldest grandkid came into my study (the others were long gone) and said; "Papa, you said to not ride through the kitchen, but how do we make it around?" You see, the tile section goes through the kitchen, but what I meant was for them to pass through the outskirts of the kitchen. Of the four grandkids, only one could not go forward because he did not want to disobey Papa.

How often when God's Word is not clear to us do we stop to get further instructions and make sure we do all that God wants us to do? How often do we seek Him to understand His ways in total surrender to Him? Jacob sought God early in this life, but once he got what he needed from God, he drifted. When things became difficult, it was God who had to tell him to return to worship Him.

Thanksgiving Day: "Thanks-living" Is Thanksgiving

Psalm 92:1–5

General Overview of the Passage

It is pleasant, excellent, delightful, and economically beneficial to declare or acknowledge the attributes of God's works. It is excellent to confess that He does deserve praise. The giving of praise is right and just because He has all authority and has displayed His nature through His works. He has provided everything for His children, which highlights the relationship He has with His people. It is because of His power and His works that believers lift their voices to sing about His faithfulness and His wondrous acts. They sing about His nature, reputation, and wonderful memories. He is exalted; we acknowledge that He is supreme and has overwhelming majesty. To talk about the Lord in this way uplifts and liberates those who praise Him.

Not only do they sing about His works, but also bring to light what was once not previously comprehended about His nature in that it is loyal and steadfast. He always maintains His obligations with His people. With kindness, He consistently fulfills His covenant. This takes place in the morning because it is always fresh, waiting, and ready to function again. He is true, unfailing and certain, like the strong arms of a parent supporting a helpless infant. It is by night, because when things are most treacherous, the Lord is unfailing.

The Sabbath is the day that is to be consecrated to God by our turning away from the business pursuits of work and applying ourselves to the praise and adoration of God. It is good—not merely good in the eyes of God, but also good for man—and beneficial to the heart to praise the name of the Lord.

Because the Lord has all authority and has a personal relationship with His people, the psalmist expends significant energy when festively rejoicing before God (failure to worship the Lord with gladness brought judgment; Deut. 28:47). The psalmist sings with much energy at the works God displays. These works are by His power and strength.

The psalmist acknowledges that the Lord is the one who has all authority and identifies with His people. His nature provides powerful and valuable activities that bless His people. His creation of new ideas and the planning and judgments that take place are very deep. As a result, the psalmist may never understand all that the Lord does, but His works manifest that He cares and is faithful to His people.

Historical Background

Establishing Context

Psalm 92 is a psalm focused on praising God for His goodness. The Psalms served as Israel's hymn book, sung in the temple, on jobs, or at home. The book covers one thousand years of Israel's history. These psalms cover times of peace, war, and exile. They express jubilation, lamenting, praise, and worship. This was a worshipful psalm that was sung during worship and praises the goodness of God. "This is the only psalm that is designated for the Sabbath. There is little indication in the Old Testament of any special worship ceremonies on the Sabbath. It has been suggested that this psalm accompanied the daily offerings on the Sabbath."[13]

There were many instruments used in worship services (e.g., see Neh. 12:27), but in this psalm, only the "ten-stringed lute," the harp, and the lyre are mentioned. "Musical instruments used by the Hebrew people were of three types: (1) stringed instruments, which used vibrating strings to make sounds; (2) percussion instruments, which were struck to produce musical sounds; and (3) wind instruments, which made sounds either by passing air over a vibrating reed or by forcing air through the instrument."[14]

When the psalmist says "to Your name" (Ps. 95:1), it signifies that he is seeking to describe God's nature, reputation, and fame. There are several names for God in this psalm and they each have different meanings. He repeats the name "Lord," which means one who has authority and power and seeks to have

---

[13] Matthews, Chavalas, and Walton, *IVP Bible Background Commentary,* s.v. Ps. 91:11–92:3.

[14] *Nelson's Illustrated Bible Dictionary.*

a relationship, with His people. This name signifies that He is always in control and He is accessible to His people. "The name of the Lord—The name of the Lord is the manifestation of his character (Exod. 3:14–15; 34:6–7). It has no separate existence apart from the Lord, but is synonymous with the Lord Himself in His gracious manifestation and accessibility to His people."[15]

The name Lord of Hosts highlights that God is supreme above all other so-called gods. It reflects on the fact that He is a warrior and He is omnipotent (all powerful). He is constantly this way. He did not become this; He is always who He is.

What Does the Context Mean?

Thanking God must become a way of life because of who He is and all He has done and continues to do. When we praise Him or thank Him, we must do so with instruments and with gladness. It must be festive, because God loves to be praised, worshipped, and adored.

Sermon Subject and Title

Sermon Title: "Thanks-living" Is Thanksgiving
Big Idea: When God's goodness is celebrated, we are reminded of what He has done and the works of His hands, which makes us glad. We may never understand all His thoughts, but His faithfulness and loving-kindness are overwhelming.

Sermon Outline (Ps. 92:1–5 NASB)

A. It Is Good to Give Thanks (vv. 1–3)

1. *Good*—It is pleasant, delightful, or economically beneficial to confess or acknowledge the attributes of God's works (Deut. 28:47). God's goodness is a set condition because there is no need for it to change, since it is complete (perfect active).
2. *Lord*—The giving of praise to one who has displayed His nature by His works, which are based on His character and relationship with His people.

---

[15] Notes in *NIV Study Bible* (Grand Rapids, MI: Zondervan, 2011), s.v. Ps. 5:11.

3. *Sing praises*—It is because of His power and His works that these individuals lift up their voices to sing about the faithfulness of the Lord's wonderful acts that He has accomplished.
4. *Name*—His wonderful works as it relates to His nature and reputation.
5. *O Most High*—This signifies the exalted, supreme, and overwhelming majesty of the Lord. To talk about the Lord in this way uplifts and liberates those who praise Him.
6. *Declare*—Bring to light or reveal to everyone what was once not understood about His nature.
7. *Lovingkindness*—He is loyal, benevolent, strong, and steadfast in that He always maintains His obligations with His people. With kindness, He consistently fulfills His covenant.
8. *Morning*—Timing—it is always fresh and waiting for us when we are ready.
9. *Faithfulness*—He is true, unfailing, and certain, like the strong arms of a parent supporting a helpless infant.
10. *Night*—It is by night because when things are most treacherous, the Lord is unfailing.
11. *Worship*—The Sabbath is the day that God is hallowed and that is to be consecrated to God by our turning away from the business pursuits of the working days and applying ourselves to the praise and adoration of God.

B. The Lord Has Made Me Glad (vv. 4–5a)

1. *Made me*—The Lord's relationship and faithfulness toward His people causes the psalmist to expend significant energy by festively rejoicing.
2. *Glad*—To rejoice in a festive manner is to worship the Lord with happiness. This should be the condition that is consistently the same every time worshippers come before Him (perfect active).
3. *Done*—Because of what the Lord's labor, practice, and behavior have produced.
4. *Sings for joy*—The psalmist sings with much energy at the works that God displays. Our singing must be continuous with no end in sight (imperfect active). This is the focus of the act of worship (Piel infinitive).
5. *Hands*—By the power and strength His hands possess, He has demonstrated He is in control of all things and causes all things to come into being.

C. We Must Continuously Praise and Trust Him (v. 5b)

1. *Great*—His nature has powerful, significant, valuable activity that blesses His people. God's greatness never changes (perfect active).
2. *Works*—Yahweh's works are great, mighty, and wonderful.
3. *Your thoughts are very deep*—God's creation of new ideas, His plans, and His judgments are very deep. The psalmist praises God for His power and His wisdom. His deep thoughts describe who He is (perfect active).
   a) His thoughts ("plans, designs" Ps. 33:10) are profound, mysterious, hard to understand. The New Jewish Version translates "subtle." God's plans are beyond human understanding (1 Cor. 2:6–9).

Author's Comments

Comments

We have been so programmed to negativism that we can probably remember all the horror stories of this year, yet have a hard time remembering the good things. Some people cannot remember the prayers God answered, but they can remember the prayers He hasn't. There was a time when Israel would not listen to God, but after seventy years in Babylon, the preaching of Ezra, Haggai, Zechariah, and possibly because of the prayer of Habakkuk, the attitude of the people finally changed. They came to a realization of how they were to live before God.

It may take people a minute to figure out all the things they want to thank God for, but if thanksgiving was their lifestyle, each day would be another day of praise. Living a lifestyle of praise is often easier said than done. But the Scriptures teach it should be a lifestyle pattern (1 Thess. 5:17), so how can we develop this lifestyle of thanksgiving before God in a depraved and negative world?

One of the first things we need to do is what the psalmist says—to reflect on all that God is and all that He is doing. Remember what James says in chapter 1:17: "Every good gift and every perfect gift is from above, and comes down from the Father of lights, with whom there is no variation or shadow of turning."

Whatever benefit a person receives in the course of any day is good because it came from above. Even if a believer faces death, there is hope for an eternal experience with God where there are no more bills, work schedules, or traffic (Rev. 21:4). Secondly, His loving-kindness and faithfulness is continuous. God steadfastly watches over especially those who are faithful (Pss. 112; 128). His love is steadfast and it is a free gift that He provides generously.

Lastly, He is God. He is supreme over everything and is always in control. He is Lord, meaning He always deserves a relationship with His people while He fights for them. Lastly, "the works of His hands" (Ps. 111:7) represents the fact that He is always in control of everything and is actively seeking to meet the needs of everyone who walks in His ways.

On your list of things, what is God not doing that can help make your life more productive or beneficial? There is absolutely nothing. Then why is it that believers find it hard to bless God? Sometimes believers do not reflect on His goodness but only on our problems. Solomon in Ecclesiastes tells us when people live under the sun their lives are empty, but when they live in reflection of God, their lives are more productive and beneficial (Eccles. 1:13–14; 8:12). This result, the psalmist says, leads to greater and better worship.

Application

What have you thanked God for lately? What prayer request that He answered did you thank Him for? Is God good and faithful? The answer is obvious, so how could there not be a reason to thank Him? Thanking God is His will for us (1 Thess. 5:17).

Illustrate It

Upon Michael Vick's return to football, Tony Dungy and Andy Reid stood next to him. He was a broken man after spending eighteen months in jail. At the pinnacle of his career and making an extraordinary amount of money, Vick had to start over. With the help of those who turned out to be Vick's friends, he apologized, stating that he was focused on doing better with his life. He praised the Eagles for taking a chance on him. He praised Tony Dungy and Andy Reid for working with him, and then went to work.

We were lost in sin and God sent His Son to die for us. His grace provides for a lot of chances. We should praise Him and adore Him as a way of life, because every day we need His power, grace, and mercy. If it were not for God and His faithful works, we would not have anyone who has the power and authority to bring us through. So thanks be to God for making us glad.

Christmas Message: The Real Gift of Christmas

1 John 5:1–5

General Overview of the Passage

Whoever has confidence and full trust that Jesus is the true anointed Messiah is a true child of God. This means that they have the divine nature of God permanently residing in them (2 Cor. 5:17; Eph. 1:3–4; Titus 3:4–81; John 2:29; 3:9; 4:7) through the ministry of the Holy Spirit (1 John 4:13). Whoever continuously and willfully demonstrates affection and concern for the Father's will vividly portrays the same kind of love for the Son of God, who is the divine nature of God. The evidence of being in a genuine relationship with God, John says, consists of a person having confidence and complete trust that Jesus is the Christ, the promised Messiah. This person further demonstrates their trust in Christ when they faithfully embrace His Word, no matter what daily pressures they encounter. David, who was a man after God's heart, shared, "Your word I have hidden in my heart, that I might not sin against You" (Ps. 119:11).

God's willingness to actively respond to our needs is demonstrated when we habitually hold to doing what He has instructed us to do. God's precepts are not a heavy burden or troublesome. The commitment to obey God's commandments leads to a true intimate experience of who God is. This is what the writer means when he says, "By this we know that we have come to know Him, if we keep His commandments" (1 John 2:3 NASB). These commandments are designed to empower a believer (the Word of God is powerful—Heb. 4:12) to overcome the evil one who has the world in his power (1 John 5:19). This is the victory that each believer can continuously experience. "You are from God, little children, and have overcome them; because greater is He who is in you than he who is in the world" (1 John 4:4 NASB).

A person's commitment to the Father, fully expressing their love for the Son, magnifies the true meaning of the gift of Christmas, Christ.

Historical Background

Establishing Context

John is writing to a church that has been infiltrated with Hellenistic Gnostic, Docetic, and Cerinthian philosophers. The Gnostics believed that the spirit of a person is good, but the flesh is entirely evil. The Docetic philosophers believed that Christ only seemed to have a body; He was really a spirit being. This complements what the Gnostics taught. Cerinthian philosophers believed that Christ joined Jesus at His baptism. "The Cerinthian Gnostics denied the identity of Jesus and the Christ. That is, they denied that the individual whom the Christian Church knew by the name 'Jesus' was also Christ."[16]

Because of these teachers, the church was being influenced to challenge the deity of Christ as explained by John. John addresses this immediately and begins the letter by explaining, "That which was from the beginning, which we have heard, which we have seen with our eyes, which we have looked upon, and our hands have handled, concerning the Word of life" (1 John 1:1). John would further say,

> By this you know the Spirit of God: Every spirit that confesses that Jesus Christ has come in the flesh is of God, and every spirit that does not confess that Jesus Christ has come in the flesh is not of God. And this is the spirit of the Antichrist, which you have heard was coming, and is now already in the world. You are of God, little children, and have overcome them, because He who is in you is greater than he who is in the world. (1 John 4:2–4)

This authentic message must be accepted with conviction.

The true test of whether a person is saved or not is based upon their convictions about the deity of Christ. John wants to stress this as the centrality of our relationship with God, which results in a relationship with others and is the power that leads us to overcome the world.

Believers lived in Ephesus and were exposed to contests and successful military campaigns. John's imagery was a vivid portrayal of what God could do for

---

[16] Keener, *IVP Bible Background Commentary*, s.v. 1 John 5:1.

them. "John calls his readers to 'overcome' or 'triumph' in the face of opposition, persecution and possible martyrdom (probably including suffering for refusal to compromise with the imperial cult)."[17]

What Does the Context Mean?

Whoever has full faith and confidence that Jesus is the true Messiah is right away confessing their salvation (Rom. 10:17). By this action alone, he is showing the depth of his care and concern for the Father. As a result, he is automatically going to demonstrate the same love and concern for the Son. This then leads the believer to love other believers because they are committed to guard the Word (Matt. 22:36–40; 1 John 2:3–6; 4:7–14). The commitment to persevere in God's command does not prove to be burdensome because of the powerful work of the Holy Spirit dwelling in them. It allows a believer to have victory continuously over a wicked world (1 John 4:4). The person who overcomes the world is a believer who truly and with deep conviction trusts that Jesus is the Christ the Son of God. Their conviction exposes their faith.

God's gift to us is His Son. He truly came in the flesh. He was not a phantom. He was fully God and fully man (1 John 4:2). We demonstrate an appreciation for the gift, no matter what difficulties we experience throughout our lives, when we commit to habitually live out His Word. This brings the gift of God, His Son, to life, by the way we love others. So our gift to others is a result of our daily experience of God's gift to us (1 John 4:7–14).

Sermon Subject and Title

Sermon Title: The Real Gift of Christmas
Big Idea: A sincere love for God leads to a true celebration of God's gift to man, Jesus the Christ, and it is this love that is manifested through us. It is this love that is a true expression of faith in Christ.

Sermon Outline (1 John 5:1–5 NASB)

A. God's Gift of Love Is His Son (vv. 1–2)

1. *Believes*—The sign that this person is saved (John 6:44; Rom. 10:9, 17), regenerated, and has the Holy Spirit in them is a confession that

[17] Ibid.

they have complete trust that Jesus is fully God and is fully human and is the true Messiah. They are confident that Jesus has the divine nature of God.

a) Here faith is described as the condition of spiritual regeneration; elsewhere John describes it as righteous behavior (1 John 2:29; 3:9–10).

2. *Born of God and loves the Father*—(Matt. 16:16–17; 1 John 2:29; 3:9; 4:7)—The decision to continuously, willfully demonstrate affection and concern for the Father only occurs because we have been regenerated by the Holy Spirit (John 6:44; Rom. 10:9, 17). This leads to a confession that Jesus is the very nature of God.
3. *Love*—To continuously have care and compassion for the children of God.
4. *Keep*—Take possession of His Word, watchfully and carefully guard it (Ps. 119:11; "a man after God's own heart").
5. *Commandments*—Expression: "We carry out His orders"; suggests the active and positive "energy of obedience."

B. God's Gift of Love Is Experienced through His Word (vv. 3–5)

1. *Love*—God serves the needs of our lives and empowers us to serve the needs of others (1 John 4:7–14). The word means to love someone based on what they need (1 John 3:16–17).
2. *Keep*—Make it a habit to preserve in His commands. It also means to guard His Word from outside influences.
3. *Burdensome*—God's precepts are not heavy, burdensome, cruel, troublesome, fierce, or hard (Matt. 11:30; 23:4; John 14:21, 23–24, 31; 15:10; 13:34–35). We can keep His Word because God, through the Holy Spirit, provides us the strength to keep His commands (John 14:16, 26).
4. *Overcome*—Powerful, continuous activity that makes us victorious; the clause serves to highlight that in the continuing struggle with evil the Christian is consistently given strength to overcome (Rom. 8:37; Phil. 2:15–16; 1 John 2:13).
5. *Faith*—The prevailing progress in battle occurs because of our full trust and deep conviction in the divine truths. This word also includes a deep confidence that God's Word is the truth.
6. *World*—The forces of the world-system of evil. The devil has saints surrounded and constantly engaged in battle in which he wants to ruin

the life of the Christian and his testimony. The believers' faith combats Satan's attacks, so that each day their faith becomes their victory (Heb. 11:6).

Author's Comments

Comments

The Gnostic, Docetic, and Cerinthian teachers did their best to influence the members of the church in Ephesus. John, who spent a lot of time serving this church, was so disturbed that he told them:

> These things I have written to you concerning those who try to deceive you. But the anointing which you have received from Him abides in you, and you do not need that anyone teach you; but as the same anointing teaches you concerning all things, and is true, and is not a lie, and just as it has taught you, you will abide in Him. (1 John 2:26–27)

The anointing he is speaking of is the ministry of the Holy Spirit (John 14:16, 26; 16:13; Eph. 1:13–14) who came to guide us to the greatest gift of all, Christ.

It is the Holy Spirit who is the Helper of Christ and it is He who came to testify about Christ (John 14:17; 1 John 4:1–3), so when the apostle John is speaking of the relationship between the Father and the Son, he is confident that there is no way a person can say they know the Father and not know the Son. For someone to claim that they experienced God and are saved, but not to believe that Jesus is the very deity of God, is evidence that they did not receive the Holy Spirit (Eph. 1:13–14). How do we know this? At the point of salvation, the Holy Spirit is deposited into the person's life (Titus 3:4–8). It is this deposit of the Holy Spirit that creates the transformation leading them to be a new creation (2 Cor. 5:17). Romans 8:9 states this in this manner: "But you are not in the flesh but in the Spirit, if indeed the Spirit of God dwells in you. Now if anyone does not have the Spirit of Christ, he is not His." This supports what John emphatically says, which is that the Holy Spirit came to testify of Christ (1 John 4:2). So, if a person knows God, the Spirit lives in them, and since He lives in them, there is no way they do not believe in Christ.

God's gift to us is His Son, and this gift is experienced through the ministry of the Holy Spirit. Without this gift being accepted true, there is no experience of God's presence in a person's life. Their claim of salvation is not true, no matter how eloquent their teaching. God's gift of Christ to us is precious, and once we experience this precious gift, our love for others will never die, no matter how difficult the relationships may become.

The true gift of Christmas is Christ, and we must make Him a treasured gift by the way we keep His commands. When we keep His commands, we are transformed by the renewing of our minds (Rom. 12:2; 8:5–9) and preserved from worldly influence. Keeping His Word stimulates the powerful influence of the Holy Spirit so we walk in the Spirit and not in the flesh (Gal. 5:16–24). When we are not in the flesh, we can love anyone, and the precious gift of Christmas is experienced all year long (Matt. 22:36–40).

Application

The hardest thing for anyone is to love people who get on their last nerve. We may have been trampled on already and our nerves are really sore. The minute we say we love these kinds of people, we end up pressing against the same nerve. But loving these people is what Christ rewards. Loving people who love us is easy (Matt. 5:43–48); we must love those who are difficult to love. John elaborates on the point by saying anyone who loves knows God (1 John 4:7–8) because it is impossible for a believer to know God and not be committed to obey God (1 John 2:3–6). Any believer who demonstrates a willingness to submit to God despite these emotions is a believer who is demonstrating that the Holy Spirit abides in them. As believers, we tend to fellowship with people who are like-minded and then rejoice about how loving we are. The true litmus test of who has the Spirit of God is obeying God in all things, even when we don't feel like it. These people can overcome the world because they are true people of faith.

Illustrate It

A boy and his father enjoyed basketball. They would play together regularly and go watch their local team play. One day while his son was talking about some of the players, his dad said to him, "These players are very good, but you should have seen the time when Michael Jordan played." The boy looked puzzled at his dad and asked, "Who is Michael Jordan?" His father, forgetting his son's age for a minute, looked at his son with amazement and said, "You don't know who Michael Jordan is?" The boy looked at his dad with a blank stare as his father spoke with excitement. "Sorry, Dad, I really don't know who he is." His father, reminding himself that his son was not even born when Michael played, said, "Yes, son, it was one of the most exciting times in the NBA." The father, thrilled to relive the past, went on to describe the ability and agility of Michael Jordan. The more his father spoke, the more the son listened. The son then said, "I wish I saw him play, Dad."

Even though this boy was not around during the time of Michael Jordan, he could visualize what took place based on what his dad said. He could feel the excitement because of his dad's passion. Their shared love for the game and the genuine nature of their relationship led them to celebrate something his son never saw.

We may not have seen Christ literally walk on earth, but John did. Since we share the same Holy Spirit and have a genuine relationship with Christ, we can believe the message and trust that Jesus is the Christ who had the very nature of God. We can know this because He lived on earth and overcame death. We can live in His power and overcome the attacks of the evil one.